Incredibly Delicious

Incredibly Delicious
Recipes for a New Paradigm

GENTLE WORLD

Introduction by Michael A. Klaper, M.D.

Gentle World Publishing
Kapa'au, Hawai'i

Gentle World Publications

The Cookbook for People Who Love Animals by Gentle World

Vegan Nutrition: Pure & Simple by Michael A. Klaper, M.D.

Artwork by Kevin Weil
Photography by Gentle Art
(Spring Rolls and Gourmet Lasagna photographed by Robin Dutson)

Published by Gentle World Inc.
P.O. Box 238
Kapa'au, HI 96755

ISBN 0-929274-25-3

Library of Congress Card Number: 99-069594

All digital photography.
Digitally printed on 100% recycled paper (30% post-consumer).
Printed in Canada

To the shared vision
of a new paradigm of peace;
not in some far-off tomorrow
when the lion lies down with the lamb;
but today, when we do.

Acknowledgments

Gentle World wishes to acknowledge, first and foremost, Marcia Katz, Jennifer Gibson-Weil, Elizabeth Flinn and Heather Potomac, who gave so generously of their time and talents in the creation of 'Incredibly Delicious'.

A heartfelt thank you to Sam Gerard for his many helpful suggestions. Another to Vince Stark for contributing in so many ways.

A note of appreciation to Freya Dinshah, Andy Walker, Andrew Fields, Patti Weill-Fields and Joan Kirson for editing and proof-reading.

For technical support, our sincere gratitude goes to Matthew Pearce, for always leaving the door open, and to Pauline Harder, for her invaluable assistance.

Table of Contents

Introduction

You are cordially invited to enjoy a cuisine for the ages – ancient yet modern, simple but elegant, a key to better health, and now – thanks to <u>Incredibly Delicious: Recipes For A New Paradigm</u> – made to taste fabulous! Through many years of innovative cooking (and endless tasting), the people of Gentle World have created this sumptuous collection of pure vegetarian recipes. The pages are lovingly filled with ideas for tasty breakfasts, lunches, dinners, soups, salads, side dishes and desserts, and richly seasoned with thoughtful quotes from across the centuries, to feed your heart, mind and spirit.

As a physician, I can attest that if all my patients adopted a diet based on these high-fiber, cholesterol-free foods, we would have a much healthier population. Lower risk of heart disease and colon cancer, as well as actual reduction of elevated blood pressure and cholesterol levels, are predictable benefits from nourishing your body on the ingredients utilized in these recipes. Witnessing the wonderful changes in people as they evolve their diet to this style of eating – becoming more energetic and functional while escaping the plagues of obesity and chronic disease – is always a great joy for this doctor. How wonderful that such powerful medicine can be created in the kitchen!

As a man who loves great-tasting food, I can also attest (after having enjoyed many of these delectable dishes myself) that you are in for a treat with every meal. As a person who wishes to bring peace and healing to my life and to our planet, I appreciate that the recipes in <u>Incredibly Delicious</u> allow me to remove the products of violence from my dining table, and thus to reduce damage and suffering in the world around me.

One could spend a lifetime eating these foods – in fact, I strongly encourage you to do so. Such a lifetime should be a long and healthy one, and sure to be filled with memorable culinary experiences. This banquet of a book celebrates the best in life and will be your guide to great eating for the next thousand years. I highly recommend it and invite you to enjoy the feast.

Michael A. Klaper, M.D.

Glossary of Ingredients

Agar-Agar ~ a gelatin replacement. It is made from sea vegetables and is a gelling agent for cold recipes, such as gelled desserts or fruit pies.

Arrowroot Powder ~ a healthier replacement for cornstarch. Use one tablespoon of arrowroot per cup of liquid. It dissolves in liquid and thickens at a simmering temperature. Used in gravies and puddings. Do not boil, as it reverses the thickening process.

Barley ~ one of the oldest cultivated grains. Scotch barley is the whole grain. The more commonly known "pearled barley", which cooks more quickly, is not a whole grain. The whole grain barley contains all nine essential amino acids.

Barley Malt ~ a thick, brown syrup, which is about half as sweet as other sweeteners, with a rich, malty flavor. It is a complex carbohydrate made from combining the grain starch with enzymes. It contains B-vitamins and trace minerals.

Bouillon ~ See page 279 for a listing of bouillons. Balanced-Mineral-Bouillon™ is a formula created by Dr. Bronner and is found in health food stores. It is wonderful for making gravies, and is a flavorful food supplement that adds minerals and vitamins to any dish.

Bragg™ Liquid Aminos ~ an unfermented alternative to tamari or soy sauce. It has a delicious, lighter flavor and less sodium content. It is certified non-GMO.

Bran ~ the husk of the grain that has been separated from the flour, either oat bran or wheat bran. Used for breading and coating in recipes.

Bulgur ~ cracked whole wheat, steamed and dried. To prepare, pour boiling water over it, cover, and let stand for one hour or until all water is absorbed and grain is softened.

Carob ~ a cocoa-like powder made from the seed pod of the evergreen carob tree. This chocolate substitute can be purchased raw or roasted. It is naturally sweet, high in fiber, low fat, and doesn't contain the caffeine that chocolate does. It contains iron, calcium, and phosphorus. Non-dairy carob chips are available in health food stores.

Cold Pressed Oils ~ extracted using pressure from a stone or hydraulic press. They are produced by a mechanical batch-pressing process in which heat-producing friction is minimized, so that temperatures remain below 120°. Most commercially produced oil is extracted using heat and a volatile solvent, which is flashed off when the oil is heated to 212° then distilled. The oil is then refined by bleaching, deodorizing, and winterizing. Cold-pressed oils are recommended. Hi-oleic safflower is a good, (mild-flavored) oil, highest in polyunsaturated fats. Cold-pressed virgin olive oil is best for salads and in raw preparation. Other good oils are hi-oleic sunflower, macadamia, sesame and flax (a rich vegetarian source of Omega-3 fatty acids). Even cold-pressed oils are exposed to some heat and all processed oil is best used in moderation. See recommended oils - page 279

Cous-Cous ~ a refined semolina product that is pre-cooked, so it conveniently cooks in just minutes. The whole wheat variety (darker in color) has a higher nutritional value.

Date Sugar ~ ground dehydrated dates. It is a source of some vitamins and minerals.

Ener-G® Egg Replacer ~ a powdered formula of starches and leavening. Mix with water to use in recipes. Ener-G® egg replacer is available in health food stores. See page 10 for egg replacement ideas.

Gluten Flour ~ used to make seitan - see page 161. It is high in protein and low in fat.

Herb Seasonings ~ mixed spice blends such as Spike™, an all-purpose seasoning with 35 herbs and spices. The first ingredient is salt, but there is also salt-free Spike. Modern Products makes a seasoning called 'Vegit', which contains kelp. Trocomare™ or Herbamare™ are herb seasoned sea salt. Both are made with fresh organically grown herbs and found in health food stores. Mrs. Dash Seasoning Original Blend (salt-free) and McCormick Salt-free All-Purpose Seasoning are found in supermarkets.

Kelp ~ a powdered seaweed with a slightly salty taste, rich in iodine, and a good salt substitute.

Maple Syrup ~ It comes in different grades of light to dark, which all contain equal levels of minerals. To make maple syrup, sap has to be collected and boiled down. During the boiling, the sap foams up, slowing down the syrup-making process. To stop this, a drop of fat or oil is added. (Lard, shortening, vegetable oil). The label does not designate this ingredient. When buying maple syrup, look for the kosher symbol, or call the company to see that they use vegetable-based defoamers. Use only 100% pure syrup, and refrigerate after opening. See page 278 for companies whose syrup is vegan.

Millet ~ a small golden grain which is the staple for nearly a third of the world's population. It is easy to digest and one of the few non-acid forming grains. It is the staple of the Hunzas, renowned for their longevity. This protein-rich grain is high in iron, calcium, magnesium, potassium, vitamins and choline.

Miso ~ a salty-flavored fermented paste from soybeans, rice or barley, rich in protein, minerals and vitamins. Purchase unpasteurized miso for nutritional benefits. Mix with water, then add to soups or gravies during the last phase of cooking, in order to keep the nutrients alive. Do not boil it or it loses its nutritional properties. Light or white misos are lower in salt content and sweeter in flavor. Keep refrigerated. Add to salad dressings.

Non-irradiated Spices & Herbs ~ Most health food stores carry a full line.

Nori ~ a high protein, sun-dried red sea vegetable, pressed into sheets.

Nutritional Yeast ~ a food supplement grown on cane/beet molasses which comes in a yellow powder or flakes with a 'cheesy' flavor. Red Star™ nutritional yeast sprinkled on your food will make vitamin B-12 supplementation convenient and delicious. (The vitamin B-12 in Red Star Vegetarian Support Formula is from a natural fermentation source; not from a synthetic or animal source. Two tablespoons will meet the daily vitamin B-12 requirements.) Nutritional yeast is to be distinguished from "Brewer's Yeast", which may have a bitter taste. Red Star Primary Grown Nutritional Yeast 'Vegetarian Support Formula' is an excellent source of protein, dietary fiber, vitamins and minerals. Avoid brands that are combined with whey.

Oat Groats ~ oats in a whole grain form. They can be soaked overnight for use in raw recipes or cooked to make healthy whole grain cereals. The more commonly known oats are groats rolled into flakes. Quick-cooking oats are flakes rolled thinner by the application of more pressure. They have the same nutritional value as thicker rolled oats. Steel cut oat groats are easily soaked for raw dishes and breakfast cereals.

Quinoa ~ (pronounced keen-wa) is a light, fluffy, fast-cooking grain. It is an ancient grain, native to the Andes, now grown organically in Colorado. It has twice the protein found in rice, barley or corn and is high in iron and B-vitamins.

Rapadura® ~ a whole, dried, unrefined evaporated juice of sugar cane. It has never been separated and retains its original vitamins and minerals. It is considered a 'living food' and is certified 100% organic. It is superb for baking, retaining its nutrients after cooking.

Rice ~ has been the staple food in most of Asia since 3000 B.C., and is currently the staple food for more than half the world's population. Rice supplies only a small amount of protein. It is a healthy carbohydrate that contains calcium, iron, zinc and almost all of the B-vitamins. There are 25,000 varieties of rice! Brown rice retains the bran and the germ; white rice has these layers polished away during refining. Long-grain rice is generally fluffier, while short-grain has a sweeter taste, and is sticky in texture.

Rice Syrup ~ (also known as "yinny") is a thick syrup, less sweet than other sweeteners. It is a healthy alternative to honey. It is used to complement vinegar in salad dressings.

Sea Salt ~ is made from evaporated sea water and retains more than 70 elements commonly found in sea water. Unrefined sea salt is high in trace minerals and contains no chemicals, sugar or added iodine. It is a good idea to regulate all salt intake. Real Salt®, a natural mineral salt, is produced by Redmond Minerals, Inc - see page 279

Seitan ~ or "Wheat-Meat" is an excellent meat substitute. It is a better protein source than beef and is low in fat. It is sold commercially or you can make it yourself from wheat gluten flour (see seitan recipe, page 161).

Sorghum Molasses ~ a dark syrup made from the sorghum plant (related to millet). The stalks of the plant are crushed and the sweet syrup released is cooked and clarified into a dark syrup, rich in minerals such as potassium, iron, calcium and B-vitamins.

Spelt Flour ~ a flavorful ancient grass and distant cousin to modern wheat. It can replace wheat flour in baking. Many wheat and gluten sensitive people can use it in their diet.

Stock ~ seasoned water that vegetables have been cooked in. Used in soups and sauces.

Sucanat™ ~ stands for Sugar Cane Natural. It is a dry, granulated evaporated cane juice sweetener. It can replace sugar in recipes. Available in organic or commercial.

Tahini ~ sesame seed butter. It comes raw or roasted. It is rich in calcium, protein and phosphorus. It needs to be mixed before use as the oil separates from the ground-up seed paste. Storage life is excellent. Combining with water in any measure, however, considerably reduces shelf life.

Tamari ~ a natural soy sauce made from fermented soybeans. It contains about 1000 mg. of sodium per tablespoon. It often contains wheat.

Tempeh ~ a fermented whole soy bean product and meat substitute, originally from Indonesia. It is usually sold frozen in health food stores. It is a perishable food, so store frozen or refrigerated. Steaming tempeh before use fluffs it up and allows it to absorb the flavors more easily. More than half of all American soybeans are genetically modified. Purchase tempeh that is labeled non-GMO to avoid possible non-vegan transgenic manipulation.

Texturized Vegetable Protein ~ (known as T.V.P.) is a hearty, high protein food made by processing defatted soy flour to extract most of its soluble sugars. T.V.P. is used in place of meat in chili, lasagna, and casseroles. It is usually fortified with Vitamin B-12.

Tofu ~ a truly versatile soy "cheese" made from soybean milk and sold in block form. It is high in protein and rich in vitamins, minerals and polyunsaturated fat, with no cholesterol. It comes in silken, soft and firm textures. The firm is best for slicing into cutlets or cubing into bite-sized chunks. The soft and silken are for mashing and blending. Tofu barely has any smell at all when it is fresh. Tofu takes on the flavor of whatever seasonings are used. Store it in a refrigerator, submerged in cold water and change the water daily. When purchasing packaged tofu, check the expiration date. If you are using tofu in uncooked dishes, submerge in boiling water to kill any bacteria. Don't leave it in the water more than a few minutes or it changes the texture of the tofu. (This does not apply to tofu bought in sealed packaged containers.) More than half of all American soybeans are genetically engineered. Purchase tofu that is labeled non-GMO to avoid possible non-vegan transgenic manipulation.

Vegan Cheese Alternatives ~ See page 274 for a listing of cheese alternatives. VeganRella™ is a 100% non-dairy alternative to cheese. It is free of soy as well. It comes in several flavors as well as cream cheese spread. It is firm when cold and melts when heated. It is found in health food stores.

Vanilla ~ Use pure, non-alcoholic vanilla. For non-baking purposes, try a vanilla powder (no alcohol). Use it in the same proportions as the liquid vanilla extract.

Vinegar ~ Two recommended vinegars to use are brown rice vinegar or unpasteurized apple cider vinegar. Rice vinegar has half the acidity.

Whole Wheat Flour ~ used for baking breads rather than for making pastry.

Whole Wheat Pastry Flour ~ a lighter flour, used for pastries and cakes.

> *"I know of no more encouraging fact than the unquestionable ability of man to elevate his life by a conscious endeavor."*
>
> HENRY DAVID THOREAU (1817-1862) ~ American essayist and naturalist

Sources of Minerals and Vitamins

Calcium ~ broccoli, green leafy vegetables (such as kale, bok choy, collard and turnip greens), tofu, blackstrap molasses, chick peas, many beans, sesame seeds, sunflower seeds, calcium-fortified non-dairy milk or orange juice, almonds, flax seeds, brazil nuts, dried figs, dried fruit, corn tortillas.

Iron ~ green leafy vegetables & sea vegetables, legumes/beans, nuts & seeds, blackstrap molasses, dried fruits, watermelon, cream of wheat, prune juice, spinach, cereals, whole grains, bran flakes.

Magnesium ~ brown rice, cooked spinach, beans/legumes, almonds/nuts, dried figs, broccoli, cooked oatmeal, wheat germ/bran, whole grains, green leafy vegetables, bananas, peanuts.

Phosphorus ~ pinto beans, cereal grains, almonds, nuts, dried beans, peas, lentils, peanuts, bread and baked goods, brown rice, avocados, spinach, many vegetables, yeast.

Potassium ~ raisins, bananas, raw and cooked spinach, potatoes, baked sweet potatoes, winter squash, raw cauliflower, avocados, kiwi, dried fruits, tomatoes, oranges, grapefruit, strawberries, honeydew melon, cantaloupe, dried apricots.

Zinc ~ pumpkin seeds, whole grains/cereals, legumes, lentils, peas, soy foods, nuts, sunflower seeds, wheat germ, yeast, maple syrup, garbanzo beans, raw collard greens, spinach, corn.

Selenium ~ brazil nuts, whole grains, kidney beans (depending on soil grown in), yeast.

Manganese ~ brown rice & whole grains, cereals, cooked oatmeal, wheat germ, nuts, seeds, legumes, cooked spinach & kale, black beans, almonds, avocados, pineapples, strawberries.

Molybdenum ~ beans, breads, cereals, cooked spinach, strawberries.

Pantothenic Acid ~ whole grain cereals, legumes, mushrooms, peanuts, soybeans, avocados, sunflower seeds, bananas, oranges, cooked collard greens, baked potato, broccoli.

Chromium ~ whole grains, nuts, broccoli, apples, peanuts, cooked spinach, mushrooms.

Biotin ~ cereals & whole grains, breads, yeast, almonds, peanuts, molasses, legumes.

Copper ~ nuts and seeds, whole grains, dried beans, mushrooms.

Folic Acid ~ legumes, lentils, oranges, whole grains, asparagus, spinach, romaine lettuce.

Fluoride ~ brewed tea, cooked kale & spinach, apples.

Iodine ~ iodized salt, iodine-rich sea vegetables, kelp, vegetables grown in iodine-rich soil.

Vitamin A ~ carrots, winter squashes (acorn and butternut), sweet potatoes, cantaloupe, apricots, spinach, kale, turnip greens, broccoli, red bell peppers and other greens.

Vitamin B1 (Thiamin) ~ brown rice & whole grains, bread, pasta, oatmeal, brewers and nutritional yeast, legumes, cereals, sunflower seeds, nuts, watermelon, raw wheat germ.

Riboflavin ~ yeast, beans, cereals, whole grains, spinach, broccoli, wheat germ, mushrooms.

Vitamin B3 (Niacin) ~ legumes, brown rice, green vegetables, potatoes, tomatoes, broccoli.

Vitamin B6 ~ whole grains, peanuts, nuts/legumes, soybeans, walnuts, bananas, watermelon

Vitamin B12 ~ Red Star 'Vegetarian Support Formula' Nutritional Yeast, B-12 fortified non-dairy milks, meat analogs and cereals. Vegan B-12 supplements: VegLife® (certified vegan) B-12 supplement, Twin Labs 'Vegetarian Formula' B-12 Sublingual Dots, etc. (see page 281).

Vitamin C ~ bell peppers, broccoli, tomatoes, strawberries, oranges/orange juice, grapefruit, tomatoes, brussels sprouts, cabbage, collard greens, turnip greens, spinach, potatoes, melon, berries, papayas, romaine lettuce, watercress.

Vitamin D ~ The most significant supply of Vitamin D comes from sunlight exposure on the skin. Most people need no extra source of the vitamin from food. Vitamin D-2 supplements are available, as well as Vitamin D fortified plant milks & cereals. Fortified vegan products contain Vitamin D-2 (ergocalciferol) as opposed to animal-derived Vitamin D-3 (cholecalciferol).

Vitamin E ~ safflower/vegetable oils, sunflower seeds, raw wheat germ, nuts, peanuts, green leafy vegetables, whole wheat flour, whole grains, spinach.

Vitamin K ~ green leafy vegetables, spinach, turnip greens, kale, parsley, brussels sprouts, broccoli, cauliflower, soybeans and soybean oil, cabbage, green tea, tomatoes.

---

*"In a gentle way
you can shake the world."*

MAHATMA GANDHI (1869-1948) ~ Hindu pacifist, spiritual leader

Preparing to Cook

· Blender - a necessary machine for dressings, milks, gravies and smoothies.

· Food processor - invaluable for many recipes in this book. A processor is used for making thicker creams, paté, dips, bean mashes, hummus, frostings and raw treats. Use for all foods that are too thick for a blender.

· Non-aluminum coated cookware - stainless steel, ceramic or glass.

· Wooden stirring spoons - use them to avoid scratching the surfaces of pots and pans with metal spoons.

· Wooden cutting boards - use separate ones for fruits & vegetables (especially onions).

· Vegetable steamer basket - place in a pot with water. Water level should not exceed the top of the steamer basket. This will keep vegetables and greens from getting limp and losing nutrients. Boil water first then add your vegetables.

· Colander - for draining pasta, beans, potatoes, etc. Washed lettuce can drain in a colander before preparing salad.

· Grater - either a hand grater or the grater blade of your food processor is a valuable tool for making raw salads.

· Vegetable peeler

· Measuring spoons and cups - cup=C., tablespoon=T., teaspoon=t.

· Garlic press

· Sifter - used for sifting flour and other dry baking ingredients.

· Citrus juicer - for orange or lemon juice (hand or electric).

· Dehydrator - helpful for many of the raw recipes in this book. If you do not own one, set the oven below 101° for dehydrating.

· Bread machine, air fryer and juice extractor.

· Champion® Juicer - A machine that grates, juices and homogenizes.

· Vita-Mix - A large extra-strength blender.

· Compost container - for fruit and vegetable peels and all leftover food. The bucket is emptied into outdoor compost piles daily to make your own vitamin and mineral-rich soil for growing food. See 'Gardening & Composting' - page 177.

Metric Conversion Chart

(adjusted slightly for simplicity)

1/4 teaspoon	(1/4 t.)	1 1/4 ml (milliliters)
1/2 teaspoon	(1/2 t.)	2 1/2 ml
1 teaspoon	(1 t.)	5 ml
2 teaspoons	(2 t.)	10 ml
1 tablespoon	(1 T.)	15 ml
1/4 cup	(1/4 C.)	60 ml
1/3 cup	(1/3 C.)	75 ml
1/2 cup	(1/2 C.)	120 ml
1 cup	(1 C.)	237 ml
1 1/4 cup	(1 1/4 C.)	300 ml
2 cups	(2 C.)	475 ml
3 cups	(3 C.)	710 ml
1 fluid oz.		30 ml
1 pint (U.S.)	2 cups	470 ml
1 pint (British)	2 1/2 cups	590 ml

Ounces to Grams:
1 oz. = 28 grams
8 oz. = 227 grams
9 oz. = 255 grams

Pounds to Kilograms:
1 lb. (pound) = 0.454 kilograms (approximately)
2 lbs. = 0.907 kilograms (kg)
2.2 lbs. = 1 kilogram
3 lbs. = 1.36 kilograms (kg)

Oven temperatures: Oven temperatures in this book are given in Fahrenheit. The Centigrade equivalents are:

275° F. = 135° C.	350° F. = 175° C.
300° F. = 150° C.	375° F. = 190° C.
325° F = 160° C.	400° F. = 200° C.

United States Measurement conversions:

3 t. (teaspoons) = 1 T. (Tablespoon)
1 & 1/2 teaspoons = 1/2 Tablespoon
2 Tablespoons = 1/8 cup
4 Tablespoons = 1/4 cup
5 1/3 T. (5 T.+ 1 t.) = 1/3 cup
8 Tablespoons (8 T.) = 1/2 cup

Baking Guide

You can create incredibly delicious, varied baked goods without eggs, milk or butter. The following tips will help to ease your transition:

Replace one egg using any of the following:
a) Ener-G™ Egg Replacer - page 276 (1 1/2 t. egg replacer + 2 T. water for each egg.)
b) Mix 1 T. soy powder with 2 T. water.
c) Soak 1 1/2 T. ground flax seeds (rich in valuable oils) in 3 T. boiling water for 15 minutes. Pour off excess water and use the gelled flax seeds.
d) Use half a mashed banana, 3 T. apple sauce or 1 T. arrowroot powder

Replace milk or cream with either of the following:
a) **Non-dairy milk**, a thick, rich soy/rice/oat or nut milk. See page 274.
b) **Tofu milk** is made by blending tofu with water.
   To prepare: Rinse and drain 8 oz. (one cup) of tofu.
   In a blender, blend tofu with one cup water. Purée until smooth.
   Add one more cup of water and blend. This will yield 2 1/2 - 3 cups of tofu milk.

Substitutes for processed sugar are evaporated cane juice, date sugar, The Ultimate Sweetener™, Rapadura®, etc. Replace honey with rice syrup, maple syrup or other liquid sweetener. (See page 278)

To reduce oil in baked goods, replace some of the oil with an equal amount of apple sauce. When baking cookies, replace oil with apple juice. See page 268.

Pre-heat your oven 15 minutes in advance and bake for specified time or until done. Half-way through baking, rotate trays/pans (move top pan to bottom and bottom pan to top) and rotate front of tray to the back for even baking.

Always mix sweetener with wet ingredients such as oil, soy milk, egg substitute and vanilla in a large bowl (some recipes blend in a blender). Sift the dry ingredients into another bowl. Mix dry ingredients into wet ingredients, unless recipe specifies otherwise. When using baking powder, do not over-mix.

To test baked goods such as cakes, cupcakes and muffins, insert a wooden toothpick or a small paring knife into the center. When fully baked, it will come out dry and clean.

"Antibiotics allowed in U.S. cow's milk: 80
Antibiotics found in soy milk: None"

JOHN ROBBINS ~ American author, Pulitzer Prize nominee for <u>Diet for a New America</u>,
author, <u>The Food Revolution</u>, Conari Press 2000

Lightly oil (and flour) baking dishes, or use baking papers or cupcake papers.

For **wheat-free baking**, spelt flour can be used interchangeably with whole wheat or whole wheat pastry flour.

Substitute non-dairy margarine for oil, measure for measure, for a richer cake or cookie. See page 274 for a listing of vegan margarines.

To melt chocolate, use a double boiler. If you do not have one, boil water in a large saucepan. Place chocolate in a smaller one and place this saucepan into the boiling water. Warm chocolate on medium heat until melted. Alternatively, place chocolate in a small saucepan on very low heat. Stir until melted.

When using baking yeast (active dry yeast) in baked breads and risen pastries, first place approximately one cup of warm water in a bowl or in a measuring cup (with a 2+ C. capacity). Make sure the water is quite warm to the touch but not hot. Mix one teaspoon of sweetener into the water then stir in the yeast. Set aside and let rise in a warm (not hot) place. Yeast will bubble up and activate in about 15 minutes, doubling in size. If it does not rise, try again. *Do not use yeast in a recipe if it does not bubble up and rise.*

To make breads using a bread machine, do so according to your machine's directions. The water usually goes in first and the yeast last to keep it dry. Use the dough setting for all breads that are baked separately in a conventional oven. When the dough cycle is complete, follow the directions given in the recipe, usually beginning at step 4 or 5. Use the whole wheat setting for a loaf that is baked from start to finish in the bread machine.

Roll pastry dough on a flat, well-floured surface, or try using wax paper. Lightly dampen a clean, flat surface and place wax paper on it. Smooth out the paper to remove all bubbles. Place dough on paper and flatten it out a bit. Cover with another piece of wax paper. Roll outward from the center, using a rolling pin, until dough is even and reaches the desired shape. Thinner pastry dough will make a lighter crust. Once rolled, transfer dough to pie plate, etc. with wax paper. When in place, gently peel paper from the back side.

> *"We stopped eating meat many years ago. During the course of a Sunday lunch, we happened to look out of the kitchen window at our young lambs playing happily in the fields. Glancing down at our plates, we suddenly realized that we were eating the leg of an animal who had until recently been playing in a field herself. We looked at each other and said, 'Wait a minute, we love these sheep—they're such gentle creatures. So why are we eating them?' It was the last time we ever did."*
>
> PAUL McCARTNEY ~ English musician, singer, songwriter

Cooking Guide for Whole Grains

Use whole grains that contain all their bran, germ and starch for greater nutrition. For portion planning, use half a cup of uncooked grain per adult serving.

Instructions: Boil water, add grain, reduce heat to a simmer and cook for specified time or until water is gone and grain is fluffy. Leave the lid on until finished.

Millet ~ 1 cup dry grain to 2 cups water. 25 minutes cooking time. Yields 3 - 3 1/2 cups of cooked grain. (Some use 3 cups water to 1 cup grain.)

Quinoa ~ 1 cup dry grain to 2 cups water. 15-20 minutes cooking time. Yields 3 - 3 1/2 cups cooked grain. Quinoa is fluffy and light.

Rice (long grain, brown) ~ 1 cup dry grain to 2 cups water. 40-45 minutes cooking time. Yields 3 cups of cooked grain. Cooks up fluffy with grains remaining separated.

Rice (short/medium grain brown) ~ 1 cup dry grain to 2 cups water. 45-50 minutes cooking time. Yields 3 cups cooked grain. Good for loaves and burgers.

Brown Basmati Rice ~ 1 cup dry grain to 2 cups water. 30-45 minutes cooking time. Cooks up fluffy with grains remaining separated. Yields 3 1/2 cups of cooked grain.

Wild Rice ~ 1 cup dry grain to 2 1/2 cups water. 40 minutes cooking time. Yields 3 cups cooked.

Cous-Cous ~ 1 cup dry grain to 1 cup water. Boil water, add cous-cous, simmer for a few minutes then shut off heat. Let stand for several minutes with the lid on, then fluff with a fork. Cover again for another five minutes. (Use whole wheat variety.)

Kasha (buckwheat groats) ~ 1 cup dry grain to 2 cups water. 20 minutes cooking time. Yields 2 cups.

Amaranth ~ 1 cup dry grain to 2 1/2 - 3 cups water. 20-25 minutes cooking time. Yields 3 cups cooked grain. Has a slightly nutty flavor and a soft, sticky consistency when cooked. Gluten-free.

Pearled Barley ~ 1 cup dry grain to 2 1/2 cups water. 50-60 minutes cooking time. Yields 3 1/2 cups of cooked grain. A hearty grain good for soups, stews and cold salads.

Kamut ~ 1 cup dry grain to 3 cups water. 100+ minutes cooking time. Yields 3 cups cooked.

Bulgur Wheat ~ can be reconstituted in boiling water. 1 cup dry grain to 2 cups water. Cover bowl and let sit for 60 minutes or until water is completely absorbed by grain. Yields 2 1/2 - 3 cups cooked. Used to make Tabouli.

Cooking Guide for Beans

Most dry beans need soaking overnight before cooking.
Soak in 4-5 cups of water to 1 cup of beans. Rinse with fresh water before cooking.
To cook beans easily and in less time, use a pressure-cooker.

1 cup dry bean yields approximately 2 1/2 cups cooked beans.

Lentils ~ 1 cup dry lentils to 3 cups water. Bring water to a boil and simmer for 30 minutes. No pre-soaking necessary. Red lentils take less cooking time.

Garbanzo Beans (chick peas) ~ 1 cup dry beans to 4 cups water. Soaked overnight, cooking time is 2-3 hours.

Soybeans ~ 1 cup dry beans to 4 cups water. Soaked overnight, cooking time is 3 hours.

Black Beans ~ 1 cup dry beans to 4 cups water. Soaked, cooking time is 60-90 minutes.

Navy Beans ~ 1 cup dry beans to 3 cups water. Soaked, cooking time is 90 minutes.

Pinto Beans ~ 1 cup dry beans to 3 cups water. Soaked, cooking time is 2-2 1/2 hours.

Great Northern Beans ~ 1 cup dry beans to 3 cups water. Unsoaked, cooking time is 90-120 minutes. Soaked, cooking time is 60 minutes.

Kidney Beans ~ 1 cup dry beans to 3 cups water. Soaked, cooking time is 60+ minutes. Unsoaked, cooking time is 90 minutes.

Lima Beans ~ 1 cup dry beans to 3 cups water. No soaking required. 90 minutes cooking time.

Split Peas ~ No soaking required. 1 cup dry beans to 3 cups water. 45-75 minutes cooking time.

Adzuki Beans ~ 1 cup dry beans to 4 cups water. Soaked 1 hour, cooking time is 1 hour. Unsoaked, cooking time is 90-120 minutes.

"Love animals: God has given them the rudiments of thought and joy untroubled. Do not trouble their joy, don't harass them, don't deprive them of their happiness, don't work against God's intent."

FYODOR DOSTOEVSKY (1821-1881) ~ Russian novelist

> *"It is from numberless diverse acts of courage and belief that human history is shaped. Each time someone stands up for an ideal, or acts to improve the lot of others, or strikes out against injustice, they send forth a tiny ripple of hope. Crossing each other from a million different centers of energy and daring, those ripples build a current which can sweep down the mightiest walls of oppression and resistance..."*
>
> ROBERT F. KENNEDY (1925-1968)
> United States Attorney General and Senator

Bread & Breakfast

Breakfast
Cereal **19–20**
Cinnamon Rolls **28**
French Toast **23**
Fresh Fruit Bowl **16**
Granola **18–19**
Hawaiian Toast **23**
Homemade Applesauce **16**
Home-style Hash Browns **22**
'Milk', Almond & Sunflower **17**
Oatmeal **19**
Pancakes **23–24**
Scrambled Tofu **22**
Tofu Cottage Cheese **18**
Tofu Yogurt **16**

Omelettes
'Cheese' **22**
Low-oil **20**
Spanish **21**
Tofu **20**
Western **21**

Breads
Banana Bread **30**
Biscuits **32**
Cornbread **29, 32, 33**
Easy Whole-Wheat/Spelt Bread **29**
Eggless Challah Bread **31**
Foccacia Bread **30**
French Baguettes **31**
Glazed Rolls **34**
Holiday Pumpkin Bread **33**
Sesame Crackers & Flat Bread **35**
Sweet Cranberry Bread **34**
Whole Wheat Burger Buns **32**

Muffins
Apple Cinnamon **24**
Banana Walnut **27**
Blueberry **26**
Blueberry Corn **26**
Bran **26**
Carrot, Party-Size **25**
Peanut Butter **27**
Sweet Corn **25**
Wheat-free Corn **27**

Bread
&
Breakfast

Fresh Fruit Bowl
yields 1 large bowl

1 mango	1 papaya or peach
1 orange	1 avocado
1 banana	1/8–1/4 C. raisins
1/4 C. raspberries or blueberries	(use any fresh fruit in season)

Peel and slice each piece of fruit into a bowl, mix and serve.
• Optional ~ Squeeze an orange over fruit bowl or top with a thick fruit smoothie.
• Optional ~ Add sunflower seeds.

Homemade Applesauce
yields 1 quart

20 small apples, peeled and cored   1 1/2 t. cinnamon

1. In a saucepan, in a little water, steam the apples on medium heat until soft.
2. Add cinnamon half-way through. When apples are soft, mash. Chill.
   • Optional ~ For raw applesauce, add lemon and use a blender or food processor instead of cooking.

Tofu Yogurt
serves 4

1 1/2 lbs. (3 C.) soft tofu	1/4 C. fruit juice
3 T. sweetener & 3 T. maple syrup	1 t. vanilla
2 bananas, peeled, frozen, sliced	1 1/2 C. frozen berries
2 bananas, ripe (spotted), sliced	1–2 T. fresh lemon juice

Rinse and drain tofu. In a blender or food processor, blend all ingredients together until creamy. Chill in the freezer then serve just before frozen.
• For a thicker consistency, use a food processor and omit some liquid if desired.

> *"There is no question that the combination of a vegan low-fat diet and daily vigorous exercise are keys to radiant good health. And, if one so desires, one can set new limits in the fields of human athletic endeavors, especially as one ages. It is my vegan diet that powers me through triathalons and marathons and 50-60 races per year!"*
>
> RUTH HEIDRICH, Ph.D. ~ Ironman triathlete

Sunflower Milk
yields 1 quart

1 quart ice cold water	*a dash of vanilla (optional)*
2/3 C. sunflower seeds	*2-3 t. sweetener, to taste*

1. Place sunflower seeds in a blender, just covering the blades.
2. Cover seeds with one cup of water and blend to a purée (about one minute).
3. Add sweetener and vanilla. Use a plastic spatula or a little water to get the pieces of seeds off the sides of the blender.
4. When the purée becomes difficult to blend, add a few more tablespoons of water until it is completely smooth.
5. Fill to the top with ice cold water while still blending.

- Optional ~ Strain milk through a fine strainer or cheese cloth.
- Use cashews in place of sunflower seeds for a rich, cream-like "milk".
- Serve with cold cereal, raisins and fruit.

Almond Milk
yields 4-5 cups

1/2 C. almonds	*2 1/2 T. maple syrup/sweetener*
1 quart ice cold water	*a dash of almond extract*

For a white, creamy milk, blanch the almonds. Pour boiling water over almonds and let sit for 5-10 minutes. Remove the outer brown layer which will come off easily.

1. Cover the blades of the blender completely with almonds.
2. Pour one cup of water (a little over the almonds) into the blender and purée until smooth and creamy. Use a plastic spatula or a little water to get the pieces of almond off the sides of the blender.
3. When the purée becomes difficult to blend, add a few more tablespoons of water until it is completely smooth.
4. Fill to the top with ice cold water while still blending. Add maple syrup and almond extract and blend again.
   - Almond milk can be strained for an even smoother consistency.

"A more secret, sweet, and overpowering beauty appears to man when his heart and mind open to the sentiment of virtue. Then he is instructed in what is above him. He learns that his being is without bound; that to the good, to the perfect, he is born."

RALPH WALDO EMERSON (1803-1882) ~ American philosopher, poet and essayist

Tofu Cottage Cheese
yields 3 1/2 cups

1 lb. (2 C.) firm tofu	2 t. onion powder
2/3 C. vegan 'mayonnaise' (pg 72)	1 t. garlic powder
1 t. sea salt (optional)	1 t. caraway seeds

Rinse tofu, drain and mash well. Mix with remaining ingredients in a bowl. Store in the refrigerator.

Baked Granola
yields 7 cups

4 C. rolled oats	1/3-1/2 C. maple syrup, to taste
1/2 C. pecans, chopped	1/2 C. sunflower seeds
1/2 C. almonds, chopped	1 t. vanilla
1 C. walnuts, chopped	1/3 C. oil
1/2 C. bran	a dash of cloves, ground
1 C. shredded coconut	1 C. raisins (optional)
1 1/2 t. cinnamon	

1. Mix all ingredients together in a bowl.
2. Lightly oil two baking sheets (or use baking papers) and bake in a pre-heated oven at 275°. Bake in the oven for 25 minutes then rotate baking sheets from top to bottom. Bake until golden-brown, another 15-25 minutes. Cool before serving and storing.

• Stores well in an air-tight container.

Raw Granola (Muesli)
yields 8 cups

4 C. rolled oats	1 C. raisins
1/2 C. almonds, chopped	1/3 C. figs, chopped
1/2 C. pecans, chopped	1/3 C. dates, chopped
1/2 C. walnuts, chopped	1/2 C. sunflower seeds
1/2 C. oat or wheat bran	1/2 C. dry sweetener
1 C. shredded coconut	2 t. cinnamon

Mix all ingredients together in a bowl. When serving, pour sunflower or almond milk over granola and top with sliced banana or other fresh fruit.

• Stores well in an air-tight container.

High Energy Granola
yields 8 cups

4 1/2 C. rolled oats	1/2 C. sweetener (maple or rice syrup)
1/2 C. bran	1/3 C. apple juice
1/2 C. wheat germ	1/4 C. safflower oil (or other)
1/2 C. nuts and/or seeds, chopped	1 1/2 C. assorted dried fruit, chopped
1 T. cinnamon	(unsulphured apricots, raisins, figs)
1/2 t. nutmeg	

1. Pre-heat oven to 350°. Lightly oil cookie sheet.
2. In a large bowl, mix together all ingredients in the first column.
3. Whisk or blend sweetener, juice and oil. Add to oat mixture. Stir until well coated.
4. Spread granola onto a baking sheet and bake for 25 minutes, stirring a few times so it browns evenly. Remove from oven and let cool on the baking sheet for 15 minutes.
5. Add dried fruit when mixture cools. Store in an air-tight container.

Oatmeal – Creamy Style
serves 3-4

4 C. water	3/4 t. cinnamon
1 t. oil (optional)	1 t. vanilla
a dash of sea salt	1/3 C. raisins
1 3/4 C. rolled oats	4-5 t. maple syrup/sweetener

1. Bring water, oil and sea salt to a boil. Add rolled oats and stir. Turn heat down to a simmer.
2. Add remaining ingredients. Stir continuously and simmer for approximately 15-20 minutes until water is absorbed and cereal is creamy. Add more water if needed.

• Serve with sunflower milk.

Hot Cereal
serves 4-5

7 C. water	2 C. rolled oats
1 t. oil	1/2 C. sweetener
1/2 t. sea salt	1-2 t. vanilla
1 1/2 C. cous-cous	1-2 t. cinnamon

1. Bring water, oil and sea salt to a boil. Add grains and simmer.
2. When grains start to absorb water, add sweetener, vanilla and spices. Stir frequently until all water is absorbed.

• Optional ~ Add raisins to cereal just before it is finished, allowing them to soften.

Three Grain Hot Cereal

serves 5-6

7 C. water	1 C. cous-cous
1 1/2 t. oil	4-5 T. dry sweetener
1/2 t. sea salt	5 T. sweetener or maple syrup
2 C. rolled oats	1 t. cinnamon
2/3 C. bulgur	1 t. vanilla

1. Bring water, oil and salt to a boil.
2. Add oats and bulgur and simmer until soft, about 15-20 minutes.
3. Add cous-cous, sweeteners, cinnamon and vanilla. Stir for several minutes and serve.

Tofu Omelette

serves 2

1 1/2 lb. (3 C.) medium-firm tofu	2-3 T. nutritional yeast
1-2 T. tahini	1 t. turmeric
2 T. tamari or substitute	1 T. safflower oil (optional)

1. Rinse and drain tofu. In a bowl, mash well, then mix with remaining ingredients.
2. Place batter in an oiled, hot skillet (or non-stick pan) and press into an omelette shape. Cook on medium heat until brown on one side. Flip and brown the other side.

• See following recipes for additional omelette ideas.

Low-Oil Omelette

serves 2-3

2 1/2 C. tofu	1 t. herb seasoning (page 3)
2 T. nutritional yeast	1/2 t. turmeric
1 T. tamari or substitute	1/4 t. sea salt
	black pepper, to taste (optional)

1. Rinse and drain tofu. In a bowl, mash well, then mix with remaining ingredients.
2. Place batter in a lightly oiled frying pan and pat down. Cook on one side, then flip. Batter will get firm and golden-brown in color.

> *"Women should be protected from anyone's exercise of unrighteous power...but then, so should every other living creature."*
>
> GEORGE ELIOT (1819-1880) ~ English novelist

Western Omelette
yields 1 large skillet

2 lbs. (4 C.) tofu, rinsed & drained	**Sauté**
1/8 C. nutritional yeast	1 C. onion, diced
1 1/2 T. tamari or substitute	3 C. red pepper, sliced
1/2 t. black pepper (optional)	1 C. mushrooms, diced
1 t. sea salt	1 T. tamari or substitute
1/4 C. scallions, chopped	1/8 C. nutritional yeast
1 t. turmeric	

1. In a bowl, mash tofu. Mix with seasonings and scallions. Set aside in a cool place.
2. Sauté onion in a little oil and/or water. Add red pepper then mushrooms and sauté until soft. Season with tamari and nutritional yeast. Add to tofu batter and mix well.
3. Pan-fry in an oiled or non-stick skillet. Flip when browned on one side.

• Variation ~ Baking the batter uses less oil and it will solidify the omelette as well. Place batter in a lightly oiled cast-iron skillet or on a baking sheet. Pat the batter firmly into shape and bake in a pre-heated oven for 25 minutes at 350°.

Spanish Omelette Pie
yields 1 large skillet

1 t. oil (optional)	1 T. nutritional yeast
3/4 C. onion, diced	1/2 t. turmeric
2 C. bell pepper (red & green)	1/4 t. paprika
3/4 C. fresh tomato	1 t. sea salt
1 t. chili powder/Mexican spice	1 T. tahini
1 T. tamari or substitute	1 C. potato, peeled and grated
1/2 C. tomato paste	1 T. oil
sea salt, paprika, dash of each	2 t. tamari or substitute
2 lbs. (4 C.) firm tofu	2 t. nutritional yeast

1. In a small saucepan, sauté the onion in oil or water. When softened, dice the bell peppers and tomatoes and add to the sauté. Add chili/Mexican spice and tamari with the tomato paste, sea salt and paprika. Cook until vegetables are tender and flavors blend, about 10–15 minutes. Set this sauce aside.
2. Rinse tofu, drain and mash in a bowl. Add the yeast, spices and tahini.
3. Fry grated potato in one tablespoon of oil, tamari and nutritional yeast. Add to mashed tofu and mix well. Batter should be firm.
4. Completely coat the bottom of a large skillet with oil (or use a non-stick pan). Fry the tofu/potato batter. Flip while cooking (in sections) so it cooks all the way through, then press back together into an omelette shape and continue cooking until browned. Allow to cool somewhat to solidify.
5. Place a serving plate over the frying pan and flip omelette onto the plate.
6. Warm the sauce (if necessary) and spread on top of the omelette. Serve.

'Cheese' Omelette
yields 1 skillet

2 lbs. (4 C.) tofu, rinsed & drained   1/2 t. turmeric
2 T. tamari or substitute   1/4 t. pepper
1 C. vegan 'cheese', grated   1/2 t. sea salt
   (page 274)   2 T. nutritional yeast

1. Rinse and drain tofu. In a bowl, mash and mix with remaining ingredients.
2. Oil a baking sheet and spread batter on it. Bake in a pre-heated oven at 350° for 25-30 minutes (or lightly fry batter in a skillet).
   • Optional ~ Sprinkle with half a cup additional grated non-dairy cheese and bake.

Scrambled Tofu
serves 2-3

1 3/4 lbs. (3 1/2 C.) tofu   1/8 t. turmeric
1 T. tamari or substitute   1 t. dill
2 T. oil   1/4 t. garlic powder
1/2 t. sea salt   1/4 t. onion powder
4 T. nutritional yeast   1/2 t. herb seasoning (page 3)

1. Rinse and drain tofu. In a bowl, mash and mix with remaining ingredients.
2. Place the batter in a heated, lightly oiled (or non-stick) skillet. Stir-fry until browned, approximately 7-10 minutes.

Home-style Hash Browns
serves

4 large potatoes, peeled & grated   1-2 T. nutritional yeast
1/3 C. onions, finely chopped   1/8 t. red or black pepper
1/2 t. sea salt   2 T. oil

1. In a medium-sized bowl, mix all ingredients (except oil) into a batter. In a cast-iron skillet, heat oil (or use a non-stick pan). Add batter to hot skillet, forming a circle.
2. Cook until golden-brown then flip to brown the other side.
   • Variation ~ Lightly oil a baking sheet and bake at 350° for 25 minutes.

> **"Only in growth, reform and change, paradoxically enough,
> is true security to be found."**
>
> ANNE MORROW LINDBURGH (1906-2001) American writer, poet and aviator

French Toast
yields 6 slices

3/4 lb. (1 1/2 C.) tofu	1/8 t. cinnamon
3 T. sweetener	a dash of nutmeg
1/2 C. water	1 T. oil
1 t. vanilla	6 slices whole wheat bread

1. Rinse and drain tofu. In a blender, blend with sweetener, water, vanilla and spices until smooth. (1/2 C. tahini can be substituted for tofu.)
2. Pre-heat oil in a skillet. Dip bread slices into mixture and grill on both sides.
3. Serve hot, and top with maple syrup or jam.

Hawaiian Toast
yields 8 slices

1 lb. (2 C.) firm tofu	8 (or more) slices bread
1 1/2 C. coconut milk	oil for cooking
2 T. maple syrup	pineapple jam or other preserves
1 t. vanilla	1/4 C. shredded coconut
a pinch of sea salt	macadamia nuts, crushed (for garnish)

1. Rinse and drain tofu. In a blender, blend with coconut milk, maple syrup, vanilla and sea salt. Blend to a smooth consistency.
2. Pour mixture into a bowl and dip two slices of bread in it, coating thoroughly.
3. In a heated, oiled skillet, place the coated pieces of bread. Cook each side until golden-brown. Repeat until all the batter is used.
4. Top with pineapple jam or maple syrup, sprinkle with coconut and crushed macadamia nuts. Serve hot.

Fluffy Pancakes
yields 9-10 small pancakes

1 1/4 C. whole wheat pastry flour	2 T. dry sweetener
1/2 t. sea salt	1/2 t. vanilla
2 t. baking powder	1 1/4 C. soy milk
1/4 t. baking soda	2 T. safflower oil *(melted coconut oil)*

Applesauce

1. Sift all dry ingredients into a bowl, except sweetener, and stir.
2. Combine sweetener and liquid ingredients in a separate bowl. Stir well.
3. Pour dry mixture into liquid mixture and stir until smooth. Do not over-mix.
4. Drop a spoonful of batter (at first to test grill) onto a hot oiled or non-stick skillet. When edges turn brown and bubbles form and remain open in the middle (approximately 1-2 minutes), flip over for another minute or two until done.
   • Spelt flour can replace whole wheat flour.

Mom's Pancakes
yields 6–8 pancakes

1 1/2 t. active dry yeast	1 t. cinnamon
1/4 C. warm water	1 1/2 T. egg replacer
1 t. dry sweetener	2 1/2 C. soy or rice milk
2 C. whole wheat pastry flour	1 T. dry sweetener
1/2 t. sea salt	1/8 C. safflower oil
1 T. baking powder	1/2 t. vanilla
1 t. baking soda	

1. Place yeast in warm water with 1 t. sweetener. Let rise in a warm spot, until it bubbles up, doubling in size. Sift dry ingredients into a bowl, except sweetener, and stir.
2. In a separate bowl, beat egg replacer with 1/2 cup of milk until frothy. Add sweetener, remaining milk, oil and vanilla. Stir well.
3. Pour wet into dry and mix until smooth. Add froth from risen yeast (without adding all the water). Mix until batter is smooth yet not thin, adding more milk if needed.
4. Pour batter to desired size onto an oiled hot grill, cast-iron skillet, or non-stick pan. When edges turn brown and bubbles form and remain open in the middle (approximately 1–2 minutes), flip over for another minute or two until golden-brown.

Easy Apple Cinnamon Muffins
yields 18 muffins

1 C. bran	1 C. dry sweetener
2 C. whole wheat pastry flour	1 C. tofu milk (page 10)
1 T. baking powder	1/2 C. oil
1/2 t. baking soda	1 C. apples, grated
1 1/2 t. cinnamon	1/2 C. raisins

1. Place bran into a bowl. Sift remaining dry ingredients into the bowl and stir.
2. In a separate bowl, mix tofu milk with oil. Add grated apple and raisins. Stir.
3. Add dry batter to the wet and mix well. Oil muffin tins. Fill cups 3/4 full. Bake in a pre-heated oven at 350° for about 35–45 minutes until a toothpick comes out dry.

*above: **Cinnamon Rolls** (page 28) ~ below: **Mom's Pancakes** (page 24)*

> *"Freedom! A fine word when rightly understood.*
> *What freedom would you have?*
> *What is the freedom of the most free?*
> *To act rightly."*
>
> JOHANN WOLFGANG VON GOETHE (1749-1832) ~ German philosopher

Sweet Corn Muffins
yields 1 dozen

1/2 C. liquid sweetener	1 1/2 C. cornmeal, sifted
1/2 C. dry sweetener	1/2 C. pastry flour, sifted
1 1/4 C. tofu milk, thick (page 10)	1 t. baking soda, sifted
1/4 C. oil	1/2 t. sea salt

1. In a large bowl, whisk the first four ingredients. Sift dry ingredients into a smaller bowl and stir. Add dry to wet ingredients and mix well.
2. Spoon batter into an oiled and floured muffin tin or use baking paper cups, filling cups 3/4 full. Bake in a pre-heated oven at 400° for 20 minutes or until golden-brown.

Carrot Muffins *(party-sized recipe)*
yields approx. 4 dozen

<u>Wet</u>

1/2 C. vegan margarine (page 274)	1 T. baking soda
1/2 C. oil	4 t. cinnamon
4 1/3 C. dry sweetener	1 t. allspice
2 C. tofu milk (page 10)	1/3 t. sea salt
5 C. carrots, grated	<u>Additional Ingredients</u>
<u>Dry</u>	1 C. raisins
8 C. whole wheat flour	1 C. walnuts, chopped
1 t. baking powder	1 C. shredded coconut (optional)

1. Mix wet ingredients in a very large bowl.
2. Sift dry ingredients into a separate bowl and stir. Mix the dry into the wet.
3. Add raisins, nuts and shredded coconut. Mix well.
4. Pour batter into an oiled and floured muffin tin, or into baking paper cups, filling each cup 3/4 full.
5. Bake in a pre-heated oven at 350° for 20 minutes or until golden-brown and a toothpick comes out dry.

above: **Twin Challah Loaves** *(page 31) ~ below left:* **Blueberry Muffins** *(page 26)*
below right: **Fresh Fruit Salad** *with* **Blueberry Tofu Yogurt** *(page 16)*

> *"It is nearly fifty years since I was assured by a conclave of doctors that if I did not eat meat, I should die of starvation."*
>
> GEORGE BERNARD SHAW (1856-1950) ~ Anglo-Irish playwright
> 1925 Nobel Prize recipient

Bran Muffins
yields 1 dozen

1 1/4 C. whole wheat pastry flour	1/3 C. oil
1 t. baking soda	1/3 C. liquid sweetener (sorghum)
1 t. cinnamon	1 t. vanilla
1 C. bran	1 C. soy milk

1. In a small bowl, sift flour, baking soda and cinnamon. Add bran and stir.
2. In a separate bowl, whisk the wet ingredients together. Add dry to the wet and mix.
3. Oil and flour a muffin tin (or use baking paper cups). Spoon batter into each cup, filling 2/3 full. Bake in a pre-heated oven at 400° for 25 minutes or until golden-brown and a toothpick comes out dry.

Blueberry Muffins
yields 1 dozen

2 C. whole wheat pastry flour	1/4 C. oil
1/2 t. baking powder	1/4 C. applesauce
1/2 t. baking soda	1/3 C. juice/water
a pinch of sea salt	1/2 t. vanilla
1/2 C. sweetener	1/2 C. blueberries

1. In a bowl or food processor, combine all dry ingredients and blend well.
2. Add all other ingredients except blueberries to the bowl/processor. Blend until creamy. Add berries and pulse or mix together, gently.
3. Oil and flour a muffin tin (or use baking paper cups). Pour batter into muffin tin, filling each cup 3/4 full. Bake in a pre-heated oven at 350° for 15–20 minutes or until golden-brown and a toothpick comes out dry.

Blueberry Corn Muffins
yields 18 muffins

Wet	Dry
2 C. dry sweetener	1 1/2 C. blue cornmeal
1/3 C. oil	1 1/2 C. w/w pastry or spelt flour
1 1/2 C. blueberries	2 t. baking soda, sifted
2 1/2 C. thick tofu milk (page 10)	1/2 t. sea salt

1. Mix wet ingredients in a large bowl.
2. Sift dry ingredients together in another bowl. Stir.
3. Add dry to the wet and mix. Pour batter 3/4 full into oiled and floured muffin tins (or use baking paper cups).
4. Bake in a pre-heated oven at 350° for 20 minutes or until a toothpick comes out dry.

Banana Walnut Muffins
yields 24 muffins

3 C. mashed bananas (approx. 6)
3/4 C. maple syrup
1/2 C. oil
1/2 T. vanilla
1 t. baking powder

3 1/2 C. pastry flour
2 t. baking soda
1/4 t. sea salt (optional)
1 t. nutmeg
1/2 C. walnuts, finely chopped

1. Combine all the wet ingredients. In a separate bowl, sift all dry ingredients together, except walnuts. Add the dry to the wet and mix thoroughly, then fold in walnuts.
2. Oil and flour muffin tins or use baking paper cups. Fill each cup 3/4 full. Bake in a pre-heated oven at 350° for 30 minutes, or until golden-brown and a toothpick comes out dry.

Wheat-Free Corn Muffins
yields 1 dozen muffins

<u>Wet</u>
1 C. dry sweetener
1 1/4 C. soy milk
1/4 C. oil

<u>Dry</u>
1 C. cornmeal
1 C. spelt flour
1 t. baking soda
1/2 t. baking powder

1. In a bowl, whisk the wet ingredients.
2. Sift dry ingredients in another bowl and stir.
3. Mix the dry batter into the wet.
4. Oil and flour a muffin tin (or use baking paper cups). Pour batter in, filling each cup 3/4 full. Bake in a pre-heated oven at 350° for 15–20 minutes, or until muffins are golden-brown and a toothpick comes out dry.

Peanut Butter Muffins
yields 12 muffins

2 C. pastry flour
1 T. baking powder
1 1/2 C. tofu milk (page 10)

1/3 C. oil
1/4 C. dry sweetener
1/4 C. peanut butter

1. Sift flour and baking powder into a bowl and stir.
2. Blend tofu milk, adding oil and sweetener. Place in a bowl and add peanut butter. Stir with a fork. Mix dry ingredients into the blended mixture. Mix well but don't beat.
3. Oil and flour a muffin tin or use baking paper cups. Fill each cup 3/4 full. Bake in a pre-heated oven at 350° for 25 minutes until golden-brown and a toothpick comes out dry.

Cinnamon Rolls
yields 2 dozen

Dough
1 1/2 C. warm water
2 t. active dry yeast (see page 11)
1 1/2 t. egg replacer
1/3 C. oil
1/2 C. dry sweetener
1 1/2 t. sea salt
4 1/2 C. pastry flour
2 t. cinnamon

Filling
1/4 C. oil (or vegan margarine)
1/2–1/3 C. dry sweetener
1/2 C. walnuts, chopped
1/3 C. raisins
3–4 T. cinnamon

Glaze
1/4 C. rice or soy milk
1/2 C. dry sweetener
1 1/2 t. vanilla

To make dough with a bread machine, do so according to your machine's directions, using the dough setting. The water should go in first and the yeast last to keep it dry. When cycle is complete, remove dough and begin here at step 5.

1. Combine one cup warm water with one teaspoon sweetener. Mix in yeast and let rise in a warm (not hot) place. Yeast will bubble up and activate in about 15 minutes, doubling in size.
2. In a separate bowl, whisk remaining 1/2 cup water with egg replacer. Mix in oil, sweetener and salt. Add the activated yeast and stir.
3. Sift the flour into a bowl and mix with cinnamon. Slowly add to the wet mixture, mixing thoroughly. Knead for ten minutes. Knead in more flour if needed to bring to a bread dough texture, not sticky or too dry.
4. Let stand for an hour in a warm, draft-free place, covered with a clean towel.
5. Punch down and let stand for half an hour. Punch down once more and cut dough in half. On a floured board, roll into a 16" x 20" rectangle.
6. Mix the filling ingredients, except the oil, in a bowl. Spread the oil or margarine on the dough and sprinkle filling on top. Roll the dough up tight, from the longest side and cut into one inch pieces. Lay pieces flat on a baking tray, leaving space in between each roll for rising. Cover and let rise for an hour in a draft-free place.
7. Bake in a pre-heated oven at 350° for 25–35 minutes until golden-brown.
8. In a small pot, mix together glaze ingredients and warm on low heat. Stir until smooth. Drip glaze over the top of warm rolls and serve.

> "Many times I am asked why the suffering of animals should call forth more sympathy from me than the suffering of human beings; why I work in this direction of charitable work more than toward any other. My answer is that I believe that this work includes all the education and lines of reform which are needed to make a perfect circle of peace and goodwill about the earth…"
>
> ELLA WHEELER WILCOX (1850-1919) ~ American poet

Easy Whole Wheat (or Spelt) Bread
yields 2 loaves

2 1/2 C. warm water	1/4 C. soy milk
3-4 T. molasses	3 t. sea salt
2 T. active dry yeast	3 t. herb seasoning (page 3)
3 C. spelt flour	2 T. egg replacer (or arrowroot)
1/4 C. vegetable oil	2 T. gluten flour (optional)
	5-5 1/2 C. spelt or w/w pastry flour

1. Mix water, 1 T. molasses and yeast together in a large bowl. Wait a few minutes for bubbles to form. Add the 3 cups of flour and mix well. Cover the bowl and set in a warm place. Let sit for a minimum of 20 minutes, two hours, or up to a day.
2. Pour in molasses, oil, soy milk, sea salt, herb seasoning, egg replacer and gluten flour. Mix. Begin adding remaining flour, 1/2 cup at a time. After the third cup, it begins to get dense. Begin kneading it in the bowl. It will be sticky; continue adding the rest of the flour. Knead for 10 minutes until it becomes smooth and elastic.
3. Cut dough into two equal parts. Shape into loaves and place them into two 8 1/2" by 6" or 7" oiled bread pans. (or make approximately 24 rolls or one loaf and 12 rolls)
4. Cover pans with a clean towel and set in a warm place until dough is doubled in size. This will take at least an hour.
5. Bake in a pre-heated oven at 350° for 30-40 minutes or until golden-brown and a paring knife comes out dry.

Sweet Cornbread
yields one 9" x 9" baking pan or skillet

2 1/2 C. tofu milk, thick (page 10)	2 C. whole wheat pastry flour, sifted
1/2 C. oil	2 C. cornmeal, sifted
2 t. vanilla	2 t. baking soda, sifted
1 1/2-2 C. dry sweetener	1/2 t. sea salt

1. In a blender, blend tofu milk with oil, vanilla and sweetener.
2. In a bowl, sift pastry flour, cornmeal and baking soda. Add sea salt and mix.
3. Pour the liquid into dry ingredients and stir.
4. Fill a lightly oiled and floured baking pan (or cast-iron skillet) half-way. Bake in a pre-heated oven at 400° for 35-40 minutes, until golden-brown and a toothpick comes out dry. It is important to bake thoroughly. Cool before cutting.

• Optional ~ For a dinner corn bread, add diced onion and seasonings before baking.

"Universal compassion is the only guarantee of morality."

ARTHUR SCHOPENHAUER (1788-1860) ~ German author and philosopher

Banana Bread
yields 1 loaf

1/3 C. dry sweetener	2 1/2 C. pastry flour, sifted
1/3 C. maple syrup	1 1/2 t. baking soda, sifted
1/2 C. oil	1/2 t. cinnamon
2 T. soy powder & 3 t. water	1/2 C. walnuts, chopped
2 C. ripe banana, mashed	1/2 C. raisins, chopped

1. In a large bowl, combine sweeteners, oil, soy mixture and mashed banana.
2. In a separate bowl, combine all dry ingredients, then add to liquid mixture. Transfer into an oiled and floured loaf pan.
3. Bake in a pre-heated oven at 350° for one hour. Test with a toothpick. If still wet inside, reduce heat to 300° and bake for another 15 minutes or until a toothpick comes out dry.

Foccacia Bread
yields 1 large or 2 small loaves

Bread	Topping
2 t. active dry yeast (see page 11)	4–5 T. olive oil
1 1/4 C. warm water	1/4 C. fresh basil, chopped
2 T. sweetener	1/2 C. chives (or onion), chopped
3 T. oil	1/4 C. garlic, minced
1 1/2 t. sea salt	1/4 C. fresh rosemary
4 1/2 C. whole wheat pastry flour	2 tomatoes, sliced or diced

To make dough with a bread maker, do so according to your machine's directions. The water should go in first and the yeast last to keep it dry. Begin here at step 3.

1. Dissolve yeast with sweetener in warm water (not hot) and let sit for at least 15 minutes in a warm place until yeast bubbles and is doubled in size.
2. Combine yeast mixture with oil and salt. Slowly add the flour until the dough no longer sticks to your fingers but is still elastic and not dry. On a floured board, knead for 10 more minutes. Let dough rise for one hour in a draft-free, warm place (covered with a towel).
3. Punch down dough and coat with 2 T. olive oil. Let rise for another 30 minutes.
4. Roll out flat onto one 16" x 20" oiled baking sheet or make two smaller loaves.
5. Cover dough with remaining olive oil and sprinkle on the toppings.
6. Bake in a pre-heated oven at 350° for 30–35 minutes.

> **"If a man earnestly seeks a righteous life,
> his first act of abstinence is from animal food..."**
>
> COUNT LEO TOLSTOY (1828-1910) ~ Russian novelist and philosopher

French Baguettes
yields 2 loaves

2 t. active dry yeast (see page 11)	2 t. sea salt
1 3/4 C. warm water	4 1/2 C. whole wheat pastry flour
2 T. sweetener	1 T. oil (optional)

1. Dissolve yeast with sweetener in warm water (not hot) and let sit for at least 15 minutes in a warm place until yeast bubbles and is doubled in size.
2. Mix the risen yeast with the sea salt. Slowly add flour until the dough no longer sticks to your fingers, but is still elastic and not dry. On a floured board, knead for at least 10 minutes. Let dough rise for one hour in a warm place (covered with a towel).
3. Lightly punch down and let rise again for another 30 minutes or until twice the size.
4. Roll out dough into a large rectangle, split in half (or thirds for three smaller loaves). Roll up tight from the longer side or make a braided baguette (see recipe below).
5. Let rise again in a draft-free place for 40 minutes. Brush lightly with oil. Bake in a pre-heated oven at 350° for 20–30 minutes, until golden-brown.

Eggless Challah Bread
yields 1 loaf

2 t. active dry yeast (see page 11)	2 t. sea salt
1/4 C. warm water	1/4 C. oil
2 T. sweetener	4 1/2 C. whole wheat pastry flour, sifted
2 1/2 t. egg replacer	<u>Topping</u>
mixed with 1 C. water	2 T. poppy seeds

To make dough with a bread maker, do so according to your machine's directions. The water should go in first and the yeast last to keep it dry. Begin here at step 4.

1. Dissolve yeast with sweetener in warm water (not hot) and let sit for at least 15 minutes in a warm place until yeast bubbles and is doubled in size.
2. Mix egg replacer with water in a bowl and add risen yeast along with sea salt and oil. Add flour slowly to the wet mixture and mix together well. Place on a floured board and knead for 10 minutes, adding flour as needed. Dough should be smooth and elastic yet not sticky. Cover and let rise for 1 1/2 hours, then punch down.
3. Divide the dough into thirds making three equal ropes. Pinch together at one end and braid together. Pinch at the other end to secure the braid. Let rise until doubled in size (about 45 minutes). Brush lightly with oil and sprinkle poppy seeds on top.
4. Bake in a pre-heated oven at 350° for 25 minutes until golden-brown.

"It is very significant that some of the most thoughtful and cultured men are partisans of a pure vegetable diet."

MAHATMA GANDHI (1869-1948) ~ Hindu pacifist, spiritual leader

Dinner Biscuits
yields 12 biscuits

2 C. whole wheat pastry flour
1 t. sea salt
4 t. baking powder

2-3 T. sweetener
1/4 C. oil
1 C. tofu milk (page 10)
1 1/2 T. egg replacer & 2 T. water

1. Sift together all dry ingredients and mix well. In a large bowl, combine all liquid ingredients. Add the dry mixture to the wet and stir lightly. DO NOT OVER-MIX.
2. Oil a muffin tin or baking sheet. Bake in a pre-heated oven at 350° for 20-25 minutes.

Whole Wheat Burger Buns
yields 8 buns

1/4 C. warm water
1 T. active dry yeast
1 t. sweetener
3-3 1/2 C. whole wheat flour

1 C. water
1/2 t. sea salt
2 T. sesame seeds

1. Dissolve yeast with sweetener in warm water (not hot) and let sit for at least 15 minutes in a warm place until yeast bubbles and is doubled in size.
2. Mix in flour, water and salt. Dough will get stiff. Knead for 10 minutes on a floured board until dough is smooth and not sticky or dry.
3. Oil a clean bowl. Place dough in bowl, cover with a damp towel and set in a warm place. Let rise for one hour or until doubled in size.
4. Press dough down. Divide into eight balls and flatten each into half inch thick rounds. Press sesame seeds on top.
5. Lay a piece of wax paper, loosely, over the top of the rolls and let rise until doubled.
6. Remove wax paper. Bake in a pre-heated oven at 375° for 15-20 minutes. Slice when cooled.

Hope's Crispy Cornbread
yields 1 skillet (1 loaf)

1 1/2 C. cornmeal
1/2 C. pastry flour
1/2 C. rice flour
1/2 C. semolina flour
1 T. sea salt

4 t. baking powder
1/4 C. oil
3-4 T. sweetener
1 C. rice milk
mexican spices (optional)

1. Sift the dry ingredients together, including baking powder. Mix.
2. Whisk oil, sweetener and rice milk and stir into the dry ingredients. Season with any desired spices, to taste. Place in an oiled cast-iron skillet.
3. Bake in a pre-heated oven at 350° for 30-40 minutes, until a toothpick comes out dry.

Fluffy Dinner Cornbread
yields 1 large loaf or 2 small cakes

2 1/2 C. thick tofu milk (page 10)
1/2 C. oil
1/4 t. tamari or substitute
1 C. dry sweetener
2 C. cornmeal
2 C. whole wheat pastry flour

2 t. baking soda, sifted
1/2 t. garlic powder
chili powder, to taste (optional)
1/2 t. onion powder
1/2 t. sea salt
1/2 t. herb seasoning (page 3)

1. In a blender, blend tofu milk, adding oil, tamari and sweetener.
2. In a bowl, sift together the remaining ingredients.
3. Pour wet mixture into dry ingredients. Mix well.
4. Pour batter into a lightly oiled baking pan, filling half-way to leave room for rising.
5. Bake in a pre-heated oven at 350° for 30–40 minutes until toothpick comes out completely dry. Be sure to bake thoroughly. Allow to cool before cutting.

• Variation ~ Finely dice half an onion and half a green pepper and fold into the batter.

Holiday Pumpkin Bread
yields 1 cake or bread loaf

2 1/4 C. whole wheat pastry flour
1 t. baking soda, sifted
1/4 t. sea salt
2 1/2 t. egg replacer (dry)
2–3 t. cinnamon
1 1/2 C. dry sweetener

1/3 C. oil
1 C. pumpkin (canned or fresh),
  cooked and blended
1/4 C. orange juice
1 t. vanilla
1/2 C. raisins
1/2 C. pecans/walnuts, chopped

1. Sift all dry ingredients together in a bowl.
2. Mix together oil, pumpkin, orange juice and vanilla. Add to dry ingredients.
3. Fold in raisins and nuts. Mix. Pour into an oiled and floured cake or bread pan.
4. Bake in a pre-heated oven at 350° for 45–50 minutes for a cake, 60 minutes for a bread loaf. The bread is done when a toothpick comes out dry.

"I know of no more beautiful prayer than that which the Hindus of old used in closing their public spectacles. It was: 'May all that have life be delivered from suffering.'"

ARTHUR SCHOPENHAUER (1788-1860) ~ German author and philosopher

Holiday Cranberry Sweet Bread
yields one 8" cake pan

2 1/4 C. whole wheat pastry flour	3/4 C. orange juice
1 t. baking soda, sifted	1/2 C. oil
1 t. baking powder, sifted	2–3 t. orange rind, grated
1 C. dry sweetener	1/2 C. walnuts
2 t. egg replacer	1 C. cranberries, halved

1. Sift the first five ingredients into a bowl and stir.
2. In a large bowl, whisk orange juice, oil and orange rinds. Add the dry to the wet batter and mix. Fold in nuts and cranberries. Place in an oiled and floured pan.
3. Bake in a pre-heated oven at 350° for 30–40 minutes, until a toothpick comes out dry.

Glazed Rolls
yields 18 rolls

Dough

2 t. active dry yeast (see page 11)	1/3 C. oil
1/3 C. dry sweetener	**Topping**
1 1/2 C. warm water	1/2 C. oil (or vegan margarine)
1 1/2 t. sea salt	1/4 C. orange peel, grated
4 1/2 C. whole wheat pastry flour	1/2 C. sweetener

To make dough with a bread maker, do so according to your machine's directions. The water should go in first and the yeast last to keep it dry. Begin here at step 4.

1. In a bowl, mix the yeast and one tablespoon sweetener with the warm water. Set aside for 15 minutes until doubled in size.
2. In a large bowl, sift the salt and flour and mix. Add yeast mixture and oil. Mix well.
3. Turn dough onto a well-floured board and knead for approximately 10 minutes until elastic and smooth, adding flour as needed. Dough should not be dry or sticky.
4. Place in an oiled bowl and turn, covering the surface of the dough with oil. Cover and allow to rise for about one hour, until doubled in size.
5. On a floured surface, divide and roll into two twelve inch ropes. Cut each rope into nine pieces.
6. In a bowl, mix topping ingredients. Dip the pieces into the topping mixture, covering each piece well.
7. Place on oiled (and floured) baking trays, spaced about half an inch apart. Cover and let rise in a warm draft-free place for 30 minutes, or until doubled in size.
8. Bake in a pre-heated oven at 350° for 20–30 minutes until golden-brown.

"Truth above all, even when it upsets us and overwhelms us."

FREDERICK AMIEL (1821-1881) ~ Swiss philosopher and poet

Sesame Herb Crackers
yields approx. 16 crackers

2 C. whole wheat pastry flour
1/2 t. baking soda
1/2 C. sesame seeds
2 T. wheat germ
1 t. sea salt

2 T. bran
1/2 t. each: oregano, basil & parsley
1/2 t. garlic powder
3/4 C. cold water
4 T. sesame oil

1. Sift flour and baking soda into a bowl. Add remaining dry ingredients and stir.
2. Mix water and oil into the dry mixture.
3. Roll dough out onto a lightly oiled cookie sheet. Gently cut into squares before baking, not cutting all the way through the dough.
4. Bake in a pre-heated oven at 350° for 17-20 minutes.
5. Cool and break crackers along pre-cut lines.
   - Variation ~ Substitute 1/4 cup onion flakes for the bran and wheat germ.
   - Variation ~ For a simple sesame cracker, do not add herbs.

Sesame Flat Bread
yields 20 flat breads

1 2/3 C. whole wheat flour
1/2 t. baking soda
1/4 t. sea salt

1 T. dry sweetener
1/4 C. oil (or vegan margarine)
1/2 C. soy milk
3 T. sesame seeds

1. Sift the dry ingredients into a large bowl and stir. Add sweetener and stir again.
2. Cut/mix in margarine or oil. Mixture will form fine crumbs.
3. Stir in soy milk and sesame seeds. Shape dough into a ball.
4. Pinch off pieces of dough and roll into one inch balls. Roll them out thin between wax paper. Lightly oil a baking sheet and place each flat bread on it. Bake in a pre-heated oven at 400° for 7-10 minutes. Cool.

> *"I went from being vegetarian to becoming a vegan... I am now in better physical health than I have ever been, with more stamina and zest for life. In my path of being vegan, my body, mind, heart, and spirit have all healed and grown stronger. And the incredible joy I receive from knowing that I am lessening my impact on this beautiful planet fulfills me in a way that a meat and dairy diet never could, and never will."*

JULIA BUTTERFLY HILL ~ author, The Legacy of Luna
quoted from The Food Revolution by John Robbins

> *"When I was 88 years old, I gave up meat entirely and switched to a plant-foods diet following a slight stroke. During the following months, I not only lost 50 pounds but gained strength in my legs and picked up stamina. Now, at age 93, I'm on the same plant-based diet, and I still don't eat any meat or dairy products. I either swim, walk, or paddle a canoe daily and I feel the best I've felt since my heart problems began."*

BENJAMIN SPOCK, M.D. (1903-1998)
pediatrician and author

Scrumptious Salads & Soups

Scrumptious Salads & Soups

"*He will be regarded as a benefactor of his race
who shall teach man to confine himself
to a more innocent and wholesome diet.*"

HENRY DAVID THOREAU (1817–1862)
American author, poet and naturalist

For additional salads, see *Rawsome Recipes* pages 185-198

Tabouli Salad
serves 4-5

2 1/2 C. bulgur
1 tomato, diced finely
1/2-1 cucumber, diced finely
1 T. oil
1/2 T. herb seasoning (page 3)
1/2 t. onion powder

2 T. fresh lemon juice
2 T. tamari or substitute
1/4-1/2 C. parsley, chopped finely
1/4 small sweet onion, diced
1/8 t. lemon pepper
1/2 t. garlic powder

1. Place the bulgur in a bowl. Pour 4-5 cups of boiling water over it and cover. Let sit for at least an hour. Allow the bulgur to get soft, then drain any excess water.
2. Mix in all the remaining ingredients. Chill and serve.

Festive Carrot Salad
serves 5-6

6-7 C. carrots, sliced, steamed
1 C. garbanzo beans, cooked
1/2 C. celery, diced
1/3 C. onion or scallion, diced
1/4 C. fresh dill weed, chopped
1/3 C. oil
1/4 C. apple cider vinegar

1/4 C. rice syrup
1/3 C. nutritional yeast
1/8 C. water
1 T. oregano
1/2 t. garlic powder
1 T. Bragg™ Liquid Aminos or tamari
1 t. herb seasoning (page 3)

1. Peel and slice the carrots, then steam. When soft, place 4-5 cups of the carrot slices in a large bowl, saving the remaining carrots for the sauce.
2. To this bowl, add the garbanzo beans (chick peas), celery, onion and fresh dill.
3. In a blender, place the steamed carrots (that were set aside) with the remaining ingredients beginning with the oil. Blend well. Pour into bowl and stir. Allow to marinate and chill before serving, stirring periodically.
   • This salad keeps well in the refrigerator.

"Veganism isn't just a strict vegetarian diet; it is a complete philosophical viewpoint. It is practical in outlook, simple to understand and aspires to the highest environmental and spiritual values. I am sure it holds the key to a future lifestyle for a humane planetary guardianship..."

HOWARD LYMAN ~ former cattle rancher, international lecturer, author, <u>Mad Cowboy</u>

Italian Basil Bulgur Salad
serves 5

2 C. bulgur	1 t. herb seasoning (page 3)
3 C. boiling water	2 t. tamari or substitute
1/4 C. parsley, chopped	1 t. dill weed
1/4 C. fresh basil, chopped	2 t. dried oregano
1/2 C. scallions, chopped	1/8 C. apple cider vinegar
1/3 C. red bell pepper, diced	1/2 t. dried basil
1/8 C. olive oil	1 T. brown rice syrup
1/8 C. safflower oil	1 t. garlic powder
1/8 C. nutritional yeast	1/2 C. water

1. Place the bulgur in a bowl and pour the boiling water over it. Cover and allow to sit for half an hour to an hour to absorb the water. Drain any excess water.
2. Chop the herbs and pepper and set aside until bulgur is soft.
3. Blend remaining ingredients.
4. When bulgur is softened, add all ingredients to it. Mix and chill before serving. (After absorbing flavors you may want to add a little lemon juice before serving).

Quinoa Salad
serves 4

3 C. cooked quinoa	2 T. tamari or substitute
1 carrot, grated	2 T. tahini
2 small scallions, chopped	1 C. sunflower seeds
1 celery stalk	2 T. sesame seeds
1/2 bell pepper, diced	1 T. parsley
2 T. lemon juice	1/2 tomato, diced (optional)

1. Boil two cups of water and add one cup dry quinoa. Simmer for 15-20 minutes. Fluff with a fork. Cover and allow to cool.
2. Combine the cool quinoa, grated carrot, scallions, celery and pepper in a bowl. Add the lemon juice, tamari and tahini and mix thoroughly.
3. In a skillet, on a medium flame, toast the sunflower and sesame seeds. Stir often.
4. Mix toasted seeds into the quinoa mixture, then add the parsley and tomato. Refrigerate until serving.

"The greatest revolution of our generation is the discovery that human beings, by changing the inner attitudes of their minds, can change the outer aspects of their lives."

WILLIAM JAMES (1842-1910) ~ American philosopher, teacher sand psychologist

Caesar Salad
serves 8 or more

1/2 lb. (1 C.) firm tofu	*2 T. nutritional yeast*
2 t. tamari	*2 cloves garlic, crushed*
1 t. turmeric	*5-6 T. fresh lemon juice*
1 T. sunflower/safflower oil	*black pepper, to taste*
2 heads romaine lettuce	*fresh herbs (optional)*
4 green onions, chopped	*1 T. tahini*
1/2 C. olive oil	*1/2 t. sea salt, to taste*
	1 C. croutons/toasted bread pieces

1. Rinse and drain tofu and crumble into a bowl. Combine with tamari and turmeric.
2. In a skillet, heat a tablespoon of oil and add crumbled tofu. Cook for several minutes on one side and turn. Lightly brown, remove from heat and allow to cool.
3. Wash lettuce, spin-dry or drain and tear into small pieces. Toss together with green onion and tofu scramble.
4. In a separate bowl, whisk remaining ingredients together, except croutons. Pour over salad and toss well. Add croutons and pepper garnish, lightly toss and serve.

String Bean Salad
serves 3

1 lb. string beans	*1 T. nutritional yeast*
2 cloves garlic, minced	*1/2 C. tahini*
1 onion, diced	*Bragg™ Aminos or tamari (to taste)*
1 T. oil	*1/2 t. herb seasoning (page 3)*
1 T. tamari or substitute	*1/2 C. water*
1/4 t. onion powder	*1/4 t. garlic powder*

1. Steam the string beans until soft.
2. Sauté the minced garlic and diced onion in a small frying pan with the oil and tamari. Season with onion powder and yeast.
3. In a small jar, mix tahini and remaining ingredients by shaking vigorously.
4. In a bowl, mash the soft beans (if desired) using a wooden utensil. Add the seasoned onions and tahini dressing and mix. Chill before serving.

> *"Come, my friends; it is not too late to seek a newer world.*
> *We are one equal temper of heroic hearts."*
>
> ALFRED LORD TENNYSON (1809-1892) ~ English poet, Poet Laureate: 1850

Yellow & Green Bean Salad
serves 8

Vinaigrette Dressing

3 small green scallions, chopped
2 T. mustard
1/4 C. vinegar

1/2 t. each: salt/red pepper/garlic powder
1/4 C. olive oil
1 T. sweetener

1. In a small bowl, whisk scallions, mustard, vinegar, salt, pepper and garlic powder. Gradually add oil and sweetener, whisking until well blended.

Salad

1 lb. green beans, trimmed
1 lb. yellow wax beans, trimmed
1 small cabbage, shredded

1 medium red onion, chopped
1/2 C. sunflower seeds, toasted
1/2 lb. (1 C.) tofu (optional)

2. In a large pot, using a steamer basket, bring water to a boil. Add beans and cook until tender. Soak in cold water until cool, then drain. Pat dry with paper towels.
3. If using tofu, rinse it, drain and crumble into a large bowl.
4. Place beans in the bowl with tofu. Add cabbage, onion and sunflower seeds.
5. Add dressing and toss gently to coat. Serve at room temperature.

Baba Ghannouj
serves 6

1 (1 lb.) eggplant
2 cloves garlic, minced
3/4 C. fresh lemon juice

1/2 C. parsley, minced
6 T. tahini
tamari, to taste
herb seasoning, to taste (page 3)

1. Trim off eggplant stem. Pierce with a fork and bake at 350° until the skin is wrinkled.
2. Let cool then scoop out the inside and place with minced garlic in a bowl or a food processor using the "S" shaped blade.
3. Mash or process with lemon juice, parsley and tahini. Season to taste with tamari and/or herb seasoning. Refrigerate for one hour before serving.

"...Dickensian compassion rescued children from sweat shops. Lincolnian empathy rescued slaves from being 'things'. Civilization weeps while it awaits one more emancipation."

PAUL HARVEY ~ American syndicated columnist

Sweet Beet Salad
yields 3 cups

3 C. beets, cubed	2 T. nutritional yeast
2 T. tahini	2 T. tamari or Bragg™ Liquid Aminos
4-5 T. vinegar	1/2 t. garlic powder
1/3 C. sweet onion, diced	

Cube or thinly slice beets. Using a steamer basket, steam until soft then drain water. Mix all ingredients together in a bowl. Chill and serve.

Quick & Easy Carrot Salad
serves 3-4

2 C. carrots, grated finely	a dash of sea salt
(through a Champion® Juicer)	1-2 onion slices, diced
4 T. vegan 'mayonnaise'	1 t. tahini (optional)
(see page 72)	1/2 t. mustard (optional)

Mix all ingredients together. Chill and serve.

• This is like a mock salmon salad. Serve as salad or on a sandwich.

Eggless Salad
serves 2

2 C. tofu, rinsed and drained	2 celery stalks, diced finely
1 T. tamari	1/2 t. sea salt
1 T. oil	1 t. turmeric
2 onion slices, diced small	4-5 T. nutritional yeast
5 T. vegan 'mayonnaise' (p. 72)	1-2 T. mustard
(or 2-3 T. tahini)	1 T. tahini (optional)

In a bowl, mash the tofu. Add the remaining ingredients and mix. Refrigerate.

• Delicious as a salad or served on sandwiches.

> *"Both breast cancer and colon cancer have been generally associated with the level of consumption of animal fat."*
>
> ARTHUR UPTON ~ Director, National Cancer Institute, Oct. 1979

Heart's Hearty Tofu Salad
serves 2-3

1 lb. (2 C.) tofu
2 T. vegan 'mayonnaise' (page 72)
3/4 T. tamari or substitute
1 1/2 celery stalks, diced
1/2 C. green pepper, diced
1/2 C. tomato, diced
1/4 C. onion, diced

1/2 C. lettuce, chopped
1/8 C. nutritional yeast
1/8 t. black pepper
1/4 t. sea salt
1/4 t. kelp
1/2 C. cilantro (optional), chopped

Rinse and drain tofu then mash. Add remaining ingredients. Chill until serving.

Tofuna Salad
serves 2-3

1 lb. (2 C.) firm tofu, frozen
1/2 C. vegan 'mayonnaise' (pg. 72)
1 T. fresh lemon juice
2 T. tamari

1-2 celery stalks, diced small
1 scallion or onion, diced
1/2 t. kelp

1. Remove tofu from freezer. Allow to thaw. Squeeze the water out of it.
2. Crumble tofu, add remaining ingredients and mix. Chill for a few hours so tofu can absorb the flavors. Season to taste.
3. Serve as a salad or on sandwiches.

Bean Salsa in Radicchio Leaves
yields 5 cups

3 C. pinto beans, cooked (page 13)
1 red onion, chopped
2 tomatoes, chopped
1 yellow bell pepper, chopped
1 C. corn kernels
2 jalapeño peppers, thinly sliced

1/3 C. cilantro, minced
1/2 C. tomato sauce
1 T. vinegar
1 t. sea salt (or to taste) no salt
radicchio leaves
  (or romaine, kale, chard)
2 avocados, cubed

1. In a large bowl, combine all ingredients, except leaves and avocados. Set aside to marinate for two hours at room temperature.
2. Place 1/4 cup of bean salsa into each leaf using a slotted spoon.
3. Garnish with avocado and serve.

• Variation ~ Toss Bean Salsa with hot or cold pasta.

Thai Tofu Salad
serves 4

4 C. romaine lettuce,
   torn into bite-sized pieces
1/2 lb. (1 C.) firm tofu,
   rinsed and drained
6 radishes, sliced thinly
2 kirby cucumbers, peeled,
   cut into 1 1/2" strips

1 large red bell pepper, cored,
   seeded, cut into 1 1/2" strips
1 small red onion, sliced thinly
1/4 C. basil leaves, chopped
1/8-1/4 C. cilantro leaves, chopped
1/8 C. mint leaves, minced

Dressing
1/4 lb. (1/2 C.) soft tofu, rinsed
2 T. tamari
2 T. lime juice
2 T. dry sweetener

1/4 t. sea salt
1/4 t. crushed red pepper
2 T. oil (safflower)
1 t. roasted sesame oil

1. Cut tofu into half inch cubes. Toss lettuce, tofu, radishes, cucumbers, pepper, onion, basil, cilantro and mint together in a large salad bowl.
2. Place ingredients for dressing in a blender or food processor using the "S" shaped blade. Process until smooth. Pour over salad and toss. Serve immediately.

• Optional ~ In place of plain tofu, add Curried Tofu Chunks (page 94) to salad.

Tomato Sesame Salad
serves 6

3 large tomatoes, diced
1 C. mushrooms, sliced
1 yellow bell pepper, diced
1 T. balsamic vinegar
1 T. sweetener
1 T. sesame oil

1 t. tamari or 1/4 t. sea salt
1 t. mustard (stoneground)
1/2 t. dried basil
black pepper and/or cayenne, to taste
2 small heads lettuce
sesame seeds, for garnish

1. In a salad bowl, toss the first three ingredients together.
2. In a mixing bowl, combine the remaining ingredients, except lettuce and garnish, and whisk well. Pour this dressing over the tomato mixture. Toss and allow to marinate for at least 10 minutes.
3. Wash lettuce, dry and tear into bite-sized pieces. Arrange in six salad bowls. Spoon 1/6 of the tomato mixture into each bowl. Sprinkle with sesame seeds and serve.

> *"Love all God's creatures, the animals, the plants.*
> *Love everything to perceive the divine mystery in all."*
>
> FYODOR DOSTOEVSKY (1821-1881) ~ Russian novelist

Pasta Salad
serves 4-6

4 C. cooked pasta shells (8 oz. dry) ~~ 1 T. fresh dill weed, chopped
2-3 T. olive oil ~~ 1 tomato, diced
2 T. tamari or substitute — 2 red onion slices, diced
1 T. apple cider vinegar — 1/4 bell pepper, diced
2 t. dried oregano ✓ — 1 cucumber, diced
1 t. dried basil — 1/4 3/4 t. black pepper (1/4)
4 t. nutritional yeast ✓ — 1 t. herb seasoning (page 3) ✓
1/2 t. onion powder ✓ — 1 t. garlic powder ✓
1/2 t. dried dill weed ✓ — 1/2 C. cooked chick peas (page 13)
black olives, sliced — (optional)

Mix all ingredients together in a bowl. Allow to marinate then serve.

Thai Noodle Salad
serves 6

16 oz. package rice noodles
2/3 C. rice vinegar
1/4 C. dry sweetener
2 cucumbers, peeled, sliced thinly
2 scallions, chopped
1/2 C. peanuts, chopped

2 T. fresh cilantro, chopped
1 T. fresh basil, chopped
  or 1 t. dried basil
1/4 C. tamari or substitute
1/2 t. crushed red pepper

1. Cook noodles in boiling water for five minutes until just tender. Rinse and drain.
2. in a small pot, combine vinegar and sweetener. Heat until sweetener dissolves. Cool.
3. In a large bowl, combine noodles, cooled vinegar mixture and remaining ingredients.
4. Toss to coat thoroughly and serve.

Curried Pasta Salad
serves 6-8

Dressing
1 lb. (2 C.) soft tofu,
  homogenized in food processor
1/2 t. salt
1/2 t. mild curry powder
1/4 t. cumin powder
1/4 t. onion powder

Salad
8 oz. package elbow pasta (cooked)
4 C. assorted vegetables
  (pepper, carrots, celery), chopped
1/2 cake (4 oz.) tempeh,
  steamed and crumbled
2 T. parsley, chopped finely

1. In a food processor, using the "S" shaped blade, blend all dressing ingredients until smooth. Rinse and drain cooked pasta and place in a bowl. Add dressing and stir.
2. Toss in vegetables and tempeh. Season again, if desired. Chill.
3. Garnish with parsley and serve.

Caribbean Spicy Black Bean Salad
serves 4

Spicy Dressing	*Salad*
1/2 t. sea salt	4 C. cooked black beans (page 13)
1/2 t. crushed red pepper	1 large bunch watercress, chopped
1/4 t. ground allspice	1 C. red & yellow bell pepper, diced
1/4 t. cumin powder	2 C. corn kernels (optional)
1/4 t. dried oregano	6 C. baby greens (loosely packed)
1/4 C. cold-pressed olive oil	2 scallions, thinly sliced
1 T. apple cider vinegar	
1 T. sweetener	

1. In a small bowl, whisk together dressing ingredients. Drain and rinse beans.
2. In large bowl, toss beans, watercress, peppers and corn with 1/4 cup of dressing.
3. Arrange greens on four serving plates. Top each with bean mixture and drizzle with remaining dressing. Sprinkle with scallions.

Tossed Tempeh Salad

10 C. mixed greens & lettuce (washed and drained)	2 cloves garlic, minced (optional)
2 carrots, grated	1 1/2 C. button mushrooms
2 tomatoes, cubed	2 T. tamari
1 cucumber, peeled, sliced	2 C. mixed cooked beans (garbanzo, kidney or your choice) (page 13)
1 sweet red pepper, sliced	Tempeh Chunks (page 93)
1 celery stalk, sliced thinly	1/2 C. sunflower seeds
1/2 sweet onion, diced	Golden Caesar dressing (page 191)

1. In a salad bowl, break up lettuce and greens into bite-sized pieces. Gently toss with carrots, tomatoes, cucumber, pepper and celery. Set aside in a cool place.
2. Sauté onion and garlic in tamari with a little water. Add the mushrooms and cook until soft. Let cool.
3. Drain beans of any excess water and place in a bowl. Mix in mushroom sauté. Add the cooled tempeh chunks and stir.
4. In a non-stick pan, toast sunflower seeds until browned. Set aside.
5. Make dressing and toss over salad. Place dressed salad into individual bowls or plates. Top with tempeh mixture and toasted sunflower seeds. Serve.

> ## "All truth is a species of revelation."
>
> SAMUEL TAYLOR COLERIDGE (1772-1834) ~ English poet and author

Cuban Black Bean Salad/Dip
serves 2

2 C. black beans, cooked, (page 13)
  drained and rinsed
1/2 C. red bell pepper, diced
1/2 C. red onion, diced
1/4 C. fresh cilantro, chopped

1/4 t. cumin powder
3 T. vinegar
3 T. olive oil
1/4 t. sea salt
1/8 t. red pepper

1. Place beans, bell pepper, onion and cilantro in a salad bowl.
2. Stir together cumin powder, vinegar and oil in a cup. Pour over bean mixture and gently stir, coating evenly. Season with salt and pepper, to taste.

  • Variation ~ In a food processor, using the "S" shaped blade, place all above ingredients along with three chopped garlic cloves and one tablespoon lime juice. Process until creamy to make a dip.

Potato Salad
serves 6-8

8 C. cooked potatoes
2/3 C. celery, diced
1/4 C. fresh parsley, chopped
1/8 C. scallions, diced
1 C. sweet onion, diced
2/3 C. carrot, grated (optional)
1 t. dried dill weed
1 T. nutritional yeast
1 t. sea salt
1/4 t. black pepper

Blender Mixture
2/3 C. oil
1/3 C. apple cider vinegar
1 C. soft tofu, rinsed and drained
1 T. Bragg™ Liquid Aminos or tamari
2-3 T. mustard
2 T. rice syrup
1/2 T. garlic powder
1/2 T. onion powder
1 t. herb seasoning (page 3)

1. Peel and cube the potatoes (approx. 4-5 lbs.). Boil until soft, but still somewhat firm. Drain and rinse. Chill to harden the potatoes.
2. In a bowl, mix chilled potatoes, celery, parsley, scallions, onion, grated carrot and dill weed. Sprinkle on the nutritional yeast, salt and pepper.
3. In a blender, blend the remaining ingredients, beginning with the oil. Pour this mixture over the potatoes in the bowl. Stir in to cover potatoes completely. Allow to marinate for several hours or overnight before serving.

> *"The problems of the world cannot possibly be solved by skeptics and cynics whose horizons are limited by obvious realities. We need men who can dream of things that never were."*
>
> JOHN F. KENNEDY (1917-1963) ~ 35th President of the U.S.A.

Potato Salad a la 'Kate'
serves 6-8

5 lbs. red potatoes, peeled
1/4 red onion, minced
1 (3.4 oz.) jar capers
1 C. vegan 'mayonnaise' (page 72)
1 T. pickle relish or sweetener

1 bunch fresh dill, chopped
1 bunch scallions, minced
6 celery stalks, diced
sea salt, to taste
black pepper, to taste

1. Cut potatoes into cubes. Boil until soft, but still firm. Drain and rinse.
2. Mix remaining ingredients with potatoes and stir. Chill and allow flavors to absorb before serving.

Curried Potato Salad
yields 6 cups

2 lbs. red potatoes
    scrubbed and cubed
1 T. mustard seeds
1 t. cumin seeds
1 t. mild curry powder
1/8 t. crushed red pepper
2 T. fresh lemon juice

1 t. fresh ginger, grated
1 t. sea salt
1 t. olive oil
1 small red onion, chopped finely
1/2-1 jalapeño pepper, seeded & minced
1 C. green peas (cooked)
1/4 C. fresh cilantro, chopped

1. Boil potatoes in lightly salted water, until just tender (20-30 minutes), then drain. Cool slightly and dice into smaller bite-sized pieces.
2. Toast mustard seeds, cumin seeds, curry and red pepper in a pan over low heat until fragrant (about one minute). Transfer to a large bowl, whisk in lemon juice, ginger, salt, then oil. Add onion, jalapeños and warm potatoes. Toss, then cool.
3. Add peas and cilantro. Serve chilled.

Creamy Cole Slaw
yields 1 large bowl

1 head green cabbage, shredded
2 C. carrots, shredded
1/4 C. sweet onion, grated
3/4 C. celery, diced
1/2 C. oil
1/2 C. apple cider vinegar

5 T. sweetener (fructose)
1/2 T. Bragg™ Liquid Aminos or tamari
1/4 t. dill weed
1/2 T. herb seasoning (page 3)
a squeeze of lemon juice
1 1/8 C. soft tofu

1. In a large bowl, mix together the cabbage, carrots, onion and celery.
2. Rinse and drain tofu. Mash and blend with remaining ingredients in a blender. Pour over the vegetables, stir well, and allow to marinate for an hour before serving.

Greek Chick Pea Salad
serves 4-6

Vinaigrette
2 T. water
2 T. olive oil (cold-pressed)
1/2 C. tomato juice
1 T. tomato paste/sauce
1 tomato, chopped
a dash of hot sauce
2 T. vinegar
2 T. sweetener

1/4 t. sea salt
1/4 C. tamari or substitute
1/4 t. garlic powder
Salad
3 C. cooked chick peas (page 13)
2 tomatoes, chopped 1/2" thick
2 C. firm tofu, rinsed and drained—no
1/2 C. black olives (pitted), sliced no
2 scallions, sliced
1/4 C. fresh parsley, chopped
cilantro

1. Blend all vinaigrette ingredients in a blender for about 15 seconds and set aside.
2. Rinse and drain tofu and crumble into a large bowl. Combine with remaining salad ingredients. Toss lightly.
3. Add vinaigrette to salad. Toss to distribute evenly and coat thoroughly. Cover and chill before serving.

Greek Lentil Salad
serves 4

2 C. cooked lentils (3/4-1 C. dry)
2 C. cooked quinoa (1 C. dry)
1/2 C. olive oil
1/4 C. vinegar
4 cloves garlic, minced
1 T. fresh oregano

1 red onion, minced
4 ripe tomatoes, chopped
1 C. kalamata olives (pitted), sliced
1/2 C. firm tofu, rinsed and drained
2 T. nutritional yeast
1/2 t. each: salt & pepper, to taste

1. Cook the lentils and quinoa separately and allow to chill (see pages 12 and 13).
2. Combine olive oil, vinegar, garlic and oregano in a small bowl and set aside.
3. Combine cooked lentils and cooked quinoa in a bowl. Cut tofu into cubes. Add onion, tomatoes, olives and nutritional yeast. Stir. Pour dressing over all and toss well. Season with salt and pepper. Refrigerate for at least 30 minutes before serving.

> **"A varied whole food vegan diet contains adequate levels of energy and protein to sustain good health in all age groups, as evidenced by studies of vegans across the world."**
>
> GILL LANGLEY, M.A., Ph.D. ~ British author, <u>Vegan Nutrition</u>, U.K.

Awesome Carrot Salad
serves 4-6

Almond Mayo
1 C. almonds, soaked & drained
3/4 C. water
1 T. onion powder
1 t. sea salt

3-4 dates, pitted (or 2 T. date sugar)
1 lemon, juiced
a dash of apple cider vinegar
1/4 C. cold-pressed oil (optional)

In a food processor, using the "S" shaped blade, or with a strong blender, thoroughly blend almonds with water. Add remaining ingredients. Process until creamy. Chill.

3 lbs. carrots, peeled & grated
2 celery stalks, diced
1 bell pepper, chopped
1 small sweet onion, diced

2 t. kelp
sea salt or substitute, to taste
1 large tomato, diced

Mix above ingredients together except tomato. Add almond mayo and mix well. Add diced tomato at the end and mix lightly. Chill until serving.

Garbanzo Salad
serves 4

2 C. garbanzo beans
  soaked, cooked and drained
2 carrots, grated
1 medium beet, grated
2 green onions, chopped
1/4 C. fresh ~~parsley~~ cilantro, minced

1-2 cloves garlic, minced
2 T. tahini — go easy like 1½ Tablespoon
2 T. balsamic vinegar
1 T. water
sea salt, to taste
black pepper, to taste

1. See instructions for preparing garbanzo beans (chick peas) on page 13.
2. In a mixing bowl, combine beans, grated carrots and beet, onions and parsley.
3. In a separate bowl, whisk together the remaining ingredients and pour over the bean mix. Toss well and serve over crisp garden greens.

> *"The obligations of law and equity reach only to mankind;*
> *but kindness and beneficence should be extended to the creatures*
> *of every species, and these will flow from the breast of a*
> *true man, as streams that issue from the living fountain."*
>
> PLUTARCH (46-120 A.D.) ~ Greek philosopher and moralist

Three Bean Salad
serves 6–8

2 C. dry pinto beans, cooked
2 C. kidney beans, cooked
2 C. green beans
1 red onion, sliced thinly
2 celery stalks, diced
2 T. balsamic vinegar

1 1/2 T. mustard (stoneground)
1 T. tamari or substitute
2 T. maple syrup
1 t. nutritional yeast
2 T. water
1 t. dried basil

1. Soak and cook pinto and kidney beans, then drain (see page 13). Steam and slice green beans.
2. In a large bowl, combine beans, onion and celery.
3. In a separate bowl, whisk all remaining ingredients together and pour over bean mixture. Toss and chill. Allow at least 30 minutes for flavors to marinate. Mix again and serve at room temperature.

Mushroom Spinach Salad
serves 4

1/4 C. veggie stock or water
2 T. balsamic vinegar
1 T. sweetener
1/2 t. sea salt & 1/4 t. red pepper
4 T. olive oil (cold-pressed)
4 bunches (12 oz.) spinach
   or arugula, stems trimmed

4 cloves garlic, crushed
8 oz. shittake mushrooms, caps
   cut into quarters
2 T. nutritional yeast
8 oz. button mushrooms, sliced
1 T. fresh parsley, chopped

1. In a small bowl, mix stock, vinegar, sweetener, salt, pepper and two tablespoons oil.
2. Wash and spin dry or drain greens. Place on a large platter and set aside.
3. In a large (cast-iron or non-stick) skillet, heat remaining olive oil on medium heat. Add garlic and cook until golden-brown. Add mushrooms and yeast and cook for 8–10 minutes, until mushrooms are browned and liquid evaporates.
4. Add stock mixture to skillet. Cook for 30 seconds, stirring. Immediately pour mushroom mixture over greens. Top with parsley and a sprinkle of nutritional yeast.

> *"If there would come a voice from God saying,*
> *'I'm against vegetarianism!' I would say, 'Well, I am for it!'*
> *This is how strongly I feel in this regard."*
>
> ISAAC BASHEVIS SINGER (1904-1991) ~ Yiddish Laureate of Literature
> 1978 Nobel Prize recipient

Cabbage, Carrot and Jicama Salad
serves 4-6

1/4 C. cilantro or mint leaves
1/2 C. fresh lime juice
1/4 C. maple syrup
1/2 t. sea salt
1/4 t. crushed red pepper
5-6 carrots, grated

1 small head green cabbage, shredded
1 medium jicama, peeled
    cut into 1/8" thick sticks
1/2 red bell pepper, cored & seeded,
    cut into 1/8" thick slices
2 T. sunflower seeds

1. In large bowl, mix chopped cilantro, lime juice, maple syrup, salt and crushed red pepper.
2. Add carrots, cabbage, jicama and bell pepper. Toss.
3. Cover and refrigerate unless serving right away. Garnish with seeds.

Waldorf Salad
serves 4-6

3 C. apples, peeled, cubed
1 T. fresh lemon juice
1/2 C. celery, chopped
1/2 C. golden raisins
1/2 C. dark raisins
3/4 C. walnuts, chopped
1/2 C. pitted dates, chopped

Vanilla Tofu Yogurt Dressing
1/4-1/2 C. apple juice
1 t. vanilla extract
3 T. maple syrup + 1 T. sweetener
1/2 lb. (1 C.) soft tofu, rinsed and drained
1 T. lemon juice
1 T. grated lemon peel
1/4 t. ground nutmeg
1 T. dry sweetener

1. In a bowl, toss apples with lemon juice. Add celery, raisins, walnuts and dates. Stir.
2. Place apple juice, vanilla, sweeteners and tofu in a blender or food processor using the "S" shaped blade. Blend until creamy. Place vanilla yogurt in a bowl and gently fold in lemon juice, lemon peel, nutmeg and sweetener.
3. Coat fruit salad with dressing. Chill and serve.

> *"Our task must be to free ourselves...*
> *by widening our circle of compassion to embrace all living*
> *creatures, and the whole of nature and its beauty."*
>
> ALBERT EINSTEIN (1879-1955) ~ German-born American physicist
> 1921 Nobel Prize winner

Corn Relish
serves 4

2 1/2 C. corn kernels, fresh (cut from cob, then cooked)	<u>Dressing</u> 1/2 t. cumin powder
2 scallions (green part), diced	1 T. lime juice
2 peppers, cored, seeded, and diced	1 T. sweetener
2 celery stalks, trimmed, diced	1 T. broth (or water)
	1 clove garlic, minced
	1/2 t. each: salt and pepper

1. Combine corn kernels, scallions, peppers and celery in a mixing bowl. Toss gently.
2. Stir together cumin, lime juice, sweetener and broth.
3. Pour dressing over salad and toss again. Season to taste with garlic, salt and pepper.

Japanese Cucumber Salad (Namasu)
serves 2-3

4 C. oriental cucumbers	1/4 C. dry sweetener
1/2 t. sea salt	2 t. herb seasoning (page 3)
1/4 C. apple cider vinegar	1 1/2 t. fresh ginger, minced (or squeeze the fresh juice)

1. Partially peel the cucumbers so some green strips show. Slice thinly. Place in a bowl and add salt. Stir and let stand for 15-20 minutes.
2. Combine the remaining ingredients in a separate bowl.
3. Press excess liquid from cucumbers. Pour vinegar dressing over the top.
4. Chill for half an hour before serving (at this point the cucumbers will still have some crunch.) Chill for four hours or overnight for a softened cucumber salad.

"I do believe that all God's creatures have the right to live as much as we have. Instead of prescribing the killing of the so-called injurious fellow creatures of ours as a duty, if men of knowledge had devoted their gift to discovering ways of dealing with them otherwise than by killing them we would be living in a world befitting our status as men .... animals endowed with reason and the power of choosing between good and evil, right and wrong, violence and nonviolence, truth and untruth."

MAHATMA GANDHI (1869-1948) ~ Hindu pacifist, spiritual leader

Creamy Vegetable Soup
serves 5-6

1 onion, sliced
2 cloves garlic, minced
1 T. oil or water
4 medium carrots, sliced
3 potatoes, cubed
2 T. tamari (or to taste)
2 celery stalks, sliced
6 C. water or stock

2-3 t. herb seasoning (page 3)
1 t. garlic powder
2 t. onion powder
2 T. fresh dill
1/4–1/2 C. cashew butter
2-3 C. assorted vegetables
   (peas, broccoli, zucchini, etc.)

1. Sauté onion and garlic in oil or water. Add carrots and potatoes. Stir and add two cups water and the tamari. Simmer. Add celery when vegetables begin to soften.
2. When vegetables are soft, remove half of the potatoes and carrots and blend in a blender with two cups of water, the remaining seasonings and cashew butter.
3. Return blended liquid to the pot and add assorted vegetables and two cups of water. (Add more or less water depending on desired consistency.)
4. Let simmer for 15-20 minutes until flavors are blended and vegetables are soft. This soup is even better when it sits for a few hours, if you can wait that long!

Tomato Vegetable Soup
serves 6-8

1/4 C. oil (optional)
2 cloves garlic, diced
2 onions, chopped
1 large potato, peeled, cubed
2 carrots, sliced
2 celery stalks, sliced
1/2 C. broccoli, chopped
1/2 C. cauliflower, chopped

1/2 C. fresh green peas
12 C. tomato sauce/stewed tomato juice
1/2 C. tamari or substitute
1 t. parsley
1/2 t. dill weed
1/2 t. garlic powder
1/2 t. sweet basil
1/2 t. sea salt

1. In a large soup pot, heat the oil or water over medium heat. Add garlic, onions, potato, carrots and celery. Sauté for five minutes. Season with half of the spices.
2. Add the remaining vegetables and cook for 3-4 minutes. Add tomato sauce, leaving two cups aside. Simmer for an hour. Add the remaining seasonings, to taste.
3. When veggies are soft, spoon half of them, especially carrots and potatoes, into a blender. Add the remaining tomato juice/sauce and purée for one minute.
4. Return mixture to the pot. Cook for one hour over low heat and serve.

> "We have committed the golden rule to memory;
> let us now commit it to life."
>
> EDWIN MARKHAM (1852-1940) ~ American poet

Summer's Split Pea Soup
serves 6-8

2-3 T. oil (safflower)
2 C. onion, chopped finely
1 T. sea salt
2 T. Tabasco™ sauce
7 cloves garlic, chopped finely
2 large potatoes, cubed

1 1/2 C. split peas, rinsed
1 1/2 carrots, sliced
3-4 celery stalks, diced
1 1/2 C. tomatoes, cubed
1/2 C. cilantro, chopped finely
10 C. water

1. In a pressure cooker, on medium-high heat, sauté onions, salt, and tabasco in oil.
2. Add garlic then the potatoes. Sauté for two minutes. Add split peas and mix well. Add four cups of water. Cook for three minutes then add carrots.
3. When water boils, add celery and six more cups of water. Put the top on the pressure cooker and cook on high until full pressure is reached. Lower the heat to medium-low and cook for five minutes. Take off heat and place under cold water until pressure dissipates. Open and add tomatoes and cilantro, then return to medium-high heat without the top. Cook until tomatoes soften. Simmer and serve.

Corn Chowder Soup
serves 6-8

3 T. oil (optional)
3 large onions, diced
4 cloves garlic, minced
5 C. corn kernels (cut from the cob)
3 T. soy powder
2 1/2 quarts water
1/4 C. tahini

3-4 potatoes, peeled, diced
2-3 carrots, sliced
3 T. tamari or substitute
1 t. garlic powder
1/2 t. dried basil
1/2 t. thyme (optional)
1 t. sea salt

1. In a large soup pot, heat the oil. Add the onions and garlic and sauté for 3-4 minutes.
2. Mix in the corn. Sauté for 3-4 more minutes. In a blender, combine 1/3 of the corn sauté with 1 T. soy powder and 1/3 of the water and blend. Set mixture aside.
3. Repeat blending two more times with remaining mixture, leaving some kernels whole if desired. Add tahini to the final blender. A thick creamy texture is desired. Pour blended mixture back into the soup pot. Add remaining ingredients. Cook until soft.

*above: **Tossed Tempeh Salad** (page 46) ~ below: **Awesome Carrot Salad** (page 50)*

> *"The vast majority of all cancers, cardiovascular diseases, and other forms of degenerative illness can be prevented simply by adopting a plant-based diet."*
>
> T. COLIN CAMPBELL, Ph.D. ~ nutritional biochemist, Cornell University, Ithica, N.Y. former Senior Science Advisor to the American Institute for Cancer Research

Light Garden Vegetable Soup
serves 4–5

1 medium onion, diced
2 C. carrots, sliced
2 C. cauliflower flowerets
3 roma tomatoes, cubed
3 C. water
3–4 T. tamari or substitute
1 t. dill weed

1/2 T. vegetable bouillon (page 2)
2 T. nutritional yeast
1 T. miso (blonde)
1 t. herb seasoning (page 3)
1 t. onion powder
1 t. dried oregano
2–3 C. zucchini, sliced in halves
1 C. green peas (optional)

1. In a soup pot, sauté onion in a little oil or water, then add carrots and cauliflower. When almost soft, add the tomatoes. Cover and simmer until soft.
2. In a blender, blend 2 1/2 cups of the cooked vegetables with remaining ingredients, except zucchini and peas. Blend well and pour back into the soup pot. Add zucchini and peas, and cook for 15 minutes. Add more water for a thinner soup.

Split Pea Soup — make this to
serves 5–6

3 C. (dry) split peas ✓
1–2 onions, diced
4–5 carrots, peeled, sliced
1–2 potatoes, peeled, cubed
1/4 t. curry powder ✓

1 T. dill weed ✓
1/4 t. cumin powder ✓
2 T. tamari or substitute
1 T. herb seasoning (page 3)
1 t. sea salt

1. Boil the split peas in their own pot with eight cups of water (see page 13).
2. In a large soup pot, sauté the onions in a little oil/water. Add the carrots and potatoes. Cook until soft, adding water as needed, then remove from heat.
3. When the split peas are cooked, scoop out two cups and place in a blender with one cup of water and the seasonings, except sea salt. Pour into soup pot.
4. Repeat the same process of blending another two cups of split peas and one cup of water. Add to soup pot.
5. Add remaining split peas to the soup pot. Season with sea salt at the end.

'Soup'erb Creamy Lima Bean
serves 6

3 C. lima beans (cooked)
1-2 T. oil (optional)
1 large onion, diced
2 C. carrots, sliced
2 C. cauliflower flowerets
6 C. water

2 T. tamari or substitute
2 T. nutritional yeast
1 t. herb seasoning (page 3)
1 t. dill weed
1 t. dried oregano
1 t. garlic powder
1/4 C. miso

1. Cook the lima beans before starting the soup (see page 13).
2. In a soup pot, sauté the onion in a little water or oil. Add the carrots, cauliflower and a little water. Cover and steam.
3. In a blender, blend two cups of water with one cup of cooked lima beans, one cup of cooked carrots and cauliflower, tamari and yeast. Pour back into the soup pot. Add an additional two cups of water to the pot.
4. In the blender, again, blend two cups of water with one cup of lima beans and pour into the soup pot.
5. Add remaining flavorings (except miso) and the remaining cup of whole lima beans to the pot and bring to a boil. Lower heat and cook for 15 minutes.
6. Remove from heat. Take out 1-2 cups of soup and mix with the miso in a bowl. Pour this mixture back into the soup pot. Stir, then serve.

Creamy Potato Soup
serves 6-8

3 cloves garlic
2 T. oil
2 T. water
2 large onions, diced
6 C. potatoes, cubed
2 C. carrots, sliced
6 C. water

2 T. cashew butter
1 T. herb seasoning (page 3)
2 T. tamari or substitute
1/2 T. sea salt
1 t. dried dill weed
1/2 t. black pepper
1/4 C. fresh dill weed, chopped

1. In a blender, blend garlic with oil and water. Pour into a soup pot.
2. Sauté the onions in this garlic oil. When the onions are partially cooked, add the potatoes then the carrots. Add two cups of water and cover. Cook until the vegetables are soft, stirring frequently.
3. In a blender, blend two cups of water, cashew butter, herb seasoning, tamari and one cup of cooked potatoes from the pot. Blend well. Pour back into the soup pot.
4. In a blender again, blend one cup of the cooked potatoes and two cups of water. Pour back into the pot. Add sea salt to taste, dill weed, pepper and fresh dill. Simmer for 15-30 minutes. Serve.

Cream of Cauliflower Soup
serves 6

2 C. cooked brown rice (page 12)
   (or use 1/2 C. cashew butter)
5 C. vegetable stock or water
1 head cauliflower, chopped
2 t. tahini

1/4 C. tamari or substitute
1/2 t. garlic powder
1/4 t. basil
1/8 t. cayenne
2 celery stalks, chopped

1. Put 1/3 of the cooked rice and 1/3 of the stock in a blender. Purée at high speed for one minute until creamy. Pour into a large soup pot. Repeat step one two more times.
2. Add half the cauliflower to the blender with water, tahini, and spices. Blend on high for one minute. Add this to the pot over medium heat. Add remaining cauliflower and celery. Cook for about an hour, stirring often, until the cauliflower is tender.

Navy Bean Soup
serves 6-8

2 C. navy or pinto beans (page 13)
10 C. water (approximately)
1/4 C. oil (optional)
1/4 C. tamari or substitute
2 onions, diced

8 cloves garlic, diced
1 t. garlic powder
2-3 bay leaves
1 carrot, sliced
1 celery stalk, sliced

1. Soak beans overnight in plenty of water. The next day, drain and rinse them and place in a large soup pot. Cover with water and place over medium heat (or use pre-cooked beans).
2. Add oil, tamari, one of the diced onions, four garlic cloves, and spices. Cook for about one hour. Add the carrot, celery, remaining onion and garlic cloves.
3. Cook for approximately an hour more, until the carrots and beans are tender. (If pre-cooked beans are used, cook for half an hour.) Remove bay leaves before serving.

above: **Thai Coconut Soup** *(page 60)* ~ *below right:* **Autumn Harvest Soup** *(page 64)*
below left: **Minestrone Soup** *(page 64) with* **Challah Bread** *(page 31)*

> *"We cannot know for sure whose domination came first,*
> *but we can see that today,*
> *the domination of women and the domination of animals,*
> *especially those exploited for food,*
> *are deeply intertwined."*
>
> CAROL J. ADAMS ~ author, The Sexual Politics of Meat, Neither Man Nor Beast

Vichyssoise Soup
serves 4–5

3 medium leeks	*2 C. soy milk*
2 T. olive oil	*1/4 t. sea salt*
4 med. potatoes, peeled and diced	*1/4 t. crushed red pepper*
3 C. water or broth	

1. Cut and discard the roots and tough leaves from the leeks. Cut the leeks in half, lengthwise, and rinse under cold water to remove dirt. Cut the leeks crosswise in quarter-inch slices. You should end up with about two cups.
2. In a medium-sized soup pot, over medium heat, place olive oil and leeks. Stir and cook for five minutes. Add potatoes and water and bring to a boil. Reduce heat to low, cover and simmer for 30 minutes.
3. Transfer the leek/potato mixture and one cup of soy milk into a blender or food processor and blend until smooth. Return to pot and stir in remaining soy milk, salt and pepper.
4. If desired, chill the soup before serving or warm over low heat.

Vietnamese Noodle Soup
serves 4

6 C. vegetable stock or water	*1 medium onion, sliced thinly*
1" piece ginger, peeled, minced	*1 bunch fresh basil, washed, chopped*
2-4 scallions, chopped	*3-4 C. bean sprouts*
4 T. tamari	*2 jalapeño chilis, sliced thinly (optional)*
8 oz. pack rice noodles, broken up	*1 lime, quartered*
1 lb. (2 C.) firm tofu	

1. In a saucepan, on medium heat, combine the first four ingredients to make a broth. Simmer for 15 minutes. Rinse and drain tofu and cut into cubes.
2. Place the rice noodles in a separate pot, in warm water. Soak for 30 minutes and drain them just before cooking. When ready to serve, cook noodles in enough boiling water to cover them, for about 2–3 minutes until soft then drain.
3. Meanwhile, heat broth and add tofu. Cook on medium heat for two minutes.
4. Divide drained noodles into four separate bowls. Also divide onion slices, basil, bean sprouts and jalapeño slices into each bowl. Spoon the broth and tofu on top.
5. Serve the soup at once with a wedge of lime.

> **"I believe that pity is a law like justice,
> and that kindness is a duty like uprightness."**
>
> VICTOR HUGO (1802-1885) ~ French poet, novelist and playwright

Thai Coconut Soup
serves 5-6

1 onion, chopped	*2 t. fresh lemon or lime juice*
3 cloves garlic, chopped	*2 T. nutritional yeast*
2-3 t. ginger, minced	*1 T. herb seasoning (page 3)*
1 T. oil or water	*2 T. tamari or substitute*
4 large carrots, sliced	*1-2 t. curry powder (mild or hot)*
1 large potato, cubed	*1/2 C. peas (defrosted if frozen)*
1 1/2 C. coconut milk	*1/2 t. sea salt*
1 t. sweetener (optional)	*2-3 T. fresh chives, chopped*

1. In oil or water, sauté onion with the garlic and ginger. Add the carrots and potato. Fill the pot with enough water to cover the vegetables and let simmer.
2. In a blender, blend two cups of cooked carrots with one cup of stock. Add coconut milk and remaining ingredients except peas and chives. Blend again. Add this to the pot when vegetables are beginning to get soft, approximately 20 minutes. Add the peas at the end. Simmer for 10-15 minutes until flavors blend. Garnish with chives.

Creamy Coconut Ginger Soup
serves 5-6

1 large onion, sliced	*1 (14 oz.) can coconut milk*
1 T. oil	*1 t. sea salt*
2-3 cloves garlic, diced	*1 t. powdered ginger*
3-4 T. fresh ginger, diced	*1 t. onion powder*
2 large potatoes, cubed	*2 t. herb seasoning (page 3)*
5 carrots, sliced	*2-3 T. tamari or Bragg™ Liquid Aminos*
2 celery stalks, diced	*1/2 C. peas or zucchini*

1. In a soup pot, sauté the onion in oil or water, adding the garlic and half of the ginger. When onions soften, add the potatoes, carrots and celery with enough water to cover the vegetables by an inch. Cover and simmer for about 15-20 minutes.
2. When the vegetables are softened, remove 1 1/2 cups of vegetables and blend with one cup of water and the coconut milk. Add the rest of the ginger and seasonings. Blend well. Pour this blended mixture back into the pot.
3. Add the peas or sliced zucchini (or any non-root vegetable) in bite-sized pieces. Cook until these vegetables are soft (8-10 minutes) adding more water if desired. Serve.

> *"Mankind's true moral test, its fundamental test (which lies deeply buried from view), consists of its attitude towards those who are at its mercy: animals."*
>
> MILAN KUNDERA ~ Czech author, poet, playwright

Vichyssoise Soup
serves 4-5

3 medium leeks	2 C. soy milk
2 T. olive oil	1/4 t. sea salt
4 med. potatoes, peeled and diced	1/4 t. crushed red pepper
3 C. water or broth	

1. Cut and discard the roots and tough leaves from the leeks. Cut the leeks in half, lengthwise, and rinse under cold water to remove dirt. Cut the leeks crosswise in quarter-inch slices. You should end up with about two cups.
2. In a medium-sized soup pot, over medium heat, place olive oil and leeks. Stir and cook for five minutes. Add potatoes and water and bring to a boil. Reduce heat to low, cover and simmer for 30 minutes.
3. Transfer the leek/potato mixture and one cup of soy milk into a blender or food processor and blend until smooth. Return to pot and stir in remaining soy milk, salt and pepper.
4. If desired, chill the soup before serving or warm over low heat.

Vietnamese Noodle Soup
serves 4

6 C. vegetable stock or water	1 medium onion, sliced thinly
1" piece ginger, peeled, minced	1 bunch fresh basil, washed, chopped
2-4 scallions, chopped	3-4 C. bean sprouts
4 T. tamari	2 jalapeño chilis, sliced thinly (optional)
8 oz. pack rice noodles, broken up	1 lime, quartered
1 lb. (2 C.) firm tofu	

1. In a saucepan, on medium heat, combine the first four ingredients to make a broth. Simmer for 15 minutes. Rinse and drain tofu and cut into cubes.
2. Place the rice noodles in a separate pot, in warm water. Soak for 30 minutes and drain them just before cooking. When ready to serve, cook noodles in enough boiling water to cover them, for about 2-3 minutes until soft then drain.
3. Meanwhile, heat broth and add tofu. Cook on medium heat for two minutes.
4. Divide drained noodles into four separate bowls. Also divide onion slices, basil, bean sprouts and jalapeño slices into each bowl. Spoon the broth and tofu on top.
5. Serve the soup at once with a wedge of lime.

> **"I believe that pity is a law like justice,**
> **and that kindness is a duty like uprightness."**
>
> VICTOR HUGO (1802-1885) ~ French poet, novelist and playwright

Thai Coconut Soup
serves 5-6

1 onion, chopped
3 cloves garlic, chopped
2-3 t. ginger, minced
1 T. oil or water
4 large carrots, sliced
1 large potato, cubed
1 1/2 C. coconut milk
1 t. sweetener (optional)

2 t. fresh lemon or lime juice
2 T. nutritional yeast
1 T. herb seasoning (page 3)
2 T. tamari or substitute
1-2 t. curry powder (mild or hot)
1/2 C. peas (defrosted if frozen)
1/2 t. sea salt
2-3 T. fresh chives, chopped

1. In oil or water, sauté onion with the garlic and ginger. Add the carrots and potato. Fill the pot with enough water to cover the vegetables and let simmer.
2. In a blender, blend two cups of cooked carrots with one cup of stock. Add coconut milk and remaining ingredients except peas and chives. Blend again. Add this to the pot when vegetables are beginning to get soft, approximately 20 minutes. Add the peas at the end. Simmer for 10-15 minutes until flavors blend. Garnish with chives.

Creamy Coconut Ginger Soup
serves 5-6

1 large onion, sliced
1 T. oil
2-3 cloves garlic, diced
3-4 T. fresh ginger, diced
2 large potatoes, cubed
5 carrots, sliced
2 celery stalks, diced

1 (14 oz.) can coconut milk
1 t. sea salt
1 t. powdered ginger
1 t. onion powder
2 t. herb seasoning (page 3)
2-3 T. tamari or Bragg™ Liquid Aminos
1/2 C. peas or zucchini

1. In a soup pot, sauté the onion in oil or water, adding the garlic and half of the ginger. When onions soften, add the potatoes, carrots and celery with enough water to cover the vegetables by an inch. Cover and simmer for about 15-20 minutes.
2. When the vegetables are softened, remove 1 1/2 cups of vegetables and blend with one cup of water and the coconut milk. Add the rest of the ginger and seasonings. Blend well. Pour this blended mixture back into the pot.
3. Add the peas or sliced zucchini (or any non-root vegetable) in bite-sized pieces. Cook until these vegetables are soft (8-10 minutes) adding more water if desired. Serve.

> *"Mankind's true moral test, its fundamental test (which lies deeply buried from view), consists of its attitude towards those who are at its mercy: animals."*
>
> MILAN KUNDERA ~ Czech author, poet, playwright

Coconut Curry Soup
serves 5-6

5 cloves garlic	2 T. cashew butter
2 T. oil	1 T. curry
2 T. tamari or substitute	1 t. onion powder
1-2 large onions, sliced	1 t. garlic powder
2 C. carrots, sliced	2 T. (additional) tamari or substitute
3 C. potatoes, cubed	2 t. herb seasoning (page 3)
1 (14 oz.) can coconut milk	1 C. broccoli, cauliflower, etc.

1. In a blender, blend the garlic with oil and two tablespoons of tamari. Pour into a large soup pot and sauté the onions in this garlic oil. When onions soften, add the carrots and potatoes with half a cup of water. Cover and simmer.
2. When the vegetables are softened, remove one cup of the vegetables and blend with two cups of water and the coconut milk. Pour this back into the pot.
3. Remove another cup of cooked veggies and blend with two more cups of water, cashew butter, curry and remaining seasonings. Pour this blended mixture back into the soup pot.
4. At this point, add some cauliflower and broccoli or any vegetables in bite-sized pieces. Cook until these vegetables are soft. Do not boil.

Creamy Carrot Coconut Soup
serves 6

1 T. oil (optional)	1 (14 oz.) can coconut milk
1 large onion, sliced	1-2 t. sea salt, to taste
4 cloves garlic, diced	1 t. onion powder
8 C. carrots, sliced	1 t. garlic powder
2 t. tamari or substitute	4 C. water

1. In a soup pot, sauté onion in oil or two to three tablespoons of water. After two minutes, add garlic and stir.
2. When the onions are getting soft, add carrots and stir in tamari. Simmer on low for three minutes, stirring often.
3. Add remaining seasonings and four cups of water. Bring to a near boil, cover and simmer on low until carrots are soft. Add coconut milk and stir.
4. Let cool, then remove and blend half of the carrots and broth in a blender, using additional water if desired. Use caution when blending anything hot; it expands in the blender and can push the top off. (Use less water for a thicker creamier soup.)

> **"The greatest man is he who chooses right with the most invincible resolution."**
>
> SENECA (8 B.C. - 65 A.D.) ~ Roman philosopher

Sea Vegetable Miso Soup
serves 4-6

4 cloves garlic, minced	1 t. parsley flakes
2 onions, diced	6 C. water or stock
3 carrots, sliced	stick of kombu
2 celery stalks, diced	(or sea vegetable of choice)
1 t. each: onion & garlic powder	6 T. miso paste
1/4 C. tamari or substitute	1 C. noodles (cooked)

1. In a soup pot, sauté the garlic and onions in a small amount of water or oil. When onions are soft, add the remaining vegetables and seasonings (except miso).
2. Add the water or vegetable stock along with the sea vegetable of choice and simmer until all vegetables are soft.
3. Remove one cup of hot broth from the pot and mix with the miso until blended. Pour this back into the soup pot. Stir. Add noodles. Serve.

'Soup'er Onion Soup
serves 4

3 onions, sliced or diced	2 T. vegetable bouillon (page 2)
3 T. tamari or substitute	1 T. onion powder
4 T. nutritional yeast	1/2 T. garlic powder
1/4 C. cashew butter	2 T. miso (blonde)
1/2 C. nutritional yeast	5 C. water

1. In a medium-sized soup pot, sauté the onions in a little oil. Add tamari and yeast.
2. When onions are soft, take out one cup and place them in the blender with three cups water, cashew butter, nutritional yeast, bouillon, onion powder and garlic powder. Blend and pour back into the soup pot.
3. Bring to a boil and stir for 5-10 minutes. Remove from flame.
4. In the blender, blend the miso with one cup of water and return this to the soup pot. Do not boil the miso. Add one more cup of water to the pot, stir and serve.

> *"How are we to build a new humanity? Only by leading people toward a true inalienable ethic of our own... reverence for life comprises the whole ethic of love, in its deepest and highest sense. It is the source of constant renewal for the Individual and for humankind."*
>
> ALBERT SCHWEITZER, M.D. (1875-1965) ~ Alsatian philosopher and medical missionary
> 1952 Nobel Prize recipient

Hearty Lentil Soup
serves 6

2 C. dry lentils	1/2 T. garlic powder
1 T. oil or water	1/2 t. dill weed
2 onions, chopped	3/4 C. lentils, cooked
3 cloves garlic, diced	1/4 C. tomato paste
2 celery stalks, diced	1 T. tamari or substitute
2 C. carrots, sliced	1 T. vegetable bouillon (page 2)
1 eggplant, diced (optional)	1/4 C. of the cooked carrots
1 T. nutritional yeast	1/4 t. cumin powder
1 T. tamari or substitute	1 t. herb seasoning (page 3)
2 C. water	1 C. zucchini, diced
	1 t. sea salt

1. Cook the lentils in a separate pot (see page 13).
2. In a soup pot, sauté the onion and garlic in oil or water, then add celery and carrots. Allow the carrots to soften then add the eggplant. Add the yeast and tamari with a little water, and cover. Cook until carrots are completely soft.
3. In a blender, blend half of the remaining ingredients except the zucchini and sea salt. Pour into the soup pot. Repeat the blender process another time.
4. Add 2-4 cups of additional water, then add the zucchini.
5. Add 2-4 cups, or the desired amount of the remaining whole cooked lentils to the pot. Add sea salt to taste. Simmer until the zucchini is soft. Serve.

Light Lentil Soup
serves 5

1 T. oil (optional)	**Blender Ingredients**
1 onion, chopped	2 C. water
3 cloves garlic, diced	1 t. garlic powder
2 celery stalks, sliced	1 t. dill
3 C. carrots, sliced	1 t. herb seasoning
2-3 potatoes, cubed	1 t. cumin powder
2 C. dry lentils (rinsed & soaked)	1 T. tamari or substitute
1 T. nutritional yeast	1 t. onion powder
tamari or substitute, to taste	1 t. sea salt
water, as directed below	

1. In a soup pot, in oil or water, sauté the onion and garlic until soft. Add celery, carrots and potatoes and stir. Add the lentils along with the yeast and tamari, with enough water to cover the lentils by two inches. Cover and simmer. Add more water as necessary as the lentils cook.
2. When lentils are soft, remove 3/4 cup of lentils with some vegetables and blend with the Blender Ingredients. Pour into soup pot. Add enough water for desired consistency. Simmer until the flavors blend, approximately 20-30 minutes.

Autumn Harvest Soup
serves 5-6

1 T. oil (optional)	1 t. sea salt
1 large onion	6-7 C. stock or water
1-2 cloves garlic	2-3 T. tamari or substitute
3 carrots, 2 sliced, 1 grated	2 T. nutritional yeast
1 large sweet potato, cubed	1 t. salt-free herb seasoning (page 3)
2 medium potatoes, cubed	1/4 t. lemon pepper
1 butternut (or sweet squash), cubed	

1. Dice onion and garlic and sauté in oil or water. Add sliced carrots, potatoes, squash and sea salt to pot with enough stock to cover vegetables by an inch. Let simmer on low heat until vegetables are soft.
2. Remove 1/3 of the cooked vegetables with a strainer and blend with remaining stock until creamy. (Use less stock for a thicker soup). Add the remaining seasonings and blend again. Return mixture to soup pot and simmer for 10 more minutes. Season to taste. Delicious served immediately and even better the next day.

Minestrone Soup
serves 5-6

2 C. cooked beans (pinto, kidney)	1/2 T. onion powder
1 large onion, diced	1/2 T. garlic powder
3 celery stalks, diced	7-8 oz. pasta ribbons or shells
2 C. carrots, sliced	1/4 C. tamari or substitute
2 zucchini, sliced & halved	1/2 t. sea salt
6 oz. tomato paste	1 T. dill weed
1/2 T. parsley	1/2 T. herb seasoning (page 3)
3 T. nutritional yeast	1/2 t. black pepper
1 1/2 T. dried oregano	fresh basil leaves, a handful

1. Prepare beans (see page 13). Drain and set aside.
2. In a medium-sized soup pot, sauté the diced onion and celery. Add the carrots. When they partially soften, add the zucchini.
3. In a blender, blend two cups of water with the tomato paste, parsley, yeast, oregano, onion and garlic powder. Return to the pot. Simmer for a while.
4. Cook pasta separately, until tender. Do not overcook. Rinse and drain.
5. Take half a cup of cooked carrots from the pot and place in the blender with 1 1/2 cups of water. Blend until creamy. Continue adding to the blender 1 1/2 cups of water, along with tamari, sea salt, dill weed, herb seasoning and pepper until thoroughly blended. Pour back into the pot.
6. Add fresh basil leaves to the soup pot. Add one to two more cups of water to the pot. Stir and simmer. Just before serving, remove basil leaves and add the pasta ribbons.

Great Gazpacho

serves 6
From The Compassionate Cook by Ingrid Newkirk

3 C. vegetable or tomato juice
1 medium onion, minced
2 medium tomatoes, diced
1 green bell pepper, minced
1 clove garlic, crushed
1 medium cucumber, diced
2 T. fresh lemon juice

2 T. vinegar
1 t. dried tarragon
1 t. fresh basil, minced
cumin powder, a pinch
a dash of hot sauce
2 T. olive oil
salt and pepper, to taste

Combine all ingredients in a bowl and chill for two hours.

Mushroom Barley Soup

serves 5-6

3/4-1 C. barley
2 cloves garlic, minced
2 small onions, diced
4 C. mushrooms, sliced
4 T. tamari or substitute

2 T. nutritional yeast
5 T. cashew butter
1 T. onion powder
1/2 T. garlic powder
1 t. sea salt, to taste

1. Cook the barley in a big soup pot (one cup dry barley to three to four cups water). Bring to a boil, then reduce heat and simmer until barley is completely cooked. This is a hearty soup. For a thinner soup, use only 3/4 of a cup of barley.
2. Remove barley from the pot. In the same pot, sauté garlic, onions, then mushrooms.
3. In a blender, blend 1 1/2-2 cups water with tamari, yeast, cashew butter and seasonings. Pour this into the soup pot.
4. Cover the blades of the blender with some cooked barley. Add water to cover the barley and blend to a creamy consistency. Add 1-2 more cups of water to the blender and blend. Pour this into the soup pot.
5. Add the remaining cooked barley to the soup pot. Simmer for 25-30 minutes. (If soup sits for a while, the barley will absorb some of the liquid and thicken the soup. To remedy this, add more liquid and seasonings.)

> *"The meat-laden, Western style diet, rather than leading us to an age of prosperity and health, has contributed to a bankrupting epidemic of degenerative diseases."*
>
> MICHAEL A. KLAPER, M.D. ~ American author and international lecturer

> *"The quality of mercy is not strained;*
> *it droppeth as gently as the rain from heaven upon*
> *the place beneath; it is twice blessed:*
> *it blesseth him that gives and him that takes."*

WILLIAM SHAKESPEARE (1564-1616)
English poet and playwright
<u>The Merchant of Venice</u>

Dips, Dressings, Sauces & Gravies

Dips, Dressings, Sauces & Gravies

"How wonderful it is that nobody need wait a single moment before starting to improve the world."

ANNE FRANK (1930–1945)
German-Jewish author, holocaust victim
The Diary of Anne Frank

Mediterranean Hummus
yields 5 cups

4 C. cooked chick peas, drained	1-2 cloves garlic
1 t. onion powder	1 t. cumin powder
1/2 C. water	1/2 t. sea salt
4 T. tahini	lemon juice, to taste (optional)
1 t. herb seasoning (page 3)	fresh herbs and/or garlic (toasted)
1 t. sea salt, to taste	(optional), to taste

1. In a food processor, using the "S" shaped blade, whiz half of the chick peas with half of the seasonings. Stop intermittently to scrape the sides of the processor with a rubber spatula and continue to whiz until creamy smooth. Repeat with the other half of the ingredients.
2. Chill and serve. The consistency should be thick and somewhat soft as it hardens when refrigerated.

Bean Dip
5-6 servings

2 2/3 C. pinto beans (cooked)	1 t. onion powder
3 T. tamari or substitute	1 t. cumin powder
2/3 C. tomato paste	1 T. apple cider vinegar
2 t. garlic powder	jalapeños, diced, to taste (optional)

In a food processor, using the "S" shaped blade, blend all ingredients. Chill.

(Upon being informed by doctors that he would die if he refused meat)

"My situation is a solemn one: life is offered to me on condition of eating beefsteaks. But death is better than cannibalism. My will contains directions for my funeral, which will be followed not by mourning coaches, but by oxen, sheep, flocks of poultry and a small traveling aquarium of live fish, all wearing white scarves in honor of the man who perished rather than eat his fellow creatures. It will be, with the exception of Noah's Ark, the most remarkable thing of its kind ever seen."

GEORGE BERNARD SHAW (1856-1950) ~ Irish-British playwright
1925 Nobel Prize recipient

Versatile Tofu Onion Dip
yields 2-2 1/2 cups

1 large onion, diced	*1 1/2 C. tofu, rinsed & drained*
2 T. Bragg™ Aminos/tamari	*4-6 T. water*
3 T. nutritional yeast	*1/2 t. sea salt*
1/4 C. safflower oil	*a dash of garlic & onion powder*

1. In a frying pan, sauté one onion in a little oil or water.
2. Add a dash of tamari, yeast and water. Cook until onions are translucent.
3. In a food processor, using the "S" shaped blade, blend all ingredients until smooth.
4. Chill and serve.
   • Perfect for baked potatoes or combine with grains to make loaves and burgers.

Tofu Herb Dip
yields 3 cups

1 lb. tofu, rinsed & drained	*1 t. garlic powder*
1/4 C. oil	*1 t. onion powder*
4 T. nutritional yeast	*1 T. chives*
1/2 C. water	*1 T. parsley*
2 t. herb seasoning (page 3)	*1 T. dill weed*
2 T. tamari or substitute	*1 T. cilantro*

Blend all ingredients together in a food processor using the "S" shaped blade.
(Add any favorite herbs.) Chill and serve.

"Dill"icious Dip
yields 2-3 cups

1/8-1/4 C. safflower oil	*a dash of garlic & onion powder*
1/2 lb. (1 C.) tofu, rinsed & drained	*1 t. herb seasoning (page 3)*
1/4-1/3 C. fresh dill weed	*2 T. tamari or substitute*
4 T. water	*2-3 T. nutritional yeast*

Blend all ingredients in a food processor using the "S" shaped blade. Chill and serve.

"Ever occur to you why some of us can be this much concerned with animals' suffering? Because government is not. Why not? Animals don't vote."

PAUL HARVEY ~ American radio newscaster, syndicated journalist

Creamy Cashew Pesto Dip
yields 2-3 cups

1 C. cashew pieces (raw)	2 T. nutritional yeast
1/4 C. oil	2 T. Bragg™ Liquid Aminos or tamari
3/4 lb (1 1/2 C.) tofu	1/4-1/2 t. sea salt
1/3 C. water	6 cloves garlic, minced
1 C. fresh basil, chopped	1 small clove garlic

1. Soak cashew pieces for 5-10 minutes in water then drain. Rinse and drain tofu.
2. In a food processor, using the "S" shaped blade, blend oil with cashew pieces until creamy smooth. Sauté minced garlic in a little oil until golden-brown.
3. Add tofu to the food processor a little at a time. Add remaining ingredients including the clove of garlic. Blend until smooth. Chill and serve.

Cheezy Dip
yields 4-5 cups

1/4 C. oil	5 T. nutritional yeast
1 lb. tofu, rinsed & drained	1/2 C. water
1/4 C. tamari or	a dash of garlic & onion powder
Bragg™ Liquid Aminos	vegan 'cheese', grated (optional)

In a food processor, using the "S" shaped blade, blend all ingredients until smooth and creamy.
- Add grated vegan 'cheese' (page 274) and whiz for an even more flavorful dip.
- Can be used as a topping for baked casseroles.

Nacho Cheeseless Dip
yields 2 cups

1 C. tofu, rinsed, drained, mashed	1/4 C. nutritional yeast
2/3 C. vegan 'cheese', grated	2 T. tamari or substitute, to taste
(see page 274)	6 T. water
1/4 C. oil	jalapeños, diced (optional)

In a food processor, using the "S" shaped blade, blend all ingredients together.

- To make nachos, pour sauce over corn chips on a baking tray. Bake for 5-10 minutes. Top with beans, salsa and guacamole if desired. Serve immediately.
- Use as a dip or spread on breads and sandwiches (as is or baked).
- Use as a topping for baked potatoes. Add to cooked grain to make burgers and loaves.

Creamy Carrot Cashew Paté
serves 5-6

2 1/2-3 C. cashew pieces (raw)
4 small carrots, peeled, sliced
1/2 small sweet onion (optional)
1-2 cloves garlic (optional)

1/4 C. oil
2-3 T. Bragg™ Aminos or substitute
1/3-1/2 C. water
sea salt, to taste

1. Soak cashew pieces in water for 15-20 minutes, until soft, then drain excess water.
2. In a food processor, using the "S" shaped blade, blend the sliced carrots as finely as you can. Add onion and/or garlic and blend again. Add oil and cashews a little at a time and blend until smooth. Add water and Bragg Aminos. Stop the machine intermittently and scrape the sides with a rubber spatula; blend again until smooth. Creaminess is essential in a paté. Chill and serve.

Pea Dip
yields 3 cups

2 1/2-3 C. green peas,
   steamed lightly
1/2 medium onion, chopped
3/4 lb. (1 1/2 C.) tofu
1 T. olive oil

2 cloves garlic, chopped
salt and red pepper, to taste
1/8-1/4 C. water
   (use less water for a thicker dip)
1/8 t. dill weed

Rinse and drain tofu. Place all ingredients in a food processor using the "S" shaped blade. Blend until smooth and creamy. (Add seasonings, to taste.) Chill and serve.

Creamy Artichoke Dip
serves 5-6

1 T. olive oil
1 medium onion, chopped
4 cloves garlic, chopped

1/2 lb. mushrooms
6-8 artichoke hearts, steamed
4 oz. (1/2 C.) firm tofu, rinsed & drained

1. Sauté the onions, garlic and mushrooms in oil. When soft, remove from frying pan.
2. Place steamed artichoke hearts and the sauté into a food processor, using the "S" shaped blade and blend until smooth. Add tofu and blend again. Season to taste with favorite seasonings, i.e. garlic powder, sea salt, sweetener. Blend. Chill and serve.

> **"As long as there are slaughterhouses,
> there will be battlefields."**
>
> COUNT LEO TOLSTOY (1828-1910) ~ Russian novelist and philosopher

Zippy Parsley Dip
yields approx. 1 1/2 cups
Contributed by Wild Ginger Restaurant - Vegan Village, U.K.

2-2 1/2 oz. fresh parsley
1 oz. onion, diced
1 1/2 T. vegan 'mayonnaise'

salt and pepper (to taste)
juice of one lemon (to taste)
4 oz. (1/2 C.) tofu, rinsed & drained

Wash and drain parsley. Discard stems. In a blender, blend all ingredients well.

Sour Cream
yields approx. 1 cup

1 C. firm tofu, rinsed & drained
2 1/2 T. lemon juice

1/4 t. sea salt
water, to thin
1 T. oil (optional)

In a food processor, using the "S" shaped blade, blend all ingredients to a smooth consistency. Chill. Keeps for 2-3 days refrigerated.

Tofu Mayonnaise
yields 2 cups – for a listing of store-bought non-dairy mayonnaise, see page 275.

1/3-1/2 C. safflower oil
3 T. apple cider vinegar
1/2 lb. (1 C.) tofu, rinsed & drained

1 t. sea salt
1 1/2-2 T. fructose (dry sweetener)
1 t. fresh lemon juice

In a blender or food processor, blend ingredients. The mixture might be thick, so add ingredients slowly, turning blender on and off. Chill. Keeps well in the refrigerator.

Oat Cheese
yields 1 1/2 cups

1/3 C. rolled oats
1/8 C. tahini
2/3 C. nutritional yeast
1 T. herb seasoning (page 3)
2-3 T. fresh lemon juice

2 C. water
1 T. onion powder
1 t. garlic powder
1 T. dill (optional)
4 T. arrowroot powder

1. Pulverize oats in a dry blender. Add remaining ingredients and blend.
2. Transfer to a saucepan. Heat on medium-low flame until thickened, stirring often. Do not bring to a boil. Use fresh for pizza and lasagna or transfer to a bread loaf pan, cool and refrigerate overnight. It will mold to a solidified consistency.

Thousand Island Dressing
yields 3 cups

1/4 C. oil
2/3 C. water
1 T. apple cider vinegar
1/2 lb. (1 C.) tofu, rinsed & drained
1/3 C. tomato paste

a dash of onion powder
1 T. mustard (stoneground)
1 T. sweetener
1 T. tamari (or sea salt to taste)
4 T. vegan sweet relish
1/3 C. sweet onion, diced (optional)

1. In a blender, blend all ingredients except half of the sweet relish and the diced onion.
2. Add remaining relish and the onion and whiz for just 30 seconds. Keeps well in the refrigerator.

Tahini Dressing
yields 1 1/2 cups

1 C. water
1/2 C. tahini

3 t. tamari or substitute
spices or herbs of choice (optional)

In a blender, blend all ingredients. (Use 1/4 cup less water for a thicker dressing to use in bakes and casseroles.) Keeps for up to two days in the refrigerator.

• Variation ~ 1 t. curry powder may be added for a delicious curry-tahini dressing.

Quick Tahini Dressing in a Jar
great for traveling!

1/2 C. tahini
2/3 C. water

2 t. tamari or substitute
1 t. nutritional yeast (optional)

Place all ingredients in a jar and shake vigorously.

House Dressing
yields 3 cups

3/4 C. water
1/4-1/3 C. oil
1/2 C. tahini
2/3 C. tofu, rinsed and drained
2 1/2 T. tamari or substitute
3 T. mustard (stoneground)

1 1/4 t. salt-free herb seasoning (page 3)
1/2 t. onion powder
1/4 t. garlic powder
2 T. nutritional yeast
1 T. herb seasoning (page 3)

In a blender, blend all ingredients until creamy. Keeps 2-3 days in the refrigerator.

French Dressing
yields 5 cups

5 carrots, sliced and steamed	garlic & onion powder, to taste
1/4-1/3 C. apple cider vinegar	2 1/2 T. tamari or substitute
2/3 C. oil	2 T. nutritional yeast
1 2/3 C. water or carrot stock	a dash of dill weed
4 T. sorghum or rice syrup	1 t. dried oregano
7-8 T. tomato paste	1 t. basil

1. Steam carrots in two cups of water until tender. Save the carrot stock to use later.
2. In a blender, add liquid ingredients, tomato paste and steamed carrots. Blend. Add remaining ingredients and blend until creamy smooth. Chill before serving.

It's Italian! Dressing
yields 2-3 cups

1 C. water	3 T. nutritional yeast
1 C. cold-pressed olive oil	2 1/2 T. herb seasoning (page 3)
3 T. apple cider vinegar	1 1/2 T. rice syrup
1 T. dried oregano	1/2-1 t. dried basil
1 t. dill weed	1 t. onion powder
1 t. garlic powder	a dash of pepper
1 clove garlic, diced	1 sweet onion slice, diced finely

In a blender, blend all ingredients together. Keeps well in the refrigerator.

Creamy Italian Dressing
yields 3 cups

1/2 C. oil	2 T. nutritional yeast
1/3 C. apple cider vinegar	herb seasoning (page 3)
1 C. water	onion & garlic powder, to taste
2 T. rice syrup (or other sweetener)	a dash of black pepper
1 T. tamari or substitute	1 T. dried oregano
1 C. soft tofu, rinsed & drained	1 t. dried basil

Place liquid ingredients in a blender. Add tofu and spices and blend until creamy.

> **"The greatness of a nation and its moral progress can be judged by the way its animals are treated."**
>
> MAHATMA GANDHI (1869-1948) ~ Hindu pacifist, spiritual leader

Sesame Miso Dressing
yields 3 cups

1/2 C. miso
1/4 C. sesame oil
~~1/4 C. oil~~
3/4 C. water
1/2 t. garlic powder

3 cloves garlic, diced
3 T. fresh lemon juice
2 T. sweetener
1-2 T. nutritional yeast
1/2 t. onion powder

In a blender, blend all ingredients together. Keeps well in the refrigerator.

Sweet and Sour Miso Dressing
yields 3-4 cups

4 T. miso (preferably blonde)
~~1 1/4 C. oil~~
1/2 C. apple cider vinegar

3-4 T. rice syrup (or other sweetener)
5 t. nutritional yeast
1 C. water

In a blender, blend all ingredients together. Keeps well in the refrigerator.

Miso Lemon Mustard Dressing
yields 2 cups

1 C. water
~~2/3 C. oil~~
5 T. fresh lemon juice
3 T. blonde miso

2 T. mustard (stoneground)
3 T. nutritional yeast
1 T. liquid sweetener *honey*

In a blender, blend all ingredients together. Keeps well in the refrigerator.

Lemon Curry Dressing
yields 2 1/2 cups

1 C. water
2 t. fresh lemon juice
1/4 C. nutritional yeast
1 T. tamari or substitute

~~1/2 C. oil~~
1 T. rice syrup (or other sweetener)
1/2 t. mild curry powder
1/2 C. tofu, rinsed, drained, mashed

In a blender, blend ingredients together until smooth. Keeps well in the refrigerator.

Papaya Seed Dressing (a favorite!)
yields approx. 2 cups

1/4 C. olive oil (cold-pressed)	*2 T. stoneground mustard*
2 T. papaya seeds	*3 T. maple syrup*
1-2 cloves garlic, minced	*1/4 C. brown rice vinegar*
1/2 t. herb seasoning (page 3)	*1/4 C. water*
1/4 C. sweet onion	*1 T. balsamic vinegar*
1/2 C. safflower oil	*1/2 t. dried basil*
1 t. sea salt or substitute, to taste	*1/2 t. dried oregano*

In a blender, blend all ingredients together. Keeps well in the refrigerator.

Lemon Ginger Dressing ✓
yields 2 cups

1 C. water	*1 T. tahini*
1/2 C. olive oil	*1-2 T. fresh ginger, minced*
2 T. fresh lemon juice	*1 T. tamari or substitute*
1 T. maple syrup	*2 T. nutritional yeast*
1/2 C. tofu, rinsed & drained	*1 t. mustard (stoneground)*

In a blender, blend all ingredients together. Keeps well in the refrigerator.

'Dill'icious Salad Dressing
yields approx. 2 cups

1/4-1/3 C. olive oil	*6 T. fresh lemon juice*
1/2 lb. (1 C.) tofu, rinsed & drained	*2-3 T. rice syrup*
3-4 T. tamari or substitute	*1/3 C. fresh dill weed*
1 T. nutritional yeast	*garlic powder, to taste*
3/4 C. water	*onion powder, to taste*

In a blender, blend all ingredients together and chill. Keeps well in the refrigerator.

Creamy Garlic Dressing ✓
yields 2 cups

2/3 C. water	*7 cloves garlic, diced, toasted*
1/3 C. oil	*2 T. tamari or substitute*
1/2 lb. (1 C.) tofu, rinsed & drained	*1/2 t. garlic powder (optional)*
1 t. onion powder	*1 T. nutritional yeast*

In a blender, blend all ingredients together. This dressing is for the real garlic lover! Keeps well in the refrigerator.

Green Goddess Dressing
yields 2 cups

3/4 C. water
1 medium avocado
3 T. fresh lemon juice

1 1/2-2 T. tamari or substitute
a dash of garlic & onion powder
1/4 C. fresh herbs, chopped

In a blender, blend all ingredients together. Serve freshly made.

No-Oil Tomato Vinaigrette
yields 1 cup

2 T. tomato paste
2 T. apple cider vinegar
3/4 C. water
a dash of lime juice

1 1/2 T. rice syrup
2 T. nutritional yeast
1 1/2 T. tamari or substitute
1 T. mustard (stoneground)

In a blender, blend all ingredients to a creamy consistency.

Creamy Dijon Dressing
yields 1 quart

1/2 C. oil
1 1/4 C. water
2 T. mustard (stoneground)
1 T. miso (blonde)

1/2 C. nutritional yeast
1 C. tofu, rinsed, drained, mashed
1 T. tamari or substitute
1/2 T. fresh lemon juice

In a blender, blend all the ingredients to a creamy consistency.

Lemon Basil Dressing
yields 2 cups

1/4 C. water
3/4 C. oil
1/4-1/3 C. fresh lemon juice
1/3 C. fresh basil

1 T. tamari or substitute
4 T. nutritional yeast
2 T. rice syrup
other fresh herbs (optional)

In a blender, blend all ingredients together. Keeps well in the refrigerator.

> ## "Harmlessness is the highest religion."
>
> JAIN (JAINISM) MAXIM

Lemon Tahini Dressing ✓
yields 2 cups

1 C. water
3/4 C. tahini
4-5 T. fresh lemon juice

1 1/2 T. tamari or substitute
1 large clove garlic
cayenne or fresh herbs (optional)

In a blender, blend all ingredients until creamy smooth.

Cole Slaw Dressing
yields 2 1/2 cups

1/2 lb. (1 C.) tofu, rinsed & drained
1/2 C. brown rice vinegar
1/2 C. safflower oil
1/3 C. fresh lemon juice
1-2 t. herb seasoning (page 3)

2-3 T. mustard (stoneground)
2 T. sea salt
1/3 C. sweetener (fructose)
fresh parsley, to taste

Blend all ingredients together. Use as a dressing for your favorite salad or add to shredded cabbage, carrot and onion to make cole slaw.

Divine Cashew Mushroom Gravy
make
yields 2-3 cups

3 cloves garlic, minced
2 small onions, diced
2 C. mushrooms, sliced
2 C. water
3 T. nutritional yeast

1 t. garlic powder
1 t. onion powder
3 1/2 T. cashew butter
2 T. tamari or substitute
1/2 t. sea salt
1 T. arrowroot powder

1. In a small sauce pot, sauté garlic and onions, then add mushrooms and simmer until vegetables are soft.
2. In a blender, blend remaining ingredients. Pour mixture into the pot and simmer, stirring often until the arrowroot thickens the gravy. Do not boil.
   • This gravy is the perfect complement for mashed potatoes and loaves.

> *"Animal fats, especially those in milk, butter, cheese and meat, are highly saturated, and an excess intake of such foods may be partly responsible for the development of atheroma, which causes atherosclerosis."*
>
> AMERICAN MEDICAL ASSOCIATION ~ Family Medical Guide

Mushroom Cheezy Gravy
yields 3 cups

1 medium onion, diced	1 T. liquid vegetable bouillon
1 C. mushrooms, sliced	1 T. tamari or substitute
2 C. water	2 T. arrowroot powder
1 C. nutritional yeast	1-2 T. molasses
1 t. herb seasoning (page 3)	1/2 t. garlic powder
1 T. oil or tahini	1/2 t. sea salt

In a small pot, sauté onion in a little oil or water. When somewhat soft, add mushrooms and sauté until soft. In a blender, blend remaining ingredients. Pour into sauté and simmer on a low flame, stirring often, until gravy thickens. Do not boil.

Holiday Mushroom Gravy
yields 2 1/2 cups

2 C. mushrooms, sliced	1 t. garlic powder
2 C. water	1 t. onion powder
1/3 C. tahini	2 t. liquid vegetable bouillon
2/3 C. nutritional yeast	4 t. arrowroot powder
2 t. herb seasoning (page 3)	1/8 t. black pepper
1 t. dried oregano	

In a little oil or water, sauté mushrooms in a small pot until soft. Blend remaining ingredients and add to the pot. Simmer on low and stir until thickened. Do not boil.

Brown Gravy
yields about 1 1/2 cups

1 T. oil	2 T. whole wheat flour
1/2 sweet onion	1 T. nutritional yeast
2 cloves garlic	1 C. water
1 T. tamari or substitute	salt and pepper, to taste

In a pan, sauté onion and garlic with oil, adding tamari and any herbs or vegetables. When soft, remove vegetables, leaving 2 T. of liquid. Add water or stock if needed. Add flour and yeast and whisk until blended. Slowly add remaining water or stock, stirring constantly until gravy bubbles and thickens.

> *"Nothing will benefit human health and increase chances for survival of life on earth as much as the evolution to a vegetarian diet."*
>
> ALBERT EINSTEIN (1879-1955) ~ German-born American physicist

No-Oil Miso Mushroom Gravy
yields 2 1/2 cups

2/3 C. onion, diced
2 1/4 C. mushrooms, sliced
2 C. water
3 T. red miso
1 1/2 T. nutritional yeast

1/2 T. tamari or substitute
1 1/2 T. arrowroot powder
1/2 T. vegetarian worcestershire sauce
1/2 t. garlic powder

1. In a small pot, sauté the onion with a little water. Add the mushrooms and simmer with the lid on, until mushrooms are soft.
2. In a blender, blend the remaining ingredients. Pour into the pot with the mushrooms and simmer on a low flame until gravy thickens, stirring often.

Rich Carrot Coconut Sauce
yields 2-3 cups

1 C. carrots, sliced
1/2 C. water
1 1/2 C. pure coconut milk
1/4 t. curry powder

2 1/2 T. Bragg™ Liquid Aminos or tamari
1 T. arrowroot powder
1/4 t. garlic powder
4-5 T. scallions, diced

1. Place the sliced carrots and water in a small gravy pot, cover, and steam until soft.
2. Place steamed carrots in a blender with steam water and remaining ingredients, except the scallions. Blend to a creamy consistency and pour into the pot. Simmer. Add the scallions while simmering. Stir continuously until gravy thickens. Remove from flame. Do not boil.

Basil Lemon Sauce
yields approximately 1 cup

1 C. soy milk or nut milk
2 T. sunflower oil (optional)
sea salt, to taste
white pepper, to taste

1 T. arrowroot powder
2 T. fresh lemon juice
2 T. fresh basil, chopped finely

1. In a saucepan, combine all ingredients except lemon juice and basil and place over medium heat, stirring continuously. Do not boil.
2. When sauce thickens, add lemon juice and basil, stir well, and remove from heat.

> *"Go to your bosom, knock there and ask your heart what it doth know."*
>
> WILLIAM SHAKESPEARE (1564-1616) ~ English poet and playwright

Tartar Sauce
yields 2 cups

1 lb. (2 C.) tofu, rinsed & drained	1 T. mustard (stoneground)
1/4 C. oil	1 1/2 t. sea salt
1/4 C. water	2 1/2 T. fresh lemon juice
1 1/2 T. sweetener (fructose)	1 T. nutritional yeast
3-4 T. vegan sweet relish	1/8 C. sweet onion, diced

1. In a food processor, blend all ingredients except the onion and 2-3 tablespoons of the relish. When mixture is smooth, fold in onion and remaining relish.
2. Chill and serve with lemon broil tempeh (page 118), breaded tofu fillet/cutlets, etc.

Chinese Sauce
4-6 servings

1/3 C. oil	3 1/2 C. stock or water
10 cloves garlic, chopped	4 T. arrowroot powder
1/2 t. fresh ginger, diced	1/3 C. tamari or substitute
	1/4 C. sweetener (rice syrup/sorghum)

In a blender, blend all ingredients together then transfer to a sauce pot and simmer on low heat until thickened, stirring continuously. Do not boil.

Tasty Marinara Sauce
yields 10 cups

1-2 T. olive oil	1 t. sea salt
6 cloves garlic, diced	2 T. garlic powder
1 onion, diced	2 T. dried oregano
2 bell peppers, diced	2 T. dried basil
8-16 oz. mushrooms, sliced	3 T. sweetener
2 (12 oz.) cans tomato paste	2 t. herb seasoning (page 3)
2 1/2 C. water	1/2 t. black pepper
1 (16 oz.) can tomato sauce	1-2 T. tamari or substitute
1 T. onion powder	2 T. nutritional yeast

1. In a large pot, sauté garlic in a little oil and a dash of water.
2. While it is simmering, add onion, peppers then sliced mushrooms. (Be sure to tip the stems of the mushrooms and clean them well).
3. When all vegetables are soft, add tomato paste, water, tomato sauce and remaining seasonings. Simmer and stir frequently for 30 minutes or longer.

Fresh Roma Tomato Garlic Sauce
yields 1 small pot

6 cloves garlic, peeled
1/4 C. olive oil
1 medium onion, diced
1 1/2 bell peppers, diced
6-7 roma tomatoes, diced

1/2 C. nutritional yeast
1/2 C. water
2 t. arrowroot powder
1/2 t. sea salt
1/4 t. black pepper

1. In a blender, blend garlic and oil. Pour into a large skillet. Add onion and sauté.
2. After one minute, add pepper and continue to sauté. Add diced tomatoes and cover. Allow to simmer for 5-10 minutes, until tomatoes are soft.
3. Remove 1 1/2 cups of the sauté (mostly tomatoes) and place back into blender. Add nutritional yeast, water and arrowroot. Blend.
4. Pour mixture into skillet. Add salt and pepper. Simmer and stir until sauce thickens (about five minutes). Do not boil. Serve over pasta.

Roasted Garlic and Basil Tomato Sauce
yields 1 medium-sized pot

1 whole bulb of garlic
1 small onion, diced
1/2 green pepper, diced
1 T. oil

1 C. fresh basil, chopped
1 T. Bragg™ Liquid Aminos
 (or 1/2 t. sea salt)
2 (14 oz.) cans tomato sauce

1. Place bulb of garlic, with peel, in toaster oven at 350° for 10 minutes, until soft.
2. In a skillet, sauté onion and green pepper in oil or water until onion is translucent.
3. Take garlic out of oven. Cool and peel. (It should be easy to peel - pop each clove out of its shell.) Dice it. Add diced garlic and chopped basil to sauté. Add Bragg's or sea salt and stir for just a moment.
4. Add canned sauce (or two cans diced tomatoes). Let simmer for 20-30 minutes until flavors are blended, adding more salt or basil if desired.

> *"A bear, who was kept in a zoological garden, displayed, so long as he had bread exclusively for nourishment, quite a mild disposition. Two days of feeding with flesh made him vicious, aggressive, and even dangerous to his attendant."*
>
> JUSTICE LIEBIG (1803-1873) ~ German chemist
> Mr. Liebig became famous for research into protein. He concluded that plants are a primary source of protein, and that plant protein is equivalent to the protein found in animals.
> Quoted in <u>The Ethics of Diet</u>, by Howard Williams, 1883.

Thai Coconut Curry Sauce
yields 1 small pot

1 large onion, halved & sliced
2-3 cloves garlic, diced
1 (14 oz.) can pure coconut milk
14 oz. can water
1/2 t. sea salt

1/4 C. cashew butter
1 T. mild curry powder
3 T. tamari or substitute, to taste
4 t. arrowroot powder

1. In a small pot, sauté onion slices and garlic.
2. In a blender, blend remaining ingredients.
3. When onions are soft, pour blended mixture into the pot and simmer for 10-15 minutes, stirring continuously, until it thickens. Do not boil. Serve over rice, Thai noodles or your favorite noodles with steamed vegetables.

Vegetable Coconut Curry Sauce (quick & easy)
serves 4-6

1 onion, peeled & sliced
3 small carrots, diced
1 zucchini, sliced, halved
<u>Blender Mixture</u>
1 C. soy milk (non-dairy milk)
1 can (14 oz.) pure coconut milk

1 t. curry powder
1 T. tamari or substitute
1/2 t. garlic powder
1 T. arrowroot powder
1/4-1/2 t. sea salt

1. Sauté the onion in a saucepan with a small amount of oil or water. When onions are softened, add carrots. Simmer until softened. Add the zucchini. Cover and simmer until soft.
2. In a blender, blend the remaining ingredients. Pour into saucepan and simmer, stirring frequently, until sauce thickens. Serve over noodles or rice.

Fresh Tomato and Green Olive Sauce
serves 4

2 lbs. tomatoes, chopped
12 large green olives, pitted
1 bunch scallions, chopped
2 cloves garlic, chopped
1 T. fresh thyme, minced
2 T. olive oil

1 t. sea salt
1 t. pepper
1 t. garlic powder
1 t. onion powder
8 oz. box of pasta (cooked)
　　or 4 C. rice (cooked)

Chop olives. Place all ingredients (except pasta/rice) in a blender or food processor. Pulse until creamy-chunky. Toss tomato-olive sauce over cooked pasta or rice.

• Variation ~ Blend all ingredients except tomatoes. Combine blended ingredients with tomatoes in a bowl. Toss in with pasta or rice.

Thai Peanut Curry Sauce
yields 3 cups

4 cloves garlic, minced
2 small onions, sliced thinly
2/3 C. peanut butter
1 1/2 T. mild curry powder
1 1/4 T. arrowroot powder

2 C. water
4-5 T. molasses
1 T. sweetener
3 T. tamari or substitute
cayenne (optional), to taste

1. In a small pot, sauté garlic and onions with a little oil or water.
2. In a blender, blend remaining ingredients.
3. When onions are tender, pour blended mixture into pot with garlic and onions. Simmer until gravy thickens, stirring continuously. Do not boil.

Sweet Potato Spread
yields 4-5 cups

1 t. oil
4 medium sweet potatoes
seasonings, to taste

2 medium onions
2 T. blonde miso
garlic powder, to taste

1. Pre-heat oven to 400°. Lightly oil a baking tray or use baking paper. Place sweet potatoes and onions on sheet. Bake until vegetables are soft, about 45 minutes. Remove from oven and allow to cool.
2. When cool enough, peel the vegetables. Transfer vegetables to food processor. Add miso and purée, using the "S" shaped blade, until smooth. Season with garlic powder and favorite seasonings.

• Variation ~ Try using butternut squash and/or carrots instead of sweet potatoes.

Sweet Ginger Sauce *make*
yields 1 1/4 cups

1 t. ginger (grated)
1 clove garlic (crushed)
2 T. tamari or Bragg™ Aminos
1 T sesame oil or water
1 1/2-2 t. sweetener

1/2 t. onion powder
cayenne, to taste
1 C. water
1 T arrowroot powder
3 green onions (diced)

1. Blend ingredients in a blender except for green onions. Strain into a small saucepan.
2. Add green onions, cook over medium heat until thickened, stirring constantly. Remove from heat before sauce boils.

Italian White Bean Topping
serves 4

4 C. cooked great northern beans or navy beans (page 13)	1/2 t. basil
	1/2 t. oregano
1/4 C. water/stock (or tomato sauce)	2 t. onion powder
1/4 C. olive oil	1/2 t. sea salt
1 T. nutritional yeast	1 T. fresh parsley, chopped
3 cloves garlic, diced	2 scallions, chopped

1. Combine beans, water/stock, oil, nutritional yeast, garlic, and spices in the food processor. Process until creamy-smooth, adding more liquid to reach desired consistency.
2. Transfer to a bowl. Top with parsley and scallions. Serve at room temperature.

Mustard Marinade
yields 1 1/2-2 cups

1 C. mustard (stoneground)	1 T. sweetener
2 T. olive oil	2 cloves garlic, crushed
2 T. vinegar	1 T. fresh ginger, minced
2 T. tamari or substitute	1/4 t. crushed red pepper
1/4 C. water	

In a small bowl or blender, whisk or blend all ingredients. If mixture is too thick, add 1/4 cup of water to turn blades.

• Serve as a marinade or over baked potatoes.

> "We must not, in trying to think about how we can make a big difference, ignore the small daily differences we can make which, over time, add up to big differences that we often cannot foresee."
>
> MARION WRIGHT EDELMAN ~ President of the Children's Defense Fund first female African-American lawyer admitted to Mississippi bar

Greek Garbanzo Dip (for Artichokes)
yields 2 1/2 cups

2 C. garbanzo beans (cooked)
1/4 C. vegetable stock
1/3 C. fresh lemon juice
1 T. garlic, minced
2 T. olive oil

2 T. parsley, finely chopped
3 scallions, sliced
1/4 t. cumin powder
1/4 t. dried oregano

1. In a blender or food processor, place the beans, stock, lemon juice, garlic and olive oil and process until smooth.
2. Transfer mixture to a bowl. Stir in the parsley, scallions, cumin and oregano.
3. Cover and refrigerate until ready to use. Spread the mixture on the soft ends of the individual artichoke leaves or use as a dip. (Enough dip for four artichokes)

To cook four medium artichokes

1. To cook and serve a whole artichoke, cut off the stem at its base so it will stand upright. Snap off the tough outer leaves and cut off the top quarter of the bud. You can also snip off the pointy tips of the exposed leaves and rub the cut portion of the artichoke with lemon to prevent discoloration. Place prepared artichokes in a bowl of water until ready to use.
2. Boil artichokes, by standing them in a deep pan, in 4-6 inches of boiling salted water. Add a little olive oil, lemon juice or herbs to the cooking water. Cover the pot and gently boil for 30-40 minutes until a petal near the center pulls out easily. Stand artichokes upside down to drain. Once cooked, artichokes are best served immediately. Serve with your favorite dipping sauce.

Salsa
yields 2 1/2 cups

1 can (14 oz.) diced tomatoes
    or 2 C. fresh tomatoes, diced
1/2 C. onion, diced
1/2 C. fresh cilantro, chopped
8 oz. tomato sauce, unflavored
1 T. nutritional yeast
1 lime, squeezed

hot chili pepper, to taste
1 clove garlic, finely chopped
jalapeño pepper, to taste, diced
1/2 t. sea salt
1 t. apple cider vinegar
1/4 t. cumin powder

In a bowl, mix all ingredients together. Chill and serve.

Zesty Barbecue Sauce
yields 3 cups

2 C. water
1/4 C. sorghum and/or molasses
2/3 C. tomato paste
2 T. vinegar
1/2 t. garlic powder
1 1/2 T. onion powder
1 T. arrowroot powder

1 T. vegan hickory smoke flavor
1 T. molasses
1 T. vegetarian worcestershire sauce
 (without anchovy, see pg 280)
2 T. liquid bouillon (see page 2)
1 1/2 t. tamari

In a blender, blend all ingredients. Pour into a small pot and simmer on low. Stir until sauce thickens. When it begins to bubble, remove from flame. Do not boil.

• If using molasses rather than sorghum, use 1 T. dry sweetener instead of 1 T. molasses.

Basil Pesto Sauce
serves 2–3

1 C. raw cashews or pine nuts
3–4 cloves garlic, diced, toasted
3 T. water
2 T. nutritional yeast

1 T. Bragg™ Liquid Aminos or tamari
1/3 C. cold-pressed olive oil
1 C. fresh basil, chopped
a dash of sea salt

1. Soak the cashew pieces in water for 5-10 minutes. Drain water.
2. Pan-fry the garlic for five minutes until golden-brown.
3. In a food processor, blend all ingredients well, including toasted garlic.

• Serve with your favorite pasta or use as a spread on breads.

---

*"I think of veganism humbly and holistically.
It's about taking personal responsibility in a world so full
of needless suffering. It's challenging one's self to open
one's eyes and question society's assumptions and habits.
It's about critical thinking and compassion and how
we would like to see the world evolve."*

MICHAEL GREGOR, M.D. ~ American lecturer and author

> "...every animal that walks the earth, or swims, or flies
> is precious beyond description,
> something so rare and wonderful
> that it equals the stars
> or the ocean or the mind of man..."
>
> JAMES MICHENER (1902-1997)
> American author and novelist
> "Where Did the Animals Go?" Readers' Digest, June 1976

Appetizers and Side Dishes

*above: **Peking Tempeh Rolls** (page 111) ~ below left: **Incredible Stuffed Mushrooms** (page 91)
below right: **Spinach Tofu Philo Wraps** (page 97) ~ following page: **Spring Rolls** (page 112)*

Appetizers
&
Side Dishes

"It is my view that a vegetarian manner of living,
by its purely physical effect on the human temperament,
would most beneficially influence the lot of mankind."

ALBERT EINSTEIN (1879–1955)
German-born American physicist
1921 Nobel Prize recipient

Tofu Rainbow Paté
yields 2 (1 1/2 quart) loaf pans

This recipe is a three layered dish. Each layer is mixed in the food processor then poured evenly into two oiled baking dishes, each layer upon the previous layer.

First Layer
2 C. carrots, sliced and steamed	1/3 C. oil
3/4 lb (1 1/2 C.) medium-firm tofu rinsed and drained	2 T. nutritional yeast
	1 t. garlic powder
1 t. Bragg™ Aminos or tamari	1 t. onion powder
1 t. sea salt	2 t. arrowroot powder

1. In a food processor, using the "S" shaped blade, blend steamed carrots. Add remaining ingredients and blend until very smooth and creamy (intermittently scraping the sides with a rubber spatula). Pour this mixture into each oiled baking dish, filling it one third of the way up.

Second Layer
2 C. beets, sliced, steamed	1 T. arrowroot powder
1/4 C. oil	3 T. nutritional yeast
1 lb. (2 C.) medium-firm tofu rinsed and drained	1 t. onion powder
	1 T. Bragg™ Aminos or tamari
1/2 t. garlic powder	2 t. herb seasoning (page 3)

2. In the processor, blend steamed beets. Add remaining ingredients and blend until smooth and creamy. Pour this mixture on top of the first layer in each baking dish.

Third Layer
1 lb. (2 C.) medium-firm tofu rinsed and drained	1/4 C. oil
	4 T. nutritional yeast
3 T. Bragg™ Aminos or tamari	1 t. turmeric powder
1 t. onion powder	1 t. arrowroot powder

3. In the food processor, blend all third layer ingredients. Pour this blended mixture on top of the second layer in each baking dish. You should now have three distinctly colored layers in each baking dish.
4. Bake, in a pre-heated oven, at 350° for 45–55 minutes. Allow to cool then chill in refrigerator overnight or for many hours, until solidified.
5. Place a plate over the bread pan and flip each baking dish onto the plate. The paté should come out easily. Slice and serve.

> **"There's no reason to drink cow's milk at any time in your life. It was designed for calves, not humans, and we should all stop drinking it today."**
>
> DR. FRANK A. OSKI ~ former Director of Pediatrics, Johns Hopkins University

Mushroom Paté
yields 1 small cake pan

3 C. mushrooms, sliced	*1 3/4 lb. (3 1/2 C.) medium-firm tofu*
1 small onion, diced	*1 1/2 T. Bragg™ Liquid Aminos*
1 t. sea salt	*2 T. nutritional yeast*
1 t. herb seasoning (page 3)	*1 t. onion powder*
	2 t. arrowroot powder

1. Wipe mushrooms clean with a damp paper or cloth towel. Rinse and drain tofu.
2. Sauté the mushrooms in a little oil and save the liquid. Sauté the onion separately.
3. In a food processor, using the "S" shaped blade, blend all ingredients except the mushrooms. Fold in mushrooms, without blending.
4. Place the mixture in an oiled baking dish. Bake at 350° until cracks appear and it turns light brown, (approximately 35 minutes). Allow to cool then chill. Serve cold in slices.

Incredible Stuffed Mushrooms
yields 10 large mushrooms

1. Wipe 10 large mushrooms clean with a damp paper or cloth towel. Remove stems. Marinate in:

2 T. tamari	*1/2 t. garlic powder*

2. In a food processor, blend:

1/2 large onion, diced, sautéed	*1 T. Bragg™ Aminos or tamari*
1 C. soft tofu, rinsed & drained	*1 T. oil*
1 T. herb seasoning (page 3)	*1 T. nutritional yeast*

3. In a frying pan, grill the mushroom caps on the top side on high heat.
4. Remove them when sizzled on one side and place onto a small baking sheet.
5. In the same frying pan, in a little oil, sauté:

2 slices whole wheat bread, cubed	*1/2 t. black pepper*
1/2 t. herb seasoning (Spike™)	*1 t. dill weed*
1 t. oregano	*1/2 t. Bragg™ Liquid Aminos or tamari*

6. Add this toasted bread to the tofu mixture. Mix together well.
7. Spoon mixture into each mushroom cap and sprinkle with paprika. In a pre-heated oven, bake at 375° for 20-25 minutes.

> *"An animal has feelings; an animal has sensitivity; an animal has a place in life, and the vegan respects this life that is manifest in the animal..."*
>
> H. JAY DINSHAH (1933-2000) ~ founder of the American Vegan Society, author

Marinated Portabella Mushrooms
serves 4-6

Marinade
5 T. toasted sesame oil
3 T. vinegar
2 T. tamari
2 T. fresh lemon juice
2 cloves garlic, minced

To Grill
4-5 portabella mushrooms
(remove stems & wipe mushrooms
clean with a damp paper/cloth towel).
1 bunch watercress or spinach
vinegar, a splash (optional)

1. Mix the marinade ingredients together in a bowl. To marinate, submerge one mushroom for just a few seconds. Remove, then shake to remove extra liquid.
2. Place mushrooms on a medium-to-hot grill. Cook for six minutes and flip, using tongs. Cook for another five minutes, until soft. While mushrooms are grilling, brush them with leftover marinade.
3. When fully cooked, place mushrooms on a cutting board. Slice into strips.
4. Place watercress/spinach on a plate and splash with vinegar or excess marinade. Sprinkle with salt and pepper (optional). Add mushroom strips.
   • Variation ~ Use grilled mushrooms to make an excellent sandwich with hot sauce.

Grilled Portabella Mushrooms with Herb Baguette
serves 2

1 1/2 lbs. portabella mushrooms
2 t. cumin powder, ground
2 t. chili powder
1 t. onion powder
1 T. dry sweetener

1-2 T. olive oil
1 French or Italian baguette (see page 31)
3 cloves garlic, minced
1 t. dried oregano
salt and pepper, to taste

1. Wipe mushrooms clean with a damp paper or cloth towel. Cut stems off if too long. In a small bowl mix cumin, chili powder, onion powder and sweetener.
2. Brush mushrooms and stems with one tablespoon olive oil. Place them in the bowl with above seasonings, tossing well to coat mushrooms.
3. Cut baguette in half and cut each piece in half again lengthwise. Place on foil, crust side down. Brush with olive oil and sprinkle with garlic, oregano, salt and pepper.
4. Place mushrooms on foil, then place on grill away from direct heat and grill for five minutes. Place bread on the grill for 2–3 minutes to toast.
5. Serve mushrooms with baguette immediately after grilling.

> *"I will continue to be a vegetarian even if the whole world started to eat meat. This is my protest against the conduct of the world."*
>
> ISAAC BASHEVIS SINGER (1904-1991) ~ Yiddish Laureate of Literature, 1978 Nobel Prize recipient

Breaded Stuffed Mushrooms
yields 20 large mushrooms

20 large stuffing mushrooms
<u>Mushroom Marinade Sauce</u>
2 T. Bragg™ Aminos or tamari
1 T. apple cider vinegar
1/2 T. garlic powder
1 T. oil
<u>Filling</u>
3 C. tortillas/bread, chopped
2 C. cooked quinoa (or other grain)
   (see page 12)

1 1/2 C. medium-firm tofu, rinsed well
1 T. salt-free Spike™ (herb seasoning)
1/2 T. dried basil
1 1/2 T. dried oregano
1 T. onion powder
1/2 C. nutritional yeast
5 T. Bragg™ Liquid Aminos or tamari
4 T. oil
2 T. tahini

1. Wipe mushrooms clean with a damp paper or cloth towel and pat dry. Remove stems, making more space for the stuffing in the mushroom cap.
2. Combine marinade mixture and place mushrooms in it. Stir periodically.
3. In a large skillet, in a little oil, pan fry the tortillas or bread. Mash tofu and add to the pan with the grain, spices and nutritional yeast. Stir and pan fry the stuffing mixture.
4. When finished, place in a bowl and add Bragg's, oil and tahini. Mix.
5. Oil the emptied frying pan. Place the marinated mushrooms in the pan with the stuffing side up. Over a high flame, brown the mushroom caps for a couple of minutes then remove from heat.
6. Fill each cap with stuffing. Pack it in tight then put another spoonful on top. Bake at 350° until the mushrooms are soft and juicy and stuffing has browned on top.

Tempeh/Tofu Chunks
yields 1 skillet

3 (8 oz.) cakes tempeh or tofu
4 T. tamari
4 T. nutritional yeast

3 T. oil or tahini
1/4 t. garlic powder
Bragg™ Liquid Aminos (optional)

If using tofu, rinse, drain and cut into bite-sized cubes, then go to step 2.
1. Steam the tempeh, allow to cool then cut into bite-sized cubes.
2. Marinate in a mixture of the remaining ingredients. Stir periodically.
3. Oil a skillet and pan fry the chunks. Add a little more Bragg's or tamari and oil (optional) while frying. Easy and filling. Serve with grains or pasta.

"There is no disease, bodily or mental, which adoption of a vegetable diet and pure water has not infallibly mitigated, wherever the experiment has been fairly tried."

PERCY BYSSHE SHELLEY (1792-1822) ~ English poet

Curried Tofu Chunks
serves 3

1 3/4 lb. firm tofu	1 T. tahini (thin) or oil
1 T. tamari or substitute	2–3 T. nutritional yeast
1/2 T. liquid bouillon (page 2)	1/4 t. onion powder
1 t. curry powder	a dash of sea salt, (optional)

1. Rinse and drain tofu, cut into 1/2" cubes and place it in a bowl. Marinate in the tamari and bouillon for several minutes. Add the remaining ingredients and stir.
2. In a lightly oiled (or non-stick) frying pan, brown the chunks on both sides, approximately 10 minutes.

   • Serve them as an appetizer on a serving platter, with a toothpick through each one or add the completed chunks to two cups of curried cooked grain of choice.
   • Variation ~ Add different seasonings other than curry, such as basil, oregano and dill weed. In addition, add a small amount of wheat germ or oat bran.

Breaded Eggplant Cutlets
serves 3-4

1–2 medium-large round eggplants, peeled
<u>Breading</u>

1 C. whole wheat pastry flour	1 t. herb seasoning (page 3)
1/2 C. wheat germ or bran	1 t. sea salt
1/2 C. fine cornmeal	1 t. garlic powder
1/2 C. nutritional yeast	1 t. onion powder

thick tahini dressing (see page 73)

1. Steam eggplants until soft. Set aside to cool for a few minutes. Slice eggplant.
2. In a bowl, mix together the breading ingredients.
3. Dip each piece of eggplant into the tahini dressing. Coat with the breading mixture. Pan fry, on both sides, in an oiled skillet (or use a non-stick pan). Drain on a paper towel. Alternatively, place on a baking tray and bake at 350° until browned on top. Serve warm as is or in a sandwich.

   • Variation ~ Cut firm tofu into chunks and prepare the same way. Serve with grain.

> **"A low-fat plant-based diet would not only lower the heart attack rate about 85 percent, but would lower the cancer rate 60 percent."**
>
> WILLIAM CASTELLI, M.D. ~ Director, Framingham Health Study; National Heart, Lung, and Blood Institute
> Excerpt from <u>The Food Revolution</u> by JOHN ROBBINS, Conari Press, 2001

Tofu Cutlets – Quick and Easy
yields 7 cutlets

1 lb. tofu, rinsed & drained	2 T. bran
2 T. tamari or substitute	garlic powder, to taste
<u>tahini dressing</u>: 2–3 T. tahini,	onion powder, to taste
2 T. water, excess marinade	favorite seasonings (optional)
3 T. nutritional yeast	2 t. salt-free herb seasoning (page 3)

1. Cut tofu into seven slices and marinate in tamari for 10 minutes.
2. Make tahini dressing, using excess tamari from marinade. Spread on one side of each cutlet. Add half the nutritional yeast, bran and seasonings.
3. Place each cutlet, coated side down, in an oiled frying pan on medium heat.
4. While frying, coat the exposed cutlet sides with the remaining dressing, yeast, bran and seasonings. Cook until browned. Flip; cook 5 more minutes. Serve on a sandwich.
   • Variation ~ Dip tofu slices in thick tahini dressing. Dip in breading. Pan fry.

Easy Lasagna Roll-Ups
yields 12 rolls

12 lasagna noodles	<u>Sauce</u>
<u>Filling</u>	1/2 t. dried oregano
3 C. medium-firm tofu	1/2 t. dried basil
1/3 C. nutritional yeast	1/2 t. onion powder
1/4 C. italian tomato sauce	1/2 t. garlic powder
3 T. tahini or oil	salt and pepper, to taste
1 T. parsley or dill	3 C. italian tomato sauce

1. Partially cook noodles so you can roll them. Rinse with cold water and drain. Separately rinse and drain tofu.
2. In a bowl, mix filling ingredients. In a separate bowl, combine sauce ingredients.
3. Spread a layer of sauce on the bottom of a casserole. Lay out noodles and spread two tablespoons of filling on each. Roll up tightly and place seam side down in casserole. Pour remaining sauce over roll-ups. Pre-heat oven to 350°.
4. Sprinkle with additional nutritional yeast. Bake for 25–30 minutes.

Mock "Chicken" Tofu
serves 2

1 lb. firm tofu	2 t. herb seasoning (page 3)
2 T. oil	2 T. tamari or substitute
1/4 t. turmeric	1/3 C. nutritional yeast

1. Rinse and drain tofu. Cut into bite-sized chunks.
2. Heat oil in frying pan on medium heat. When hot, add tofu and cook until one side is crispy.
3. Flip and brown tofu for another five minutes. Add seasonings, cover and simmer.

Grilled 'Cheese' & Tomato Sandwich

grated VeganRella™ (see page 5)   1–2 tomatoes, sliced
1–2 T. oil   Nacho Cheeseless Dip (optional -
bread slices, quantity desired   see recipe page 70)

· This sandwich can be baked for a healthier choice or grilled in a frying pan for a more authentic taste.

1. Grate the vegan 'cheese' (any flavor you choose - see page 274). The quantity will depend on how many sandwiches you are making.
2. If frying, spread 'cheese' on two pieces of bread adding a slice of tomato to one piece. Grill on medium-high heat in an oiled or non-stick frying pan for a couple of minutes. Then put one slice over the other, press down with spatula, cover with a lid and simmer for about a minute or two. Shut off flame and allow the cheese to melt.
3. If baking, simply sprinkle grated 'cheese' on bread or toast. Add a slice of tomato, then bake until 'cheese' is melted. Another option is to spread some Nacho Cheeseless Dip on slices of bread (instead of or with the 'cheese'), add a slice of tomato and bake until spread is golden-brown in color.

California Grills
yields 2 sandwiches

6 slices of eggplant, 1/2" thick   4 slices red onion, 1/2" thick
3 T. olive oil   2 tomatoes, sliced 1/2" thick
salt and pepper, to taste   4 slices whole wheat bread
1 red bell pepper, cut in half,   1 T. mustard (stoneground)
  cored and seeded

1. Pre-heat grill to medium-high. Brush eggplant slices with olive oil on both sides, sprinkle with salt and pepper and grill for 4–5 minutes on each side.
2. Grill the bell pepper halves, skin down, until browned. Place in a bag and seal (to steam) about ten minutes. Slip off any charred areas and discard.
3. Lightly brush onion and tomato slices with oil on both sides and grill 5–7 minutes each side. Sprinkle with salt and pepper.
4. Brush both sides of bread with oil and grill or toast until golden-brown.
5. For each sandwich, spread mustard on both pieces of bread. Top one piece with three eggplant slices, two slices of onion, one sliced tomato and one red pepper half. Cover with the other slice of bread. Cut in half to serve.

"All beings tremble before violence. All fear death. All love life. See yourself in others. Then whom can you hurt? What harm can you do?"

The BUDDHA (circa 563-483 B.C.) ~ Indian avatar

Spinach Tofu Philo Wraps
serves 4

1 package philo dough wraps
   (whole wheat or regular)

Spinach Filling
1/2 C. vegetable stock
1 medium onion, chopped
2 cloves garlic, diced
1 C. mushrooms, sliced
2 C. spinach, chopped

Tofu Filling
1 lb. (2 C.) firm tofu, rinsed & drained
1 T. oil
1/2 t. garlic powder
1/4 t. sea salt
1 T. sesame seeds
1/4 t. paprika
1/4 t. dry mustard

1. Put stock, onions and garlic in a skillet, over medium heat. Cook until soft. Add mushrooms and spinach and let simmer for several minutes.
2. Drain the sauté, remove from skillet and set aside.
3. In a bowl, mash tofu into a chunky batter and combine with oil and the seasonings. Add spinach filling and mix.
4. Spread one full sheet of philo wrap flat and lightly oil using a pastry brush or spray lightly with a vegetable oil spray.
5. Fold sheet in half. Place about 3-4 T. of filling in the center of each philo piece. Fold dough around filling, wrapping like a package. Alternatively, fold into a triangle and gently bend in half. Place on a lightly oiled baking sheet or use baking papers.
6. Repeat steps 4 & 5 until all the filling is used. (You will have extra philo dough.) Bake in a pre-heated oven at 350° for 20 minutes, until golden-brown.

Broccoli Almondine Casserole
serves 3-4

3 heads broccoli
4-6 cloves garlic, peeled
2-3 T. olive oil

3/4 C. almonds, finely sliced
2 T. tamari or substitute

1. Wash broccoli and cut into bite-sized pieces. Steam until just tender. While broccoli is steaming, blend two cloves of fresh garlic in a blender with olive oil.
2. Finely chop the remaining cloves of garlic and sauté in a pan, using the garlic oil just made. Add sliced almonds to the cooking oil and toast them, then add the tamari.
3. When broccoli is steamed, put in a baking dish and pour sauté mixture over it. Stir.
4. Place in oven at 300°, covered for 10-15 minutes. Serve.

> *"Compassion alone stands apart from the continuous traffic between good and evil proceeding within us. Compassion is the anti-toxin of the soul."*
>
> ERIC HOFFER (1902-1983) ~ American philosopher

Middle-Eastern Broccoli with Sesame
serves 2

1 small head broccoli	*1 T. tamari*
2 T. sesame seeds	*1/8 t. crushed red pepper*
1 T. toasted sesame oil	*1 T. vinegar (optional)*
2 t. fresh ginger, peeled & grated	*2 green onions, chopped*

1. Remove stems from broccoli and cut into bite-sized pieces. Steam for 5-7 minutes until tender yet still firm, then drain.
2. Lightly toast sesame seeds in a toaster-oven or frying pan.
3. Heat sesame oil in a cast iron skillet or non-stick pan. Add ginger and cook for 30 seconds over low heat. Add tamari, red pepper and vinegar.
4. Stir broccoli into the sesame oil mixture and simmer for about three minutes to coat well.
5. Sprinkle green onions over broccoli with toasted sesame seeds.

'Cheezy' Onions
serves 2-3

2 onions, sliced or diced	*2 1/2 T. tamari or Bragg™ Liquid Aminos*
2 T. oil	*5 T. nutritional yeast*
3-4 T. water	*sea salt & pepper, to taste*

In a frying pan, sauté the onions in oil, then add remaining ingredients. Continue to cook until onions are thoroughly soft. Serve as a topping or side dish.

Cabbage & Onion Sauté
serves 5

1 T. oil	*3 T. nutritional yeast*
4 cloves garlic, diced	*1 head cabbage, shredded or sliced thinly*
2 onions, diced	*3/4 t. garlic powder*
3 T. tamari or substitute	*1 t. dill weed*

1. Sauté the diced garlic in a frying pan with oil. Add onions and sauté until tender. Add a portion of the tamari and yeast to the cooking onions.
2. Add cabbage to the pan with remaining seasonings. Stir-fry until soft.

> ***"The high-minded man must take care more for truth than for what people think."***
>
> ARISTOTLE (384-322 B.C.) ~ Greek philosopher, scientist, logician (student of Plato)

Tofu Caraway Cabbage
serves 4

2 T. caraway seeds
1 T. oil
3 cloves garlic, diced
1 large onion, diced
2 T. water
2 T. tamari or substitute

2 T. apple cider vinegar
1 large head cabbage, sliced
1/2 lb. (1 C.) soft tofu, rinsed & drained
2 T. fresh lemon juice
1/4 t. sea salt
black pepper, to taste (fresh ground)
1/4 C. fresh parsley

1. In a skillet, heat caraway seeds until they start to pop. Add oil and garlic and sauté. Add diced onion and cook until soft. Add water, tamari, and vinegar and stir well. Add the cabbage, cover, and simmer for 10-15 minutes or until cabbage is tender.
2. In a blender, combine tofu, lemon juice and salt. Blend until smooth. Pour over cabbage and heat for one more minute. Season with pepper and garnish with parsley.

Asparagus with Hollandaise Sauce
serves 3-4

1-2 bunches asparagus, trimmed
1 C. soft tofu, rinsed & drained
1/8 C. oil
1/8 C. fresh lemon juice
1 C. water

1 T. miso (blonde)
1 T. Bragg™ Aminos or sea salt, to taste
1 T. arrowroot powder
1/2 t. sea salt
1/4 C. nutritional yeast

1. Cut or break the hard bottoms off the asparagus stalks. Steam the asparagus in a steamer basket until soft (approximately five minutes). Place in a casserole dish.
2. In a blender, blend remaining ingredients and pour into a small pot. Simmer and stir frequently for about 10 minutes until thickened. Do not boil. Pour over asparagus.

Cream of Cauliflower
serves 4

2/3 C. onion, diced
1 T. oil (optional)
1 stalk celery, sliced
1 whole cauliflower, cut bite-sized
1 t. sea salt (or to taste)
1 1/2 C. soft tofu, rinsed & drained

1 T. fresh lemon juice
1 t. onion powder
1 t. garlic powder
4 T. nutritional yeast
1/4 t. black or lemon pepper

1. In a frying pan, sauté onion in oil or a small amount of water. Add celery, cauliflower and sea salt. Simmer on a low flame, adding water if needed.
2. In a blender, purée tofu thoroughly, with just enough water to turn it into a cream, then add remaining ingredients. Pour over cauliflower, stir, and place in a casserole dish. Sprinkle with additional nutritional yeast. Pre-heat oven to 275°. Bake for 10-15 minutes then serve.

Baked Butternut Squash
yields 1 squash

1 butternut squash	*1 T. tamari or substitute*
2 T. oil	

1. Bake squash in a pre-heated oven at 375° until soft (approximately an hour). Remove from oven and let it cool enough to touch. Slice in half, lengthwise. Remove seeds.
2. Cut lines in both directions down the inside of the squash halves, opening it up for a marinating mixture to seep in. (Don't cut through the shell.) Spread 1+ T. oil and 1/2 T. tamari on each half. Bake for another 10-15 minutes.

Yellow Summer Squash on the Half Shell
yields 14 halves

7 yellow crookneck squash	*1 t. salt-free herb seasoning (page 3)*
2 T. nutritional yeast	*1 T. tamari or substitute*
1 t. garlic powder	*1/4 C. water*
1/2 t. each: oregano and parsley	*1/2 T. tahini (thin)*

1. Wash the squash and slice in half, lengthwise.
2. Use a fork to make grooves on the inside for the marinade mixture to seep into. Line up each piece, with the grooves facing up, in a baking dish with sides.
3. Mix together the remaining ingredients and brush over the top of the squash. Pre-heat oven to 375°. Bake for 15-25 minutes until very tender. Serve immediately.

Spaghetti Squash on the Half Shell
yields 2 halves

1 large spaghetti squash	*2 T. tamari or substitute*
1 t. onion powder	*1 t. parsley flakes*
1/2 t. garlic powder	*2 T. nutritional yeast*
2 T. water	

1. Bake squash in a pre-heated oven at 375° until it softens (approximately an hour). Remove from oven and let it cool enough to touch. Slice in half lengthwise. Remove seeds. Place back in the oven for another 15 minutes. Mix the remaining ingredients.
2. Remove from oven and loosen the inside of the squash with a fork. Mix in the seasoning mixture and place back in the oven for another 10-15 minutes.

"You have discovered as much love as you live."

LIGHT ~ President and co-founder of Gentle World

Spaghetti Squash Marinara
yields 2 halves

1 large spaghetti squash	1 t. garlic powder
1-2 T. oil (optional)	2 T. nutritional yeast
2 T. tamari or substitute	1/2 C. tomato sauce (see pages 81 & 82)

1. Bake the squash in a pre-heated oven at 375° until soft (approximately an hour). Remove from oven and cool enough to touch. Slice in half lengthwise. Remove seeds.
2. Using a fork, loosen up the squash. Mix remaining ingredients into both halves of the squash (using only half of the yeast and tomato sauce). Spread the rest of the sauce and yeast on top of squash. Bake until completely soft (approximately 20 minutes).

Stuffed Tomatoes
serves 6

6 large tomatoes	fresh ground pepper, to taste
3 green onions, chopped	1/2 t. basil
1 T. balsamic vinegar	1/2 t. oregano
1 T. stoneground mustard	sea salt, to taste
1/4 C. fresh parsley, chopped	1 C. basmati rice, cooked (see page 12)
2 t. tahini	curly lettuce, to garnish plate

1. Slice half an inch off the top of the tomatoes and scoop out the insides using a sharp knife and a spoon. Save the insides in a bowl. Turn the tomato shells upside down on a paper towel to drain for five minutes.
2. Add the remaining ingredients to the tomatoes in the bowl, except the rice and lettuce. Stir and allow to marinate for 10 minutes.
3. With a slotted spoon, remove 1/3 of the mixture and set aside for later as a garnish. Stir rice into the remaining mixture and allow to stand for another five minutes.
4. Arrange the lettuce on six salad plates. Spoon the rice mixture back into the tomato shells, and place one on each plate. Top with remaining tomato mixture garnish and serve at room temperature.

"A reduction in beef and other meat consumption is the most potent single act you can take to halt the destruction of our environment and preserve our natural resources. Our choices do matter. What's healthiest for each of us personally is also healthiest for the life support system of our precious, but wounded planet."

JEREMY RIFKIN ~ President of The Foundation on Economic Trends
author, <u>Beyond Beef</u>, Dutton, New York

Stuffed Zucchini Boats
yields 12 boats

6 zucchini, sliced in half lengthwise	1 T. nutritional yeast
1 onion, diced	1/8 C. water
3 C. mushrooms, sliced	1 t. herb seasoning (page 3)
2 T. tamari or substitute	1/2 t. salt-free herb seasoning (page 3)
2 C. tofu, rinsed, drained, mashed	1 t. onion powder
2 T. oil	1 C. cooked grain of choice (see page 12)

1. Wash zucchini and remove stems. Slice in half, lengthwise. Carefully cut out insides, leaving enough to make a firm container for the filling. Set aside zucchini insides.
2. Sauté the diced onion until soft. Remove from pan and place in the food processor.
3. Sauté mushrooms with 1 T. tamari. When finished, place in a mixing bowl.
4. Chop the zucchini insides into bite-sized pieces and sauté with 1 T. tamari. When cooked, add it to the bowl with the mushrooms.
5. In the food processor, using the "S" shaped blade, blend tofu with the onion sauté. Add remaining ingredients, except for the grain, and process until smooth. Add this to the bowl with mushrooms and zucchini. Add the grain and mix.
6. Oil a large, shallow baking pan and add a dash of tamari. Place the zucchini halves in the pan and fill them generously with the stuffing. Pre-heat oven and bake at 375° for about 30–40 minutes. First place the tray on the lower shelf in the oven. Half-way through baking, switch to the upper rack. They are finished when filling is golden-brown and the zucchini is soft.

Simply Delicious Baked Zucchini
yields 14 halves

7 zucchini (smaller size)	1 T. nutritional yeast
1/3 C. oil	3 T. tamari or substitute
1/4 C. water	1/2 t. garlic powder

1. Wash zucchini and remove stems. Slice in half, lengthwise. (For larger zucchini slice into thirds or quarters making wide thin strips.)
2. Using a fork, make grooves on the inside of each piece, from one end to the other. Place each piece with the grooves up, on a baking sheet with baking paper.
3. In a blender or in a bowl, blend or whisk the remaining ingredients.
4. Spoon this mixture onto the tops of the zucchini. Bake in a pre-heated oven at 350° until tender and golden-brown on top, about 20–30 minutes.

> *"An unrefined plant-based diet, together with appropriate exercise consistently followed, would eliminate most of the degenerative diseases that curse our western world."*
>
> RAY FOSTER, M.D., FACS

Zucchini Pizzas
yields 6 half shells

3 medium zucchini, sliced in half
1 T. oil
1 T. tamari or substitute
1 T. water
1/2 t. dried oregano

1/4 t. dill weed
1/4 t. dried basil
1 C. tomato sauce
'Cheezy' Dip (see recipe page 70)

1. Wash zucchini and remove stems. Slice the zucchini in half, lengthwise.
2. Using a fork, make grooves on the inside of each piece, from one end to the other. Place each piece with the grooves up, on a baking sheet with baking paper.
3. Mix oil, tamari, water, and herbs. Spoon this mixture evenly into the grooves. Cover with tomato or marinara sauce. Then cover with 'Cheezy' Dip. Bake at 350° until zucchini are quite soft, 30-40 minutes.

Italian Eggplant Stir-Fry
serves 4

3 cloves garlic, diced
1 onion, sliced in half moons
1 large eggplant, peeled & cubed
2 C. mushrooms, sliced
1 bell pepper, sliced in strips
2 T. tamari or substitute

2 tomatoes, cubed
1/4 C. fresh basil, chopped
1/3 C. fresh dill, chopped
1/4 t. black pepper
1 T. nutritional yeast
1 t. sea salt

1. In a skillet, sauté the garlic in a little oil then add the onion slices.
2. Add the eggplant and cover, allowing it to soften. In a couple of minutes, add the mushrooms, then the pepper. Season with tamari. Cover and simmer for a couple more minutes. Add tomatoes and remaining seasonings. Simmer briefly until tomatoes are soft.

• Serve as is or over grain or pasta.

> *"In the American Journal of Clinical Nutrition, there was a recent series of letters and commentaries saying that people should probably get their omega-3 fats from vegetables and not from fish, because the omega-3 fish oils do seem to have a variety of negative effects, one of which is that they promote the production of free radicals. Free radicals can damage tissues and lead to cancer."*
>
> MILTON R. MILLS, M.D. ~ Physicians Committee for Responsible Medicine

Ratatouille
yields 1 large skillet

4 cloves garlic, diced	1 t. garlic powder
1 onion, diced	1/2 t. black pepper
2 bell peppers, diced	2 t. herb seasoning (page 3)
4 C. mushrooms, sliced	3 T. nutritional yeast
7 C. eggplant, peeled & cubed	4 t. sweetener
2 T. tamari or substitute	2 T. oregano
2 zucchini, diced	1/2 t. dill weed
1 (15 oz.) can tomato sauce	1/2 t. sea salt
3 T. tomato paste	2 T. dried basil

1. In a large cast-iron pan or skillet, sauté the garlic and the onions. When they are partially cooked, add the peppers then the mushrooms. When they soften a bit, add the eggplant. Season with tamari, cover with a lid and allow to cook until soft. Add the zucchini pieces and cover again.
2. When the vegetables are almost cooked, add the tomato sauce and paste. Add all the remaining seasonings and spices and simmer, stirring frequently.
3. When sauce turns darker in color, remove from heat and allow to sit and absorb flavors. Serve warm as is or over grain or pasta.

Steamed Greens

greens of choice
collard greens
kale (different varieties)   *tamari or substitute (optional)*
mustard greens   *oil (optional)*
swiss chard
bok choy, pok choy & totsoi
spinach

1. Wash the greens well as they often have sand particles. Slice into small strips.
2. Steam using a steamer basket at the bottom of a pot. Add water, not exceeding the height of the steamer basket. (If water is filled too high, the greens will shrink as they cook and fall into the water, losing nutrients.)
3. Soft leaf greens, like chard, don't need anything added to them. When they soften they melt in your mouth. Collards, a thicker leaf, tend to need a dash of oil added to the pot to make them more tender, as well as delicious!
  • The less the greens are steamed the more vitamins and nutrients are retained.

> *"The best way to fight evil is by making energetic progress in the good."*
>
> I CHING (Ancient Chinese Book of Changes)

Magical's Steamed Vegetables
for steaming green beans, broccoli, cauliflower, corn, potatoes, etc.

vegetables of choice   herb seasoning (page 3)
cold-pressed olive oil   nutritional yeast

1. In a large pot, using a steamer basket, bring water to a steaming boil.
2. Drop vegetables into steamer basket. Leave for a few minutes on high heat; then reduce to medium-high. Steam until tender, but still crisp. The color will be retained. Remove steamer basket with the veggies from the hot water immediately.
3. Serve dressed with cold-pressed virgin olive oil, seasoning and nutritional yeast.

Baby Bok Choy & Mushroom Stir-Fry
serves 4

8 oz. shittake mushrooms (dried)   1 T. sesame oil
3 1/2 C. water   1 T. sweetener
2 T. tamari or substitute   2 heads baby bok choy
2 T. chili sauce or 1/2 t. red pepper 1 T. sunflower oil
2 T. arrowroot powder   2 C. sliced mushrooms (fresh)

1. Soak shittake mushrooms in water until completely soft, 15–20 minutes.
2. In a small bowl, combine one cup of the soaking liquid with tamari, chili sauce (without sugar) or red pepper, arrowroot powder, sesame oil and sweetener.
3. Slice the shittake mushrooms. Cut off root end of bok choy and separate into stalks. Wash well. Cut crosswise into one inch slices.
4. Heat oil in a skillet or wok over high heat. Add shittakes and bok choy and stir-fry for three minutes. Add fresh mushrooms and sauté until softened, about one minute. Add tamari mixture and cook until it thickens, about two minutes longer. Serve over rice or noodles.

"Lobsters are fascinating. They have a long childhood and an awkward adolescence. They use complicated signals to explore and establish social relationships with others. Their communications are direct and sophisticated. They flirt. Their pregnancies last 9 months. Some are right-handed, some left-handed. They've even been seen walking hand-in-hand. Some can live to be more than 150 years old, though few (1%) survive the world's most devastating predator – the species with whom lobsters share so many traits – the human being."

INGRID NEWKIRK ~ National Director, People For The Ethical Treatment of Animals
quoted from Save the Animals; 101 Easy Things You Can Do

Mediterranean Eggplant Sauté
serves 4-5

1-2 T. oil or water
1/2 large onion, diced
5 C. eggplant, peeled & cubed
1 t. garlic powder
1-2 t. onion powder
1/2 t. paprika
2 1/2 T. tamari
2 1/2 C. mushrooms, sliced thick

1-2 t. cumin powder
1/8 t. black pepper
1 T. oregano
1 T. nutritional yeast
1 C. cooked chick peas (see page 13)
1 T. tamari or substitute
1 T. vinegar (optional)

1. Sauté onion in oil or water. When soft, add eggplant. Season with garlic, onion powder, paprika and tamari. Cover and simmer for five minutes. Add mushrooms, the next four seasonings and cover. Allow the eggplant to soften, 20-30 minutes.
2. Place the chick peas in a small bowl with the tamari and vinegar and stir. Mix into the sauté and cook for several minutes. Let sit with the lid on for 5-10 minutes. Serve.

Scalloped Potatoes
yields 1 large casserole

8-10 russet potatoes
1/2 C. oil
1 C. tofu, rinsed, drained, mashed
1 C. water
1 T. tamari or substitute
3 T. nutritional yeast
1 T. cashew butter

1 onion, sliced
4-5 cloves garlic, sliced
1 t. onion powder
1/2 t. garlic powder
sea salt and pepper, to taste
paprika

1. Peel potatoes and slice thinly. Cover with water and drain before using in step 3.
2. In a blender, blend oil, tofu, water, tamari, yeast and cashew butter.
3. In a large bowl, mix the blended sauce with sliced potatoes, onion and garlic. Pre-heat oven to 350° and bake in a large, oiled baking dish. Stir periodically while baking.
4. When potatoes are almost thoroughly cooked (in 40 minutes, pull one out to test it), add sea salt and pepper, to taste. Sprinkle with paprika. Cook until potatoes are completely soft.

> *"People often say that humans have always eaten animals, as if this is a justification for continuing the practice. According to this logic, we should not try to prevent people from murdering other people, since this has also been done since the earliest of times."*
>
> ISAAC BASHEVIS SINGER (1904-1991) ~ Laureate of Literature, 1978 Nobel Prize recipient

Mashed Potatoes – Creamy Style
serves 4-6

7 C. potatoes, cubed	4-5 t. oil or cashew milk
1 onion, diced	2 t. tamari or substitute
1 T. oil + 3 T. water	1 t. dill weed
5 T. nutritional yeast	1 T. soy milk (optional)
4 T. potato stock	1 t. sea salt

1. Boil a large pot of water and cook the cubed potatoes until soft.
2. Sauté the onion in 1 T. oil, 3 T. water and 2 T. nutritional yeast, until soft.
3. Drain the potatoes, saving a small amount of the potato water as stock. Mash the potatoes with the stock, 3 T. nutritional yeast and the remaining ingredients. Stir in the onion sauté.

   • Serve with Cashew Mushroom Gravy (page 78) or Tahini Dressing (page 73).

Potato Latkes
serves 8

4 large potatoes (2 1/2 lbs.)	1/2 t. black pepper (fresh ground)
1 medium onion	3 T. tahini
1-2 t. sea salt	2 T. Matzoh Meal (or wheat germ)
	safflower oil

1. Coarsely grate the potatoes and onion with a hand grater or a food processor using the grater blade. Place in a colander. Set over a large bowl and squeeze out liquid.
2. Pour off the liquid from the bowl, leaving the potato starch that has settled to the bottom. Add the potatoes, onions, salt, pepper, tahini and matzoh meal. Mix well.
3. Over medium heat, heat enough oil to cover the bottom of a large skillet. Use a heaping tablespoon of batter to form each pancake. Flatten them with the back of a spoon as you add them to the skillet. Pan fry until golden-brown, turning once. Add more oil and adjust heat as needed. Drain on a paper towel before serving.

> *"I know many people are on a continuum, evolving their diet from red meat to one predominantly based on chicken and fish, with or without dairy products. The logical progression is toward a vegan dietary style, completely free of animal products. If you are in this continuum, I urge you not to linger in 'chicken-and-fish-land' too long."*
>
> MICHAEL A. KLAPER, M.D. ~ author and international lecturer

Potato Omelette
serves 4

3 large potatoes, grated	1/2 lb. (1 C.) tofu, rinsed and drained
1 large onion, grated	1/4–1/2 t. sea salt
1/2 t. sea salt	1/2 t. garlic powder
1/8 t. crushed red pepper (or black)	1/2 t. onion powder
2 T. olive oil	1/8 t. paprika
1 bell pepper, chopped finely	1/8 t. crushed red pepper

1. In a bowl, thoroughly mix the grated potato, onion, salt and pepper. Add this mixture to a skillet with 1 T. olive oil, and pan fry over medium heat, until potatoes and onions are golden-brown. Add chopped bell pepper and cook for four more minutes.
2. In a bowl, mash tofu and season with salt, garlic powder, onion powder, paprika and red pepper. Add the cooked potatoes, onions and pepper to the tofu and mix well.
3. In the same skillet, over medium heat, add 1 T. olive oil. Place the tofu-potato batter in the pan. Lightly brown on one side and flip to brown the other. Serve.

Home Fries
serves 2–3

2 T. oil	1 t. onion powder
4 C. cooked potatoes,	1/2 t. sea salt
(cut into bite-sized cubes)	1/2 t. paprika
1 1/2 T. tamari or substitute	1/4 t. black pepper
2 T. nutritional yeast	

1. Heat 2 T. oil in a skillet on medium heat, or use less oil and a non-stick pan.
2. Place the cubed potatoes (leftover baked potatoes work well) in the skillet and season with tamari. Add the yeast and onion powder. If potatoes are sticking, add another tablespoon of oil. Just before the potatoes are browned, add sea salt, paprika and pepper and pan-fry for another minute.

French Unfries
yields 2 small trays

7 large potatoes	1 t. sea salt
2 T. oil	1 T. nutritional yeast
1 T. tamari or substitute	1/2 t. paprika

1. Peel and cut the potatoes into strips like French fries.
2. Place in a bowl and mix with the remaining ingredients.
3. Pre-heat oven to 375˚. Lightly oil two small baking sheets (preferably lipped). Place the potatoes on the trays and bake for 20–40 minutes until golden-brown, switching the trays half-way through. Use a spatula to flip the fries periodically. Lightly salt, to taste.

'Cheezy' Creamed Potatoes (no-oil)
serves 4

5-6 large potatoes (approx. 9 C.) peeled and cubed	1/2 T. tahini
<u>Blender Mixture</u>	1 t. garlic powder
2 C. soy milk	1 t. herb seasoning (page 3)
8 oz. (1 C.) tofu, rinsed & drained	2 t. sea salt
1/2 C. nutritional yeast	1/2 t. mild curry powder
	1 T. arrowroot powder

1. Bring water to a boil in a pot using a steamer basket. When water is boiling, place potatoes in the steamer basket and steam on high until soft.
2. In a blender, blend the remaining ingredients.
3. When potatoes are soft all the way through, remove steamer basket from pot and drain the potato water. Pour potatoes back into the pot without the steamer basket.
4. Pour sauce into the pot with the potatoes and cook on medium heat. When sauce begins to bubble, reduce heat to medium-low. Cook for another 20 minutes, stirring often. Allow to cool slightly and serve immediately.

Holiday Candied Yams
serves 4-6

5 medium-large yams (or sweet potatoes), sliced	1 T. nutritional yeast
1 T. tamari or substitute	1 T. sweetener
3-4 T. maple syrup	1 T. vanilla
	1/8 C. oil

1. Peel and slice the yams. Steam in a pot until softened, about 20-30 minutes.
2. In a blender, blend the remaining ingredients.
3. Place the yams in a casserole and pour blender mixture over it. Be sure to scrape the sides of the blender with a rubber spatula. Spread evenly on the yams and bake in a pre-heated oven at 350°. Stir occasionally and continue baking for about half an hour. Allow to cool slightly before serving.

> *"If you change to a vegan diet, and do it very vigorously, you have enormous power. You can reverse heart disease. You can prevent it. You can, I believe, prevent most cases of cancer if you combine dietary changes with avoiding tobacco. You could prevent probably 70% or 80% of cancers, just by those steps alone. And, obviously, there's a whole host of other diseases that you would be able to live without."*
>
> NEAL BARNARD, M.D. ~ President, The Physicians Committee for Responsible Medicine

Thai'd Veggie Rolls
yields approximately 24 small rolls

1 bunch scallions	1/4 C. orange juice
1 T. olive oil	1/2 C. cilantro, chopped
2 C. carrots, shredded	1 T. sesame oil
2 C. cabbage, shredded	1/2 t. ginger powder
2 red bell peppers, sliced thinly	salt and pepper (to taste)
2 C. snow peas, sliced diagonally	12 sheets of nori, cut in half

1. Cut the green tops from the scallions and set aside. (You will need 24 strands for tying the rolls.) Mince enough of the white part of the scallion to make 1/4 cup and set aside.
2. Heat oil over medium heat, in a large skillet or non-stick pan. Sauté minced scallions, carrots, cabbage, peppers and snow peas for three minutes. Add orange juice and continue cooking, uncovered, until juice is almost evaporated, about 3 minutes.
3. Place vegetables in a bowl and toss with cilantro, sesame oil and ginger powder. Sprinkle with salt and pepper to taste.
4. Lay out half a sheet of nori and place one tablespoon of vegetable filling in the center. Roll up carefully and tie up each roll with a green scallion.
5. Serve with Thai Dipping Sauce - see recipe below.

Thai Dipping Sauce
yields 1 1/2 cups

3/4 C. peanuts (roasted)	1/4 C. tamari or substitute
2 thin slices fresh ginger, peeled	2 T. rice vinegar
2 cloves garlic, minced	1 C. vegetable stock (warm)
2 T. sweetener	2-3 T. lime juice
1/2 t. crushed red pepper	

In a blender or food processor, using the "S" shaped blade, combine all ingredients except vegetable stock and lime juice. Process until smooth, adding stock slowly and blending on a low speed. Finally, add the lime juice. Serve at room temperature.

> *"Most nutrition professionals agree that moving away from an animal product-based diet to a plant-based diet is the single most important improvement Americans (and others who eat similarly) can do to improve their well-being. I personally have eaten vegan (totally vegetarian) for over 15 years and have raised my two children that way since birth."*
>
> GEORGE EISMAN ~ registered dietitian, author

Peking Tempeh Rolls
serves 6

2 C. long grain brown rice (cooked)	3 T. rice vinegar
1 T. sesame oil	1/2 t. salt
6 scallions, cut into 1" pieces	1 T. ginger, grated
4 T. sesame seeds, toasted	1/3 lb. snow peas (ends trimmed)
2 C. red cabbage, shredded finely	6 whole wheat tortillas
1 C. carrot, shredded	3 T. spicy mustard
8 oz. cake tempeh, steamed	

1. After cooking rice (see page 12), combine cooked rice with sesame oil, scallions and two tablespoons of sesame seeds. Set aside. Crumble tempeh into a non-stick pan with one tablespoon of tamari and sauté until browned.
2. In a bowl, combine cabbage, shredded carrots, tempeh, vinegar, salt and ginger. Mix.
3. Bring a small saucepan of water to a boil. Add snow peas and cook for 30 seconds. Drain and rinse under cold water. Pat dry and cut lengthwise into thin strips. Add to cabbage mixture.
4. Lay tortillas flat on work surface. Spread each with half a tablespoon of mustard. One inch from the bottom edge, place a strip of the cabbage mixture and top with a strip of the rice mixture.
5. Roll up until tortilla just covers ingredients and tuck in ends. Continue to roll into a tight cylinder. Serve immediately.

Vegetable Curry
serves 8

<u>Curry Sauce</u>	1 lb. carrots, peeled and
1 1/2 C. soy milk (thick)	cut into chunks
1 C. corn kernels	1 large onion, sliced
1 C. coconut milk	1/2 lb. small mushrooms
1 T. curry powder	1/2 t. cumin seeds (optional)
1" piece fresh ginger,	<u>Ingredients to set aside</u>
(peeled, chopped)	2 C. cooked chick-peas (see page 13)
2 large cloves garlic	2 C. green peas
<u>Vegetable Base</u>	fresh cilantro, chopped
1 head cauliflower, cut into florets	roasted cashews
5 red potatoes, cubed	

1. In blender, purée soy milk, corn kernels, coconut milk, curry powder, ginger and garlic until smooth. Pour into a large bowl.
2. Place <u>Vegetable Base</u> ingredients into the bowl with the curry sauce and toss until vegetables are well coated. Place mixture into an oiled casserole dish and cover.
3. Bake in a pre-heated oven at 375° for 30–40 minutes. Uncover, stir in chickpeas and green peas. Cover and bake for five more minutes or until vegetables are tender. Serve over Basmati rice and garnish with cilantro and cashews.

Spring Rolls
yields 15 rolls

Tofu Scramble
2 1/2 C. tofu, rinsed & drained
2 T. nutritional yeast
2 T. water
1 t. sea salt
1/2 t. onion powder
1/2 t. garlic powder
1/4 t. turmeric

Sauce
2 T. stock from vegetable sauté
1 T. tamari or Bragg™ Aminos
1 T. sesame oil or water
1 t. arrowroot powder

Vegetable Sauté
1 T. sesame oil or water
1 onion, diced
2 t. ginger, grated
2 cloves garlic, crushed
1/3 C. green onion, diced
1 small carrot, finely chopped
2 stalks celery, finely chopped
1/2 C. red bell pepper, diced
5 button mushrooms, sliced
2 1/2 C. green cabbage, shredded
2 C. mung bean sprouts

1. Mash <u>Tofu Scramble</u> ingredients together and mix well. Cook in a non-stick frying pan until browned, stirring often. Set aside.
2. In oil or water, sauté the first five vegetables for two minutes.
3. Add the rest of the vegetables and sauté until tender; drain the stock and set it aside.
4. Mix all <u>Sauce</u> ingredients in a small saucepan. Cook on medium heat until thickened, stirring constantly.
5. Add sauce to the sauté and mix, then add this to the tofu scramble and stir.

Wrapping
15 Lumpia/egg roll wrappers
1/2–1 C. oil

2 t. arrowroot powder & 3 T. water

1. Place wrappers in between two clean, damp towels to keep them from drying out.
2. Separate one wrap and place on tray, being sure to cover the remaining wraps.
3. In a small bowl or cup, mix arrowroot and water thoroughly. Spoon 2–3 heaping tablespoons of filling onto the bottom half of the middle of the Lumpia wrap.
4. Roll up from the bottom. Tuck sides in, and continue rolling. Before you roll it up all the way, spoon a little arrowroot/water mixture onto the edge to stick it together. Set this one aside and continue with the rest of the rolls.
5. Pour the oil into a shallow bowl. Gently coat each spring roll in oil and place on a baking sheet, at least half an inch apart. (Baking paper makes the clean-up easy.)
6. Bake in the oven at 350° for 15–20 minutes or until golden-brown.
7. Serve with Thai Peanut Curry Sauce or Sweet Ginger Sauce on page 84.

> *"The moral duty of man consists of imitating the moral goodness and beneficence of God, manifested in the creation, toward all His creatures."*
>
> THOMAS PAINE (1737-1809) ~ English-born American patriot, political thinker and author, <u>The Age of Reason</u>

Quinoa Spicy Pilaf
serves 6–8

1 C. cooked chick-peas	1/4 t. black pepper
6 C. cooked quinoa	1/4 t. mild curry powder
1/4 t. cayenne pepper	1/2 t. cumin powder
1/4 t. paprika	2 T. oil
1/2 t. dried oregano	1 T. tamari or substitute
1 T. nutritional yeast	1 t. herb seasoning (page 3)
1/2 t. onion powder	1/2 t. garlic powder

1. Cook chick-peas and drain (see page 13). Cook quinoa (see page 12). Pre-heat oven to 350˚. Mix all the ingredients together in a casserole.
2. Bake 20–25 minutes. Serve as a side dish or as a bed for vegetable medley and sauce.

Potato Rolls
yields 22 rolls

12 C. potatoes (peeled and cubed)	1 t. onion powder
1/8 C. oil	1 t. herb seasoning (page 3)
1 1/2 T. tamari or substitute	1 T. nutritional yeast
1 1/2 t. sea salt	1/2 t. dill weed
1/4 t. black pepper	2 C. frozen peas, defrosted
1/4 C. soy/rice/oat milk	1 package Lumpia or spring roll wrappers
1 t. garlic powder	cornstarch & water mixture

1. Boil the cubed potatoes until soft. Drain water. Place in a large mixing bowl and mash thoroughly. Add the remaining ingredients, except the peas, Lumpia wrappers, corn starch and water mixture. Mix well. Fold in the peas and mix again.
2. After opening the wrappers, place them in between two damp dish towels to keep them moist. Place about 2-3 heaping tablespoons of potato batter onto the bottom edge of each wrapper. Roll up, folding sides in. (A mixture of cornstarch and water will make a glue for closing the wrappers or use a little oil.)
3. Place each roll on an oiled baking sheet. When all rolls are on the baking sheet, baste each with oil (using a basting brush) on the tops and ends. Bake (or convect) in a pre-heated oven at 375˚ for 20–30 minutes until golden-brown and crispy on the outside. Serve with Tofu 'Mayonnaise' page 72.

> *"Running the ranch paid well; it was challenging; it was my family tradition. But my conscience told me that I needed to speak out about this industry – there's just too much that the cattle industry hides from the public."*
>
> HOWARD LYMAN ~ former cattle rancher, international lecturer, author, <u>Mad Cowboy</u>

Entrées

Entrées

"As man advanced gradually in intellectual power and was enabled to trace the consequences of his actions; as his sympathies became more tender and widely diffused, extending to men of all races and finally, to the lower animals, so would the standard of his morality rise higher and higher."

CHARLES DARWIN (1809–1882)
English naturalist and biologist

Wish Kabobs with Marinated Tempeh
yields 6 skewers

2 C. tempeh, steamed, cubed
  or 1 lb. firm tofu
1 medium-sized red onion,
  cut into chunks
1 red pepper, cut into 1" pieces
1 zucchini, cut in rounds
12 button mushrooms, wiped clean
  with a damp towel, stems removed

Marinade
6 T. mustard (stoneground)
3 T. rice vinegar
3 T. olive oil
1/2 C. apple juice & 1/2 C. orange juice
1 t. each: salt and pepper
2 cloves garlic, crushed

1. (For tempeh begin at step 4) Rinse and drain tofu. Place the whole block on a plate. Place another plate directly on top of tofu and place a weight on top of the plate, for example, a teapot filled with water. After 30 minutes, pour off collected water.
2. Repeat step one. After draining, cut into four small rectangles and wrap in plastic. Freeze for 12-48 hours. (Freezing tofu makes it easier to handle and changes its texture.) Unwrap and thaw by placing tofu in a bowl of hot water for 20-30 minutes.
3. Do not pull pieces apart until completely thawed. Gently squeeze and drain.
4. In a shallow dish, mix the marinade ingredients. Add tofu/tempeh and coat well. Marinate for at least two hours. Remove from marinade, then marinate the vegetables.
5. Cut tofu/tempeh into cubes, then thread onto wooden skewers, alternating with veggies.
6. Grill over medium-high heat for 10-20 minutes, turning occasionally. Brush with marinade frequently. Vegetables should be slightly browned on the outside, tender on the inside.

Polenta with Pesto Sauce
serves 4

2 C. polenta (coarse cornmeal)
2 T. herb seasoning (page 3)
1 t. garlic powder
1 t. onion powder

1 t. dried basil
Creamy Cashew Pesto Dip (see page 70)
1/2 C. mushrooms, sliced
  (or zucchini or onion)

1. Bring seven cups of water to a boil. Add polenta slowly, stirring with a whisk. Add all seasonings and continue to whisk for 7-10 minutes. When thickened and cooked, pour polenta mixture into a dish and let cool. Refrigerate, allowing it to solidify.
2. When cooled, slice. Fry with a little oil or bake until the outside is crisp. Serve with fresh cashew pesto and top with sautéed mushrooms, onions or zucchini.

"Life is not complex. We are complex. Life is simple, and the simple thing is the right thing."

OSCAR WILDE (1854-1900) Irish poet and playwright

Creamy Polenta with Tempeh Onion Sauce
serves 4-6

Sauce
1 T. olive oil
1 1/2 medium onions, chopped
4 cloves garlic, minced
1 t. oregano
1/4 t. crushed red pepper

1 cake tempeh, steamed,
  drained, and chopped
2 large tomatoes, chopped
1/3 C. vinegar (optional)
1 t. sea salt
1 T. dry sweetener

Polenta
4 C. water
2 C. corn kernels
1 1/2-2 C. stoneground
  yellow cornmeal
1/3 C. nutritional yeast

sea salt, to taste
cayenne or black pepper, to taste
1/4 C. parsley, chopped
  (for garnish)
olive oil, (to top with)

To Prepare Tempeh Onion Sauce
1. Heat olive oil in a large skillet over medium-high heat. Add onions, garlic, oregano, red pepper and tempeh. Sauté, stirring frequently, until onions are tender, about five minutes. Add tomatoes to skillet along with vinegar, salt and sweetener. Quickly bring to a boil. Reduce heat to low and simmer for 15 minutes, stirring occasionally.

To Make Polenta
2. Bring water to a low boil in a saucepan. Add corn kernels. Slowly add cornmeal, stirring often with a wooden spoon, until cornmeal is no longer grainy (taste it to check), 5-6 minutes. Lower heat. Stir in nutritional yeast. Batter should be creamy. If too thick, add some hot water. Stir in salt and pepper to taste.
3. Spoon polenta into shallow bowls. Top with tempeh onion sauce. Sprinkle with chopped parsley. Drizzle olive oil over the tops. Serve immediately.

> *"It is increasingly obvious that environmentally sustainable solutions to world hunger can only emerge as people eat more plant foods and fewer animal products.*
> *To me it is deeply moving that the same food choices that give us the best chance to eliminate world hunger are also those that take the least toll on the environment, contribute the most to our long-term health, are the safest, and are also far and away the most compassionate toward our fellow creatures."*
>
> JOHN ROBBINS ~ American author, Pulitzer Prize Nominee for <u>Diet for a New America</u>, author, <u>The Food Revolution</u>, Conari Press 2000

Lemon Broil Tempeh
serves 2-3

2 (8 oz.) cakes tempeh	2 T. water
2 T. fresh lemon juice	1/2 t. garlic powder
2 T. tamari or substitute	4 T. fresh lemon juice
1/2 lb. (1 C.) tofu, rinsed & drained	2 T. Bragg™ Liquid Aminos or tamari
4 T. nutritional yeast	1 t. onion powder
2 T. vegan sweet relish	1-2 T. oil

1. Steam the tempeh (in a steamer basket) for about 5-10 minutes until warm. With a sharp knife, cut each cake in half, to make two squares. Carefully slice each piece in half through the center like a burger bun, ending up with eight pieces.
2. Marinate the tempeh in two tablespoons lemon juice and two tablespoons tamari.
3. In a blender or food processor, blend the remaining ingredients, beginning with the tofu.
4. Dip and thoroughly coat each piece of tempeh in this batter.
5. Place each piece on an oiled baking sheet (or use baking papers) and bake in a pre-heated oven, at 350° until the coating turns golden-brown. Serve with Tartar Sauce (see recipe page 81).

Tempeh Pizzas
serves 4-5

1/4 C. vegetable stock or water	1 t. dried basil
1 medium onion, chopped	1 t. garlic powder
1 bell pepper, chopped	1 t. crushed red pepper
8 oz. tempeh (steamed 5 minutes)	2 1/2 C. italian tomato sauce
3 T. tamari or substitute	6 whole wheat pita pocket bread
1 t. oregano	(or 8 whole wheat tortillas)
	nutritional yeast, to sprinkle

1. In a large skillet, sauté the onion and pepper in the vegetable stock or water. Crumble the steamed tempeh and add to the skillet. Stir in and cook for five minutes.
2. Add tamari, oregano, basil, garlic and red pepper. Stir in tomato sauce. Simmer for another five minutes.
3. Put pita bread or tortillas on a baking tray and place under a hot broiler to toast lightly. When toasted, spread the tempeh mixture evenly over the bread, top with nutritional yeast and bake in a pre-heated oven at 375° for 10 minutes.

> *"Being all fashioned of the self-same dust,*
> *Let us be merciful as well as just."*
>
> HENRY WADSWORTH LONGFELLOW (1807-1882) ~ American poet

Coconut Curry Tempeh & Vegetables
serves 4

2 cakes tempeh, in small cubes
4 cloves garlic
1/4 C. oil
2 t. mild curry powder
3/4 C. hot water & 1 bouillon cube
1 medium-large onion, diced
5 C. potatoes, cubed
   (a mix of white and sweet)

2 C. carrots, sliced thinly
corn kernels from 3 ears of corn
1 (14 oz.) can pure coconut milk
1 C. soy milk
1 T. Bragg™ Liquid Aminos or tamari
3 T. arrowroot powder
2 T. nutritional yeast (optional)

1. Place tempeh in a shallow dish. In a blender, blend garlic, oil, 1 t. curry powder, bouillon and water. Pour over the tempeh and allow it to marinate. Peel and cut the vegetables.
2. Pour the liquid from the marinating tempeh into a large skillet. Add onion, potatoes and carrots. Cook on medium-heat (covered) until potatoes soften. Stir frequently. Add corn, then add the tempeh and stir-fry.
3. In a blender, blend remaining ingredients, including remaining curry powder. Pour into the skillet. Simmer on low heat until sauce thickens.

   • Optional ~ Add one cup of green peas and mix.
   • Serve over your favorite grain or noodles.

Tempeh Cacciatore
serves 4-6

2 T. oil
2 cakes tempeh, sliced in strips
2 carrots, julienned
2 yellow crookneck squash, sliced
1 bell pepper, sliced
1 C. tomato paste
2 C. vegetable stock

2 T. balsamic vinegar
2 T. garlic, minced
1 T. fresh basil or 1 t. dried
1 T. fresh oregano or 1 t. dried
2 T. arrowroot powder
sea salt and pepper, to taste
1/2 lb. bag penne pasta (cooked)

1. Over medium heat, in a large oiled skillet (or non-stick pan) place tempeh (that has been steamed for 10 minutes). Sauté for 6–8 minutes, until tempeh starts to brown. (Optional: Add two tablespoons of tamari to tempeh while in the skillet.) Remove tempeh and set aside.
2. On medium heat, put one tablespoon of oil in the pan. Add carrots and squash. Two minutes later, add the pepper strips. Sauté until softened. Remove from skillet and set aside.
3. In the same skillet, place tomato paste, stock, vinegar, garlic and herbs. Stir well over medium heat for about eight minutes. Sift in arrowroot powder and keep stirring until it homogenizes into a sauce and thickens. When sauce is thick, add cooked vegetables and tempeh, and stir until it bubbles. Do not boil. Season with salt and pepper, to taste. Serve over cooked penne pasta.

Neat Loaf
yields 1 large skillet or casserole

2 onions, diced, sautéed
1 bell pepper, diced, sautéed
4 C. seitan, ground
1 cake tempeh, ground
tamari/nutritional yeast, to taste
2 C. millet (cooked) or other grain
1/4 C. oil
1/2 t. black pepper

1 C. tofu, rinsed, drained, mashed
1 T. liquid bouillon (page 2)
1 1/2 C. tomato paste
1 1/2-2 T. dried oregano
2 t. salt-free herb seasoning (page 3)
1 t. cumin powder
1 t. sea salt
2 T. nutritional yeast + 1-2 T. oil

1. Sauté onions in a little oil. When soft, remove from pan and put half of them aside. Put the rest in a large mixing bowl. Sauté bell pepper and add to onions in bowl.
2. In a food processor, using the "S" shaped blade, grind the seitan then the tempeh. Fry together in a large skillet, season with tamari and yeast, to taste. When browned, place this in the mixing bowl. Add cooked millet (see page 12).
3. In the food processor, blend oil, remaining onion sauté, black pepper, tofu, bouillon and one cup of tomato paste. Stir this into the mixture in the large bowl. Add oregano, herb seasoning, cumin, sea salt and the half cup of tomato paste. Mix well.
4. Place into an oiled casserole or large cast-iron skillet. Sprinkle with nutritional yeast and spread 1-2 T. oil on top. Bake in a pre-heated oven at 350° for 50 minutes.

Easy Carrot Grain Loaf
yields 1 loaf

2 C. brown rice (uncooked)
1 C. grain of choice (uncooked)
2 C. carrots, grated
1/2 lb. (1 C.) tofu, rinsed & drained
1/3 C. water
1-2 t. each: garlic & onion powder

1 large onion, diced, sautéed
3 T. nutritional yeast
1/4 C. tamari or substitute
1/2 C. tahini dressing (see recipe page 73)
1/2 t. sea salt
2-3 T. mustard (optional)

1. Cook grains and set aside to cool (see Cooking Guide for Grains on page 12).
2. In a food processor, using the "S" shaped blade, blend all ingredients except grains, carrots and onions until smooth. In a large bowl, mix this into the grains and carrots.
3. Place into an oiled casserole and bake at 350° for 30 minutes or until golden-brown.

*above: **Black Bean Tostadas** (page 150) ~ below: **Wish Kabobs** (page 116)*

"If human civilization is going to invade the waters of the earth, then let it be, first of all, to carry a message of respect — respect for all life."

JACQUES COUSTEAU (1910-1997) ~ renowned sea explorer, film-maker

Mexican Rice and Lentil Loaf
yields one 9" x 12" baking pan

1-2 T. garlic oil (see below)	2 T. tamari or substitute
1 large onion, diced	1 t. garlic powder
8 C. cooked brown rice	onion sauté (the 1 diced onion)
1 C. dry lentils, cooked, drained	<u>Final Ingredients</u>
<u>Processor Ingredients</u>	1 t. sea salt
1/4 C. oil	1 C. vegan 'cheese', grated
1 C. tofu, rinsed, drained, mashed	paprika, sprinkle
1 C. vegan 'cheese' (see page 274)	

1. In a blender, blend two cloves garlic with two tablespoons oil. Sauté onion in the garlic oil. Set aside for step 3.
2. Place cooked rice and lentils in a large mixing bowl (see pages 12 & 13).
3. In a food processor, blend the <u>Processor Ingredients</u> and add to rice and lentils. Mix.
4. Add the sea salt and 'cheese'. Mix thoroughly and place in an oiled baking pan. Sprinkle with paprika. Bake in a pre-heated oven at 350° for 35-40 minutes.

Savory Carrot Tofu Loaf
yields one 9" x 12" casserole

<u>Blended Mixture</u>

3 C. carrot, grated	1/3 C. oil
2 lbs. (4 C.) tofu, rinsed & drained	1 1/2 C. tofu, rinsed, drained, mashed
3 C. dry millet, cooked (page 12)	1/8 C. tamari or substitute
1 T. salt-free seasoning (page 3)	1/8 C. mustard (stoneground)
1 T. dried oregano	3 T. nutritional yeast
2 t. garlic powder	1 T. onion powder
1 t. herb seasoning (page 3)	a dash of pepper
1/2 t. turmeric	1 t. sea salt
3/4 C. vegan 'cheese', grated (page 274)	

1. Sauté the onion. Set aside for the blended mixture in step 3. In a large bowl, mash the tofu and mix with the grated carrot, millet and seasonings. Mix in the grated 'cheese'.
2. In a food processor, blend the remaining ingredients along with the sautéed onion.
3. Pour the wet mixture into the dry batter and mix thoroughly. Place in an oiled casserole dish. Bake in a pre-heated oven at 350° for 45 minutes until golden-brown on top, rotating casserole from top to bottom racks.

above: **Zucchini Mushroom Omelette** *(page 154) ~ below:* **Gourmet Lasagna** *(page 139)*

> ## "The more noble a soul is, the more objects of compassion it has."
>
> FRANCIS BACON (1561-1626) ~ English philosopher, statesman and essayist

Barley Pecan Loaf
yields 1 large baking casserole

5 cloves garlic	1 T. herb seasoning (page 3)
1/4 C. oil	2 T. nutritional yeast
1 1/2 C. tofu, rinsed & drained	8 C. cooked barley (see page 12)
1 C. water	2 C. carrots, grated
2 T. tahini	1/2 C. pecans, chopped
1/2 t. curry powder	1 t. paprika
1/2 t. pepper	

1. In a blender, blend garlic in 1/4 cup oil (just covering the blender blades). Blend in mashed tofu, water, tahini and spices, except paprika.
2. In a large bowl, combine blended mixture with the barley, carrots and pecans. Mix well.
3. Place into a large oiled casserole and sprinkle with paprika. Bake in a pre-heated oven at 350° for 45–60 minutes. Allow to cool slightly before serving. Serve with a gravy.

Tofu Loaf
serves 4–6

2 cloves garlic, diced	2 T. oil
1 onion, diced	3 T. tamari or substitute
1 red bell pepper, diced	1/2 t. garlic powder
1 celery stalk, diced	1 C. nutritional yeast
1 carrot, diced or grated	1 C. tahini
1 T. oil & 1 T. tamari	1/2 t. basil
2 lbs. (4 C.) tofu, rinsed & drained	1/2 t. turmeric
4 slices whole wheat bread	1/2 t. oregano

1. In a medium-sized skillet, sauté garlic, onion, pepper, celery and carrot (in that order) in one tablespoon of oil. Season with one tablespoon of tamari. Mash tofu.
2. When vegetables are tender, add them to the mashed tofu in a bowl.
3. Cut bread into small crouton-sized pieces and quick-fry in 1 T. oil adding 1 T. tamari, 1/2 t. garlic powder and 5 T. nutritional yeast.
4. Add croutons, tahini and remaining seasonings to tofu mixture. Stir well.
5. Place mixture in a well-oiled, medium-sized casserole and bake in a pre-heated oven at 350° for 35 minutes. Allow to cool. Slide a butter knife along the sides to remove.

• Serve at holidays or any occasion with a gravy, or slice and use for sandwiches.

> *"Ethics are responsibility without limit towards all that lives."*
>
> ALBERT SCHWEITZER, M.D. (1875-1965) ~ Alsatian philosopher and medical missonary
> 1952 Nobel Prize recipient

Indian Curry Loaf
yields one 9" x 7" casserole

4 C. cooked lentils	1 t. curry powder
8 C. cooked short grain brown rice	1 t. cumin powder
<u>Blender Ingredients</u>	<u>Final Seasonings</u>
1 C. tofu, rinsed, drained & mashed	1/2 t. sea salt
1/4 C. oil	1/2 t. curry powder
1/2 C. water	1/2 t. cumin powder
1/8 C. tamari or substitute	1/4 t. turmeric

1. In a large mixing bowl, place the cooked lentils and rice (see pages 12 & 13).
2. In a blender, blend all the <u>Blender Ingredients</u>. Pour into the mixing bowl and mix well with rice and lentils. Add the final seasonings and mix again.
3. Oil a shallow baking casserole and place the mixture into it. Pack down and smooth the top. Bake in a pre-heated oven at 350° for 45 minutes until top is golden-brown.

Millet Tempeh Burgers
yields 16 burgers

Excellent! 3/19/19 I'm allergic to millet (!)

1 onion, diced	
1 cake tempeh	2 T. mustard (stoneground)
1 1/2 T. tamari or substitute	1/4 t. black pepper
3 T. nutritional yeast	1 t. garlic powder
1/4-1/3 C. oil	1 t. onion powder
1 C. tofu, rinsed, drained & mashed	1 t. herb seasoning (page 3)
1 T. tahini	6 C. cooked millet (see page 12)

add chickpeas - cooked 1 can

1. Sauté diced onion in 1 teaspoon of oil, 1 tablespoon tamari and 1 tablespoon yeast.
2. In a food processor, use the "S" shaped blade to grind the tempeh into small chunks.
3. When onions are soft, remove from frying pan. Fry the ground tempeh with a small amount of tamari, oil and one tablespoon nutritional yeast.
4. In the food processor, using the "S" shaped blade, blend oil, tofu, tahini, mustard, *chickpeas,* remaining yeast and seasonings along with the sautéed onion.
5. In a large mixing bowl, combine the cooked millet, tempeh and the blended creamy *chickpea +* tofu mixture. Mix well.
6. Form into patties and bake in a pre-heated oven at 350° for 20–30 minutes, until golden-brown. *chickpeas to hold it together!*

Peanut Millet Burgers
yields 15 burgers

6 C. cooked millet (see page 12)
1 C. celery, diced
2 C. onion, diced
3/4 C. tofu, rinsed & drained
1/3 C. peanut butter
1 T. herb seasoning (see page 3)

1/3 C. oil
2 T. tamari or substitute
1 t. cumin powder
1 T. oregano
2/3 C. vegetable sauté
1/3 C. water

1. In a frying pan, sauté celery and onion until soft.
2. In a food processor, using the "S" shaped blade, blend remaining ingredients, adding 2/3 cup of the vegetable sauté and 1/3 cup water.
3. In a mixing bowl, mix the remaining vegetable sauté, millet and the blended mixture. Shape into patties.
4. Bake in a pre-heated oven at 350° for 25 minutes, until crispy golden-brown.

Sweet Potato and Black Bean Burgers
yields 12–15 burgers

2 T. oil
2 medium onions, diced
4 cloves garlic, minced
2 carrots, grated finely
2 C. cooked black beans (page 13)
10 sun-dried tomatoes,
  soaked in hot water until soft
2 C. dried shittake mushrooms,
  soaked in hot water until soft
2 baked sweet potatoes,
  (scooped out of skin)

2 C. cooked quinoa (page 12)
1 1/2–2 C. home-made breadcrumbs
  or wheatgerm or bran
2 T. caraway seeds
1 t. sea salt
1 t. onion powder
1 t. crushed red pepper or 1/4 t. cayenne
1/2–1 C. tomato sauce (page 81 & 82)
4 T. mustard (stoneground)
2 T. balsamic vinegar

1. Heat oil in a skillet over medium heat. Add onions and garlic and lower heat. Cook until lightly browned. Chop mushrooms and tomatoes and add to skillet with carrots and beans and cook for an additional 4–5 minutes, stirring occasionally. Turn off heat. Mash slightly in pan, until beans are half crushed.
2. Place skillet mixture in large bowl with remaining ingredients, and mix thoroughly. If mixture is moist, add more breadcrumbs.
3. Form into patties and cook over medium heat in oiled skillet, about four minutes on each side or until heated through and slightly crispy on the outside. (Patties can also be baked on a cookie sheet in a pre-heated oven at 350° for 25 minutes.)

> *"The love for all living creatures*
> *is the most noble attribute of man."*
>
> CHARLES DARWIN (1809-1882) ~ English biologist and naturalist

High Protein Quinoa Burgers
yields 24 medium burgers

10 C. cooked quinoa
3 C. firm tofu, rinsed & drained
Processor Ingredients
1/2 C. oil
1/4 C. tamari or substitute
1/2 T. garlic powder
1/2 T. onion powder
1 C. firm tofu, rinsed & drained

1/2 C. tomato paste
1/2 T. herb seasoning (page 3)
1/2 C. nutritional yeast
2 T. peanut butter
3 T. mustard (stoneground)
1 T. tahini (thin)
sea salt, to taste
favorite seasonings, to taste
3/4 C. water

1. In a large bowl, mash tofu and mix with the cooked quinoa (see page 13).
2. In a food processor, using the "S" shaped blade, blend remaining ingredients. Add blended mixture to quinoa/tofu mixture and mix well.
3. Form the mixture into medium-sized burgers. Place on two oiled cookie sheets. Bake in a pre-heated oven at 350° until crispy on one side (25–30 minutes). Flip and continue to bake until the outside of the burgers are crispy (about 15 more minutes).

Light and Easy Quinoa Burgers
yields 18 burgers

9 C. quinoa (cooked – see page 12)
  (about 2 1/2 C. uncooked)
1 onion, diced
1/2 C. oil
2 C. tofu, rinsed & drained
3 T. tamari or substitute

2 T. nutritional yeast
3/4 t. sea salt
1/4 t. black pepper (or cayenne pepper)
1/2 T. onion powder
1/2 T. garlic powder
1/4 C. water

1. Place quinoa in a large mixing bowl. In a small frying pan, sauté onion until softened.
2. In a food processor, blend remaining ingredients, adding the onion sauté. Combine blended mixture with quinoa in bowl. Mix well.
3. Form into small patties and place on an oiled baking sheet. Bake in a pre-heated oven at 350° until crispy on the top side (25–30 minutes). Flip and continue to bake until the outside of the burgers are crispy (about 15 more minutes).

"To live without killing is a thought which could electrify the world, if men were only capable of staying awake long enough to let the idea soak in."

HENRY MILLER (1891-1980) ~ American author

Super Vegan Burgers
yields 12 large burgers

1 1/2 C. oats	1 T. hickory smoke (optional)
1/2 C. sunflower seeds, ground	1 1/2 T. mustard (stoneground)
1/4 C. oil	2 1/2 C. seitan, ground
1 C. tomato paste	2 T. tamari or substitute
1 C. tofu, rinsed & drained	1/4 C. nutritional yeast
1 T. garlic powder	1 T. herb seasoning (page 3)
1 T. onion powder	2 1/2 C. cooked millet (see page 12)
1 T. herb seasoning (page 3)	

1. In a food processor, using the "S" shaped blade, grind oats and sunflower seeds to a fine meal. Set aside in a mixing bowl.
2. In the same food processor, whiz together the next eight ingredients and set aside.
3. Grind the seitan, using the "S" shaped blade, and add to the mixture.
4. Add remaining ingredients and mix well. Form into burger patties, place on an oiled baking sheet. Bake in a pre-heated oven at 350° until browned, about 45 minutes.

Chick Pea Tempeh Burgers
yields 11 burgers

2 cakes tempeh, ground	1/2 T. herb seasoning (page 3)
1/4 C. oil	1 t. onion powder
2 T. tamari or substitute	1/2 t. garlic powder
2 1/2 C. cooked chick peas	1/2 C. water
1 T. tahini	paprika for sprinkling

1. In a food processor, using the "S" shaped blade, grind the tempeh into small pieces.
2. Sauté the ground tempeh in a frying pan with oil and tamari.
3. In the food processor, combine all the ingredients (except for the tempeh and paprika) with half a cup of water and blend well.
4. Mix tempeh with blended mixture and form into burgers. Place them on an oiled baking sheet and sprinkle with paprika. Bake in a pre-heated oven at 350° for 30–40 minutes. Switch racks and rotate baking sheet from front to back during baking.

> "In all the round world of Utopia, there is no meat. There used to be, but now we cannot stand the thought of slaughterhouses. We never settled the hygienic aspect of meat-eating at all. This other aspect decided us. I can still remember as a boy the rejoicings over the closing of the last slaughterhouse."
>
> H.G. WELLS (1866-1946) ~ English novelist and historian, A Modern Utopia

Greek Spaghetti
serves 3–4

16 oz. spaghetti (cooked)
4 cloves garlic
3 T. oil
2 T. tamari or substitute
1 onion, sliced in half moons
4 roma tomatoes, cubed
1 red bell pepper, sliced in strips
1 zucchini, diced

1 C. soy milk (or any non-dairy milk)
1/4 C. oil + 2 T. cashew butter
1 T. rice syrup
1/2 C. water
4 T. nutritional yeast
3 T. arrowroot powder
1/4 t. black pepper
4 T. fresh lemon juice
1 (16 oz.) can black olives

1. In a blender, blend the garlic, oil and tamari. Pour into a saucepan.
2. Sauté the onion. When softened a bit, add the tomatoes. Add the pepper strips then the zucchini and cook until soft. Cook spaghetti in plenty of boiling water then rinse.
3. In a blender, blend the remaining ingredients, except the olives. Pour it into the saucepan when the vegetables are soft. Stir and simmer until sauce thickens. Add the sliced olives to the thickened sauce. Serve over spaghetti.

Greek Rice and Tofeta
serves 4

2 C. brown basmati rice (uncooked)
<u>*Tofeta Cheese*</u>
1 1/2 lb. (3 C.) firm tofu
3 T. tahini
1 t. lemon pepper
1 t. herb seasoning (page 3)
3 T. fresh lemon juice
1/2 T. nutritional yeast
<u>*Sauté*</u>
1 T. oil
1/2 red & 1/2 yellow pepper, diced

2 C. mushrooms, sliced
4 small tomatoes, cubed
1 large bunch spinach, chopped
1 T. fresh lemon juice
1 T. Bragg™ Liquid Aminos or tamari
1 T. vegan Worcestershire sauce (pg. 280)
1/2 T. garlic powder
1 t. black pepper
1 T. oregano
1 1/2 C. black olives, sliced
1/4 C. pine nuts

1. Cook the rice in water seasoned with a dash of oregano, lemon pepper and garlic. Set aside. Rinse and drain tofu and crumble it into a bowl.
2. Combine tofu with remaining <u>Tofeta Cheese</u> ingredients, stir well, chill to marinate.
3. Sauté the pepper and mushrooms. Add tomatoes, then spinach and seasonings. Finally, add olives and pine nuts. Remove from flame. Cover.
4. Serve the sauté over the rice and top with Tofeta Cheese.

> **"To avoid causing terror to living beings,
> let the disciple refrain from eating meat."**
>
> The BUDDHA (circa 563-483 B.C.) ~ Indian avatar

Greek Eggplant Moussaka
yields one 13" x 9" pan

2 C. dry chick peas, soaked
2 C. cooked millet
2 medium eggplants
<u>Flour Batter</u>
1/3 C. gluten flour
3/4 C. pastry flour
1/2 C. nutritional yeast
1 t. garlic powder
1/4 C. bran
1/2 t. onion powder
1/2 t. sea salt
1 T. dried oregano
1/2 T. dried basil
1 t. herb seasoning (page 3)
1/2 T. salt-free herb seasoning
2 C. Tahini Dressing (page 73)
(to reduce oil, substitute water)

1 medium onion, diced
1 T. tamari or substitute
1 (12 oz.) can tomato paste
1 T. fresh oregano
1 T. fresh basil
1/2–2/3 C. oil
1/2 C. water
2 T. tamari or substitute
1/2 T. herb seasoning (page 3)

<u>Topping</u>
1 C. tofu, rinsed and drained
1/2 C. nutritional yeast
1/4 C. vegan 'cheese', grated (see pg. 274)
1/4 C. oil
1 T. Bragg™ Liquid Aminos or tamari
1/4 t. sea salt

1. Cook chick peas until soft. Cook millet (see page 13) and set aside.
2. Peel eggplant and slice into quarter inch slices.
3. Mix together <u>Flour Batter</u> ingredients, including the salt-free herb seasoning.
4. In a separate bowl, place two cups of tahini dressing (or water). Dip eggplant slices in dressing and then lay them in the flour batter. Spoon flour mixture over each piece.
5. Fry each piece on both sides in an oiled pan and set aside on a plate.
6. Sauté the onion with one tablespoon of tamari.
7. In a large bowl, combine tomato paste, cooked millet, onion sauté, oregano, basil, three cups chick peas (mashed or whizzed through the food processor), oil, water, tamari and herb seasoning.
8. In a food processor, blend the topping ingredients and set aside.
9. Place half of the chick pea/tomato/millet mixture into a long, shallow, oiled baking pan and press it in firmly. Add a layer of breaded eggplant slices. Add the other half of the chick pea mixture. Again, add another layer of the eggplant slices. Finish by spreading on the topping. Bake in pre-heated oven at 325° for 40 minutes.

"One farmer says to me: 'You cannot live on vegetable food solely, for it furnishes nothing to makes bones with,'
walking all the while he talks behind his oxen, who,
with vegetable made bones, jerk him and his
lumbering plow along in spite of every obstacle."

HENRY DAVID THOREAU (1817-1862) ~ American author, poet, naturalist

Hungarian Sweet & Sour Stuffed Cabbage
yields 1 large casserole

1 large head cabbage	2 t. herb seasoning (page 3)
2 C. seitan, ground	1/4 C. water
2 C. cooked rice	4 T. nutritional yeast
1 C. cooked quinoa or millet	2 T. tamari or substitute
1 C. texturized vegetable protein	1 t. sea salt
1 clove garlic, diced finely	1/4 t. parsley
1 onion, diced finely	1/2 t. oregano
1 T. oil	1/2 t. garlic powder
1 (12 oz.) can tomato paste	12 oz. can tomato paste, & water (to thin)
<u>Tofu Mixture</u>	sweetener, to taste
1/2 lb. tofu, rinsed & drained	fresh lemon juice, to taste

1. Boil water in a large pot. In the pot, place one head of cabbage (remove core to reduce cooking time).
2. While cabbage is cooking, grind the seitan in a food processor, using the "S" shaped blade. Cook the rice and quinoa (see page 12). Pour boiling water over the T.V.P. and let it absorb the water.
3. Stir-fry garlic and onion in one tablespoon oil.
4. In a large mixing bowl, place grains, seitan, T.V.P, garlic powder, onion powder and one can of tomato paste.
5. In a food processor, blend the tofu mixture ingredients and add to the mixing bowl. Mix well.
6. Carefully remove cabbage leaves and let cool for five minutes. Put 1–2 tablespoons of batter in each and roll up, making sure batter is completely covered with the leaf.
7. Mix tomato paste, sweetener and lemon juice. Cover the bottom of a baking dish with this mixture. Place rolls on top of mixture. Before adding second layer, spread more mixture on top of rolls. End with the tomato paste sauce on top of rolls. (Add a little water while baking, if necessary.) Bake in a pre-heated oven at 350° for one hour. Cool a little before serving.

• Stuffed cabbage stores well in the freezer.

> *"Devoted as I was from boyhood to the cause of the protection of animal life, it is a special joy to me that the universal ethic of 'Reverence for Life' shows the sympathy with animals which is so often represented as a sentimentality, to be a duty which no thinking man can escape."*
>
> ALBERT SCHWEITZER, M.D. (1875-1965) ~ Alsatian philosopher, medical missionary, 1952 Nobel Peace Prize recipient

Hungarian Goulash
serves 6

2 T. oil
2 large onions, sliced
2 cloves garlic, chopped
1/4 C. sweet paprika
3-4 potatoes, cubed and boiled
2 lbs. seitan, in bite-sized cubes

1 small cabbage, shredded
3 C. tomatoes, diced + 4 T. tomato paste
3 C. broth (2 bouillon cubes in 3 C. water)
1 1/2 t. sea salt
1/4-1/2 t. black pepper
1 C. thick tofu milk (page 10)
   or 1 C. soy milk with 3 T. arrowroot

1. In a large saucepan, heat oil over medium heat. Add onions and cook for seven minutes. Stir in garlic and cook for four minutes longer, stirring often. Add paprika and cook for 30 seconds.
2. When potatoes are softened, add them to the pot.
3. Add seitan, cabbage, tomatoes (with their juice), tomato paste, broth, salt and pepper. Heat on high until boiling; then simmer on medium-low heat for about 30 minutes. Lastly, stir in the tofu milk, and heat thoroughly. Do not boil. If using packaged soy milk, sift and mix the arrowroot into the soy milk, then add to the pot. Simmer on low until sauce thickens.

• Serve over your favorite noodles.

Veggies Taj Mahal
serves 6

From The Compassionate Cook *by Ingrid Newkirk & PETA*

1 T. vegetable oil
1 T. vegan margarine (page 274)
2 cloves garlic, minced
3/4 t. cinnamon
1/2 t. cardamom
1 1/2 t. cumin powder
1 T. fresh cilantro, minced
1/2 t. fennel seeds
3/4 t. turmeric
2 t. ground ginger

1/2 t. cayenne pepper
1 1/2 C. onions, chopped
1 C. tomatoes, chopped
2/3 C. carrots, sliced
1 C. peas (frozen), thawed
2 C. potatoes (white and/or sweet),
   peeled and diced
salt, to taste
3/4 C. water
1/4 C. slivered almonds

1. Heat the oil and margarine in a large frying pan over medium heat. Add the garlic and spices all at once and reduce the heat to low. Cook for approximately one minute, making sure not to burn the spices.
2. Add the onions and sauté for a few more minutes, until soft. Add the tomatoes and stir in the carrots, peas, potatoes, salt and water. Bring to a boil over high heat, cover and reduce the heat to a simmer. Cook until the potatoes are soft, about 15 to 20 minutes.
3. Serve the veggies over a bed of rice and garnish with slivered almonds.

Spanish Rice with Seitan
serves 4-6

1 T. oil	3 1/2 C. water
2-3 T. garlic, minced	1 bouillon cube or 1-2 T. of tamari
1 1/2 C. onion, diced	1 1/2 C. green bell pepper, diced
4 C. roma tomatoes, diced	1/4 C. fresh cilantro, chopped
2 C. brown rice (uncooked)	3 C. seitan, in bite-sized cubes
1 t. chili powder or seasoning	1 T. tamari or substitute
1 t. cumin powder	2 T. nutritional yeast
1 t. mexican blend/taco seasoning	1 t. garlic powder

1. In a large skillet or pot, sauté the garlic and onions in oil for several minutes. Add the tomatoes. Cover and cook for 5-7 minutes. Add the rice and stir-fry on medium heat. Add the three spices. Add water to the skillet along with bouillon or tamari). Raise heat to high. When boiling, stir again, lower to medium-low and simmer.
2. Prepare pepper and cilantro. After the rice has been simmering for 15-20 minutes, add the bell pepper and cilantro. Stir. Simmer until water is absorbed.
3. Lightly coat a separate frying pan with oil. Stir-fry the seitan with the tamari, yeast and garlic powder for 5-10 minutes. When water from the rice is absorbed, add the seitan cubes and stir. Allow to sit, covered, for at least 15 minutes before serving.

African Stew   *make this add peanut butter*
serves 4

2 T. oil	5 C. vegetable broth or water
1 medium onion, chopped	1/2 t. sea salt
4 cloves garlic, chopped	1 C. bulgur wheat
1/2 t. paprika	1/2 C. fresh cilantro, chopped
1/8 t. crushed red pepper	1/4 C. fresh mint, chopped
1 C. tomatoes, diced	2 C. cooked garbanzo beans

1. Heat oil in a saucepan, over medium heat. Add onion and sauté until tender. Stir in garlic, paprika and crushed pepper, and cook for two minutes, stirring continuously. Add tomatoes and vegetable broth/water and bring to a simmer. Stir in salt and bulgur. Cover and reduce heat to a simmer, stirring occasionally, until bulgur is tender (about 25 minutes). Remove from heat, uncover and cool.
2. Place stew in food processor. Add cilantro and mint. Process until almost smooth. Return stew to pot, stir in garbanzo beans, and re-heat.

> **"What is philosophy but a continual battle,**
> **an ever-renewed effort to transcend the sphere of blind custom**
> **and so become transcendental."**
>
> THOMAS CARLYLE (1795-1881) ~ Scottish-born English historian, biographer and essayist

South of the Border Stew with Tempeh and Tofu
serves 4-5

1/2-1 T. oil	2 C. boiled water, 2 bouillon cubes (pg. 279)
4-5 cloves garlic, diced	3-4 medium potatoes, diced small
1 medium onion, diced	2 C. carrots, cut in big chunks
1-1 1/2 C. mushrooms, sliced	2 T. nutritional yeast
1 C. roma tomatoes, diced	1 t. each: chili powder and cumin
1 cake tempeh	3/4 C. tomato paste
1 lb. (2 C.) tofu, rinsed & drained	2 C. corn kernels
1/4 t. cayenne pepper (optional)	1/3 C. fresh cilantro, chopped

1. In a large sauce pot, sauté the garlic and onion in oil. After a minute, add the mushrooms then the tomatoes. Cook until tomatoes soften. Cube the tempeh and tofu and add to the sauté. Add the cayenne pepper if desired.
2. Dissolve bouillon cubes in boiling water and add to the pot. Add the potatoes and carrots. Cook until carrots are soft. Add the yeast and spices while cooking.
3. In a blender, blend one cup of boiled/hot water, tomato paste, and one cup of the cooked and softened carrots from the pot. Mix back into the pot and stir. Add the corn kernels and cilantro. Simmer for another 15 minutes, stirring continuously.

Moroccan Vegetable Stew
serves 5

3 1/2 C. cooked garbanzo beans	1/2 C. pitted prunes, chopped
1 T. oil	1/4 t. cinnamon
2 medium carrots, in 1/4" slices	1/2 t. sea salt
1 medium butternut squash, peeled and cut into 1" cubes	1/4 t. crushed red pepper or cayenne
	2 C. water
1 medium onion, chopped	2 C. cous-cous
3 C. tomatoes, diced	2 T. fresh cilantro or parsley, chopped
1 1/2 C. water	

1. Prepare garbanzo beans (see page 13). In a large pot, over medium-high heat, place oil, carrots, squash and onion. Cook, covered, for about 10-15 minutes. Stir often.
2. Stir in beans, tomatoes, water, prunes, and spices. Heat to a boil. Reduce heat to medium-low, cover and simmer for 30 minutes or until the vegetables are tender.
3. In a separate pot, boil 2 cups of water. Add cous-cous, stir and cover for one minute. Remove from heat. Let sit for 3-5 minutes. Remove cover and fluff grain with a fork. Cover and let sit. Stir cilantro or parsley into stew and spoon over cous-cous to serve.

> *"We can judge the heart of a man by his treatment of animals."*
>
> IMMANUEL KANT (1724-1804) ~ German philosopher

Tempeh Teriyaki
yields 1 large skillet

make this

4 cakes tempeh	1 red bell pepper, sliced in strips
2–3 T. sesame oil	3 1/2 C. water
1 t. tamari	3 T. liquid bouillon (see page 2)
1–2 cloves garlic	3 T. molasses
4 T. fresh ginger, minced	1 T. garlic powder
1 T. garlic, minced	1 T. onion powder
tamari, for marinating	1 t. ginger powder
1 onion, sliced in half moons	3 1/2 T. arrowroot powder
10 button mushrooms, sliced	3 T. miso (dark)
1/2 green bell pepper, sliced	nutritional yeast, sprinkle

1. Steam tempeh (in a steamer basket) until warm all the way through and let cool.
2. In a blender, blend oil, tamari, garlic cloves, one tablespoon ginger and just enough water to cover the blades. It will blend into a thick, creamy marinade.
3. Cut tempeh into large bite-sized cubes and marinate in blended mixture along with extra tamari. Stir to coat.
4. In a large saucepan, sauté remaining fresh ginger and garlic in sesame or other oil. Add onion, mushrooms and peppers and cook until softened, about seven minutes.
5. In a blender, blend 3 1/2 cups of water, bouillon, molasses, garlic powder, onion powder, ginger powder, arrowroot and miso. Pour this mixture into pot with the vegetables. Allow to thicken, stirring continuously. Do not boil.
6. In a large, oiled cast-iron skillet, fry tempeh chunks with a sprinkle of nutritional yeast. When they have browned a bit, add the thickened sauce to the skillet and bake for an hour at 350°, allowing the sauce to saturate tempeh. (If using a regular skillet to fry tempeh, transfer to a casserole dish before baking.) Serve over a grain.

> *"Reverence for life, for the smallest and most insignificant, must be the inviolable law to rule the world from now on. In so doing, we do not replace old slogans with new ones and imagine that some good may come out of high-sounding speeches and pronouncements. We must recognize that only a deep-seated change of heart, spreading from one man to another, can achieve such a thing in this world."*
>
> ALBERT SCHWEITZER (1875-1965) ~ Alsatian philosopher and medical missionary
> 1952 Noble Prize recipient

Teriyaki Vegetable Rice
serves 6–8

Teriyaki Sauce

2 T. fresh ginger, grated	3 C. pineapple juice
or 1 T. ginger powder	1/2 C. tamari or substitute
6 cloves garlic, minced	2 t. dry mustard
2 T. sesame oil	1/2 t. cayenne pepper

1. Combine the above ingredients in a blender. Blend well and set aside.

2 bunches young asparagus	2 C. cauliflower, chopped
4 T. arrowroot powder	1 red onion, cored & halved,
4 C. teriyaki sauce (see above)	cut into 1/4" strips
2 T. sesame oil	4–5 C. cooked brown basmati rice
2 C. broccoli flowerets	4 T. sesame seeds, toasted in a
2 C. carrots, chopped	dry skillet until lightly browned

2. Gently bend each asparagus stalk to break off the tough, woody ends and discard. Cut the stems diagonally into 1 1/2–2" sections, leaving 2" of tips. Separate thicker lower stems from the upper stems and tips.
3. Dissolve the arrowroot in two cups of the teriyaki sauce. Set aside.
4. Heat half of the sesame oil in a large skillet over high heat. Add thicker asparagus stalks and stir-fry for two minutes. Add broccoli, carrots and cauliflower. Stir-fry for two minutes. Add one cup teriyaki sauce (without arrowroot). Cover and cook for two minutes, or until vegetables are almost tender. Then remove from pan, cover and set aside.
5. Add remaining sesame oil to skillet and heat. Add remaining asparagus and red onion. Stir-fry for 2–4 minutes. Add the last cup of teriyaki sauce (without arrowroot). Cover and cook for two minutes or until vegetables are tender.
6. Add remaining teriyaki sauce (containing arrowroot) to skillet and simmer for 1–2 minutes, stirring. Add vegetables that have been set aside, stirring continuously until sauce thickens. Do not boil.
7. Serve immediately over basmati rice with toasted sesame seeds.

"Patients fed a vegan (meat and dairy free) diet during an intensive 12-day live-in program experienced an average reduction of 11% in total cholesterol levels. Most patients also lost weight and had improved blood pressure levels."

JOURNAL OF THE AMERICAN COLLEGE OF NUTRITION, 1995

Chinese Medley
yields 1 casserole

1 T. sesame oil
3 cloves garlic, minced
1 onion, sliced
1 red pepper, sliced
12 mushrooms, sliced in half
1/3 C. almonds, blanched
3 T. tamari or substitute
2 carrots, sliced diagonally
4 C. cabbage, shredded
3 T. apple cider vinegar

2 T. sweetener
1 zucchini, quartered, diced
2 C. cauliflower flowerets
2-3 C. broccoli flowerets
1 t. garlic powder
2 C. snow peas
2 C. mung bean sprouts
1-2 C. bok choy or pok choy
1 T. tamari or substitute
1/2 t. ginger powder

1. In a large skillet, sauté garlic and onion in sesame oil. Add the pepper and mushrooms. Stir and cover to simmer. At one minute intervals, add each of the remaining ingredients and seasonings, stirring and simmering. The peas, sprouts and greens should be added last and cooked for a few minutes. Save the liquid from the sauté for the Chinese sauce. Serve immediately over rice or add the following:

Tempeh Chunks
1-2 T. oil
2 cakes tempeh, steamed, cubed
3 T. tamari or substitute

1 t. ginger powder
1/2 t. garlic powder
1 t. nutritional yeast (optional)

2. In an oiled skillet or non-stick pan, over medium-high heat, pan fry the cubed tempeh with the remaining ingredients, until crisp. Add to the vegetable medley.

Chinese Sauce
1 T. oil
2 T. garlic, minced, sautéed
3 T. fresh ginger, minced
2 C. liquid from sauté and water
2 T. tamari or substitute
1/4 C. sesame oil
1-2 T. sorghum (liquid sweetener)

2 T. apple cider vinegar
5 T. sweetener
1 t. onion powder
1/2 t. garlic powder
1/2 t. ginger powder
3 T. arrowroot powder

3. Sauté the minced garlic and ginger in oil. In a blender, whiz all ingredients and pour into a small pot. Simmer and stir until sauce thickens, never allowing a rapid boil.
4. Serve Chinese Medley over rice, add Tempeh Chunks and top with Chinese Sauce.

• Use sauce over fried rice, eggless foo yung (page 136), spring rolls (page 112), etc.

> *"I believe if the viewing of slaughter was required to eat meat, most folks would become vegetarians."*
>
> HOWARD LYMAN ~ ex-cattle rancher, international lecturer, author, <u>Mad Cowboy</u>

Veg Foo Yumm!
yields 13 patties

<u>Sauté</u>
1 onion, diced
2 C. mushrooms, sliced
1 T. tamari or substitute
1 C. zucchini, diced
2 C. snow peas, tipped, cut
1–2 C. mung bean sprouts
1 t. ginger powder
1 t. garlic powder
<u>Tofu Mixture</u>
2 lbs. (4 C.) firm tofu, rinsed & drained
1 C. whole wheat pastry flour
1/2 T. onion powder

2 T. tamari or substitute
1 t. sea salt
1/4 C. nutritional yeast
1/4 t. black pepper
1 t. baking soda
1 T. baking powder
<u>Blender Mixture</u>
3/4 C. liquid from sauté and water
1 C. soft tofu, rinsed & drained
1/2 T. onion powder
1 T. tamari or substitute
1 T. egg replacer
1/2 T. herb seasoning (page 3)

1. In a pan, sauté the onion in water or oil. Add mushrooms, tamari and zucchini. Cook for two minutes. Add snow peas, mung bean sprouts and seasonings and cover to simmer. After several minutes, remove from flame. Drain the liquid from the sauté and set aside.
2. In a bowl, mash the firm tofu and add the remaining <u>Tofu Mixture</u> ingredients.
3. Blend soft tofu with the remaining <u>Blender Mixture</u> ingredients. Add to the bowl and mix. Finally, add the sauté to the bowl and mix thoroughly.
4. Oil two baking sheets well (or use baking papers). Drop batter onto the sheet using a serving spoon. Flatten and form each of them into round patties (there will be about 13–14). Bake in a pre-heated oven at 375° for 50 minutes, switching racks in the oven half-way through baking, to avoid burning the bottom batch. They will be golden-brown on the outside when ready.

Coconut Curry Veggies – *simple and delicious!*

2 (14 oz.) cans pure coconut milk
1 T. vegan margarine or oil
5 T. curry powder
1 t. fresh ginger, grated
1 t. coriander

1 carrot, diced
1 head cauliflower, in bite-sized pieces
1 C. mixed vegetables of choice
1–2 t. sea salt, to taste
2 C. peas

1. Place coconut milk, margarine and spices in a frying pan. Cook on low heat for about five minutes until mixed well. Add veggies and simmer until soft (about 25 minutes).
2. Add sea salt to taste. Serve hot over a bed of rice.

> **"Sooner or later, the truth comes to light."**
>
> WILLIAM SHAKESPEARE (1564-1616) ~ English poet, playwright

Delicious Curried Vegetables
serves 3-4

1/8 C. sesame or safflower oil
2 medium onions, chopped
2 T. fresh ginger, finely chopped
3 cloves garlic, finely chopped
1 t. cumin powder
1/2 t. turmeric
1/4 t. cayenne
1 1/2 t. curry powder

1 t. sea salt (or substitute)
1 (16 oz.) can tomato sauce
  (or 2-3 tomatoes, peeled – see step 2)
1 medium eggplant, peeled, sliced
2 potatoes, sliced and par-steamed
1 1/2 C. snow peas
1 1/2 C. fresh spinach, washed & drained
  (or other vegetables)

1. Sauté onions in oil or water. Add ginger and garlic, stirring frequently. When onions are translucent and the mixture is "melted" together, add spices and continue to stir.
2. Add tomato sauce or tomatoes. (Place tomatoes in very hot water for five seconds and the skins come off easily. Dice.) Mix thoroughly with sauté.
3. Add vegetables, starting with the hardest (i.e. eggplant and potatoes). Let simmer until veggies are soft, but not overdone. Add spinach at the end. Serve over rice.

Curried Tempeh Cutlets
yields 12 cutlets

3 cakes tempeh, steamed
Marinade
1/3 C. water
2 T. tamari or substitute
1 t. mild curry powder
2 T. oil
Coating
1/3 C. water

1 T. cashew butter
1 C. tofu, rinsed, drained, mashed
1/2 t. garlic powder
2-3 T. oil
3 T. nutritional yeast
1 T. tamari or substitute
1 t. mild curry powder

1. With a sharp knife, cut each cooled tempeh cake in half, making two squares. Slice each square in half through the middle, like a burger bun, creating 12 pieces.
2. Put marinade ingredients in a bowl and whisk with a fork. Add tempeh cutlets, allowing them to marinate, for approximately an hour.
3. In a blender, blend Coating ingredients. Pour mixture into a bowl and dip each cutlet into the coating. Get a good, thick coat on each piece and place on an oiled baking sheet. Bake at 350° until coating turns golden-brown, about 30 minutes.

> *"Compassion is the foundation of everything positive, everything good. If you carry the power of compassion to the marketplace and the dinner table, you can make your life really count."*
>
> RUE McCLANAHAN ~ American actress

Curried Cous-Cous with Lima Beans
serves 5-6

2 C. cooked lima beans	1/2 t. curry powder (to taste)
3 C. water	1/2 t. cumin powder
1 T. liquid bouillon (page 2)	1 t. garlic powder
3 C. whole wheat cous-cous (dry)	1/4-1/2 t. sea salt
2 t. herb seasoning (page 3)	1/4 t. black pepper (or cayenne)
1/4 C. scallions, diced	

1. Cook the lima beans (see page 13).
2. Boil water with the bouillon. When water boils, add cous-cous. Cook for one minute then remove from flame. Cover and let steam for several more minutes. Fluff with a fork. Cover again.
3. Add the spices and beans. Mix with a fork. Serve with the following sauce.

1 C. soy milk	2 T. miso (blonde)
1 T. rice syrup	1 T. Bragg™ Liquid Aminos or tamari
2 T. nutritional yeast	1 t. arrowroot powder
1/2 t. curry powder (to taste)	

4. Blend all ingredients together in a blender. Pour into a small sauce pot and simmer for approximately 8-10 minutes until sauce thickens, stirring often. Do not boil.

Vegetable Cous-Cous
serves 6

3 C. water or vegetable broth	1 T. cumin powder
2 C. whole wheat cous-cous (dry)	1 t. paprika
1 T. oil	1/2 t. salt
1 zucchini, halved lengthwise, thinly sliced	1/4 t. red pepper flakes
1 yellow pepper, thinly sliced	1 t. curry powder
	4 C. chick peas (cooked)
	1/2 C. slivered almonds

1. In a medium-sized saucepan, bring two cups of water/broth to a boil. Add cous-cous. Cover and remove from heat; set aside. In a skillet, over medium-high heat, add oil and vegetables. Sauté for 2-5 minutes to soften. Add seasonings and mix.
2. Stir in chick peas and remaining broth. Cover and cook for two minutes, until heated through. Stir in cous-cous. Transfer to a bowl and top with almonds.

> *"Animals have the same source as we have. Like us, they derive the life of thought, will and love from the Creator."*
>
> ST. FRANCIS OF ASSISI (1182-1226) ~ Christian saint and mystic

Gourmet Lasagna
yields one 9" x 12" deep casserole

5 + C. Marinara Sauce (page 81)
10 oz. package lasagna noodles
'No-Meat' Layer
1 C. texturized vegetable protein
1-2 cakes tempeh or
   1-2 lbs. seitan (page 161)
   or see substitutes page 275
2-3 T. oil
tamari or substitute, to taste
1 1/2 T. oregano
1 t. dried basil
1 t. garlic powder
1/2 t. sea salt
1/2 t. black pepper
2 T. nutritional yeast

Tofu 'Uncheese' Layer
2 C. soft tofu, rinsed & drained
2 C. firm tofu, rinsed & drained
1 t. sea salt
2 t. tamari or substitute
1/4-1/2 t. black pepper
1 t. onion powder
5-6 T. nutritional yeast
1 t. dried oregano
4 t. oil
'Cheesy' Topping
1 C. soft tofu, rinsed & drained
1 T. tamari or substitute
4 T. oil
5-6 T. nutritional yeast
1/2 t. sea salt

1. Partially cook the lasagna noodles in boiling water for 6-8 minutes. (Cook in a flat pan, if you have one.) Rinse noodles, separate, flatten out and set aside in cold water.
2. Place T.V.P. in a bowl and pour 1 1/2 cups of boiling water over it. Cover and allow it to soak up the water. (You can substitute T.V.P. with tempeh or ground seitan.)
3. In a food processor, grind tempeh or seitan with the "S" shaped blade, into tiny chunks. Pan fry the ground tempeh/seitan until slightly crisp with 2 T. oil and tamari. Add remaining spices and yeast. Mix in one cup tomato sauce and cook for 5-10 minutes. Use any combination of T.V.P, ground seitan and ground tempeh)
4. When the water is absorbed in the T.V.P. (you may need to drain it), add it to the tempeh in the pan. Season with tamari. Sauté and remove from flame.
5. In a bowl, mash all Tofu 'Uncheese' ingredients together. Chill.
6. In a food processor, homogenize the 'Cheesy' Topping ingredients. Set aside.
7. Spread one cup of tomato sauce over the bottom of an oiled 9" x 12" pan. Lay four noodles down and spread 1/2 cup tomato sauce over them. Flatten in the "no-meat" layer and pour another 3/4 cup of sauce over it.
8. Place another layer of four noodles, then spread another 1/2 cup of sauce over the noodles. Mash and flatten in the tofu layer and then another noodle layer. Spread one cup of tomato sauce over the noodles and sprinkle with oregano (optional).
9. Spread and swirl the 'Cheesy' Topping over the top. Bake in a pre-heated oven for 40-50 minutes at 350°. Cool somewhat before slicing. Serve with sauce on top.

> *"That which we are, we are; and if we are ever to be any better, now is the time to begin."*
>
> ALFRED LORD TENNYSON (1809-1892) ~ English poet, Poet Laureate: 1850

Penne 'Cheese' Bake
serves 4-6

16 oz. Penne pasta	*2 t. arrowroot powder*
6 cloves garlic	*1/2 t. sea salt*
1/4 C. olive oil	*1/4 t. pepper*
1 onion, diced	*1 C. tofu, rinsed & drained*
1 1/2 bell peppers, diced	*1 package vegan 'cheese', grated (pg. 274)*
6-7 roma tomatoes, cubed	*1/2 C. water*
1/2 C. nutritional yeast	*4 t. nutritional yeast*
1/2 C. water	*1/8 C. Bragg™ Liquid Aminos or tamari*

1. In 4 quarts of boiling water, cook pasta al denté (about 5 minutes). Drain and rinse.
2. In a blender, blend garlic and oil. Pour into a frying pan and add onion, peppers and tomatoes. Cook until soft (about 5-7 minutes). When done, ladle 1 1/2 cups of this sauce back into the blender, adding 1/2 cup nutritional yeast, 1/2 cup water and the arrowroot. Blend and return to pan. Add salt and pepper and simmer until thickened.
3. In a blender, blend mashed tofu, half of the grated 'cheese', 1/2 cup of water, 4 t. nutritional yeast, and 1/8 cup Bragg™ Liquid Aminos or tamari.
4. Pour the pasta into an oiled casserole and mix thoroughly with the blended 'cheesy' mixture. Mix in red sauce. Sprinkle with the remaining half of the grated 'cheese'. Bake in a pre-heated oven at 350° for 35 minutes.

Oil-free Whole Wheat Pizza Crust
yields 1 medium crust

2 1/2 t. dry active yeast (page 11)	*1/2 t. salt*
1 C. water (warm)	*1 t. molasses (or other sweetener)*
2 t. dry sweetener	*3 C. whole wheat flour*

1. Dissolve yeast in 1/2 cup of warm water with sweetener. Let sit for 10-15 minutes until doubled in size. Separately, add salt and molasses to remaining warm water.
2. In a large bowl, combine the two liquids. Mix in flour and knead for about 10 minutes until dough is firm and not sticky.
3. Let rise for about 15 minutes, punch down and roll out on a pizza pan, making a lip around the edges. Add sauce, vegan 'cheese' and your favorite toppings.
4. Bake in a pre-heated oven at 375° for about 25 minutes until bottom is crisp.

> *"My refusing to eat meat occasioned an inconveniency, and I have been frequently chided for my singularity. But my light repast allows for greater progress, for greater clearness of head and quicker comprehension."*
>
> BENJAMIN FRANKLIN (1706-1790) ~ American statesman, inventor and author

Veggie Pizza
yields 1 large pizza

'Cheesy' Topping
1/3 C. oil
1 lb. (2 C.) tofu, rinsed & drained
4 T. nutritional yeast
4 T. water
1/3 C. grated 'cheese' (pg. 274)
2 T. tamari or substitute
Dough
1 packet active dry yeast
  (see page 11)

2 C. warm water
2 T. sweetener
2 t. olive oil
2 1/2 C. whole wheat flour
2 t. sea salt
Toppings
tomato sauce
2 T. fresh basil and oregano (or 2 t. dried)
vegetables of choice
grated vegan 'mozzarella' (see page 274)

1. In a food processor, blend all the 'Cheesy' Topping ingredients. Set aside.
2. Dissolve yeast in 1/2 cup of warm water with 1 T. of sweetener. Set in a draft-free place for approximately 15 minutes, until yeast is risen and almost doubled in size.
3. Thoroughly mix together flour and salt. Mix the remaining water and oil, separately. Combine the dry and the wet ingredients, adding the activated yeast last. Mix well.
4. Turn out dough on a flat, floured surface and begin to knead. (If the dough is too wet and sticks to your fingers, add more flour.) Knead for about 10 minutes until dough is smooth. Cover and let sit in a warm (not hot) place for 20–30 minutes.
5. Punch down and let rise again for 45 minutes until doubled in size. Roll into two small circles or one large circle, or rectangle depending on your pan. After rolling out the dough, let sit for another 25 minutes.
6. Spread the tomato sauce on the risen dough and then the cheesy topping. Sprinkle with herbs and grated 'cheese'. Top with veggies. Bake in a pre-heated oven at 375° for 20 minutes or until the bottom crust is golden-brown.

Pizza Crust
yields 2 crusts

1 packet fast-rising baking yeast
1 t. sweetener
1 C. warm water

2 t. olive oil
2 1/2 C. whole wheat flour
additional olive oil

1. Dissolve yeast and sweetener in warm water. Allow to bubble and rise (see page 11).
2. Add oil and flour. Knead until dough is firm and not sticky. Let rise for half an hour.
3. Divide into two equal parts. Roll each out into an 8" circle or onto two pizza pans.
4. Brush with olive oil. Spread tomato sauce on top, add 2 C. of grated vegan 'cheese' and toppings. Bake in a pre-heated oven at 350° until crust is lightly browned.

> *"All things must change to something new."*
>
> HENRY WADSWORTH LONGFELLOW (1807-1882) ~ American poet

Calzone (pizza pie)
yields 6

use Pizza Crust page 141,
   adding these ingredients:
1/2 t. herb seasoning (page 3)
1/2 t. garlic powder

1 T. fresh basil
1 t. onion powder
1 T. fresh oregano

Sauce
2 1/2 C. Tasty Marinara Sauce (see page 81)

Tofu Filling
1/2 lb. (1 C.) tofu, rinsed & drained   2 T. nutritional yeast
1 1/2 T. tamari or substitute

Sauté together in 1–2 t. oil
1 medium onion or 3 scallions
3 yellow zucchini, sliced or diced

2 small japanese eggplants, peeled,
   sliced thinly
6 mushrooms, sliced

8 slices vegan 'cheese' or 1 C. Cheesy Topping (see Veggie Pizza page 141)

1. Follow the recipe for the pizza crust, adding the additional ingredients to the dry mixture.
2. When dough is ready to roll out, cut it in half. Roll one piece flat onto a paper baking sheet. Cut into three large rectangles. Spread half of each rectangle with tomato sauce, keeping sauce away from the edges.
3. Mash tofu and mix with tamari and yeast.
4. On the tomato sauce side of the rectangle put one sixth of the tofu filling and sautéed vegetables, as well as a slice of vegan cheese or cheesy topping.
5. Fold the dry side of the dough over each and seal edges, wrapping the underside up. Repeat process with the two other rectangles, and three more rectangles made from the second half of the dough. Using a fork, make air holes in the top.
6. Place paper baking sheets on a baking tray, and bake in a pre-heated oven at 375° for 20–30 minutes until crust is golden-brown and firm.

"Our survival as people and a planet, depends not so much on our superiority or dominion over nature, but rather in humility and the willingness to learn what our fellow creatures are trying to teach us, that ALL LIFE is sacred and that Love is the answer."

JAMES CROMWELL ~ American actor (Farmer Higgins in Babe)

Italian Vegetable Polenta
yields one 9" x 9" casserole

4 C. water
1 C. polenta (coarse cornmeal)
1 t. garlic powder
1 T. herb seasoning (page 3)
1 t. dried oregano
1/2 t. salt-free herb seasoning
1/4 C. fresh basil, chopped
2 T. nutritional yeast
<u>Filling</u>
1 onion, diced
1 bell pepper, diced
4 C. eggplant and/or zucchini, sliced

2 T. tamari or substitute
4 C. kale, sliced thinly
   (or other greens of choice)
1 t. onion powder
1 t. parsley flakes
1 t. dill weed
1/2 t. sea salt
1/2 C. tomato paste
a dash of pepper
1/2 C. water
<u>Topping</u>
2 T. nutritional yeast
1 T. oil

1. In a saucepan, bring water to a near boil. Add the polenta. (In order to prevent lumps, dry cornmeal is usually poured very slowly into hot water, stirring constantly or mix cornmeal with an equal amount of cold water then stir it into the hot water.) Add the seasonings and fresh basil. Stir continuously. Add the yeast and keep stirring until it thickens.
2. Pour into an oiled pan. Bake in a pre-heated oven at 350° for 25 minutes, then remove. (After it has cooled, work it up on the sides as much as possible, forming a lip. It will slide down off the edges.)
3. Slice eggplant and zucchini. In the empty saucepan, sauté the onion and pepper. Add the eggplant and/or zucchini along with a drop of water if necessary. Season with tamari. Cover and simmer. When vegetables are soft, add the thinly sliced greens and cover again for a minute. Add the seasonings, tomato paste and water. Sauté and stir for eight more minutes, then pour into the center of the polenta crust.
4. Top with the yeast and oil and spread. Place the whole mixture back in the oven and bake for 30–40 minutes. Allow to cool and solidify a bit before serving.

"The first reason why I don't consume dairy products, and why I think other people should not, is the fat content. The fat is saturated fat, and you may as well be eating beef tallow. The fat in these dairy products encourages heart disease and numerous other problems. It's a risk factor for some forms of cancer as well."

NEAL BARNARD, M.D. ~ President, Physicians Committee for Responsible Medicine, author, <u>Turn Off The Fat Genes</u>

Basil Tempeh Casserole
serves 6

3 (8 oz.) cakes tempeh (5 grain)
3 T. fresh lemon juice
2 T. tamari or substitute
Blender Ingredients
1 C. water
4 T. fresh lemon juice
2 cloves garlic
1 C. fresh basil, chopped
1 C. tofu
1/4 C. nutritional yeast
1 t. sea salt
1 t. onion powder
1 T. Bragg™ Aminos or tamari
1/2 t. garlic powder

Breading
1/2 C. pastry flour
1/4 C. soy powder
2/3 C. nutritional yeast
2 t. salt-free herb seasoning (page 3)
1 t. onion powder
1/2 t. sea salt
Toppings
3 C. mushrooms, sliced thinly
1 T. tamari or substitute
1/2 t. garlic powder
1 1/2 T. nutritional yeast
2 tomatoes, cubed
1 t. sea salt
1 (6 oz.) can black olives, sliced

1. Steam the tempeh in a steamer basket. Cut each cake into six strips then cut each strip in half, making two long strips. Marinate in the lemon juice and tamari.
2. Rinse, drain and mash tofu. In a blender, blend with remaining <u>Blender Ingredients</u>.
3. Place the tempeh flat in a pan and pour the blender mixture over it. Refrigerate and allow to marinate for half an hour. (Use any extra basil sauce to make salad dressing.)
4. In a separate bowl, combine the <u>Breading</u> ingredients.
5. Coat each marinated tempeh stick with the breading mixture. Pan fry. Let it crisp on one side, then flip and let the second side crisp. When finished, place in a long casserole.
6. Sauté the mushrooms with tamari, garlic powder, and half a tablespoon of nutritional yeast. Set aside.
7. Sauté the tomatoes in a lightly oiled skillet with remaining nutritional yeast and sea salt. When cooked, combine with mushroom sauté and sliced black olives. Mix. Pour over the top of the tempeh and gently mix. Serve.

"There are many other sources of calcium besides the milk of cows. Green vegetables contain significant amounts of calcium as do grains, legumes, nuts, and seeds. Calcium-fortified orange juice, soy milk, and other beverages are widely available. My medical experience affirms that many health problems - from asthma to colitis - respond favorably to the removal of dairy products from the diet."

MICHAEL A. KLAPER M.D. ~ American author and international lecturer

Eggplant Parmesanless
yields one 8" x 10" casserole

2 large eggplants	1 T. wheat gluten flour
1 large onion	1/3 C. corn meal
1 C. water	2 T. bran
2/3 C. tahini	1/2 t. dill weed
1/2 C. tofu, rinsed & drained	1 t. garlic powder
3 T. tamari or substitute	1/4 t. pepper
1/2 t. sea salt	1 t. dried basil
4-5 C. 'Cheezy' Dip (see page 70)	2 t. herb seasoning (page 3)
2/3 C. nutritional yeast	1 T. oregano
1 C. pastry flour	1 t. onion powder
	3-4 C. tomato sauce (see pages 81 & 82)

1. Peel eggplant and onion and slice thinly. Set aside. In a blender or food processor, blend water, tahini, mashed tofu, tamari and salt. Pour into a large bowl.
2. In a food processor, make the 'Cheezy' Dip to use as a topping.
3. In a separate bowl, make a breading mix with the remaining ingredients except the tomato sauce.
4. Dip eggplant slices into tahini batter and then into the breading mix. Don't move them around; just spoon the breading mix over the slices. (Avoid having your dry batter get clumpy or sticky from too much wet batter getting in it.)
5. Pan fry both sides of each cutlet in an oiled skillet until coating turns crispy brown. Stack them on a plate covered with a paper towel to absorb excess oil.
6. Spread half a cup of tomato sauce across the bottom of an oiled 8" x 10" casserole. Lay in the cutlets covering each layer with half a cup of tomato sauce and a good layer of 'Cheezy' Dip. Lay in the onion slices. Repeat process, covering the last layer with a full cup of tomato sauce and the remaining 'Cheezy' Dip. Bake in a pre-heated oven at 350° for 40 minutes. Cook an additional 15 minutes at 200°, then serve.

"In the next ten years, one of the things you're bound to hear is that animal protein is one of the most toxic nutrients of all that can be considered."

~

"Quite simply, the more you substitute plant foods for animal foods, the healthier you are likely to be. I now consider veganism to be the ideal diet. A vegan diet — particularly one that is low in fat — will substantially reduce disease risks. Plus, we've seen no disadvantages from veganism."

T. COLIN CAMPBELL, Ph.D. ~ nutritional biochemist, Cornell University, Ithaca, NY. Director, Cornell-China-Oxford Project on Nutrition, Health and Environment 1983-1990

Stuffed Manicotti
yields 10 stuffed manicotti

8 oz. package manicotti shells	1/2 t. herb seasoning (page 3)
3 C. Italian tomato sauce	1/2 t. sea salt
1 lb. (2 C.) firm tofu, mashed	<u>Cheesy Topping</u>
1 C. soft tofu, rinsed & drained	1/2 C. water
1 lb. fresh spinach, sliced, steamed	3 T. oil
1/3 C. vegan 'mayonnaise' (pg. 72)	1 C. soft tofu, rinsed & drained
3 T. nutritional yeast	1/4-1/3 C. nutritional yeast
1/4 t. black pepper	1 T. Bragg™ Liquid Aminos or tamari
2 T. tamari or substitute	1/4 t. sea salt

1. Cook the shells al denté (about five minutes) in rapidly boiling water. Drain, rinse and set aside.
2. Prepare tomato sauce (see recipes page 81 & 82) or have store-bought set aside.
3. Rinse and drain tofu and mash in a bowl. Mix with the remaining ingredients, except <u>Cheesy Topping</u>.
4. Cover the bottom of a long casserole dish with tomato sauce. Stuff each manicotti shell with the tofu-spinach filling and place in the casserole. Cover with the remaining tomato sauce.
5. In a blender, blend the <u>Cheesy Topping</u> ingredients. Pour this over the manicotti. Bake at 350° for 30-40 minutes. Cool slightly before serving.

Saucy Italian Eggplant
serves 3-4

3 cloves garlic, diced	1/4 C. each: fresh dill & basil, chopped
1-2 T. oil	1/2 C. nutritional yeast
1 onion, sliced thinly	1/2 C. water
1 bell pepper, sliced in strips	1 t. sea salt
1 large eggplant, peeled & diced	1 t. dried oregano
2 T. tamari or substitute	1 t. arrowroot powder
2 C. mushrooms, sliced	black pepper, to taste (optional)
2 tomatoes, in large chunks	

1. In a large skillet, sauté the garlic in oil. Add the onion and pepper and sauté for a minute or two, then add eggplant. Season with tamari and stir. Cover and simmer for a few minutes. Add the mushrooms and cover again for a minute or two. Finally, add the tomato chunks and fresh herbs.
2. When the tomatoes are soft, pull out 1/3 cup of the cooked tomatoes and place in a blender. Blend them with the yeast, water, spices and arrowroot.
3. Pour this back into the frying pan and simmer while stirring for a few minutes until it thickens. Do not boil. Serve over grain or noodles.

Mexican Enchilada Pie
9 large servings

Red Sauce
1/2 large onion, diced
2 bell peppers, diced
7 mushrooms, sliced (optional)
1 1/2 C. water
1 (12 oz.) can tomato paste
1 t. garlic powder
2 T. tamari or substitute
1/2 t. chili powder
1/2 C. fresh cilantro, chopped
1 t. cumin powder
1 chili pepper (optional), diced

Tofu Layer
2 lbs. (4 C.) firm tofu
1/4 C. fresh cilantro, chopped
2 T. oil
3 T. nutritional yeast
1 t. sea salt
2 T. tamari or substitute

Cheesy Topping
1 C. tofu, rinsed & drained
4 T. nutritional yeast
1/2 t. sea salt
1/8 C. oil (or water for a low-oil recipe)
2 T. Bragg™ Liquid Aminos or tamari

'No-Meat' Layer
3 C. texturized vegetable protein
2/3 C. of the Red Sauce
3 T. nutritional yeast
1 t. cumin powder
2 t. sea salt
1/2 t. black pepper
1 t. onion powder
1 t. garlic powder

1 1/2 packages corn tortillas
1 (12-16 oz.) can black olives, sliced
garnish: fresh cilantro, chopped

1. In a saucepan, sauté onion and peppers, then mushrooms. Add water, tomato paste and seasonings. Stir and cook for 20-30 minutes. (This amount of sauce is just enough for the pie itself; additional sauce may be desired for serving.)
2. Rinse and drain tofu. In a bowl, mash tofu and mix with remaining Tofu Layer ingredients. Set aside.
3. In a food processor, blend together Cheesy Topping ingredients.
4. Boil 4-5 cups of water. Pour the boiled water over the T.V.P. (texturized vegetable protein), cover and allow it to absorb all the water. Set aside.
5. Cover the bottom of a large, oiled casserole with one cup of the red sauce.
6. Layer the bottom with corn tortillas. Press in the tofu mixture, evenly.
7. Add another layer of corn tortillas and another layer of red sauce.
8. When all the water is absorbed by the T.V.P. (drain any excess), add the remaining 'No-Meat' Layer ingredients to it and mix. Place this layer on top of the casserole, and firmly pack it in.
9. Sprinkle with sliced olives and another light layer of red sauce. Again, cover with a layer of tortillas. Cover with a thick layer of sauce and top with Cheesy Topping. Garnish with sliced olives and chopped cilantro. Bake at 350° for 40-45 minutes.

"Reasonable minds are open to persuasion."

PLUTARCH (46-120 A.D.) ~ Greek philosopher

Homemade Chili
yields 1 medium to large sized pot

1 2/3 C. dry beans (pinto, red or
   kidney) soaked overnight
5 cloves garlic, diced
1 large onion, diced
1 bell pepper, diced
1 (12 oz.) can tomato paste
1 (12 oz.) can tomato sauce
1/4 C. fresh cilantro, chopped
jalapeño peppers, diced, to taste

1 T. sweetener
1 T. tamari or substitute
3 T. nutritional yeast
1 T. cumin powder
1 T. vegetable bouillon (page 2)
1/2-1 T. chili powder
1/4 t. sea salt
garlic & onion powder, to taste
2 C. T.V.P. (p. 5) (or ground tempeh/seitan)
1 C. bean stock (see step 1)

1. Rinse and cook soaked beans (see page 13) one hour before beginning chili preparation. Drain beans and set aside one cup of liquid.
2. In a separate pot, sauté garlic, onion and pepper. When cooked, add tomato paste, tomato sauce and all other ingredients except T.V.P. (texturized vegetable protein), beans and bean stock. Continue simmering.
3. Place T.V.P. in a separate bowl. Cover with 2-3 cups of boiling water and simmer, covered. When the T.V.P. absorbs all the water, add it (or the ground tempeh/seitan) to the chili pot. Stir frequently. When beans are cooked thoroughly, add them to the pot with one cup of the bean stock. Simmer for another half an hour.
4. Serve in taco shells, over rice or with corn bread (see recipes pages 32 & 33).
   • Optional ~ Grate some vegan 'cheese' (see page 274) over the top of chili tacos and bake in oven until it melts.

Maui Baked Beans
yields 1 large casserole

2 cloves garlic
1/8 C. oil
1/2 T. tamari or substitute
4 C. seitan, sliced and cubed
4 T. nutritional yeast
1/2 C. tomato paste
1/4 C. molasses
1/4 C. oil

1 T. vegetable bouillon (page 2)
1 t. garlic powder
6 C. beans, cooked (great northern/pinto)
1/2 onion, diced
1/3 C. molasses
1/3 C. tomato paste
1 T. tamari
1/4 T. onion powder

1. In a blender, blend garlic with oil, tamari and 1 T. water. Pour garlic oil into a skillet and sauté cubed seitan for 5-10 minutes, adding 2 T. of nutritional yeast.
2. Blend one cup water, tomato paste, 1/4 C. molasses, oil, 2 T. nutritional yeast, bouillon and garlic powder. Add this blended mixture to a casserole dish with the beans, onion and seitan.
3. Bake covered at 350° for approximately 35 minutes, or until onions are soft. Remove from oven.
4. Blend 1/3 C. molasses, tomato paste, tamari and onion powder. Mix into casserole leaving a lot of sauce on top. Bake for another 30-45 minutes, uncovered.

Burritos with Refried Beans
yields 6 burritos

3 1/3 C. pinto beans (cooked)	2 t. chili powder
3 T. tamari or substitute	1 t. cumin powder
2/3 C. tomato paste	1 T. apple cider vinegar
2 t. garlic powder	diced jalapeño pepper, to taste
2 t. onion powder	6 tortillas

1. In a food processor, using the "S" shaped blade, blend two cups of the pinto beans (see page 13) with the remaining ingredients, except tortillas.
2. When blended, add 2/3 of a cup of whole pinto beans to the blended mixture.
3. Pan fry in an oiled skillet for several minutes.
4. Fill tortillas with the refried beans, diced tomato, diced onion, shredded lettuce, salsa, avocado and grated vegan 'cheese' (optional - see page 274). Wrap filling in tortilla, tucking in ends.

Southern Black Beans
serves 4-6

1 1/2 C. dry black beans, washed, soaked and drained	1 green bell pepper, seeded & diced
	3 roma tomatoes, diced (or 2 diced tomatoes)
1/2–1 T. oil	2 C. corn kernels (fresh/frozen)
3 cloves garlic, diced	1 t. sea salt
1 medium onion, chopped	1 t. cumin powder
1 jalapeño pepper, seeded & diced	2 T. fresh cilantro, chopped
1 red bell pepper, seeded & diced	2 t. dry oregano

1. Boil the beans (pre-soaked) in water until tender, about an hour (see page 13). Drain and rinse.
2. In a large skillet or non-stick pot, heat the oil to medium and sauté the garlic, onion and peppers for 5–6 minutes. Add the tomatoes, corn and spices and cook until tomatoes are soft. Add the beans and mix well. Cook for several more minutes, stirring occasionally.
   • Serve with rice or other grain.

"Today about 1.3 billion cattle are trampling and stripping much of the vegetative cover from the earth's remaining grasslands. More than 60 percent of the world's rangeland has been damaged by over-grazing during the past half century."

JEREMY RIFKIN ~ President, The Foundation on Economic Trends, author, <u>Beyond Beef: The Rise and Fall of the Cattle Culture</u>

Black Bean Tostadas
serves 6–8

2–3 T. oil	1 t. cumin powder
1 onion, chopped	sea salt, to taste
2 cloves garlic, minced	8 corn tortillas
3 C. cooked black beans	Green Chili Sauce (see recipe below)
(1 1/3 C. dry beans)	1 C. vegan 'cheese', grated (page 274)
1/2 C. liquid from cooked beans	2 C. lettuce, shredded
1 t. dried oregano	2–3 C. tomatoes, chopped

1. Heat 1 T. oil in a large skillet. Add onion and sauté over low heat until translucent. Add garlic and sauté. Add beans, liquid and spices. Sauté for 20–25 minutes, stirring occasionally. Be sure there is enough liquid to keep everything moist and bubbling. Remove lid at the end of cooking to evaporate moisture.
2. Heat remaining oil in another skillet. When oil is very hot, individually crisp tortillas on both sides. Drain on paper towels.
3. Place one tortilla on each dinner plate. Spread half a cup of the black-bean mixture over each, followed by 2 T. of Green Chili Sauce. Sprinkle with 2 T. grated 'cheese', shredded lettuce and chopped tomatoes.

• Optional ~ Spread vegan sour cream (see page 72) on tortilla and top with guacamolé (page 193).

Green Chili Sauce

1 T. oil	1 C. = 2 (4 oz.) cans green chilis,
1 onion, finely chopped	drained and chopped
1 clove garlic, minced	1/2 C. water
1 T. whole wheat flour	1/2 t. sea salt

Heat oil in a small saucepan. Add onion and sauté until translucent. Add garlic and sauté. Sprinkle in flour and cook, stirring until mixture begins to brown slightly. Stir in chilis, water and salt. Simmer over low heat for 15 minutes, covered.

> *"1.5 million deaths per year in the U.S. are from diseases associated with diets high in saturated fats and cholesterol. The major dietary sources of fat in the American diet are meat, poultry, fish, dairy products and fats and oils...Dietary cholesterol is found only in foods of animal origin...Reduce consumption of saturated fat and cholesterol...Increase consumption of whole grain foods and cereal products, vegetables and fruits."*
>
> THE SURGEON GENERAL'S REPORT ~ on nutrition and health, 1988

Southern Pot Pie
serves 6

Cornmeal Pastry
1 1/2 C. whole wheat pastry flour
3/4–1 t. sea salt

1 C. yellow cornmeal (fine grain), sifted
2/3 C. oil

Filling
2 T. oil
3 scallions, cut into 1/2" pieces
   (or 1 onion, diced)
2 carrots, diced
2 t. chili powder
4 T. whole wheat pastry flour
1 C. soy or rice milk
1/2 C. veggie stock/broth

1 C. firm tofu, rinsed, drained & cubed
2 C. black beans (cooked)
2 C. corn kernels
1 green bell pepper, diced
1 red bell pepper, diced
1 t. sea salt
1/4 t. garlic powder
Optional: 2 T. fresh cilantro

Pastry
1. Combine flour, salt and sifted cornmeal in a medium-sized bowl using a whisk. Mix in oil and stir until pastry is moist enough to hold together.
2. Shape pastry into a ball. Cover with plastic wrap. Pastry can be prepared and refrigerated for later use.

Filling
3. Heat oil in a large skillet over medium-high heat. Add scallions, carrots and chili powder. Cook, stirring occasionally, until carrots are slightly soft (about 6–8 minutes). Stir in flour, stirring constantly for one minute or until smooth and bubbly. Stir in soy milk and broth. Cook, stirring constantly until mixture thickens (1–2 minutes). Stir in tofu, black beans, corn kernels, peppers, salt and garlic powder.
4. Using a floured rolling pin, roll out the pastry on a lightly floured surface into a rectangle 1" larger than a baking casserole.
5. Spoon the filling into a baking dish. Center pastry over filling. Fold overhang back over the top of pastry. Press to form edge.
6. Using a sharp knife, cut vents in pastry.
7. Bake in a pre-heated oven at 350° for 35–40 minutes until crust is golden-brown and filling is bubbly.

> *"The Christian argument for vegetarianism is simple:*
> *since animals belong to God, have value to God and live for God,*
> *then their needless destruction is sinful."*
>
> REV. DR. ANDREW LINZEY ~ Anglican (Episcopalian) priest, Professor of Theology
> chaplain Oxford University, author of 13 books

Mushroom Pepper Tofu Bake
yields 1 small baking pan

4-6 mushrooms, sliced	1 3/4 lb. (3 1/2 C.) tofu, rinsed & drained
2 t. nutritional yeast	1 t. sea salt
garlic powder, to taste	1/2 t. black pepper
1 1/2 onions, diced	2 T. nutritional yeast
	1 T. oil & tamari

1. Sauté mushrooms with 2 T. water, 2 t. nutritional yeast, and garlic powder. Set aside.
2. Sauté the onion with a little water or oil. When soft, set aside.
3. In a bowl, mash 1 1/2 C. of the tofu. Add sea salt, pepper and yeast, then mushrooms.
4. In a food processor, using the "S" shaped blade, blend remaining tofu with one tablespoon oil, the onion sauté and a dash of tamari. Add the blended tofu mixture to the tofu-mushroom mix and stir them together.
5. Bake in a shallow baking pan at 350° for 30 minutes or until golden-brown.

A "Quiche to Build a Dream on"
yields 1 large skillet

1 onion, diced	**Blender Ingredients**
1-2 cloves garlic, minced	1/4 C. oil
1 T. tamari or substitute	1 T. tamari or substitute
1 red bell pepper, diced	3/4 C. tofu, rinsed, drained & mashed
1 zucchini, sliced	1/3 C. water
6 mushrooms, sliced	1 t. onion powder
2 lbs. (4 C.) tofu, rinsed & drained	**Add to batter at end**
2 T. nutritional yeast	1/2 t. sea salt, or to taste
1/2 t. black pepper	1/2 t. baking powder, sifted
1 t. herb seasoning (page 3)	1 T. nutritional yeast

1. Sauté the diced onion and garlic in one tablespoon of tamari and a little oil or water. When soft, add red pepper, zucchini, and mushrooms, cover and simmer until soft.
2. In a bowl, mash the tofu and add the following three seasonings.
3. In a blender, whiz the blender ingredients. Pour this into the mashed tofu. Add the sea salt, baking soda and yeast. Mix well.
4. Pour into an unbaked pie crust or an oiled casserole dish. Bake at 350° for 30-40 minutes or until golden-brown. Cool and allow to partially solidify before serving.

*above: **Tempeh Teriyaki** (page 133) ~ below: **"Quiche To Build a Dream On"** (page 152)*

> **"Being a vegan is one of the most important roles I will ever play."**
>
> RIVER PHOENIX (1970-1993) ~ American actor

Spinach Mushroom Tofu Pie
yields one 13" x 9" x 2" baking pan

15 mushrooms, tipped and sliced

Crust

1 onion, diced
1/2 C. oil
1/2 lb. (1 C.) tofu, rinsed & drained
liquid from mushroom sauté
2 T. nutritional yeast
tamari or substitute, to taste
3 C. millet (cooked)
1 C. brown rice (cooked)
2 T. whole wheat pastry flour

2 lbs. (4 C.) tofu, rinsed and mashed
2 C. brown rice (cooked)

Filling

1 C. spinach, chopped & steamed
1 T. sea salt
1 t. egg replacer
2 T. tamari or substitute
1/2 t. pepper
3 T. nutritional yeast
4 t. blended tofu mixture (see below)

1. Sauté mushrooms and onions separately in a little oil or water. Drain and save liquid from mushroom sauté. In a food processor, blend oil, tofu, onion sauté, liquid from mushroom sauté, yeast, one tablespoon tamari and your favorite seasonings to taste. Set aside four teaspoons of this blended tofu mixture for pie filling.
2. In a mixing bowl, combine cooked millet, one cup cooked rice, pastry flour and your favorite seasonings with creamy tofu mixture. Mix well. Firmly pat this batter into a well-oiled 13" x 9" baking pan, forming a crust around the sides and bottom.
3. In a bowl, mash four cups of tofu. Add the rice and remaining filling ingredients. Add mushrooms. Mix well. Pour this filling into the crust.
4. Bake at 350° until golden-brown and firm, approximately 30-45 minutes. Serve with Cashew Mushroom Gravy (page 78) for an elegant dish.

Potato Tofu Stir-Fry — *great!*
serves 4-6

10 small red potatoes
1 lb. (2 C.) firm tofu
1/2 t. sea salt
1/2 t. garlic powder
1/2 t. paprika
1/8 t. cayenne or black pepper

4 T. olive oil
3 T. nutritional yeast
1/8 C. vegetable stock/broth
4 cloves garlic, chopped
2 medium onions, diced

1. In a saucepan, cover potatoes with water and bring to a boil. Cook until potatoes are tender, yet firm. Do not overcook. Drain and slice thinly.
2. Rinse and drain tofu, then marinate it by placing it in a bowl with spices, 3 T. olive oil, yeast and stock. Stir and let sit for 25 minutes.
3. In a large skillet, over medium heat, add the remaining olive oil, garlic and onions, and sauté for three minutes. Add the tofu marinade and sauté for 4-5 minutes until tofu starts to brown. Add the potato slices and cook for three more minutes. Re-season to taste if desired. Variation ~ Bake for 20 minutes.

*above: **Veggie Pizza** (page 141) ~ below right: **Half-Moon Pot Pies** (page 158)*
*below left: **Cashew Mushroom Alfredo** (page 156) ~ **Not Roast Beef** (page 163)*

Zucchini Mushroom Baked Omelette
serves 4

1 onion, diced	*2 lbs. (4 C.) tofu, rinsed & drained*
8–9 mushrooms, sliced	*2 T. oil*
2 medium-sized zucchini, diced	*1 t. turmeric*
a dash of tamari or substitute	*2 T. nutritional yeast*
1/2 t. dill weed	*2 T. tamari or substitute*
a dash of garlic & onion powder	*1/2–1 T. herb seasoning (page 3)*
nutritional yeast	

1. Sauté onion in oil or water until translucent. Add mushrooms and zucchini with a little tamari, dill, garlic and onion powder and a sprinkle of nutritional yeast. Cook until soft. Mash tofu into a bowl. Add remaining ingredients and mix.
2. Add sauté to the tofu batter and mix well.
3. Flatten batter onto an oiled baking sheet (batter should be about one inch high). Bake in a pre-heated oven at 350° for 30 minutes or until golden-brown.

Zucchini Fritatta
serves 4

1 onion, diced	*3 T. tamari or substitute*
3 medium-sized zucchini, diced	*2 T. oil*
2 1/4 lbs. (4 1/2 C.) soft tofu	*2 T. nutritional yeast*
1/2 t. mild curry powder	*1 t. turmeric*
1 T. garlic powder	*1 t. black pepper*
1 T. herb seasoning (page 3)	*2 T. herb seasoning (page 3)*
1 T. onion powder	*3 T. pastry flour*
1/2 T. egg replacer	

1. Sauté onion and zucchini with a dash of tamari and nutritional yeast.
2. In a bowl, mash tofu with remaining ingredients. Add the sauté and mix.
3. Flatten mixture onto an oiled baking sheet (batter should be about an inch high). Bake in a pre-heated oven at 350° for half an hour, or until golden-brown.

> **"The protein of animal muscle (steak, chicken, meat, fish fillets, etc.) is far more concentrated and acidic than the plant protein found in whole grains, legumes, and green vegetables. This concentrated acidic protein load can promote the leaching of calcium from the bones, contributing to the process of osteoporosis."**
>
> MICHAEL A. KLAPER, M.D. ~ American author and international lecturer

Easy Linguine Mushroom Stroganoff
serves 4-6

1/2 onion, diced	1/2 t. garlic powder
4 C. mushrooms, sliced	1/4 t. black pepper
2 T. Bragg™ Aminos or tamari	5 t. arrowroot powder
3 C. soy milk	1 t. liquid bouillon (see page 2)
2 1/2 T. nutritional yeast	1 t. onion powder
1/2 t. sea salt	16 oz. linguine noodles

1. In a large pot, sauté the onion then add the mushroom slices, along with the tamari. Cover and simmer until soft.
2. In a blender, blend the remaining ingredients, except the linguine. Pour this mixture into the pot with the onions and mushrooms. Simmer and stir frequently until sauce thickens. Do not boil.
3. In a separate large pot, boil four quarts of salted water with a dash of oil. Bring to a rapid boil and add the linguine. Cook until tender. Drain noodles well in a colander, then place the linguine into the large pot of sauce and stir. Serve.

Mushroom Eggplant Stroganoff
yields 1 large skillet

	Blender Ingredients
4 cloves garlic	2 C. water
4 T. oil	1/3-1/2 C. cashew butter
1/4 C. water	4 T. Bragg™ Liquid Aminos or tamari
9 C. eggplant, peeled, cubed small	3 T. nutritional yeast
2 C. mushrooms, sliced	2 T. arrowroot powder
1 T. tamari or substitute	1/2 t. sea salt
1/2 T. onion powder	

1. In a blender, blend the garlic with the oil and 1/4 cup water. Pour this into a large skillet and add the eggplant chunks. Stir and cover. Allow to simmer. Be sure to cook the eggplant until soft.
2. Add the mushrooms. Season with tamari and onion powder. Cover with lid and simmer until mushrooms are soft.
3. In a blender, blend the remaining ingredients. When vegetables are thoroughly cooked, add the liquid. Simmer and stir for 5-10 minutes. Serve over linguine.

> *"Meat, which contains cholesterol and saturated fat, was never intended for human beings, who are natural herbivores."*
>
> WILLIAM C. ROBERTS, M.D. ~ Editor in Chief of American Journal of Cardiology
> (Vol.66, October 1, 1990 pg. 896)

Cashew Mushroom Alfredo Sauce over Pasta
serves 4

1 onion, diced	*1/4 C. cashew butter*
3 cloves garlic, diced	*2 T. nutritional yeast*
1 T. oil or water	*1 t. tarragon*
1/2 bell pepper, diced	*3 T. Bragg™ Liquid Aminos or tamari*
5 C. mushrooms, sliced thick	*1 t. onion powder*
3 T. fresh dill weed, chopped	*2 t. herb seasoning (page 3)*
1/4 C. water	*1 t. garlic powder*

1. Sauté onion and garlic in oil or water. Add pepper and cook until soft, then add mushrooms. One minute later, add dill weed and stir.
2. In a blender, blend water with cashew butter and remaining seasonings. Pour over cooking vegetables. Simmer on low heat and stir for five minutes. Serve warm over pasta.

• Optional ~ Add steamed vegetables to pasta and top with sauce.

Rick Browning's Macaroni and 'Cheese'
serves 3-4

4 C. elbow macaroni	*1 1/2 t. garlic powder*
1/2 C. olive oil	*a dash of turmeric*
1/2 C. whole wheat flour	*2 T. tamari*
4 C. boiling water	*1 C. nutritional yeast*
1 t. sea salt	*paprika, sprinkle*

1. Cook the pasta in plenty of boiling water and drain.
2. In a pot, heat the olive oil and whisk in the flour. Whisk in the boiling water, sea salt, garlic powder, turmeric and tamari. Then whisk in the yeast. (Large flakes are best.)
3. Mix most of the topping with macaroni in a bowl. Place mixture in a casserole and top with the remaining creamy sauce. Sprinkle with paprika. Bake for 15 minutes at 350° in a pre-heated oven. Broil for two minutes to brown the top after baking.

> **"This (video footage from the movie Babe) is the way Americans want to think of pigs. Real life "Babes" see no sun in their limited lives, with no hay to lie on, no mud to roll in."**
>
> MORLEY SAFER ~ 'Pork Power', 60 Minutes, ABC television show, aired 9/19/97

Vegetable Potato Kugel
serves 4

1/2 C. onion, diced	6 large potatoes, peeled & grated
1/2 C. carrots, diced	1 large onion, grated
1/2 C. cauliflower, diced	1 t. baking soda
1/2 C. broccoli, diced	1/4 C. parsley, chopped
1-2 T. oil	1/4 C. fresh dill weed, chopped
1 1/2 t. sea salt	1/2 C. frozen peas, defrosted
1 1/2 t. garlic powder	1/2 C. matzoh meal (optional)
1/2 t. onion powder	paprika, sprinkle
4 T. nutritional yeast	

1. Sauté diced vegetables in oil and 1/2 t. each of sea salt, garlic and onion powder, as well as 2 T. nutritional yeast.
2. Grate the potatoes and onion, strain off excess water and mix with the vegetable sauté. Add baking soda, remaining sea salt, garlic powder, yeast, parsley, dill weed, peas and matzoh meal.
3. Place in a well-oiled, shallow pan and pat down. Oil the top for browning and sprinkle with paprika. Bake at 375° for about 30 minutes.

Herb Roasted Potatoes and Sweet Potatoes
serves 6 ~ quick & easy

4 medium sweet potatoes	1 t. dried thyme
4 medium baking potatoes	1/2 T. dried oregano
4 cloves garlic, minced	1 t. dried rosemary
2 T. olive oil	1 t. tamari or substitute
2 T. water	1/4 t. black or cayenne pepper

1. Peel and cut each potato and sweet potato lengthwise into eight pieces and combine in one large bowl.
2. Combine garlic, olive oil, water, and seasonings in a small bowl. Add this herb mixture to the potatoes and toss to coat.
3. Place the entire mixture into a baking casserole dish and cover. Bake in a pre-heated oven at 400° for 45-50 minutes or until the potatoes are tender.

> *"Other things being equal, I judge that a strict vegetarian will live ten years longer than a habitual meat eater, while suffering on the average, less than half so much from sickness."*
>
> HORACE GREELEY (1811-1872) ~ American newspaper publisher
> founder of New York Herald Tribune

Potato Zucchini Fritters
yields approximately 12

2-3 medium zucchini	4 T. unbleached flour
1/3 C. soy powder & 2/3 C. water	1/4 t. salt
1 lb. russet potatoes	1/4 t. garlic powder
4 large scallions, chopped	4 T. oil

1. Trim zucchini ends and grate in a food processor fitted with a shredding blade.
2. In a large bowl, whisk soy powder and water then add grated zucchini.
3. Peel potatoes and grate immediately in the food processor. Blot dry on paper towels. Add to zucchini in bowl along with scallions, flour, salt and garlic powder. Stir well.
4. In a large skillet, over medium-high heat, put 2 T. oil. Using 1 T. per pancake, drop batter into the skillet making 5-6 pancakes. Press mounds of batter flat with back of spoon or spatula. Cook 4-5 minutes until crispy. Turn carefully. Cook 4-5 minutes longer until crispy. Remove pancakes and place on paper towels to remove excess oil.
5. Repeat procedure using remaining batter and additional oil if needed. Serve hot.

Half-moon Pot Pies
yields 10 pies

	Sauce
3/4 C. water	1 1/2 C. cashew pieces
1 onion, diced	1 1/2 C. water
4 cloves garlic, minced	1 C. spinach, steamed, chopped
4 red potatoes, cubed	1 t. sea salt
4 C. butternut squash, cubed	1 t. garlic powder
2 carrots, cubed	2 T. tamari or substitute
1/2 t. sea salt	2 t. onion powder
2 C. green peas	2 1/2 t. dill

1. In a medium-sized pot with a lid, sauté onion and garlic (in a little oil or water). Add water, potatoes, squash, carrots and salt. Cook until tender, adding peas at the end.
2. In a blender, blend sauce ingredients until creamy. Add to sauté and mix gently.
3. Prepare dough. Roll out into 6 inch rounds and place the filling on half of the dough. Fold over and pinch sides making a half-moon. Or make a single pie using a pie plate.
4. Place on an oiled baking sheet (or use baking papers). Bake in a pre-heated oven at 350° until golden-brown, approximately 25-30 minutes.

> *"No great improvements in the lot of mankind are possible until a great change takes place in the fundamental constitution of their modes of thought."*
>
> JOHN STUART MILL (1806-1873) ~ English author and philosopher

Potato Wellington
yields 2 rectangular 12" loaves

<u>Crust</u>
1/2 C. oil
1/4 C. orange juice
1 t. herb seasoning (page 3)
1/4 t. garlic powder
1/4 t. onion powder
1/2 t. dill weed
2 C. whole wheat pastry flour, sifted
<u>Filling</u>
1 onion, diced
1 T. tamari or substitute

1 T. oil
2 T. nutritional yeast
7 C. potatoes (cooked), mashed
  (3–5 lbs. potatoes, uncooked)
2 t. dill weed
2 t. onion powder
2 t. garlic powder
2 t. sea salt
4 T. potato stock
3 T. oil
1 T. tamari or substitute

1. In a bowl, whisk oil and orange juice. Separately, sift crust spices and flour together. Mix the dry into the wet forming a ball of dough. (Dough should be moist but not sticking to bowl.) Chill for 15 minutes.
2. In a frying pan, sauté onion with 1 T. tamari, 1 T. oil, 2 T. nutritional yeast, and 3 T. water, creating a cheesy onion sauté. Cook until onions are soft.
3. Cut potatoes into small chunks and boil. Drain when cooked. Mash. Add onion sauté to potatoes and mix with all the remaining seasonings, potato stock, additional oil and tamari. Set aside to cool for wrapping in the dough.
4. Separate dough in half. With a rolling pin, roll out each piece of dough into a long rectangle between two sheets of wax paper.
5. Place potato filling along the center of the dough rectangles leaving enough dough on both sides to fold over the potatoes. Pinch or fold in the ends and seal. Fork vents into the top.
6. When potato filling is folded into the dough, transfer loaves onto an oiled baking sheet, flipping so the seam is on the bottom. Bake in a pre-heated oven at 350° until the crust turns golden-brown.

• Serve with Cashew Mushroom Gravy (page 78).

> *"...Again, there may be some people in the future who...being under the influence of the taste for meat, will string together in various ways sophistic arguments to defend meat eating...but...meat eating in any form in any manner and in any place is unconditionally and once for all prohibited."*
>
> The BUDDHA (circa 563-483 B.C.) ~ Indian Avatar, <u>Lankavatara Scripture</u>

Stuffed Baked Potatoes
yields 15-17 potatoes

10 lbs. large potatoes	1-2 large onions, diced
4 cloves garlic	4-5 T. nutritional yeast
6 T. oil	4 C. tofu, rinsed, drained & mashed
3 T. tamari or substitute (to taste)	1 t. sea salt
4 C. mushrooms, sliced	paprika, for sprinkling

1. Bake potatoes in oven. When soft, make a slit in the top of each potato, and another crossing it. (Don't slit all the way to edges.) Push both ends towards the middle, opening the potato & loosening it from its skin. (Use a towel to protect your fingers from burning.) Allow them to cool.
2. In a blender or processor, blend garlic in 3 T. oil and 1 T. tamari. Pour into a large frying pan.
3. Add mushrooms and sauté. When finished, drain liquid from mushrooms and put it in the food processor. Set the mushrooms aside in a large mixing bowl.
4. In the frying pan, sauté the onions with a dash of tamari, water and 2-3 T. yeast.
5. Using a food processor, purée half of the onion sauté with two cups of mashed tofu, 2-3 T. oil, 2 T. tamari, 2 T. yeast. Add to the mushrooms in the large mixing bowl. Repeat this step. Mix in the sea salt.
6. Scoop the potatoes out very carefully (don't hurt the shape of the skins, for stuffing purposes). Mash potatoes together with the tofu-mushroom mixture.
7. Stuff each potato skin with this mixture. Sprinkle with paprika and bake again at 325° for 25-30 minutes. This is an easy gourmet treat!

Potato Kugel - Mike Dunetz Style
yields one shallow 10" x 6" casserole

5 lbs. potatoes (about 7 large russet)	1/4 C. oil (plus oil for baking)
1 large onion, or to taste	1 t. garlic powder
2 t. baking powder	2 t. sea salt or tamari
1/2 C. Matzoh Meal	1 t. herb seasoning (page 3)
1/2 t. black pepper	2 t. onion powder
2 t. egg replacer & 4 T. water, mixed	

1. Grate potatoes and onion into a bowl. Drain liquid. Add remaining ingredients. Mix.
2. Oil a shallow casserole dish and pour mixture into it. Spread a light layer of oil on the top. Bake in a pre-heated oven at 375° for an hour or more, until browned on top.

> *"It is man's sympathy with all creatures that first makes him truly a man."*
>
> ALBERT SCHWEITZER, M.D. (1875-1965) ~ Alsatian philosopher and medical missionary
> 1952 Nobel Peace Prize recipient

Seitan (Wheat-Meat)

Wheat gluten is the natural protein portion of wheat that is extracted after wheat is milled into flour. In its processed form, wheat gluten is a fine tan flour consisting of about 75–80% protein.

Seitan is made from wheat gluten flour and can be used for many purposes. It is one of the best meat substitutes for flavor absorption as well as texture. It is high in protein and low in fat. Once prepared, it can be sliced into strips and served with different sauces or ground for tacos, lasagna, chili, etc.

Seitan (basic recipe)
yields five 3" x 3" pieces

18-20 C. water (for boiling)	1 T. herb seasoning (page 3)
1/2 t. sea salt	1 t. onion powder
4 1/2 C. gluten flour	1 t. oregano
1/2 C. nutritional yeast (optional)	3 1/2 C. water
1 t. garlic powder	1/4 C. molasses
1 t. dried basil	1/4 C. tamari or substitute
1 t. sea salt	

1. Add sea salt to the water and bring to a boil.
2. In a medium-sized bowl, combine the dry ingredients (flour, yeast & spices). Stir well.
3. In a separate bowl or measuring cup, mix together the remaining liquids.
4. Add liquid to the dry and mix thoroughly until dough is consistent (solid and firm, yet not dry).
5. Pour onto tray and knead dough until all air is removed. Form a rectangular loaf on the tray and cut into even pieces (approximately 3" x 3").
6. Place the cut dough into boiling water. Boil for 45–50 minutes.
7. Remove a piece and cut it to see if it is done. (It should be firm all the way through).
8. Take out and cool on a tray. If not for immediate use, leave in large pieces and freeze. Keeps well in the freezer. When removing from freezer, defrost then prepare as directed in recipe. See recipes pages 162-168.

> *"...the wolf shall dwell with the lamb...the lion shall eat straw like the ox...and no one shall hurt nor destroy in all of God's holy mountain."*
>
> THE BIBLE ~ Isaiah 11: 6-9

Sweet and Saucy Seitan Stew
serves 4-6

3-4 cloves garlic, diced	2 T. herb seasoning (page 3)
2 small onions, chopped	3 T. tamari or Bragg™ Liquid Aminos
1 bell pepper, chopped	1 t. cumin powder
6 carrots, sliced	1-2 T. oregano
3 potatoes, cubed	6 T. + 1 C. tomato purée
2 sweet potatoes, cubed	5 large chunks seitan (see page 161)
1 small beet, cubed	(cut into bite-sized cubes)
1 t. onion powder	1/4 C. oil blended with 2-4 cloves garlic
1 t. garlic powder	tamari & nutritional yeast, for sauté
1 t. dill weed	pepper & basil, to taste

1. In a large pot, sauté garlic, onions then pepper in a little oil or water. After a few minutes, add carrots and allow them to partially soften. Add potatoes and beet. Allow to simmer with onion powder, garlic powder, dill weed, herb seasoning, 2 T. tamari, 1/2 t. cumin, oregano and six tablespoons of tomato purée. (Add a little water if necessary.) For a saucier stew, blend more carrots and tomato purée together.
2. While the vegetables are cooking, fry seitan in garlic oil, tamari and nutritional yeast.
3. When the carrots are soft, remove two cups of them and place in a blender. Blend with one cup of tomato purée and a dash of tamari. You may need to add a little water to get the blades moving.
4. Pour this blended mixture back into the stew pot and stir. Add the seitan and mix. Simmer and add pepper and basil. Allow to sit and absorb flavors after simmering. Serve alone or over grains.

• Optional ~ Add some steamed cauliflower, broccoli, eggplant or zucchini.

"So much more efficient is a vegetarian diet that less than one half the current agricultural acreage would be needed...We would not have to cut down forests and destroy habitats to create land on which to grow feed for livestock. We wouldn't have to force our acreage and squeeze every last possible yield from it. We could dispense with synthetic fertilizers and toxic pesticides, and still have vast surpluses of food. Our world would be a far greener one, with far less pollution, cleaner air, cleaner water and a more stable climate."

JOHN ROBBINS ~ American author, Pulitzer Prize Nominee for <u>Diet for a New America</u>, author, <u>The Food Revolution</u>, Conari Press 2000

Seitan Stir-Fry
yields 1 large skillet

3 cloves garlic	1 tomato, cubed
1/4 C. oil	4 C. seitan, sliced
2 T. tamari or substitute	4 T. nutritional yeast
1 large onion, in half slices	1/4 t. black or cayenne pepper
1 pepper, sliced in strips	1 t. sea salt

1. In a blender, blend garlic, oil and one tablespoon tamari. Pour half of this blended mixture into a large skillet. Add onion slices and pepper. When they soften, add tomato. When the vegetables are almost cooked, remove from skillet and put aside.
2. Pour remaining garlic oil into the skillet and add sliced seitan. Season seitan with one tablespoon of tamari and the nutritional yeast and allow to crisp on both sides.
3. Add sautéed vegetables back to the skillet. Season with pepper and salt. Cook for five to ten more minutes, allowing seitan to absorb the flavors.

Not Roast Beef
serves 4-5

4-5 C. seitan, sliced in strips	1 1/2 T. tamari or substitute
2 T. oil	1/8 C. miso (blonde)
2 T. tamari or substitute	2 T. molasses
3 T. nutritional yeast	1/4 t. turmeric
<u>Sauce</u>	1/4 t. black pepper
2 1/2 C. water	1/2 T. parsley (fresh or dried)
1/4 C. nutritional yeast	1 T. onion powder
1/2 C. tomato paste	1/2 T. garlic powder

1. Grill or pan fry the seitan slices in the oil and season with tamari and yeast. Brown on both sides. (If desired, grill some sliced onions and mix in.)
2. In a blender, blend the <u>Sauce</u> ingredients. Pour into a saucepan and simmer for 25 minutes. Stir frequently, never bringing sauce to a rapid boil.
3. Pour sauce over the seitan and pan fry once again or bake in the oven. (Baking in the oven or letting it sit in the refrigerator with the sauce will allow the seitan to absorb the sauce and its flavors.)

"A six-year study of 88,000 nurses
by Boston's Brigham and Women's Hospital
found that those who ate meat every day were more than
twice as likely to get colon cancer as those who avoided meat."

NEW ENGLAND JOURNAL OF MEDICINE ~ 13 December 1990

Seitan Peppersteak
yields 1 large skillet

4-5 C. seitan slices
2-3 T. oil, 2-3 cloves garlic and a dash of tamari
nutritional yeast, tamari, seasonings, to taste
<u>Peppersteak Sauce</u> (yields 4 C.)

4-5 cloves garlic, diced	1 1/2 T. arrowroot powder
2 onions, sliced like half moons	1 t. herb seasoning (page 3)
2 bell peppers, thinly sliced (1 red)	1 C. tomato paste, or thick tomato sauce
8 mushrooms, sliced	1/2 T. garlic powder
3 C. water	1 t. onion powder
3 T. liquid bouillon (see page 2)	2 T. nutritional yeast
1 1/2 T. dried basil	3 T. sorghum or molasses
1/2 T. veggie pepper or 1 t. pepper	1 1/2 T. tamari

1. Slice seitan into wide, quarter-inch thick slices then cut each in half.
2. In a blender, blend garlic with oil and tamari. Pour this oil into a cast-iron skillet and sauté the seitan pieces in it. Add nutritional yeast, tamari and seasonings, to taste. (To use less oil, don't use garlic oil. Simply add sauce to the seitan and bake.)
3. In a saucepan, using a dash of oil (or water), sauté the garlic, then the onions, peppers and mushrooms (in that order). Cover and allow to soften.
4. In a blender, blend the remaining ingredients. Pour in with the vegetables. Simmer over a low flame for 20-25 minutes, stirring often until sauce thickens. Do not boil.
5. Add most of the sauce to seitan in the skillet and stir. Bake for 30-40 minutes at 275°. Add remaining sauce, warm and serve.

Seitan Sloppy Joes
yields 1 large skillet

4 C. ground seitan	4 C. Marinara Sauce
1-2 T. oil	(see recipe page 81)
1 t. garlic powder	3 T. molasses
a dash of pepper	1/2 T. tamari or substitute

1. In a food processor, grind the seitan.
2. In a large skillet, sauté the seitan in oil; season with garlic powder and pepper. Add the marinara sauce, molasses, and tamari to the seitan in the pan. Stir and simmer.
 • Serve over whole wheat buns or bread.

"Vegan living demonstrates in the physical world, the spiritual ideal of compassion, which is the heart of love."

SUN ~ co-founder Gentle World

Baked Ziti with Seitan
yields one 4 quart casserole

4 C. sliced seitan
4 cloves garlic
1/8 C. olive oil
1/3 C. water
1 T. vegan 'cream cheese'
   (page 274)
1/4 C. nutritional yeast
1/2 t. sea salt
1 1/2 T. nutritional yeast

Blender Mixture
1/4 C. oil
1/2 C. water
1 C. tofu, rinsed, drained & mashed
1/4 C. nutritional yeast
2 T. tamari
2/3 C. vegan 'cheese', grated (page 274)

16 oz. ziti shells
4-5 C. Marinara Sauce (page 81)
1 package 'cheese', grated

1. Thinly slice seitan and set aside.
2. In a blender, blend garlic cloves with oil, water, 'cream cheese' and yeast. Pour this blended mixture into a large skillet or frying pan.
3. Place the seitan slices in the pan and simmer, stirring thoroughly. When most of the liquid is absorbed, sprinkle with sea salt and 1 1/2 T. nutritional yeast. Continue cooking to brown seitan on both sides. Remove from heat.
4. In the blender, whiz <u>Blender Mixture</u> ingredients, up to the ziti shells in column 2.
5. Boil water and cook the ziti, but don't overcook. Drain and rinse.
6. Oil a baking dish. Place seitan and ziti in the casserole with most of the tofu blender mixture (save enough to layer the top of the casserole). Stir two cups of marinara sauce into the pasta and seitan. (Optional: sprinkle grated vegan 'cheese' throughout the pasta and seitan.)
7. Flatten down the pasta then layer two more cups of marinara sauce on top. Spread the remaining tofu blender mixture on top of the sauce and sprinkle with additional grated 'cheese'.
8. Bake in a pre-heated oven at 350° for 45 minutes, rotating casserole halfway through baking from bottom to top rack in the oven for even baking. A gourmet delight!

> *"Tenderness and mercy and gentility, and all the spiritual qualities that set man off so greatly from beasts of prey, are lacking in the lion, tiger, wolf and other carnivores. The claim that man has evolved to such a high mental plane and spiritual plane that he must have meat is exactly the opposite of the facts. He must crush and harden his higher nature in order to hunt and fish and prey."*

DR. HERBERT M. SHELTON (1895-1985) ~ father of Modern Natural Hygiene

Baked Seitan and 'Cheese' Tacos
yields 18 small tacos

2 T. oil	1 T. sweetener
1 onion, diced	1 t. herb seasoning (page 3)
3 cloves garlic, diced	1 1/2 t. cumin powder
2 bell peppers, diced	4-5 C. seitan, ground
2 C. mushrooms, sliced	2 T. oil
1/2 C. fresh cilantro, chopped	2 T. tamari or substitute
hot chili pepper, diced, to taste	1 T. garlic powder
1 (12 oz.) can tomato paste	12-18 taco shells
1 1/2 C. water	vegan 'cheese', grated (page 274)
4 T. nutritional yeast	

1. In a large pot, sauté the onion and garlic in oil. Add the peppers; then the mushrooms. Cover and simmer until vegetables are soft. Add cilantro, chili pepper, tomato paste and water. Stir. Add 2 T. yeast, sweetener, herb seasoning and cumin powder. Stir and simmer.
2. In a food processor, using the "S" shaped blade, grind seitan into an imitation ground-meat consistency.
3. Oil a frying pan with 2 T. oil and pan fry the seitan. Season with tamari and 2 T. nutritional yeast. When browned, add this to the cooked red sauce. Season with garlic powder and stir together.
4. Crisp the taco shells for several minutes in the oven then remove. Line the shells up in a casserole pan. Fill them with the taco mixture. Sprinkle grated 'cheese' on the top of each shell and bake until it melts.
   · Optional ~ Top with shredded lettuce, diced tomato and onion.

Seitan Barbecue
serves 4-5

4-5 C. seitan, sliced	1/4 T. garlic powder
2-3 T. oil	1/2 T. onion powder
2-3 T. tamari or substitute	1 T. hickory smoke flavor (page 280)
2-3 T. nutritional yeast (optional)	(Wright's Concentrated)
Sauce	1 T. molasses
2 C. water	1/2 T. tamari or substitute
1/4 C. sorghum	1 T. arrowroot powder
2/3 C. tomato paste	2 T. liquid bouillon (page 2)
2 T. apple cider vinegar	

1. Pan fry the sliced seitan in the oil and season with tamari. Add yeast and brown on both sides. Shut off flame.
2. In a blender, blend the <u>Sauce</u> ingredients and pour into a saucepan. Simmer and stir for about 25 minutes, never bringing sauce to a boil.
3. For a quick and easy barbecue, simply add some of the sauce to the seitan and pan fry. A second option is to add the sauce to the seitan slices and bake in the oven, allowing the seitan to absorb the flavors.

Seitan Kabobs

From The Gentle Persuasion Cookbook by Brook Katz
serves 6-8

Pepper Glaze
1/4 C. water
1/3 C. vinegar
1/3 C. tamari or substitute
1/2 C. sweetener
1 T. arrowroot powder, sifted
1/4 t. black pepper

6-8 skewers
1 lb. seitan, cubed
12-16 shallots (or onion chunks)
2 bell peppers (cut into large pieces)
1 C. pineapple, cubed (optional)

1. Combine glaze ingredients in a small saucepan. Stir over low heat until thickened.
2. To each skewer, alternately add the seitan, shallots, pepper and pineapple.
3. Brush kabobs with pepper glaze and grill or broil, turning and brushing with glaze until browned. Serve immediately.

Seitan Macaroni and 'Cheese' Casserole

yields an 8" x 12" casserole

1 lb. macaroni noodles
1 C. water
3/4 C. tofu, rinsed & drained
a squeeze of lemon juice
1/4 C. oil
1 T. tamari or substitute
1/2 t. sea salt
1/4 C. nutritional yeast
garlic & onion powder, to taste
1 T. tahini

1 T. oil
3 C. seitan, bite-sized chunks
garlic & onion powder
1 T. nutritional yeast
Topping
1/2 C. water
1/3 C. tofu, rinsed, drained & mashed
1 T. cashew butter or tahini
2 T. oil
1/2 t. sea salt
6 T. nutritional yeast

1. In boiling water, cook pasta.
2. In a blender, blend the water, mashed tofu and remaining ingredients in first column.
3. When noodles are cooked, drain and set aside in an oiled casserole dish.
4. In an oiled skillet, pan fry the seitan chunks with garlic/onion powder & yeast.
5. Add the seitan chunks to the pasta in the casserole and pour the blended mixture over. Mix. Bake in a pre-heated oven at 350° for 20 minutes, stirring periodically.
6. In a blender, blend the Topping ingredients. Pour over the casserole and bake for 20-30 more minutes.

> *"What ever creed be taught or land be trod,*
> *man's conscience is the oracle of God."*
>
> LORD BYRON (1788-1824) ~ English poet

Sweet and Sour Seitan
yields 1 large skillet

2 T. Bragg™ Aminos or tamari	2 T. liquid bouillon (page 2)
2 T. oil	1/4 C. tomato paste
4 cloves garlic	2 T. sweetener
1 t. fresh ginger, minced	1 T. oil
8 C. seitan, cut in thin strips	1 t. garlic powder
1/4 C. apple cider vinegar	1 t. onion powder
1/3 C. sorghum	1 t. ginger powder
1 1/2 C. water	1 T. arrowroot powder

1. In a blender, blend tamari (or substitute), oil, garlic and fresh ginger until smooth. Pour into a large skillet and add seitan. Pan fry the seitan, stirring frequently.
2. In a blender, blend remaining ingredients and pour into a small saucepan. Stir and simmer until it thickens. Mix into the seitan in the skillet.
3. Bake in a pre-heated oven at 350° for 30 minutes. Allow to cool and marinate.

Seitan with Spicy Peanut Sauce
From The Gentle Persuasion Cookbook by Brook Katz
serves 6-8

2 T. nutritional yeast	cayenne pepper, to taste (1/8 t.)
8 oz. peanut butter (natural)	2 t. arrowroot powder
3 1/2 C. water	2 lbs. seitan, cubed
2 T. tamari or substitute	2 lbs. (dry weight) flat wide noodles (cooked, rinsed, and drained)

1. In a saucepan, combine the first five ingredients.
2. Combine arrowroot with half a cup of water and add to main mixture. Cook over medium heat, stirring frequently until sauce thickens. Do not boil.
3. Add seitan, stir well and serve over noodles.

"The Utopians feel that slaughtering our fellow creatures gradually destroys the sense of compassion, which is the finest sentiment of which our human nature is capable."

SIR THOMAS MOORE (1779-1852) ~ Irish author and poet

Holiday Stuffed Butternut Squash
serves 4

2 butternut squash	1/2 t. cumin powder
2 C. brown rice (cooked)	2 T. tamari or substitute
1 C. onions, chopped	1/2 t. garlic powder
1/2 C. celery, chopped	1/2 t. onion powder
1/2 C. bell pepper, chopped	1 C. walnuts, chopped
1/2 t. dried basil	1/2 C. pecans, chopped
1 t. dried oregano	3 T. tahini
1/2 t. herb seasoning (page 3)	3 slices of toast

1. Slice butternuts in half and scoop out the seeds. Bake in a pre-heated oven at 350° for 20-30 minutes, until tender. Remove from oven and let cool.
2. Carefully scoop out insides without breaking shells. Mix squash with rice. Save shells.
3. Sauté vegetables then add them to this mixture. Add seasonings, nuts and tahini.
4. Slice the toast into small squares like croutons and add to mix.
5. Stuff mixture into hollowed squash shells.
6. Bake for another 20 minutes and serve with gravy.

Holiday Sweet Potato Pie
yields 2 pies

3 large sweet potatoes, sliced	<u>Filling</u>
<u>Crust</u>	1/2 T. arrowroot powder
1/4 C. oil	a dash of sea salt
1 C. tofu, rinsed & drained	1 T. dry sweetener
2 T. tamari or substitute	4 T. maple syrup
3 C. cooked brown rice	2 T. nutritional yeast
1 C. carrots, grated	4 T. oil

1. Steam sweet potatoes in a pot using a steamer basket. When soft, allow to cool.
2. In a food processor, blend oil, tofu and tamari adding 1-2 T. water.
3. In a large mixing bowl, place blended tofu mixture, rice, and the grated carrots. Mix.
4. Press rice mixture into two oiled pie plates, evenly along the sides and bottom, forming a pie crust. In a food processor, blend all filling ingredients with sweet potatoes. Pour into the two pie shells.
5. Bake in a pre-heated oven at 350° for 30-35 minutes until golden-brown. Cool.

> *"Among the attributes of God, although they are all equal, mercy shines with even more brilliancy than justice."*
>
> MIGUEL DE CERVANTES (1547-1616) ~ Spanish playwright and novelist

Festive Stuffed Chard Leaves
yields 18-19

2 small onions, diced	3-4 T. oil
1-2 bell peppers, diced	2-3 T. herb seasoning (page 3)
2 stalks celery, diced	1 1/4 T. mild curry powder
2 C. mushrooms, sliced	4 C. cooked brown rice (short grain)
6 T. tamari or substitute	1 C. pecans or walnuts, chopped
5 T. nutritional yeast	1 T. vegetable bouillon (page 2)
5 carrots, grated	2 T. oregano
1-2 T. garlic powder	1/2 T. basil
1-2 T. onion powder	1/2-1 T. dill weed
1 1/2 lb. (3 C.) soft tofu	18 large swiss chard leaves

1. In a frying pan, with a dash of oil, sauté onions, peppers, celery and mushrooms with 2 T. tamari and 1 T. yeast. Add carrots along with garlic and onion powder. Remove from frying pan and put in a large mixing bowl.
2. Rinse and drain tofu and cut into small pieces and place in a frying pan with a dash of oil. Sauté with 2 T. tamari, 1 t. herb seasoning, a dash of garlic and onion powder and 1/4 T. curry powder.
3. Add tofu, rice and chopped nuts to the bowl and mix together well.
4. Add oregano, basil, 2 T. herb seasoning, 4 T. nutritional yeast, bouillon, dill weed, 3 T. oil, and 1/2 T. curry powder. Mix well.
5. Lightly oil two long casserole pans. Remove the thick bottom stem of each chard leaf. Drop 3-4 spoonfuls of mixture onto each leaf, starting at the top, thinner part of the leaf. Roll (from the top down) pressing sides in, if possible, and place the rolled leaf into the pan. Pack each wrap closely together.
6. Cover lightly with your favorite gravy (or a mixture of oil, tamari and water) and bake in a pre-heated oven at 350° until leaves are tender, approximately 35-40 minutes.

> *"Fish is by far the most polluted of all the flesh foods, regularly containing toxic chemical pollutants known to cause cancer, kidney failure, nerve damage and birth defects. Besides, we are running out of fish. Day and night, fleets of huge factory fishing ships let out thousands of miles of nets, scooping up all free-swimming marine life, while bottom-scraping trawlers devastate the fragile sea beds in their relentless vacuuming of sea animals. The current rate of fish consumption is simply not sustainable... The number of fish and most other species of large sea life are dwindling throughout the world's oceans. Humans must learn to nourish themselves optimally on plant-based foods."*
>
> MICHAEL A. KLAPER M.D. ~ American author and international lecturer

Savory Shepherd's Pie
serves 8

2 lbs. potatoes, peeled and
   cut into 1" cubes
3/4 C. soy milk (non-dairy milk)
1 T. olive oil
1/4 C. nutritional yeast
1/4 t. each: salt, garlic powder, & oregano
1 1/2 lbs. seitan, (ground in food
   processor with "S" shaped blade)
1/2 t. sea salt
1 medium onion, chopped finely

1 large yellow or red bell pepper,
   cored, seeded & cut into strips
4 cloves garlic, crushed
3 tomatoes, cubed
1 C. broth (from cooked veggies)
2 T. tamari or substitute
1/2 t. rosemary leaves, chopped
   or 1/4 t. dried, crumbled
1/2 t. hot red pepper flakes
4 T. whole wheat flour

1. Place potatoes in a large saucepan and add enough water to cover them by an inch. Bring to a boil. Reduce heat to medium. Simmer, covered, 15–20 minutes until tender.
2. Drain well and return potatoes to saucepan. Add soy milk, olive oil, nutritional yeast, salt, garlic powder, and oregano. Mash potatoes just until smooth. Set aside.
3. In a large oiled skillet, over medium-high heat, combine ground seitan and sea salt. Cook, stirring frequently, until lightly browned (about five minutes). Then place in a lightly oiled square baking dish.
4. Wipe skillet clean. Lightly oil and place over medium-high heat. Add onion, pepper and garlic. Cook for 3–4 minutes, stirring frequently, until vegetables are tender yet still firm. Add tomatoes, half a cup of broth, tamari, rosemary and red pepper flakes. Bring to a low boil. Reduce heat to low and simmer, covered, for five minutes.
5. Meanwhile, in a small bowl, stir remaining half a cup of broth into flour until blended and smooth. Stir this into mixture in skillet. Simmer for two minutes longer, stirring continuously until slightly thickened.
6. Remove from heat. Gently stir vegetable mixture and pour onto seitan in baking dish. With a spatula, swirl the mashed potatoes into a layer over the vegetables.
7. Bake in a pre-heated oven at 350° for 20 minutes until tips of potato swirls are golden-brown.

> *"Let a man begin to think about the mystery of his life
> and the links which connect him with life that fills the world,
> and he cannot but bring to bear upon his own life
> and all other life that comes within his reach,
> the principle of reverence for life."*
>
> ALBERT SCHWEITZER, M.D. (1875-1965) ~ Alsatian philosopher and medical missionary
> 1952 Nobel Prize recipient

Thanksgiving Shepherd's Pie (Thanksgiving Stuffing)
serves 5-6

mashed potatoes (see step 1)	3 T. tahini
(use 5 large potatoes)	1/4 C. oil
1 loaf of bread, cut into small cubes	1/2 T. garlic powder
2 onions, diced	2 T. oregano
3 cloves garlic	1/2 T. onion powder
3 celery stalks	4 T. nutritional yeast
1 T. oil & tamari, a dash	3 T. tamari or substitute
1/4-1/2 C. potato water or stock	paprika, sprinkle

(To make plain stuffing, begin at step 2 and bake without the mashed potatoes on top.)

1. Boil water for the mashed potatoes. Follow instructions on page 107.
2. Cut bread into small cubes, the size of croutons.
3. Sauté the onions, garlic and celery in one tablespoon of oil and a dash of tamari, until soft, on medium-low heat.
4. Mix the remaining seasonings and liquids and pour over bread cubes. Mix. Spread on a tray and toast in oven at 350° for 15 minutes, stirring occasionally.
5. Stir the vegetable sauté into the toasted bread mixture (stuffing). Press into the bottom of an oiled long baking dish.
6. Spread mashed potatoes on top of stuffing. Sprinkle with paprika and bake in a pre-heated oven at 350° for 25 minutes.

• Serve with Cashew Mushroom Gravy. See recipe page 78.

Herb Roasted Vegetables
serves 4-6

8 small red potatoes	1/4 C. olive oil
12 small zucchini	1/4 C. tamari
12 small carrots	1/4 C. balsamic vinegar
1 bunch small beets	1/4 C. sweetener
3-4 small red onions	3 cloves garlic, minced
1/2 lb. button mushrooms	1 T. fresh ginger, minced
2 red bell peppers	3 T. fresh herbs, chopped

1. Pre-heat the oven to 400°. Scrub potatoes, zucchini, carrots and beets. Peel the onions and leave whole. Wipe mushrooms clean with a damp towel. Core and seed the bell peppers and cut into strips. Place all the vegetables together in a large mixing bowl.
2. In a small bowl, whisk together the remaining ingredients to make a topping.
3. Pour this topping over the vegetables. Stir to coat evenly. Pour vegetables into a roasting pan and roast until they become tender, (about an hour) turning them over and brushing on more topping from the roasting pan, every 15 minutes.
4. Serve immediately.

Eggplant Tomato Tahini Bake
yields 1 large baking casserole

2–3 medium-sized eggplants	2 T. tamari or substitute
3 large ripe red tomatoes	2 t. salt-free herb seasoning (page 3)
1 onion, sliced	garlic oil for sauté
1 1/4 C. water	3 C. mushrooms, halved
3/4 C. tahini	1 T. tamari or substitute
2 cloves garlic	1/4 C. scallions, diced
1/4 C. nutritional yeast	paprika, sprinkle

1. Peel and slice eggplant in thin slices. Slice the tomato and onion.
2. In an oiled casserole dish, place a layer of eggplant covered with a layer of sliced tomato and onion.
3. In a blender, blend water, tahini, garlic, nutritional yeast, tamari and herb seasoning.
4. Pour a thin layer of this mixture over the layered vegetables. Add another layer of vegetables along with some more dressing.
5. Fill almost to the top with layers of tomato, onion, eggplant and sauce, leaving some sauce aside for later. Begin baking at 375° in a pre-heated oven.
6. In a blender, blend 1–2 cloves garlic with 1–2 tablespoons oil. In a small frying pan, sauté the halved mushrooms in the garlic oil. Season with tamari.
7. When eggplant is partially cooked, remove from oven. Mix the mushroom sauté with the sauce saved from step 5. Pour this mixture over the top of the casserole, and spread out evenly. Sprinkle with diced scallions and paprika. Bake until eggplant is melt-in-your-mouth soft, approximately an hour.

• Variation ~ Try a zucchini tahini bake. Replace eggplant and tomatoes (if desired) with zucchini and extra onions. This bake will take a little less cooking time and is also rich and delicious.

> "The superior man will watch over himself when he is alone. He examines his heart that there may be nothing wrong there; and that he may have no cause for dissatisfaction with himself."
>
> CONFUCIOUS (551-479 B.C.) ~ Chinese philosopher

Rawsome Recipes

'Rawsome' Recipes

"I am only one, but still I am one.
I cannot do everything, but still I can do something.
I will not refuse to do the something I can do."

HELEN KELLER (1880–1968)
American essayist

Live Foods

In the pages ahead you will find a bountiful array of uncooked dishes. Colorful, nutritious salads, sauces, entrées, smoothies, desserts and other fresh delights. This section also includes directions for growing sprouts and recipes for making sprouted breads and crackers.

In a raw food diet, lunches and dinners can center around tossed salads and fruit or vegetable trays with sauces and dips. A fruit salad can be prepared in minutes and served as a light breakfast or lunch. The water and fiber content of fruit is high and the sugars are burned easily, making fruit less fattening. Fully ripened fruit is sweeter, more digestible and has greater nutritional value than immature fruit. For example, a green banana has 2% fruit sugar while a ripe one has 20%.

Live foods are packed with minerals and vitamins and are a good foundation for a healthy diet. These live foods add valuable nutrients necessary for optimum health and contain enzymes to break themselves down, providing more energy with less digestive effort. Taking time to prepare beautiful salads will help you enjoy eating more live foods.

Each person must find his or her point of balance between cooked and raw foods. This balance may change with the seasons, with your needs for nutrition and your evolving tastes. We hope this section will encourage people to increase their intake of live, fresh fruits and vegetables, seeds, nuts, sprouted grains and legumes, by offering recipes that make this transition easy and incredibly delicious.

"Raw plant food is beautiful. Creating and eating this food is an art. Every ingredient is a new color. Each meal is a cloud or a stream or a flower — a piece of the magnificent painting that you are becoming. Every bite is a detailed brush stroke on your work of art in progress. What we see as the world is only a reflection of the work of art we are inside. We find that once we become pure and polished within, everything outside of us also becomes that and more. To me, the raw vegan ideal represents not only a way to live in peace, love and harmony with nature and the animals, but also it represents the highest aspirations of beauty in the human spirit."

DAVID WOLFE ~ author and international lecturer
author, <u>Eating for Beauty</u> & <u>The Sunfood Diet Success System</u>

Gardening and Composting

Vegan-organic gardening avoids chemicals as well as livestock manures and animal remains. Soil fertility is maintained with vegetable compost, green manure, crop rotation, mulching, and other sustainable, ecological methods. By growing our food vegan-organically, there is a greater hope of eliminating transmittable diseases and bacteria. Fertilizers to avoid are blood and bone meal, sludge, fish emulsion (parts/oils), and manures that are derived from the abuse of animals. These products may carry Mad Cow Disease and other dangerous diseases. Vegan-organic gardening is a healthier, more compassionate alternative.

Soil conditioners and fertilizers that are vegan-organic include lime, gypsum, rock phosphorus, dolomite, rock dusts, rock potash, wood ash, hay mulch, composted organic matter (fruit/vegetable peels, leaves and grass clippings), green manures/nitrogen-fixing cover crops (fava beans/clover/alfalfa/lupines), liquid feeds (such as comfrey or nettles), and seaweed (fresh, liquid or meal) for trace elements. Seaweed is best used harvested fresh from the sea rather than washed up on beaches where it has been sitting. If it has been, stack it and allow rain to wash out the salt. Some plants do not like too much salt. Marigolds have a root system that improves the soil and they also deter some insect pests.

You can successfully create rich, nutritious soil from composting fruit/vegetable peels and kitchen scraps, leaves, grass clippings and any trimmings of trees and bushes that are in their green, soft state. (Woody material takes a longer time to break down.) Untreated sawdust, rock dust and gypsum, as well as seaweed, can be added to the compost pile. The manure of a pet horse, bunny rabbit or cow (naturally vegan animals) can be utilized in the compost. Manure is a good source of nitrogen, but is often obtained from sources that exploit animals. Following is a recipe for a basic veganic soil, to be seasoned with whatever nutrition is needed, depending on your location:

1. Save all fruit and vegetable peels and leftovers in a sealed container or bucket in your kitchen. When full, take to an outdoor compost pile.

2. Compost piles should be somewhere near the garden, away from the house, in a shady, cool spot. Begin a pile with prunings or other course materials. Then add the kitchen waste, i.e. fruit/vegetable rinds, and cover with whatever assortment of covering material you have available (grass clippings, hay, leaves, etc.). The object is to create layers of food material alternating with covering material to allow aeration.

3. When the pile is a few feet high, place extra cover material on it. Cover with a black plastic sheet, weed mat or ground cloth to protect it from rainfall and contain its heat. Then let nature's master recycling plan take its course for about two to three months, depending on the climate.

4. After that time period, the pile needs to be uncovered and turned. Turning requires flipping the entire pile so that the bottom of it becomes the top. Cover it again and your soil should be ready within a couple of months. You can make or buy a compost container that has moveable layers to make this job easier.

Growing Wheatgrass

SUPPLIES
1. Large wide mouth jars
2. Screens or other porous cloth; (cheese cloth, screening, nylon stockings)
3. Strong rubber bands to hold screen on
4. Wheat berries
5. Healthy soil in trays.

Wheatgrass juice is a rich, green chlorophyll drink, extremely high in enzymes and nutrition. Wheatgrass is easy to grow and ensures a supply of fresh, live vitamins and minerals. It can be juiced or simply chewed to extract the juice and remove pulp. Sprouted wheat berries can be made into delicious essene breads. See pages 214-216.

Use about 1 1/2 C. dry wheat berries to grow one garden flat of wheatgrass.

1. Begin by inspecting the seeds. Rinse them once in a jar.
2. Fill the jar with water two inches above the berries. Soak for 10-12 hours.
3. Pour out water and rinse again. Cover the mouth with a screen and hold in place with a strong rubber band or a mason jar lid. Place jar on a rack, at a 45° angle, to drain. Cover with a towel or shade cloth. Continue rinsing and draining 2-3 times a day for 2-3 days until the sprout's tail is at least 1/8 inch long.
4. Sprouted wheat berries can be planted to grow wheatgrass or used in this sprouted state to make Essene breads. See pages 214-216.
5. To prepare soil, a good mixture is 75% top soil and 25% peat moss or 50% top soil, 25% compost and 25% peat moss. You can also use a prepared potting soil (see page 285). Mix soil in a bucket or box. Fill trays at least 1 1/2 inches high with soil. We have also had great success growing wheatgrass in raised garden beds. Use 15 lbs. dry wheat berries for a 4' x 10' raised bed, flipping soil over after harvesting.
6. Sprinkle berries on top of soil, keeping them close but not piled on top of each other. Water and cover with a shade cloth. Keep them shaded for the first three days and then partially shaded for the remaining days. Water at least once a day. In hot climates, water more often.
7. Harvest in 5-7 days from planting. Wheatgrass harvesting requires a sharp knife, scissors or grass clippers. Cut half an inch above the base. Cut fresh, only what you need, and let the rest continue growing. It is overgrown at 8-9 days. The second growth does not have the same potency, so it is suggested to harvest only once, and then compost the roots & soil.
8. Any problems can usually be solved by a slight change in the growing process. Mold may grow if the seeds are too damp, planted too closely or have poor ventilation. Use shade cloth to increase aeration, and water less. A sparse crop can happen if the seeds were soaked too long or not watered properly. Pale grass may be caused by insufficient sunlight. Protect it from birds. (Wheat berries can be attractive to some animals and birds.) Wheatgrass likes filtered sunlight better than direct hot sunlight.
9. It takes approximately seven days from soaking to harvest. One pound of wheatgrass should yield at least 10 oz. of wheatgrass juice.

See page 290 for recommended wheatgrass juicers

Sprouting

A tiny seed appears lifeless. Then quite magically, with the help of fresh water, air and sunshine, a sprout comes forth, bursting with life. It is packed with enzymes, vitamins and nutrients that contain the elements the body needs for optimum growth and health. Sprouts are rich in chlorophyll and are a great source of protein.

Growing sprouts is great fun and well worth the effort. It is a quick, easy and inexpensive way to get fresh, vital nutrients into your diet, even if you are living in an area that does not have fresh foods in season. The process is rewarding as well as meditative, and will pay for itself many times over. The cost of the seeds is nominal and they grow into a bounty of nutrition.

Sprouts are full of vitamins and minerals in their purest form, which are easily digested with the help of the many enzymes they contain. They are actually germinated seeds, legumes and grains that, in the sprouting process, become powerful enzyme-makers, converting carbohydrates into simple sugars, complex proteins into amino acids and fats into fatty acids. These conversions make the assimilation and absorption of their valuable nutrients easier. The nutrient content of grains, seeds and legumes can increase 10–20% when they are sprouted. Many sprouted grains and legumes also contain the essential amino acids. Sprouts are a wonderful way to ensure that you are getting the nutrition your body needs.

There are two ways to grow sprouts. Some sprouts are grown hydroponically, using water and sunlight, like alfalfa seeds and mung beans - see page 180. There are also sprouts that you can plant and grow in the soil, like sunflower and buckwheat - see page 181.

"The individual is capable of both great compassion and great indifference. He has it within his means to nourish the former and outgrow the latter...Nothing is more powerful than an individual acting out of his conscience, thus helping to bring the collective conscience to life."

NORMAN COUSINS ~ American journalist, author, lecturer

Sprouts
hydroponic jar, bag or basket method

SUPPLIES
1. Wide mouth glass jars
2. Screens or cheese cloth to cover the opening of the jar
   (cut the screen to fit well over the jar's mouth - usually about a 6" square)
3. Strong rubber bands to secure screen
4. Organic seeds, legumes and grains are sold at most health food stores.

UNHULLED SEEDS	LEGUMES	GRAINS
Alfalfa - 1 1/2 T.	Lentils - 3/4 C.	Wheat Berries, soft - 1 C.
Clover - 1 1/2 T.	Adzuki Beans - 3/4 C.	Millet - 1 1/2 C.
Radish - 1 1/2 T.	Mung Beans - 3/4 C.	Rye - 1 C.
Fenugreek - 1 1/2 T.	Green Peas - 1 C.	Barley - 1 C.
	Garbanzo Beans - 1 C.	Quinoa - 1 C.

SOAKING

Inspect seeds and remove any that are broken. Place them in a jar, rinse and drain. Fill with spring or filtered water, about 2-3 inches above seeds or legumes. Soak overnight, approximately eight hours. After eight hours, drain water.

RINSING & DRAINING

Rinse soaked seeds. Place jars in a rack or bowl (mouth down) at a 45 degree angle so air can circulate. Make sure seeds do not totally cover mouth of jar. Cover with a towel to keep dark for the first days. This will ensure germination. Rinse and drain 2-3 times a day. Legumes and grains do not need sunlight and will be ready in 1-2 days when the sprout tail is 1/8 inch long. For unhulled seeds, such as alfalfa, clover and radish, continue rinsing and draining for 2-3 more days and place in indirect sunlight until the leaves are deep green.

HARVEST

To harvest grains and legumes, just rinse and serve. For unhulled seeds and some legumes (such as mung beans), place in a container and submerge the sprouts until the hulls rise to the surface. Skim them off and place sprouts back in the jar to drain. Refrigerate all sprouts after they are fully sprouted to maintain freshness. They will last 5-7 days in refrigeration. Once wheat berries are sprouted, they can be used to make uncooked Essene breads and other healthy treats.

> *"God said, 'Behold! I have given you every herb bearing seed which is upon the face of all the earth, and every tree, in which is the fruit of a tree yielding seed. To you it shall be for meat.'"*
>
> THE BIBLE, GENESIS 1:29

Sprouts
planted

SUPPLIES
1. Organic seeds are sold at most health food stores.
2. Healthy soil
3. Garden flats or cafeteria trays with holes
4. Box or basket with holes to drain, or gutters around the side
5. Strainer or screening material for rinsing seeds before planting

1 3/4 C. Sunflower Seeds (whole, unhulled) for one flat of sprouts
1 2/3 C. Buckwheat Seeds for one flat of sprouts

SOAKING, RINSING & DRAINING
Inspect seeds and remove any that are broken. Place them in a jar, rinse and drain. Fill with spring or filtered water, about 2-3 inches above seeds. Soak for 12 hours. Rinse and drain 2-3 times a day for 1-2 days until the sprout shoot is growing.

SOIL PREPARATION
A good mix is 75% top soil & 25% peat moss or 50% top soil, 25% peat moss and 25% compost. A prepared vegan-organic potting soil can also be used. A small amount of fresh sand, rock dust or kelp/seaweed adds to the potency of the sprouts. Mix soil in a bucket or box, and fill trays at least one inch thick with soil.

PLANTING & GROWING
Sow seeds onto soil and spread out. Seeds should touch, but not be bunched on top of each other. Water them daily and cover with shade cloth or towel. After three days uncover and put in indirect sunlight. More sun = larger leaves.

HARVESTING
Harvest 5-8 days from planting when sprout is just over 2 inches tall with deep green leaves. Harvest with a serrated knife or scissors, trying not to pull plants up by the roots. Remove hulls with fingers. Brushing the tops of the sprouts with your hands before harvesting helps to remove the hulls.

SOLVING POSSIBLE PROBLEMS
Mold may grow if the seeds are too damp, planted too closely or have poor ventilation. Use a shade cloth to cover instead of towels or newspaper and water less. A sparse crop can happen if the seeds were soaked too long or not watered properly. Pale sprouts may be caused by insufficient sunlight.

"Sprouts and immature greens are the most nutritious of live, raw, organic foods that are available on this planet."

VICTORAS P. KULVINSKAS, M.S. ~ author, Survival into the 21st Century

Breakfast

Applesauce
yields 1 bowl

10 apples, small
2 T. date sugar (or dates, to taste)
1 t. cinnamon
1/8 t. nutmeg (optional)

1. If using dates, remove pits and soak for 15-20 minutes. Peel and core apples.
2. Blend all ingredients in a food processor, using the "S" shaped blade.

Fresh Fruit Salad
serves 1-2

1 apple/avocado
1 mango/5 strawberries
1 banana
1 papaya or peach (or any fruit in season)
1 orange
1/8 C. raisins

Peel and slice each piece of fruit into a bowl. Add raisins, mix and serve.
• Optional ~ Squeeze an orange over fruit bowl and sprinkle with sunflower seeds.

Sunflower 'Milk'
yields 1 quart

1 quart (4 C.) ice water
2/3 C. sunflower seeds
a dash of vanilla (optional)
2-3 dates (pitted), soaked in 1/2 C. water

1. Place sunflower seeds in a blender, just covering the blades.
2. Cover seeds with one cup of water and blend to a purée (about one minute).
3. Add soaked dates and vanilla. Use a plastic spatula or a little water to get the pieces of seeds off the sides of the blender.
4. When the purée becomes difficult to blend, add a few more tablespoons of water until it is completely smooth.
5. Fill to the top with ice cold water while still blending.

• This milk is quick, easy and delicious over breakfast cereals. Use raw cashews in place of sunflower seeds for a rich, cream-like, whiter milk.

> *"The fate of animals is of greater importance to me than the fear of appearing ridiculous; it is indissolubly connected with the fate of men."*
>
> EMILE ZOLA (1840-1902) ~ French novelist and critic

Almond 'Milk'
yields 1 blender

1/3 C. almonds, soaked & drained	*3–4 dates (pitted), soaked in 1/2 C. water*
4 C. ice cold water	*a dash of almond extract (optional)*

1. Cover the blades of the blender completely with almonds. Pour 3/4 cup of water (or enough water to cover the almonds plus a little extra) into the blender and purée until smooth and creamy. Add the soaked dates along with water enough to purée.
2. Pour a little water down the sides of the blender, getting all the little pieces to fall into the purée. When completely smooth, add ice cold water to fill the blender nearly to the top. Add a drop or two of almond extract. Blend.

• For a smoother consistency, strain before serving.

Granola Mix
yields approximately 8 cups

4 C. rolled oats	*1 C. raisins*
1/2 C. almonds, chopped	*1/3 C. figs, chopped*
1/2 C. pecans, chopped	*1/3 C. dates, chopped*
1/2 C. walnuts, chopped	*1/2 C. sunflower seeds*
1/2 C. oat or wheat bran	*1/2 C. date sugar, to taste*
1 C. shredded coconut	*1 t. cinnamon*

Mix all ingredients together in a bowl and store in a sealed container.

• Serve with sunflower or almond milk.

"When we dare to think of the environmental threats facing our planet: air pollution, water pollution, land contamination, soil erosion, wildlife loss, desertification (the turning of verdant land into a condition resembling natural desert), rain forest destruction and global warming. Humankind's profligate consumption of animal products has made a significant contribution to all of these ills, and it stands as the leading cause of many of them. Certainly these problems wouldn't disappear overnight if the world suddenly became vegetarian, but no other lifestyle change could produce as positive an impact on these profound threats to our collective survival as the adoption of a plant-based diet."

HOWARD LYMAN ~ ex-cattle rancher, international lecturer, author, <u>Mad Cowboy</u>

Tasty Dried Granola
yields 4 cups

1 large, ripe papaya	3 C. whole oats
1 banana	1/2 C. raisins
1 T. cinnamon	1/4 C. walnuts
1 1/2 t. vanilla	1/4 C. pecans
1/2 C. date sugar	1/4 C. dried banana

1. Soak all nuts for at least 10 minutes. In a food processor, using the "S" shaped blade, whiz the papaya, banana, cinnamon, vanilla and date sugar. Add oats and whiz again. Mixture should be thick and sticky. Place in a bowl.
2. Place nuts, raisins and dried bananas in the food processor and pulse to chop nuts.
3. Fold chopped nuts and dried fruit into the mix.
4. Crumble onto dehydrator sheets so it looks like granola. Dehydrate at 105° for six hours or until desired crunchiness is reached.

Almond Raisin Whip
yields 1 cup

2/3 C. almonds, soaked	2 dates (pitted), soaked
1/2 C. raisins, soaked in 1/2 C. water	

1. Soak almonds for at least six hours then drain and rinse.
2. In a blender, blend the ingredients together. Use as a spread on Essene bread or crackers - see pages 214 & 215.

above: **Mexican Mostadas** *(page 208)* ~ *below:* **Cucumber Vinaigrette** *(page 193)*

> " 'Thou shalt not kill' does not apply to one's own kind only, but to all living beings; and this Commandment was inscribed in the human breast long before it was proclaimed from Sinai."
>
> ~
>
> "The vegetarian movement ought to fill with gladness the souls of those who have at heart, the realization of God's kingdom on earth."
>
> COUNT LEO TOLSTOY (1828-1910) ~ Russian novelist and moral philosopher

Almond 'Milk'
yields 1 blender

1/3 C. almonds, soaked & drained	*3-4 dates (pitted), soaked in 1/2 C. water*
4 C. ice cold water	*a dash of almond extract (optional)*

1. Cover the blades of the blender completely with almonds. Pour 3/4 cup of water (or enough water to cover the almonds plus a little extra) into the blender and purée until smooth and creamy. Add the soaked dates along with water enough to purée.
2. Pour a little water down the sides of the blender, getting all the little pieces to fall into the purée. When completely smooth, add ice cold water to fill the blender nearly to the top. Add a drop or two of almond extract. Blend.

• For a smoother consistency, strain before serving.

Granola Mix
yields approximately 8 cups

4 C. rolled oats	*1 C. raisins*
1/2 C. almonds, chopped	*1/3 C. figs, chopped*
1/2 C. pecans, chopped	*1/3 C. dates, chopped*
1/2 C. walnuts, chopped	*1/2 C. sunflower seeds*
1/2 C. oat or wheat bran	*1/2 C. date sugar, to taste*
1 C. shredded coconut	*1 t. cinnamon*

Mix all ingredients together in a bowl and store in a sealed container.

• Serve with sunflower or almond milk.

"When we dare to think of the environmental threats facing our planet: air pollution, water pollution, land contamination, soil erosion, wildlife loss, desertification (the turning of verdant land into a condition resembling natural desert), rain forest destruction and global warming. Humankind's profligate consumption of animal products has made a significant contribution to all of these ills, and it stands as the leading cause of many of them. Certainly these problems wouldn't disappear overnight if the world suddenly became vegetarian, but no other lifestyle change could produce as positive an impact on these profound threats to our collective survival as the adoption of a plant-based diet."

HOWARD LYMAN ~ ex-cattle rancher, international lecturer, author, Mad Cowboy

Tasty Dried Granola
yields 4 cups

1 large, ripe papaya	3 C. whole oats
1 banana	1/2 C. raisins
1 T. cinnamon	1/4 C. walnuts
1 1/2 t. vanilla	1/4 C. pecans
1/2 C. date sugar	1/4 C. dried banana

1. Soak all nuts for at least 10 minutes. In a food processor, using the "S" shaped blade, whiz the papaya, banana, cinnamon, vanilla and date sugar. Add oats and whiz again. Mixture should be thick and sticky. Place in a bowl.
2. Place nuts, raisins and dried bananas in the food processor and pulse to chop nuts.
3. Fold chopped nuts and dried fruit into the mix.
4. Crumble onto dehydrator sheets so it looks like granola. Dehydrate at 105° for six hours or until desired crunchiness is reached.

Almond Raisin Whip
yields 1 cup

2/3 C. almonds, soaked	2 dates (pitted), soaked
1/2 C. raisins, soaked in 1/2 C. water	

1. Soak almonds for at least six hours then drain and rinse.
2. In a blender, blend the ingredients together. Use as a spread on Essene bread or crackers - see pages 214 & 215.

above: **Mexican Mostadas** *(page 208)* ~ *below:* **Cucumber Vinaigrette** *(page 193)*

> " 'Thou shalt not kill' does not apply to one's own kind only, but to all living beings; and this Commandment was inscribed in the human breast long before it was proclaimed from Sinai."
>
> ~
>
> "The vegetarian movement ought to fill with gladness the souls of those who have at heart, the realization of God's kingdom on earth."
>
> COUNT LEO TOLSTOY (1828-1910) ~ Russian novelist and moral philosopher

Salads Galore

Tossed Dressed Salad
serves 5

1 head romaine lettuce
1 small sweet onion, thinly sliced
1 C. yellow/red bell pepper, diced
1/2 pint cherry tomatoes, halved
1 long cucumber, sliced
2-3 T. nutritional yeast

1/2-1 T. herb seasoning (page 3)
1/2 t. garlic powder
1/8 t. black or cayenne pepper (optional)
1 T. apple cider vinegar
2 T. fresh lemon juice
1/2 T. olive oil
sea salt or Bragg™ Aminos, to taste

1. Wash the lettuce and spin dry or allow to drain.
2. Prepare the vegetables and toss with the lettuce. Sprinkle with dry seasonings.
3. Just before serving, add the vinegar, lemon juice, olive oil and salt/salt substitute. Toss for several minutes. Serve immediately.

Garden Salad
serves 4-5

1 head leaf lettuce
5 large spinach leaves, chopped
1/2 C. purple cabbage, shredded
broccoli & cauliflower flowerets

4 carrots, grated
2 beets, grated
1 cucumber, sliced
1-2 tomatoes, diced small
1 yellow/red bell pepper, sliced

1. Wash the greens and spin dry or allow to drain. Prepare the vegetables.
2. Toss the shredded purple cabbage, broccoli and cauliflower flowerets, grated carrots and sliced pepper in the salad.
3. Don't mix in the grated beet as it turns the salad red; decorate the top with it. Place the cucumbers and tomatoes around the edges of the salad; don't mix in. (Tomatoes and cucumbers mixed in will limit the shelf life of the salad.)
4. Serve with your favorite dressing.

above: **Delightful Sprout Salad** *(page 190)*
below: **Vegan-organic gardens, New Paradigm Center, New Zealand**

"...I was so moved by the intelligence, sense of fun, and personalities of the animals I worked with on 'Babe' that by the end of the film I was a vegan..."

JAMES CROMWELL ~ American actor (who played Farmer Higgins in Babe)
Excerpt from The Food Revolution by John Robbins

Sprout & Spinach Salad
serves 4

4 C. sprouts (any combination)
1/2 head of lettuce or spinach
2 slices purple onion, diced small
4 carrots, grated

3 mushrooms, sliced
1 cucumber, peeled, diced
1 yellow/red bell pepper, sliced
1 tomato, diced

Toss all ingredients except the cucumbers and tomatoes. Toss with dressing of choice. Add cucumber and tomato to the top.

Champion Carrot Salad
serves 4

2 C. carrots, grated
1 stalk celery, diced finely
1/4 sweet onion, diced small

1 T. dill weed (or to taste)
1 C. thick tahini dressing (pg. 199)
a dash of garlic & onion powder
sea salt, to taste

1. Grate carrots through a Champion® Juicer. (Rather than assembling with the juicing screen, assemble leaving that space open.) Another option is to use a food processor with the grater blade or a hand grater and grate as finely as possible.
2. Mix all ingredients together. Chill. Garnish with extra dill weed.

Oriental Cabbage Salad
serves 5

1 small head cabbage, grated
1/4 C. purple cabbage, grated
2-3 carrots, grated
1 scallion, diced
3 stalks celery, diced
2 cloves garlic, diced

2 T. fresh ginger, diced
2 T. miso (blonde)
sea salt/Bragg™ Liquid Aminos, to taste
2 t. raw apple cider vinegar
1 T. date sugar (or 2-3 dates, soaked)
4 T. water (or more if needed)

1. Prepare vegetables and mix together in a bowl.
2. In a blender, whiz the garlic and ginger with the miso, sea salt, vinegar, sweetener and water. Be sure to thoroughly blend the ginger and garlic.
3. Pour the mixture over the vegetables and mix well. Marinate and chill for an hour before serving.

> **"A man can not be comfortable without his own approval."**
>
> MARK TWAIN (1835-1910) ~ American humorist, novelist

Curried Cauliflower Salad
serves 3

2 1/2 C. cauliflower, chopped
1/2 C. leeks or scallions, diced
1 1/2 C. carrots, grated
sea salt/Bragg™ Aminos, to taste

1/4 C. raw tahini
1 t. mild curry powder
1/4 C. water

1. Place the vegetables in a small bowl.
2. In a separate cup, mix together the tahini and remaining ingredients.
3. Pour over the vegetables, mix and allow to marinate before serving.

Rainbow Salad
serves 5-6

1/2 C. cabbage, shredded
3/4 C. red bell pepper, diced
1 C. carrot, grated
1/2 C. purple cabbage, grated
1 stalk celery, diced small
2 1/2 C. broccoli flowerets
1/3 C. scallions, diced

1/2 tomato, diced
1/4 C. fresh lemon juice
2 T. oil
sea salt/Bragg™ Liquid Aminos, to taste
1/2 T. herb seasoning (page 3)
2 T. nutritional yeast
1/2 t. black pepper

Mix all ingredients together in a bowl. Allow to marinate a short time and serve.

Grate Beet Salad
yields 6 cups

4-6 beets, peeled & grated
3/4 C. sweet onion, diced
<u>Dressing</u>
1 C. water
1 T. sweet onion, diced

1/2 C. raw tahini
2 T. raw apple cider vinegar
2 T. nutritional yeast
1 clove garlic
3 dates, pitted (optional)

1. Grate beets and place in a mixing bowl. Add the diced onion.
2. In a blender, mix the dressing ingredients. Pour over the shredded beets. Marinate for several hours and serve.

" 'Do unto others as you would that they should do unto you'
applies to animals, plants and things, as well as to people..."

ALDOUS HUXLEY (1894-1963) ~ English author

Vibrant Italian Salad
serves 4-6

3 C. fresh tomatoes, cubed
2-3 C. english cucumbers,
    peeled & sliced
1/2 sweet onion, diced small
1 1/2 C. broccoli flowerets
<u>Blender Ingredients</u>
1/4 C. water
1/4 C. cold-pressed olive oil
1 t. onion powder
1 clove garlic
1 t. garlic powder

1 T. date sugar (or 2-3 dates, soaked)
sea salt/Bragg™ Liquid Aminos, to taste
3 T. nutritional yeast
<u>Final Ingredients</u>
1 1/2 large avocados, cubed
1 t. herb seasoning (page 3)
1/8 C. raw apple cider vinegar
1/2 T. basil
1 T. oregano
1/4 t. black pepper
1/2-1 t. sea salt

1. Place the tomatoes, cucumber, onion and broccoli flowerets in a large mixing bowl.
2. In a blender, whiz the <u>Blender Ingredients</u>. Pour over vegetables and marinate for an hour. After marinating, add the avocado and final ingredients. Stir and serve.

Mexicavo Salad
serves 4-6

4 ears of corn
4 tomatoes, diced
1/4 C. red bell pepper, diced
1 bunch pok choy or bok choy
1/2 C. sweet onion, diced
<u>Blender Ingredients</u>
1/4 C. raw apple cider vinegar
1/4 C. cold-pressed olive oil

1 t. nutritional yeast
sea salt/Bragg™ Aminos, to taste
1 small clove garlic
a dash of pepper
1 t. herb seasoning (page 3)
<u>Final Ingredients</u>
5-6 avocados (hass), cubed
1/2 C. fresh cilantro, chopped

1. Cut corn kernels from cob. Place in a bowl with the next four ingredients.
2. In a blender, whiz the <u>Blender Ingredients</u>. Pour onto vegetables in bowl and allow to marinate for 1/2-1 hour.
3. Finally, just before serving, add the avocado and fresh cilantro. Stir well and serve.

> *"We have a great deal more kindness than is ever spoken.*
> *Despite all the selfishness that chills the world like east winds,*
> *the whole human family is bathed with*
> *an element of love, like a fine ether."*
>
> RALPH WALDO EMERSON (1803-1882) ~ American philosopher, poet and essayist

Pink Passion Salad
serves 5-6

1 small head green cabbage
1/2 small head red cabbage
  (thinly sliced or shredded)
1 beet, grated
1 red bell pepper, diced
1 tomato, diced
2 T. fresh basil, chopped

2 red onion slices, diced
1 lemon, juiced
sea salt or substitute, to taste
4 T. nutritional yeast
2 T. fresh dill, chopped
2 T. olive oil
fresh herbs of choice (optional)

1. Prepare vegetables and mix in a bowl. Dress with the remaining ingredients.
2. Chill for several hours before serving, allowing it to marinate.

Sprouted Lentil Salad
serves 4-5

4 C. sprouted lentils
2 carrots, grated
1/4 C. onion, diced
1/4 C. parsley, chopped
1-2 T. olive or cold-pressed oil

1/4 C. fresh lemon juice
3 dates, pitted, soaked in 1/4 C. water
sea salt or substitute, to taste
3 T. nutritional yeast

1. In a bowl, combine the sprouted lentils, grated carrots, diced onion and fresh parsley.
2. In a blender, blend the remaining ingredients (including date soak water). Pour over the vegetables and mix. Chill and serve.

Simple Cabbage Salad

1 small head cabbage, shredded
2 T. fresh lemon juice
1/4 sweet onion (optional)

sea salt or substitute, to taste
3-4 T. raw tahini
a dash of water

Mix tahini with water and lemon juice, then add to remaining ingredients. Let chill for a few hours or serve immediately.

"Recognize the eternal essence that exists in every living thing and shines forth with inscrutable significance from all eyes that see the sun!"

ARTHUR SCHOPENHAUER (1788-1860) ~ German author and philosopher

Delightful Sprout Salad
serves 4-5

1 1/2 C. cabbage, finely grated	**Dressing**
1/2 C. lentil sprouts	1 T. fresh lemon juice
(or other sprouted legume)	2 T. fresh basil, chopped
1/2 C. clover or alfalfa sprouts	2 T. fresh dill, chopped
2 carrots, grated	sea salt/Bragg™ Liquid Aminos, to taste
1 bell pepper, diced	2 T. nutritional yeast
1/8 C. sunflower sprouts or seeds	3 T. raw tahini

1. Combine grated and diced veggies, sprouts and seeds.
2. Mix dressing ingredients separately; then pour over the top of the vegetables. Mix well. Marinate for 20-30 minutes if desired.

Aramé (Sea Vegetable) Salad
serves 4-5

1.75 oz. package of aramé	2 T. olive oil
4 C. water	sea salt or substitute, to taste
1 tomato, diced	1 T. raw apple cider vinegar
1 small sweet onion, diced	1/2 t. herb seasoning (page 3)
1 cucumber, diced	1/2 red bell pepper, diced
1 clove garlic, diced	

1. Rinse aramé and soak in water for 15-30 minutes. Rinse again and drain all water.
2. Place soaked aramé in a bowl. Add remaining ingredients. Toss and serve.

Aramé & Cabbage Salad
serves 4

2 C. dry aramé	2 T. cold-pressed olive oil
4 C. water	sea salt or substitute, to taste
2 C. green cabbage, shredded	1 T. raw apple cider vinegar
1 C. red cabbage, shredded	2 T. tahini, mixed with 3 T. water
1/2 C. cilantro, chopped	1/2 t. onion powder

1. Rinse aramé and soak in water for at least 15 minutes. Rinse and drain all water.
2. Place soaked aramé in a bowl and add the remaining ingredients. Mix well and serve.
   • Optional ~ Add 1/4 sweet onion or scallion, diced.

"Our bodies are our gardens, to which our wills are gardeners."

WILLIAM SHAKESPEARE (1564-1616) ~ English poet, playwright

Parsley Salad
serves 2-4

1 bunch parsley, chopped
1 can of olives, pitted, sliced
2 cloves garlic, diced
1 tomato, diced (optional)

2 T. fresh lemon juice
1-2 T. cold-pressed olive oil
Bragg ™ Aminos or sea salt, to taste

Mix all ingredients in a bowl. Marinate and serve.

Pok Choy Miso Salad
yields 8 cups

6 C. pok choy or bok choy
2 stalks celery, diced
2 C. grated carrot
1 T. water

1 clove garlic, pressed
2 T. miso
1 T. cold-pressed oil
1 T. parsley, chopped

Chop the pok choy and mix with celery and carrot. Mix remaining ingredients in a cup or blender to liquefy the miso. Pour over salad. Mix well.

Golden Caesar Salad
yields 1 medium-sized bowl

12 C. baby mixed greens, loosely packed
   (totsoi, bok choy, spinach)
1 yellow bell pepper, sliced thinly
6 mushrooms, sliced thinly
<u>Sprinkle</u>
1/2 C. raw macadamia nuts
1/2-1 T. nutritional yeast
1/4 t. sea salt

<u>Dressing</u>
3 dates soaked in 1/2 C. water
1 T. mustard (stoneground)
2 T. cold-pressed olive oil
1/2 t. nutritional yeast
1/4 t. sea salt
2 t. fresh lemon juice

1. Wash and dry mixed greens and place in a salad bowl with pepper and mushrooms.
2. In a small blender cup (or blender), place macadamia nuts, yeast and salt. Pulse enough to chop nuts into small pieces but not into a paste. Set aside.
3. In a blender, blend the <u>Dressing</u> ingredients. Toss the salad with the dressing just before serving. Sprinkle with macadamia topping.

"I wish no living thing to suffer pain."

PERCY BYSSHE SHELLEY (1792-1822) ~ English poet

Sprouted Mung Bean Salad
serves 5

5 C. sprouted mung beans
2 C. carrot, grated
2 C. pok choy, spinach
  or totsoi, chopped
1 T. raw apple cider vinegar
1 t. dried oregano

2 T. fresh lemon juice + 2 T. oil
1/4 t. garlic powder
1 t. herb seasoning (page 3)
1 T. nutritional yeast
1/2 t. dill weed
sea salt or substitute, to taste

Mix all ingredients together in a bowl. Allow to marinate before serving.

Creamy Cole Slaw
serves 4

1 head cabbage, shredded
1 C. water
1/2 C. raw tahini
1/8 C. raw apple cider vinegar

1-2 t. sea salt, to taste
3 t. onion powder
1/4 C. fresh lemon juice
2 t. stoneground mustard (optional)

1. Shred the cabbage finely and set aside in a bowl.
2. Place remaining ingredients in a blender and blend thoroughly. Pour over shredded cabbage, mix well and allow to marinate.

Spicy Raw Slaw
serves 4-5

1 small head cabbage, shredded
2 C. beet, grated
1/4 C. onion, diced
2 T. raw tahini
1 T. raw apple cider vinegar

sea salt or substitute, to taste
1/2 t. mild curry powder
1/4 t. cumin powder
1 T. water

Mix all ingredients together in a bowl. Marinate for an hour before serving.

> *"...If man was what he ought to be,*
> *he would be adored by the animals..."*
>
> HENRI-FREDERIC AMIEL (1821-1881) ~ Swiss philosopher and poet

Cucumber and Cherry Tomato Salad
serves 3-4

1 C. cherry tomatoes, halved
2 long seedless cucumbers, diced
1 small sweet onion, diced
1/2 C. bell pepper, diced
1+ T. cold-pressed olive oil
1 1/2 T. apple cider vinegar
1 T. nutritional yeast

1/4 t. garlic powder
1/8 t. black pepper (or cayenne pepper)
1/4 t. dill weed
1/2 t. dried oregano
sea salt or Bragg™ Aminos, to taste
1/2 t. herb seasoning (page 3)

In a bowl, mix all ingredients together. Stir. Marinate before serving if desired.

Cucumber Vinaigrette
serves 3-4

4 C. cucumbers, sliced
4 t. cold-pressed olive oil
1 t. herb seasoning (page 3)
1 1/2 T. raw apple cider vinegar
1 T. fresh lemon juice

1/2 sweet onion, sliced thinly
1 T. nutritional yeast
sea salt/Bragg™ Liquid Aminos, to taste
1 t. dried oregano
1/4 t. black pepper (or cayenne pepper)

Mix all ingredients together in a bowl. Chill and marinate for an hour or less. Serve.

Guacamolé Dip
serves 2-3

5 small avocados (hass)
1/2 small sweet onion, diced
2 1/2 t. lemon juice (or lime)
1 tomato, diced

1 clove garlic, minced
1/2 t. garlic powder
a dash of cayenne pepper
sea salt or substitute, to taste

Mash the avocados and mix in the remaining ingredients. Serve as a dip or spread.

"Parents usually educate their children merely in such a manner that however bad the world may be, they may adapt themselves to its present conditions. But they ought to give them an education so much better than this, that a better condition of things may thereby be brought about by the future."

IMMANUEL KANT (1724-1804) ~ German philosopher

Tossed Confetti Cabbage
serves 4-6

1/2 head green cabbage, grated
2 medium beets, grated
3-4 carrots, grated
1 1/2 T. cold-pressed olive oil

1 T. nutritional yeast
3 T. raw apple cider vinegar
1/4 C. sunflower seeds
sea salt or substitute, to taste

1. In a food processor, grate the cabbage, beets and carrots and place in a bowl.
2. Sprinkle olive oil over cabbage and toss. Add remaining ingredients, toss and serve.

Stuffed Avocados
serves 4

2 large avocados (hard shelled)
2 scallions, diced
1-2 cucumbers, diced
2 tomatoes, diced
2-3 carrots, grated
1/2 C. lentil sprouts

sea salt or substitute, to taste
1/2 t. herb seasoning (page 3)
1/2 t. garlic powder
1 t. sesame seeds
2 T. nutritional yeast
a squeeze of lemon juice

Slice the avocados in half and remove the pit. Gently scoop out the avocado, removing any dark spots. Mash avocado and mix with remaining ingredients in a bowl. Place back into the shells. Decorate the top with colorful raw veggies and serve.

Avocado Tomato Jubilee
serves 2-4

5 small avocados, cubed
1-2 tomatoes, cubed
2 T. fresh dill weed, chopped
1 T. fresh lemon juice

2 slices sweet onion, diced
sea salt or substitute, to taste
a dash of cayenne pepper (optional)

Mix all ingredients together in a bowl and serve.

"If you have men who will exclude any of God's creatures from the shelter of compassion and pity, you will have men who will deal likewise with their fellow men."

ST. FRANCIS OF ASSISI (1182-1226) ~ Christian saint and mystic

Avocado Marinade
serves 4

5-6 avocados
sea salt or substitute, to taste
1 T. raw tahini
2 T. nutritional yeast

1 small sweet onion, diced
1 T. raw apple cider vinegar
1/2 t. garlic powder
a squeeze of fresh lemon juice

1. Slice the avocados in half and remove the pits. Slice into large bite-sized pieces and scoop out with a spoon. Do not mash.
2. In a bowl, mix all other ingredients with the avocado pieces. Chill and serve.

Sprouted Quinoa Salad
serves 4

1 C. sprouted quinoa
1 small tomato, diced
1/2 red bell pepper, diced

1/2 T. raw apple cider vinegar
sea salt or substitute, to taste
1 T. nutritional yeast
2 t. stoneground mustard

Soak quinoa for six hours and sprout for one day, to maintain freshness. Mix all ingredients together in a bowl. Allow to marinate for 10-30 minutes before serving.

Shittake Snow Pea Salad
serves 2-4

1 large avocado, cubed
1/2 lb. snow peas (in pods),
  washed and stemmed
1/2 C. mung bean sprouts
3 scallions, chopped
1 bunch watercress,
  washed and chopped

1/2 C. shittake mushrooms
  stemmed and sliced
1 lemon, juiced
2 T. sesame oil
sea salt or substitute, to taste
black or cayenne pepper, to taste
sesame seeds, for garnish

1. In a mixing bowl, combine avocado and vegetables and lightly toss.
2. In a separate bowl, whisk the lemon, oil, sea salt and pepper. Pour over the vegetables and toss again.
3. Place in a serving bowl and garnish with sesame seeds.

> **"A thought may touch the edge of our life with light."**
>
> JOHN TROWBRIDGE (1827-1916) ~ American author

Almond Beet & Carrot Salad
serves 4

1 3/4 C. almonds	sea salt or substitute, to taste
1 C. beet, grated	1–2 T. raw tahini
2 carrots, grated	1 1/2 t. nutritional yeast

1. Soak almonds for two to six hours, rinse, drain and slice.
2. Mix almonds with remaining ingredients. Refrigerate for 15 minutes before serving.

Lemon Walnut Salad
serves 6

2 C. walnuts	4 T. fresh lemon juice
4 C. carrots, grated	2 T. nutritional yeast
1 1/2 C. red cabbage, shredded	sea salt or Bragg™ Aminos, to taste
1/8 C. sweet onion, diced	

1. Soak walnuts for one hour. Rinse, drain and slice.
2. Mix vegetables with the walnuts. Add the remaining seasonings and stir well.

Cucumber & Snow Pea Salad
serves 4

2 C. cucumber slices	1 T. raw apple cider vinegar
1 C. snow peas	sea salt or substitute, to taste
1/4 C. red bell pepper, sliced	2 T. fresh dill, chopped
1/2 C. broccoli flowerets	2 T. cold-pressed oil (optional)

Peel and slice cucumber; mix with the vegetables. Add seasonings and herbs. Chill before serving.

"Compassion is a natural human quality, not the province of a particular religion. But unless we cultivate it in relation to ourselves and others, we will never achieve peace."

TENZIN GYATSO, 14th DALAI LAMA ~ Tibetan Buddhist priest

Chinese Cabbage Pecan Salad
serves 4-5

1 head chinese cabbage
1 C. carrots, grated
1 C. pecans, chopped
1 yellow bell pepper

sea salt or substitute, to taste
2 T. raw apple cider vinegar
2 T. nutritional yeast
1/2 t. herb seasoning (page 3)

Finely slice chinese cabbage. Mix all ingredients in a bowl. Allow to marinate and serve.

Dressed Spinach Salad
serves 2-4

4 C. spinach
1/2 yellow bell pepper, diced
2 C. mushrooms, sliced
1 long english cucumber, sliced
2 C. carrots, grated
1/4 C. raw cashews
2 T. sweet onion, diced

2-3 small tomatoes, chopped
1 T. oregano
1 1/2 T. cold-pressed olive oil
sea salt/Bragg™ Liquid Aminos, to taste
2 T. raw apple cider vinegar
1 T. nutritional yeast
1/8 t. black or cayenne pepper

1. Wash and de-stem the spinach and spin dry or drain. Tear into bite-sized pieces.
2. In a bowl, mix spinach with remaining vegetables and cashews.
3. Add the remaining ingredients. Toss. Chill and serve.

Creamy Curry Sprouted Lentil Salad
serves 4-6

4 C. sprouted lentils/mixed sprouts
2/3 C. sweet onion, diced finely
1 C. carrot, grated
Sauce
1/8 C. cold-pressed oil

1/2 C. water
1 C. cashews (soaked a little and drained)
sea salt or substitute, to taste
1/2 T. mild curry powder
1 T. fresh lemon juice

1. Place the first three ingredients in a bowl.
2. In a blender, blend the Sauce ingredients until thick and creamy. Pour over the vegetables. Mix well. Chill and allow to marinate for several hours before serving.

> *"Do unto animals as you would have them do unto you."*
>
> LIGHT ~ President and co-founder of Gentle World

Awesome Carrot Salad
serves 4-6

3 lbs. carrots, peeled, grated
2 celery stalks, diced
1 bell pepper, chopped
1 small sweet onion, diced

1 large tomato, diced
sea salt or substitute, to taste
1 1/4 C. almond "mayo" (see recipe below)
2 t. kelp

Mix all ingredients together and serve.

Almond "Mayo"
yields 1 1/4 cups

1 C. almonds (soaked 1-6 hours)
3/4 C. water
1 T. onion powder
1 t. sea salt

2-3 T. dates, pitted
1 lemon, juiced
raw apple cider vinegar, a dash
1/8 C. cold-pressed oil (optional)

1. In a food processor using the "S" shaped blade (or with a strong blender), thoroughly blend almonds with water. Add the remaining ingredients, except the oil. Process.
2. Slowly add oil or extra water, while processing, and mixture will become thick and smooth. Chill. Use in the Awesome Carrot Salad, see recipe above.

Brazil Nut "Mayo"
yields 3 cups

2 C. brazil nuts
1/8 C. cold-pressed olive oil
1 t. sea salt, to taste

1/2 C. fresh lemon juice
1/2 C. water
3 dates, soaked (optional)

1. In a food processor, using the "S" shaped blade, process the brazil nuts.
2. Slowly add oil while still processing. Add remaining ingredients. Process. Chill.

"There is nothing more difficult to take in hand, more perilous to conduct or more uncertain in its success than to take the lead in the introduction of a new order of things."

~

"Where the willingness is great, the difficulties can not be great."

NICCOLO MACHIAVELLI (1469-1527) ~ Florentine statesman

Dressings, Dips, Soups and more!

Green Goddess Dressing
yields 2 cups

3/4 C. water
1 avocado (hass)
3 T. fresh lemon juice

sea salt or substitute, to taste
a dash of garlic & onion powder
1/4 C. fresh herbs (parsley, cilantro, basil)

In a blender, blend all ingredients until creamy. Serve fresh.

Avocado Dressing
yields 2 cups

1/4 C. cold-pressed olive oil
1/4 C. fresh basil
1 clove garlic, minced
1/2 T. fresh herbs of choice
1/4 t. onion powder
1/8 t. cayenne pepper (optional)

1/4 C. avocado
2 T. nutritional yeast
sea salt or substitute, to taste
1 C. water
2 T. fresh lemon juice

In a blender, blend all ingredients until creamy. Serve fresh.

Tahini Dressing
yields 1 1/2 cups

1 C. water
1/2 C. raw tahini
Bragg™ Aminos or substitute, to taste

1/2 T. fresh lemon juice (optional)
curry or other spices, to taste (optional)

In a blender, blend all ingredients. Use 1/4 cup less water for a thicker dressing.

> *"Every man who has ever been earnest to preserve his higher or poetic faculties in the best condition, has been particularly inclined to abstain from animal food."*
>
> HENRY DAVID THOREAU (1817-1862) ~ American author, poet, naturalist

Cucumber Walnut Dressing
yields 2 cups

1 C. water
1/2 C. walnuts
1 small cucumber
sea salt or substitute, to taste
3-4 t. nutritional yeast

1 small tomato
  (or 1/2 of a large tomato)
1/2 t. garlic powder
2 bunches parsley (stems removed)
1/2 t. onion powder

In a blender, blend all ingredients until smooth.

Tomato Vinaigrette
yields 1 1/4 cups

3/4 C. tomato, diced
1/2 C. cucumber, diced
2 T. red or green onion, diced
2 T. fresh lemon juice
sea salt or substitute, to taste
1 T. olive oil (optional)

1 T. nutritional yeast
a dash of garlic-pepper
1/4 t. onion powder
2 T. water
1/2-1 T. oregano
1/2 T. basil

In a blender, blend all ingredients until creamy. Chill and serve.

Sunny Dressing
yields 2 1/4 cups

3/4 C. sunflower seeds,
  soaked a few minutes in water
1 1/2 C. water
2 T. raw tahini
2 T. fresh parsley, chopped
1 T. red onion, diced

1/2 C. scallion, diced
1/4 t. garlic-pepper
a dash of cayenne pepper
3/4 T. nutritional yeast
sea salt or substitute, to taste
2 T. fresh herbs of choice

In a blender, blend the seeds with half a cup of water until creamy and smooth. Add the remaining water and ingredients. Blend, chill and serve.

> *"The decision to go vegan has been one of the most rewarding choices I have ever made.*
> *Not only do I feel great, but my taste buds have been opened to a whole new world of culinary delight."*
>
> ALICIA SILVERSTONE ~ American actress

Sweet Dill Dressing
yields 2 cups

6 dates (pitted), soaked in water
1 C. fresh dill, packed into cup
1/4 C. fresh lemon juice
1/4 C. cold-pressed olive oil

1 T. nutritional yeast
1 T. mustard (stoneground)
2 T. miso (unpasteurized)

1. Soak dates in 1 1/2 cups of water until softened. In a blender, blend dates with their water. Add dill and blend until smooth.
2. Add remaining ingredients and blend thoroughly.

Oriental Dressing
yields 2 cups

7 dates, pitted, soaked in water
1/4 C. sesame or olive oil
2 cloves garlic, diced
1/2 t. ginger, peeled, diced

2 t. miso
1/4 C. raw tahini
1/4 t. sea salt
1 t. mustard (stoneground)

1. Soak dates in two cups of water until softened.
2. In a blender, mix olive oil, garlic and ginger with one cup of date soak water, thoroughly blending the garlic and ginger pieces.
3. Add dates with remaining water and ingredients and blend until smooth.

Fresh Salsa
yields 1 small bowl

2 C. fresh tomatoes, diced
3 T. sweet onion, diced
sea salt or substitute, to taste
1 T. nutritional yeast

1/2 T. raw apple cider vinegar or lemon
1/4-1/2 C. fresh cilantro, chopped
1/2 t. mexican seasoning and/or cumin
fresh garlic/hot pepper, to taste, minced
cayenne, to taste (optional)

1. Place tomatoes and onions in a small bowl.
2. Mix in remaining ingredients. Stir, chill and serve.

• Optional ~ Blend some of the tomato with the seasonings and stir into salsa.

(looking into an aquarium)
"Now I can look at you in peace; I don't eat you any more."

FRANZ KAFKA (1883-1924) ~ Austrian-Czech author

Pesto Sauce
serves 2-3

1 C. pine nuts (or raw cashews)
3-4 cloves garlic, diced
3 T. water

sea salt or substitute, to taste
1/3 C. cold-pressed olive oil
2 C. fresh basil, chopped

1. Soak the pine nuts in water for 5-10 minutes then rinse and drain water.
2. In a food processor, using the "S" shaped blade, blend all ingredients until smooth.

Spicy Mexican Tomato Sauce
serves 4

1 lb. tomatoes, chopped
1 red onion, diced
3 large cloves garlic, diced
1 jalapeño pepper, seeded & diced
3 T. fresh cilantro, minced
1 red bell pepper, chopped

1 red bell pepper, chopped
1 T. fresh lemon juice
sea salt, to taste
cayenne pepper, to taste
1 t. chili powder
1 t. cumin powder

1. Blend tomatoes, onion, garlic and jalapeño pepper in a blender. Place in a bowl and add cilantro, peppers, lemon juice and seasonings.
2. Allow to stand for 30 minutes at room temperature. Stir and re-season if needed.
3. Serve over greens and veggies with avocado.

Nacho Sauce
yields 2 cups

1 C. raw cashews, soaked
1/4 C. water
1/2 C. fresh salsa
3 T. nutritional yeast
sea salt or substitute, to taste

2 t. mexican blend spice
1/2 t. garlic powder
1 t. onion powder
1/2 t. kelp
1 t. fresh lemon juice

1. Soak cashews for five minutes and drain. Thoroughly blend with water in a food processor, using the "S" shaped blade. When creamy, add the remaining ingredients and blend.
2. Serve with sunflower corn chips (page 216) or as a dip.

> **"Vegetarianism is the cure for 99% of the world's problems. Think about it..."**
>
> CASEY KASEM ~ American top 40 radio announcer

Italian Tomato Sauce *(rich and creamy)*
yields 2 1/2 cups

3 oz. sun-dried tomatoes
3 dates (pitted)
1 large tomato
1/4 C. cold-pressed olive oil

1 T. oregano
sea salt or substitute, to taste
2 T. nutritional yeast
1/2 C. fresh basil

1. Place dried tomatoes in a bowl and cover with water. Soak for at least one hour (until soft). Cover dates with water and soak for 20 minutes.
2. Place all ingredients in a blender, including all soak water and blend thoroughly, adding more water only if needed. Sauce should be thick and creamy.
3. This is a great Italian sauce, used in pizza (page 209) and stuffed peppers (page 210).

Oriental Sauce
yields 1 1/2 cups

1/4 C. olive/sesame oil (cold-pressed)
2 cloves garlic, diced
1/2 t. ginger, diced
7 dates (pitted), soaked in 1 C. water

1 t. miso
1 t. mustard (stoneground)
1/4 t. sea salt

Blend olive oil, garlic and ginger with dates and half a cup date soak water, blending thoroughly. Add remaining ingredients and blend.
• Serve over soaked and sprouted wild rice with diced vegetables.

Miso Tahini Dipping Sauce
yields about 1 1/2 cups

2/3 C. water
2-3 T. miso
1/2 C. raw tahini

2 T. nutritional yeast
1/2 t. stoneground mustard
1/2 t. fresh lemon juice

In a blender or bowl, thoroughly mix all ingredients. Serve in a bowl circled with fresh vegetables. Use as a dip or as a spread for sprouted breads and crackers.

Curry Almond Sauce *(use with Mock Salmon Loaf - page 212)*

1/2 C. almonds (soaked 1-6 hours)
1 C. carrot juice
2 t. curry powder

1/4 t. herb seasoning (page 3)
1/2 t. tomatillo juice

Soak and drain the almonds. Blend all ingredients in a blender until creamy. Add more almonds for a thicker sauce.

Cashew Carrot Paté *(a favorite!)*
serves 3-4

2 carrots, peeled and chopped
1 celery stalk, chopped
2-3 cloves garlic, diced
1 slice sweet onion

1 C. cashews (soaked for 15 minutes)
Bragg™ Aminos or substitute, to taste
1/4 C. cold-pressed oil
sea salt, to taste

1. In a food processor, using the "S" shaped blade, blend the vegetables to a fine consistency.
2. Drain the water from the cashews. Add them to the processor and process along with the remaining ingredients. (Or use soaked almonds or sunflower seeds instead of cashews.) Stop periodically and scrape the sides with a rubber spatula. Continue to blend until creamy. Chill and serve.

Pesto Paté
yields 3 cups

1 C. brazil nuts
1 1/2 C. walnuts
1/2 C. almonds
1/3 C. nutritional yeast
3/4 C. water
1/4 sweet onion, chopped
2 T. cold-pressed olive oil

3/4 t. sea salt
1 clove garlic
1 t. onion powder
1/2 t. garlic powder
1/2 C. fresh parsley
3 1/2-4 C. fresh basil, firmly packed

1. Soak all nuts for 15 minutes then drain and rinse. In a food processor, using the "S" shaped blade, whiz the basil and parsley. Remove from processor.
2. Process the drained nuts and remaining ingredients until smooth.
3. Add the basil and parsley and process until creamy. Chill before serving.

> *"I have lived primarily on sprouted seeds, beans, grains and nuts for more than two decades. Not only have I healed my body of colitis and arthritis following such a regimen, but I have also achieved a greater level of vitality and health than I had even as a child – and I am no child at seventy-seven. And my hair has returned to its natural brown color, too!"*
>
> ANN WIGMORE, D.D. (1909-1994) ~ teacher, author, living foods proponent
> quoted from <u>The Sprouting Book</u>

Pink Paté
yields approx. 2 1/2 cups

1 clove garlic, diced	*1 3/4 C. cashews (soaked 10 minutes)*
1/2 C. sweet onion, diced	*1 C. beet, grated*
2 T. cold-pressed oil	*1/4 C. fresh corn kernels (cut from cob)*
sea salt or substitute, to taste	

In a food processor, whiz the garlic, onion and liquids first; then add the softened cashew pieces. Add the beet and corn kernels. Process until smooth and creamy, occasionally scraping sides with a rubber spatula. Chill to solidify before serving.

Sunny Almond Paté
serves 2–3

2 small carrots, sliced	*sea salt or substitute, to taste*
1/4 of a beet, sliced	*4 T. water*
2 slices sweet onion	*2 T. cold-pressed oil*
1/2 C. almonds, soaked	*1 t. herb seasoning (page 3)*
1/2 C. sunflower seeds, soaked	

1. In a food processor, using the "S" shaped blade, blend the carrots, beet and onion finely. Add the soaked nuts and remaining ingredients. Process until smooth and creamy. Use a rubber spatula to scrape the sides periodically.
2. Chill to solidify before serving. Great as a healthy sandwich spread or use as a dip.

Raw Hummus
serves 4

1 1/2 C. garbanzo beans	*2 cloves garlic*
sprouted (see page 180)	*2 T. fresh lemon juice*
3 T. fresh parsley, finely chopped	*2 t. herb seasoning (page 3)*
1 1/2 T. raw tahini	*1 t. cumin powder*
	sea salt, to taste

In a food processor, using the "S" shaped blade, homogenize sprouted garbanzo beans. Add remaining ingredients and process until smooth. Chill and serve.

"Pity melts the mind to love."

JOHN DRYDEN (1631-1700) ~ English poet and playwright

...rn Soup

...t corn kernels
...d
...ini

1 T. nutritional yeast (optional)
1-2 T. green onion, chopped
1/4 t. sea salt

...tes in one cup of water until softened. (If corn is very sweet, filtered water can replace date water.)
2. Remove corn from cob. Blend all ingredients in a blender and serve.

Corn Sesame Chowder
yields 3 cups   recipe from Optimum Health Institute

1 1/2 C. sesame milk (see below)
2 C. corn (removed from cob)
1 green onion
1/3 avocado

1 t. Bragg™ Liquid Aminos
   (or sea salt, to taste)
1/4 t. coriander
1/8-1/4 t. fresh nutmeg, grated

1. In a blender, blend 1/3 C. sesame seeds with a small amount of water and purée. Add additional water to make 1 1/2 cups of milk.
2. Put 1 1/3 cups of corn and remaining ingredients in the blender. Blend until very smooth (about three minutes).
3. Put remaining corn kernels into individual bowls, add soup, stir and serve.

Spinach Cilantro Soup
yields 3 1/2 cups   recipe from Optimum Health Institute

3 C. spinach leaves
1 C. fresh cilantro
1 1/2 C. fresh tomato juice
1 C. fresh carrot juice
1 large avocado

2 cloves garlic
4 green scallions
1/2 t. kelp
1/2 t. basil
1/2 t. onion powder

1. Wash and remove stems from spinach and cilantro.
2. Place juice and all ingredients in a Vita-Mix or strong blender. Blend thoroughly and serve fresh or chilled.

> **"The conscience is God's presence in man."**
>
> EMANUEL SWEDENBORG (1688-1772) ~ Swedish theologian, scientist and philosopher

Rawsome Entrées

Sunflower Vegetable Burgers
yields 8-10 burgers

1/2 C. almonds	5 carrots, grated finely
4 C. sunflower seeds	1 beet, grated finely
2 celery stalks, diced	sea salt or substitute, to taste
1/2 bell pepper, diced	1 T. raw tahini
2 scallions/small sweet onion	3 T. nutritional yeast

1. Soak the almonds for 4-5 hours and the sunflower seeds for at least half an hour. Drain the nuts and seeds and put them through the food processor using the "S" shaped blade or Champion® juicer to homogenize (not juice) them. Save 1/4-1/2 cup of whole sunflower seeds for texture.
2. Dice celery, pepper and onions and place in a bowl.
3. Mix the processed nuts and seeds with the diced vegetables. Add the finely grated carrot and beet. (These can also be put through the processor/juicer for a smoother consistency.) Add the seasonings, tahini and nutritional yeast, and mix well.
4. Form into patties and dehydrate for three or more hours (in the oven at 101°) until dry on the outside, and firm. They can also be enjoyed un-dehydrated.

Oat Groat Energizer
serves 4-5

2 C. oat groats	Bragg™ Aminos or sea salt, to taste
2 celery stalks, diced small	4 T. fresh lemon juice
1 C. sprouts, chopped	2 T. cold-pressed oil
(buckwheat or sunflower)	2 T. nutritional yeast
1/4-1/2 sweet onion, diced	a dash of cayenne pepper
2 T. fresh parsley, chopped	

Soak oat groats in water for 10-12 hours, rinse and drain. Mix all ingredients together in a bowl. Allow to marinate before serving.

"To admit that we have the right to inflict unnecessary suffering is to destroy the very basis of human society."

JOHN GALSWORTHY (1867-1933) ~ English novelist and dramatist
recipient of 1932 Nobel Prize for literature

Mexican Mostadas
serves 5-6

Tostada

1 1/4 C. fresh water	1 t. onion powder
sea salt or substitute, to taste	1 t. garlic powder
2 T. nutritional yeast	2 C. flax seeds
1 T. mexican spice	1 C. grated carrot
a dash of cumin powder	1 C. raw pumpkin seeds

1. Mix together water, sea salt, nutritional yeast, mexican spice, cumin, onion powder and garlic powder. Add flax seeds and let sit for 30 minutes until gelled.
2. Add carrots and pumpkin seeds; mix.
3. Spread onto Teflex® (non-stick) dehydrator sheets into four flat circles per sheet.
4. Dehydrate at 101° for two hours (in dehydrator or oven). Flip crackers over and dehydrate for two more hours or until crispy.

Guacamolé
6 hass avocados
1 cob sweet corn
1 (6 oz.) can olives
sea salt or substitute, to taste

Mash avocados. Cut corn off the cob. Slice olives. Mix all ingredients together until creamy.

Salsa: double the Fresh Salsa recipe (page 201)
Other ingredients: sunflower or alfalfa sprouts

Putting together Mexican Mostadas

1. Spread guacamole on tostada.
2. Spread salsa on guacamolé.
3. Top with fresh sprouts and a spicy Nasturtium flower.
4. To keep tostadas crisp, serve immediately.

"Justice and power must be brought together, so that whatever is just may be powerful and whatever is powerful may be just."

BLAISE PASCAL (1623-1662) ~ French moralist

Beets-a-Pizza
yields 6-7 small pizzas

Crust	White Sauce
2 C. flax seeds, soaked 10 min.	2 1/2 C. brazil nuts or cashews (soaked)
1 t. sea salt	1 1/2 T. fresh lemon juice
2 T. fresh basil	1-2 t. sea salt
1 T. fresh oregano	1 t. Bragg™ Aminos (or extra sea salt)
1 t. each onion & garlic powder	1-1 1/4 C. water
1/4 C. onion	1/4 C. nutritional yeast
1 beet, grated	Toppings
2 C. sunflower seeds, soaked 15 min.	1 C. beets, grated
3 medium ears of corn	1 C. carrots, grated
1 large clove garlic	2 tomatoes, diced
Red Sauce	1 C. olives, sliced
3 dates (pitted)	1/2 C. fresh basil, chopped
3 oz. sun-dried tomatoes	1/2 C. onion, diced
1 whole tomato	Sprinkle
sea salt or substitute, to taste	1 C. walnuts or almonds
1 T. oregano	1 T. nutritional yeast
1/2 C. fresh basil	2 t. dried oregano
1/4 C. cold-pressed olive oil	1 T. dried basil
2 T. nutritional yeast	1 t. sea salt

1. Soak flax seeds, adding dry seasonings to the water. In a food processor, using the "S" shaped blade, chop the beet into fine pieces. Add soaked sunflower seeds to the processor and process into a paste, adding a little water if necessary. Remove from processor. Place remaining crust ingredients, including soaked flax seeds, into processor and blend. Combine with first mixture. Thoroughly mix in a bowl. Form into 3-4 inch flat circles on dehydrator sheets and dehydrate for 5-7 hours until crust is firm. (Remember to flip crusts over half-way through.)
2. Red Sauce: Soak dates and dried tomatoes together until soft, with just enough water to cover. Blend all ingredients in a blender, including date and tomato soak water.
3. White Sauce: Drain nuts & process ingredients in a food processor until smooth.
4. When ready to serve, place crust on a plate. Spread on red sauce then white sauce. Top with grated beet, carrot, diced tomato, olives, onion and fresh herbs.
5. Pulse Sprinkle ingredients in a food processor or blender cup and sprinkle on top.

Raw Parmazano (alternative topping for pizza)
yields 3/4 cup

1/2 C. almonds/walnuts, ground	1/2 t. herb seasoning (page 3)
1/4 C. nutritional yeast	

1. Pulse almonds in a food processor using the "S" shaped blade. Do not make a paste.
2. Put in a jar and add nutritional yeast and herb seasoning; mix.
3. Sprinkle on your salad, pasta, raw pizza, etc.

Pesto Pizza
yields 6 small pizza pies

Raw Pizza Crust
4 C. sprouted wheat berries
1 t. onion powder
1 t. dried basil
1 t. dried oregano
1/2 t. garlic powder
Pesto Sauce
1 C. pine nuts
1-2 cloves garlic, diced
1-2 C. fresh basil, chopped

1/8 C. water
sea salt or substitute, to taste
1 T. nutritional yeast
Toppings
1/2 C. carrots, grated
1/2 C. beets, grated
1-2 tomatoes, diced
1/3 C. onion, diced
1/3 C. peppers, diced
1/3 C. mushrooms, sliced

1. Put sprouted wheat berries through a Champion® juicer. Use the juicing screen. This will remove some of the excess gluten. Discard the liquid.
2. Thoroughly mix the remaining dough ingredients in with the wheat berries.
3. Press dough into small, personal-sized circles on flat dehydrating sheets (4 per sheet). Dehydrate at 100° for three hours; turn over and continue for another three hours until dough is firm but not dried out. (If you don't have a dehydrator, place the pizza crusts in an oven at 100° for several hours, or use a solar dryer.)
4. Blend all pesto sauce ingredients in a food processor until creamy. Spread on finished rounds of pizza crust. Add toppings and serve.

Stuffed Sweet Peppers
yields 10

10 sweet yellow bell peppers
2 tomatoes, diced
1 cucumber, diced
2 T. fresh basil, chopped

1/4 t. sea salt
2 T. nutritional yeast
Italian tomato sauce (page 203)

1. Cut stem end off peppers, and remove core and seeds. Trim off and save any good pepper from this. Place peppers in a dish with sides where they fit tightly and hold each other up.
2. Dice the extra pepper pieces and mix in a bowl with tomato, cucumber, basil, sea salt and nutritional yeast.
3. Make Italian tomato sauce and mix half a cup of the sauce in with the tomato cucumber mixture. Pour this into each pepper, filling to just below the top.
4. Top peppers with extra tomato sauce and sprinkle with Raw Parmazano (pg. 209).
5. Serve with extra tomato sauce on top or on the side.

Tasty Wild Rice Burritos
serves 5

2 C. dry wild rice = 4 C. sprouted
sea salt or substitute, to taste
1/4 t. cumin powder
2 T. nutritional yeast
1 clove garlic, diced finely

1 (6 oz.) can olives
2-3 avocados, cubed
1-2 tomatoes, diced
1/8-1/4 C. cilantro, chopped
chard leaves or lettuce leaves

1. Soak wild rice for two to three days (until soft). It will take longer in colder climates. Drain and rinse each day, and again before use. Store in refrigerator.
2. Place soaked wild rice in a bowl. Add sea salt, cumin, nutritional yeast and garlic and mix well.
3. Dice olives, avocados, tomatoes and cilantro and fold into the rice mixture.
4. Wrap like a burrito in lettuce leaves or dark green leaves of choice.

Stuffed Tomatoes
serves 4

4 large tomatoes (ripe but not soft)
2/3 C. carrot, grated
1 C. avocado, cubed
1/2 C. avocado, mashed
1 t. sea salt
1 T. cilantro, chopped
1 t. fresh lemon juice
1 T. dill, chopped (optional)

Sauce
drained juice from tomatoes
4 T. cashews (soaked & drained)
3 T. avocado
sea salt or substitute, to taste
1 t. fresh lemon juice

1. Remove stem and slice 1/8" off the top of the tomato. Gently scoop out the inside and put it in a strainer, over a bowl. Save the liquid, on the side, for the sauce.
2. Mix strained tomato insides with other stuffing ingredients (all but the sauce ingredients). Then fill the tomato shells with this mixture. Place on a serving plate.
3. In a blender, blend sauce ingredients, adding water only if needed. Sauce should be thick. Pour over tomatoes. Garnish and serve.

> *"On a diet of raw plant foods, the diseased cells heal,
> the emaciated ones recuperate, the inactive
> regain their vitality...Raw nutrients spread throughout
> the body, relax the organs, and grant health,
> strength, vigor, long life and success."*
>
> WOLFE, ARLIN & DINI ~ American authors, <u>Nature's First Law; The Raw Food Diet</u>

Seed Balls
serves 12   recipe from The Optimum Health Institute

1 red bell pepper	1/2 C. sesame seeds
1 bunch green onions	1 C. sunflower seeds
1 bunch celery	1 T. dehydrated basil
1 yellow onion	1 T. caraway or dill
1 bunch parsley	1-2 t. dulse (a seaweed)
3 small zucchini	1-2 t. garlic powder

1. Finely mince green pepper, green onions, celery, yellow onion and parsley. Place in a bowl. Shred zucchini and add to the bowl. Mix.
2. Grind seeds to a fine powder and add to bowl. Grind basil and caraway/dill. Add to bowl and mix well. Add dulse and garlic and mix thoroughly.
3. Form into balls. Dehydrate at 102° until firm, but not hard; about six hours.

Mock Salmon Loaf with Almond Curry Sauce
serves 4   recipe from The Optimum Health Institute

2 C. almonds (soaked & drained)	2 t. kelp
2 medium carrots	1 t. curry powder
1 C. celery, diced	1/4 C. carrot juice
1/2 C. green onions, diced	1/4 C. tomatillo juice

1. With a Champion® juicer, using the blank insert, homogenize the almonds and carrots alternating one and the other.
2. In a bowl, mix celery, onion, seasonings and juice. Add the homogenized carrots and almonds; then mix thoroughly.
3. Shape mixture into a loaf. (Also delicious made into veggie burgers and dehydrated.)
4. Top loaf or burgers with Curry Almond Sauce (page 203).

The Optimum Health Institute of San Diego
6970 Central Ave., Lemon Grove, CA. 91945
(619) 464-3346
optimum@optimumhealth.org

"Diabetes is not necessarily a one-way street.
Early studies suggest that persons with diabetes can improve
and, in some cases, even cure themselves of the disease
by switching to an unrefined, vegan diet."

ANDREW NICHOLSON, M.D. ~ Physicians Committee for Responsible Medicine

Italian Zucchini Boats
yields 4 boats

2 medium-large zucchini
1/2 T. fresh lemon juice
sea salt or substitute, to taste
1/8 C. cold-pressed oil
2 C. carrot & 2 C. beet, grated
1/2 t. oregano
1/2 t. basil

1/2 t. garlic powder
2 t. nutritional yeast
1/4 C. scallions, diced
1/2 t. dill weed
1/2 t. herb seasoning (page 3)
1 T. raw apple cider vinegar

1. Wash the zucchini and remove stems. Slice in half lengthwise. Gently cut out the insides (avoiding breaking the outer shell).
2. Place the zucchini shells in a shallow plate or dish with lemon juice, sea salt and oil to marinate (1/8 cup water can replace oil).
3. Grate or dice the insides of the zucchini, carrots and beets. Mix together and season with the remaining ingredients.
4. Fill the shells with the grated vegetable mixture. Chill and serve.

Raw Nori Rolls
yields 6 rolls

6 nori sheets
2 C. paté/spread (pg. 204 & 205)
1 C. carrots, shredded
1 C. beets, shredded
1 avocado, sliced
4 C. baby greens or sprouts

1 C. mushrooms, sliced
(marinated in oil, Bragg's, spices, vinegar or lemon)
<u>Dipping Sauce</u>
2 T. water & sea salt, to taste
1 t. nutritional yeast
a dash of cayenne

1. Lay out the nori sheets. Place a scoop of paté at the bottom of one sheet and spread to the edges.
2. Sprinkle with shredded beet and carrot. Add sliced avocado. Top with sliced marinated mushrooms and a small layer of baby greens or sprouts. Roll up tightly, wetting the top of the nori edge to help it stick together.
3. Slice each roll into 6–8 rounds. Serve with a bowl of dipping sauce.

"In fact, every kind of creature that does not eat meat was there, living peaceably and happily with the others in this land where vegetable food abounded..."

HUGH LOFTING (1889-1947) ~ British author, from <u>Dr. Dolittle's Post Office</u>

Dehydrated Breads and Crackers

Sprouted breads have been around for centuries, and are becoming a staple in the raw food diet. Whole wheat berries have more gluten and make a sweeter more doughy bread. Juicing the wheat berries first removes the gluten and makes a lighter, crispier bread. Directions for sprouting wheat berries are given on page 180.

Sweet Wheat Essene Bread
yields 8 loaves

4 C. sprouted wheat berries	1/4+ C. raisins
2 small bananas, sliced	1 T. maple syrup (optional)

1. Homogenize wheat berries through the Champion® juicer. (Use the juicing screen, to remove some gluten and excess liquid.)
2. Mix in raisins, bananas, and sweetener.
3. Flatten or make small thin loaves on a tray to dehydrate. Dehydrate for five hours. Flip over for another 3-4 hours until bread is firm and not sticking to tray.

Herb Essene Bread
yields 8-10 loaves

4 C. sprouted wheat berries	3 T. fresh parsley
1/2 C. carrots, finely grated	2 T. fresh basil
1-2 t. sea salt (or substitute) to taste	(or use your favorite herbs)

1. Homogenize wheat berries through the Champion® juicer. (Use the juicing screen, to remove some gluten and excess liquid.)
2. Mix in grated carrots, seasonings and herbs to the dough.
3. Flatten or form into thin loaves and put on trays to dehydrate. Dehydrate for four hours; flip over and continue dehydrating until firm. If a dehydrator is not available, dehydrate in the oven below 101°.

> *"So act that your principle of action might safely be made a law for the whole world."*
>
> IMMANUEL KANT (1724-1804) ~ German philosopher

Flax & Sesame Crackers
yields 8-9 dehydrator sheets

4 C. dry flax seeds	*2 t. sea salt*
5 1/2 C. water	*1 1/2 C. sesame seeds*
1 t. onion powder	*1/2 C. carrots, grated (optional)*

1. Place all ingredients into a bowl and mix well. Set aside to gel for 20-25 minutes.
2. Spread into flat rounds on Teflex®(non-stick) dehydrator sheets and dehydrate for four hours. Turn each round over onto a mesh sheet and dehydrate for four more hours until crisp.

Sprouted Chapati
yields 1 large chapati

4 C. sprouted wheat berries	*2-3 t. fresh herbs*
3 T. sesame seeds	*1 t. cold-pressed olive (or other oil)*

1. Juice wheat berries through Champion® juicer; mix in fresh herbs or other seasoning.
2. Lightly oil the baking sheet or dehydrating tray and sprinkle with sesame seeds. Roll or flatten out dough and place on sheet, on top of the sesame seeds.
3. Dehydrate at 101° for three hours; flip over for another 2-3 hours or until firm.

Carrot Sunflower Crackers

3 C. sunflower seeds	*2 cloves garlic*
1/2 C. walnuts	*1/4 sweet onion*
7 large carrots	*3 T. fresh basil, chopped*
2 beets	*1-2 T. fresh herbs*

1. Homogenize all ingredients, except herbs, in a food processor using the "S" shaped blade, or through a Champion® juicer using the blank plate, not the juicing screen.
2. Mix well, adding the herbs.
3. Roll or flatten onto dehydrating tray and dehydrate for four hours at 104°. Cut to cracker size, spread out on tray and continue to dehydrate until crisp.

"God offers to every mind a choice between truth and repose.
Take which you please...you can never have both"

~

"The greatest homage we can pay to truth is to use it."

RALPH WALDO EMERSON (1803-1882) ~ American philosopher, poet and essayist

Sunflower Corn Chips

1 2/3 C. sunflower seeds	1 1/2 C. fresh corn kernels
2 carrots	1/2 t. sea salt
1/4 C. flax seeds soaked in 1/4 C. water	

1. Soak (hulled) sunflower seeds for one hour. Rinse and drain.
2. Peel and cut carrots and blend in a food processor with the "S" shaped blade until finely chopped. Add remaining ingredients and blend thoroughly.
3. Press into circles on Teflex® (non-stick) sheets and dehydrate for 5-6 hours until crisp, flipping half-way through. Serve with nacho sauce or a dip (pages 202 & 204).

Carrot Sesame Crackers

carrots (20 medium-sized)	3/4 C. almonds (soaked)
1 beet, sliced	1/4 C. walnuts
2 cloves garlic	1/4 C. fresh basil
3 C. sunflower seeds (soaked)	1/2 C. sesame seeds
1/4 C. fresh parsley	2-3 t. herb seasoning (page 3)

1. Peel the carrots and homogenize through the Champion® juicer with the rest of the ingredients, except the sesame seeds and herb seasoning. (Do not use juicing screen.)
2. Thoroughly mix together in a bowl, adding the herb seasoning and sesame seeds.
3. When mixed, roll or press onto dehydrating sheets. Dehydrate for 3-4 hours at 104° on one side; turn and dehydrate for three more hours on the second side, until crisp.

Sunflower Spread *(for crackers)*

2 C. sunflower seeds	2 T. fresh dill
5 carrots, peeled and sliced	sea salt or substitute, to taste
3 T. water	3 T. nutritional yeast
2 T. fresh herbs	1/4 C. sweet onion, diced

Soak sunflower seeds for one hour. Rinse and drain. In a food processor, blend seeds and carrots using the "S" shaped blade. Add water to help blade spin; then add the remaining seasonings. Process until smooth. Serve chilled.

above: **Tasty Wild Rice Burritos** *(page 211)* ~ *below:* **Aramé & Cabbage Salad** *(page 190)*

"So with a boundless heart should one cherish all living beings."

THE BUDDHA (circa 1563-483 BC) ~ Indian avatar

Rawsome Treats and Beverages

Frozen Bananas

1. Freeze only very ripe bananas (peels should be speckled).
2. When bananas are ripe, remove peels. Tip ends if necessary and cut away any bruised spots. Place in a plastic bag and freeze overnight or longer.
3. Use frozen bananas for smoothies, sorbéts, yogurt and 'Nice Cream' (a soft ice cream alternative - see below). Slice bananas and dip in carob sauce or tahini-maple syrup sauce for a quick and delicious treat.

Banana 'Nice Cream'

> *6 bananas, frozen*
> *2 T. raw tahini (or any nut butter)*

Homogenize frozen bananas through a Champion® juicer. Add tahini or nut butter for a richer ice cream. (Blend in food processor if you don't have a Champion.) Eat immediately or freeze for a firmer 'Nice Cream'.
- Variation ~ Make a serving of carob-tahini fudge (page 220) and swirl through the 'Nice Cream' before freezing.

Banini or Vanilla (Malted) Shake
yields 1 blender

> *ice cold water*   *1/4 C. raw tahini*
> *4 bananas, peeled & frozen, sliced*   *1 T. maple syrup (optional)*
> *1 t. vanilla*   *1 fresh banana, peeled*

In a blender, start with one cup of ice cold water. Add the remaining ingredients and blend. If too thick, add more water. Sweeten to taste. Suggested variations ~ add fresh strawberry, carob or mint.

Carob Smoothie

> *1 C. ice cold water*   *1 T. date sugar or maple syrup*
> *1 3/4 C. frozen banana slices*   *1 T. carob powder*
> *2 1/4 T. nut butter or tahini*   *1/8 t. mint oil (optional)*

In a blender, blend all the ingredients. Use ice cold water for best results.

*above: **Blueberry Cream Pie** (page 221)*
*below left: **Papaya Pleasure Smoothie** (page 219) ~ below right: **Aloe Orange Julius** (page 219)*

Orange Banana Smoothie
yields 2 glasses

> 1 C. fresh orange juice
> 1 1/2-2 C. banana, frozen (pg. 217)
>
> 1 T. maple syrup (optional)

Slice frozen bananas. Blend all ingredients in a blender. Refreshing and delicious!

Fresh Mango Smoothie
yields 2 glasses

> 1 mango (medium-sized Hayden)
> 1 C. fresh orange juice
>
> 1 1/2 C. banana, frozen and sliced

Remove mango from pit and place in a blender (including juice). Add orange juice. Add the frozen banana slices, a little at a time, and blend. Serve immediately.

Tropical Fruit Smoothie
yields 4 cups

> 1 papaya (fresh or frozen)
> 1 C. fresh mango
> 1/2 C. pineapple, cubed
>
> 2 bananas (peeled & frozen), sliced
> 1 1/2 C. fresh orange or pineapple juice

Cut the fruit into small pieces and place in a blender. Add half of the juice and blend. Add the remaining juice and blend thoroughly.

Summer Harvest Blend
yields 4 cups

> 2 bananas (peeled & frozen), sliced
> 1 C. strawberries
> 1/2 C. blueberries or raspberries
>
> 2 peaches or nectarines
> 1 1/2 C. apple juice

Slice the bananas and peaches. Place half of the fruit in a blender with half of the juice and blend. Add the remaining fruit and juice and blend thoroughly.

> *"The gods created certain kinds of beings to replenish our bodies...they are the trees and the plants and the seeds."*
>
> PLATO (circa 428-347 B.C.) ~ Greek philosopher

Papaya Pleasure Smoothie
yields 3/4 of a blender

2-3 small strawberry papayas
1 C. ice cold water
2 bananas (peeled & frozen)

1/2 t. vanilla
1-2 T. maple syrup
1 fresh banana

Slice frozen bananas. In a blender, blend all ingredients until smooth.

Fresh Fruit Sorbét
serves 2-3

3 bananas (peeled & frozen)
1 C. mango (frozen), sliced
1 C. papaya (fresh or frozen)

1/2 C. pineapple (frozen), sliced
1/2 C. fresh orange juice

Slice frozen banana. Mix all ingredients together in a food processor (or Vita Mix®) a little at a time, blending into a cream. Delicious and creamy served immediately or freeze to make sherbet.)

Wheatgrass/Orange Juice Cocktail
serves 2

2 C. fresh orange juice
2 oz. fresh wheatgrass juice

a squeeze of lime

Mix the above ingredients and drink immediately for full vitality.

Aloe Orange Julius

1 1/2 C. orange juice
4 T. fresh aloe (scooped out from skin)
1 oz. wheatgrass juice (optional)
1/2 frozen banana, sliced (optional)

Blend all ingredients until smooth. Serve.

"The world has been harsh and strange.
Something is wrong; there needeth a change."

ROBERT BROWNING (1812-1889) ~ English poet

Coconut Cashew Balls
yields 12 balls

3/4 C. cashew pieces
6 dates, pitted (medjool)
3 T. maple syrup

3 T. raw tahini
6 T. coconut (fresh), shredded

1. Place all the ingredients in a food processor and blend, using the "S" shaped blade.
2. Roll into balls and refrigerate or freeze before serving.

Carob Tahini Fudge
yields about 2 cups

1 C. raw carob powder
1/2 C. raw tahini
2 dates, pitted, soaked

1/4 C. maple syrup
1/8 C. water (from date soak)

Blend all ingredients thoroughly in a food processor. Freeze and serve.

Carob Chunkies
yields 8

1/3 C. raw tahini or nut butter
1/4 C. raw carob powder
1/4 C. maple syrup

1/4 C. sunflower seeds
1/3 C. raisins
1/4 C. shredded coconut

Mix ingredients in a bowl. Drop by spoonful onto a plastic plate and freeze.

Rich Carob Fudge/Carob Cream Pie
yields 3 cups

4-5 hass avocados
20 dates (pitted), soaked
1 1/2 C. water

1 1/4 C. raw carob powder
1-2 bananas
pie crust (page 223) (optional)

1. Soak dates in water for 15 minutes, do not drain.
2. Blend all ingredients, until creamy, in a food processor using the "S" shaped blade. Add a little water if too thick. Freeze for fudge or chill for a creamy pudding.
3. To make a pie, place mixture in a raw pie crust lined with sliced bananas, chill for a few hours and serve.

"Let us ask what is best, not what is customary..."

SENECA (c. 5 B.C.-65 A.D.) ~ Spanish-born Roman philosopher and statesman

Raw Apple Pie
yields 1 pie

<u>Crust</u>
1/4 C. water (or date soak water)
3/4 C. walnuts, soaked
1/2 C. almonds, soaked
3/4 C. pecans, soaked
8 dates, pitted, soaked
1 C. raisins
1 1/2 C. oats
1 t. apple pie spice

<u>Filling</u>
2-3 ripe bananas, sliced
1 T. maple syrup
6 C. apples, peeled (3 C. grated, 3 C. diced)
1/2 C. raisins (optional)
1/8 C. lemon juice (optional), with additional sweetener
6 dates, pitted, chopped
Garnish: pecans, strawberries, raisins

1. Soak all nuts, dates and raisins for 20-30 minutes.
2. In a food processor, using the "S" shaped blade, blend the oats and pie spice (cinnamon, nutmeg and allspice combination) until it becomes a flour. Remove from processor. Optional ~ blend in 1/4 cup of dry almonds.
3. Add the date soak water, dates, raisins and nuts to the processor and blend. Add the oat flour mixture to it. Batter should be fairly dry. If too wet, add some more oats.
4. Press into a pie shell forming a bottom and sides.
5. Slice two bananas into 1/4" rounds. Lay each slice flat next to each other to cover the pie shell bottom.
6. In the food processor, blend the remaining banana, maple syrup, and one cup of grated apples until creamy.
7. Add mixture to the remaining five cups of grated apples. Optional: add 1/2 cup raisins and/or 1/4 cup lemon juice (if adding lemon juice, add more maple syrup). Add dates. Mix.
8. Place the filling into the pie shell on top of banana slices. Garnish with pecan halves and raisins or strawberry slices. Chill for several hours and serve.

Blueberry Cream Pie
yields 1 pie

<u>Crust</u>
1/4 C. dates, pitted, soaked
1/2 C. walnuts
1/4 C. almonds

<u>Filling</u>
2-3 medium bananas
1 lb. blueberries (fresh or frozen)
1/2 C. dates, pitted

1. In a food processor, using the "S" shaped blade, blend the crust ingredients well.
2. Pat mixture into the bottom and sides of a pie plate, forming a crust.
3. Slice the bananas into 1/4" rounds, leaving 1/4-1/2 of one banana for the creamy filling. Cover the bottom of the pie shell with a layer of banana pieces.
4. In a food processor, blend one cup of the blueberries with the remaining piece of banana and 1/2 cup of dates. Mix in the remaining blueberries (whole). Pour this over the sliced bananas in the pie shell. Garnish with walnuts. Chill and serve.

Raw Fruit Pie
yields 1 pie

Crust	Filling
2/3 C. whole oats	1 apple, peeled, diced small
2/3 C. walnuts	1/2 C. raisins
1/3 C. cashew pieces	2 ripe bananas, sliced
3/4 C. dates, pitted	2-3 kiwifruit
1/3 C. almonds, soaked 15 minutes	1 large mango (or 2 small), sliced
2 T. maple syrup + sprinkle of carob	2 T. agar-agar

1. In a food processor, using the "S" shaped blade, grind the oats into a flour. Drain soaked almonds then blend all ingredients in the first column.
2. Sprinkle a little carob on the bottom of the pie plate, then press batter into it, forming a crust. (The carob helps to keep it from sticking.)
3. Place the apple, raisins, one sliced banana, half of the mango and one diced kiwifruit in the pie shell.
4. In a processor, blend the other half of the mango and one ripe banana. Add two tablespoons of agar-agar. Pour this mixture over the fruit and mix together.
5. Decorate the top with remaining sliced kiwifruit and/or strawberries and raisins. Chill for several hours before serving.

Tropical Mango Banana Pie
yields 1 pie

Crust	Filling
	2 C. mango (2-3 mangoes)
3/4 C. almonds, soaked 15 minutes	1 1/2 bananas
3/4 C. pecans	2 bananas, sliced
3-4 dates, pitted	fruit of choice, sliced
1/2 C. raisins, soaked 1 minute	1/2 C. raisins

1. In a food processor, using the "S" shaped blade, blend the crust ingredients. Remove and press evenly into a pie plate and chill.
2. In food processor, blend one cup of mango and 1 1/2 bananas.
3. Slice two bananas into 1/4" rounds and layer on the bottom of the pie crust. Slice remaining mango and place over bananas with sliced fruit of choice then sprinkle in the raisins. Spread in some of the mango-banana sauce and mix it with the fruit. Pour remaining sauce on top.
4. Decorate and chill for several hours. (Place in the freezer 1/2 hour before serving.)

> **"Where mercy, love and pity dwell,**
> **there God is living too."**
>
> WILLIAM BLAKE (1757-1827) ~ English poet

Outrageous Raw Pie Crust
yields 2 pie crusts

1 3/4 C. rolled oats	3/4 t. cinnamon
1 3/4 C. pecans/walnuts/almonds (mix)	1/4 C. macadamia oil (cold-pressed)
4 dates, pitted, soaked 10 minutes	1/2 C. dried bananas
1 1/2 t. vanilla	3/4 C. maple syrup

1. In a food processor, using the "S" shaped blade, grind the oats. Remove oats and set aside. Add the nuts and grind finely. Add the remaining ingredients to the food processor and blend. Mix with the oats.
2. Press and shape into a pie plate and fill with your favorite fruit medley.

Marble Nice Dream Pie
yields 1 pie

Crust
1/3 C. dried shredded coconut	1/2 t. vanilla
1/2 C. walnuts	6 dates, soaked 10 minutes
1/2 C. almonds	1/2 C. sunflower seeds, soaked 15 minutes
1/3 C. raw carob powder	1/3 C. raisins

1. Blend crust ingredients in a food processor using the "S" shaped blade.
2. Sprinkle a little dry carob into the bottom of a pie plate. Press crust into pie plate.

Carob Sauce
4 T. raw tahini	1 banana, peeled & frozen
8 dates, soaked 10 minutes	3/4 C. raw carob
1/2 t. vanilla	date soak water, small amount

In a blender, blend all ingredients until thick and creamy. Freeze until ready to use.

'Nice Dream' Filling
12 bananas, peeled & frozen	5 T. raw tahini
15 dates, soaked 10 minutes	2-3 T. shredded coconut

1. Homogenize using a food processor or a Champion® juicer, alternating ingredients.
2. Mix half of the 'Nice Dream' Filling with Carob Sauce, to make carob 'Nice Dream'.
3. Put the carob and vanilla 'Nice Dream' into the pie crust and swirl. Top with shredded coconut. Cover and freeze overnight. Remove from freezer five minutes before serving. For a soft freeze, serve immediately.

"Peace above all earthly dignities: a still and quiet conscience."

WILLIAM SHAKESPEARE (1564-1616) ~ English poet and playwright

Fig Bars
yields 32 delicious raw goodies!

<u>Crust</u>
3 C. rolled oats
1 1/2 C. walnuts
1 1/2 C. almonds
25 dates (soaked 10 minutes)
1/2 t. cinnamon
1 1/2 t. vanilla

<u>Filling</u>
60 black mission figs (small),
   de-stemmed, soaked 10–15 minutes
1 C. dates, soaked in water
1 t. vanilla

1. In a food processor, using the "S" shaped blade, process the oats into a flour. Remove from the processor.
2. Process the nuts until fine. Add oat flour and blend. Remove from processor.
3. Return half the mixture to the processor and add half of the soaked dates, 1/4 t. cinnamon and 1/2 t. vanilla. Process together then remove. Do the same with the other half. Remove from processor.
4. In the food processor, blend the soaked figs with one cup of the date soak water, along with 1 t. of vanilla.
5. Take half the crust and roll it onto a flat cookie sheet. (Wax paper on top will prevent the crust from sticking to the rolling pin.) Cut into 2" by 2" squares and set aside.
6. Take the rest of the crust, roll it onto a flat cookie sheet and evenly spread all of the fig mixture on top.
7. Place the pre-cut squares of crust on top of the fig filling. Cut each square through to the bottom crust.
8. Lift each fig bar gently off the tray with a spatula onto a serving dish or into a sealed container to stay fresh. It will keep well in the refrigerator for about a week.

Maple Coconut Treats
yields 9–10 balls or cookies

1 1/4 C. coconut, shredded
1 C. raisins
3 T. maple syrup

4 dates (medjool), chopped finely
1/3 C. raw tahini

1. Mix all ingredients together in a bowl.
2. Form into cookies and refrigerate, or freeze for a more solid treat.

"A raw and living food diet is loaded with enzymes, crammed with vitamins and minerals, abundant in oxygen, complete with available proteins, and is especially high in fiber."

BRIAN R. CLEMENT ~ <u>Hippocrates Health Program</u>

Carob Coconut Cookies
yields 12 cookies

1 C. raw carob powder	*1/4 C. maple syrup*
1/2 C. coconut, shredded	*1/4 C. water*
1 banana	*1/2 t. vanilla*
3 dates, pitted, soaked 10 minutes	*1 C. shredded coconut*

1. In a food processor, thoroughly blend all ingredients, except the shredded coconut.
2. Spread shredded coconut on a tray. Scoop out 2 T. of the blended mixture and place on the dry coconut. Flatten and turn over so the coconut coats the entire outside.
3. Place flat on a sheet for dehydration and repeat with the rest of the carob mixture. Dehydrate or freeze for two hours to help the cookie maintain form.

Oat Cookies
yields 18 medium cookies

3 ripe bananas	*1 C. oat flour*
2 T. maple syrup	*4 C. whole rolled oats*
2 t. vanilla	*3/4 C. raisins*
1/2 C. date sugar	*1/2 C. walnuts, chopped*
3 t. cinnamon	*1/2 C. almonds, chopped*

1. Mix bananas, maple syrup, vanilla and date sugar. Separately mix the remaining three dry ingredients. Add the dry to the wet and mix. Soak raisins, walnuts and almonds for 15 minutes. Rinse and drain. Chop nuts and fold with raisins into the batter.
2. Pat into cookies and dehydrate at 102° for one hour, flip and dehydrate for one more hour. (For a cereal or snack, use the same batter sprinkled on dehydrator sheet; dehydrate until firm.)

Date Nut Cookies
yields 15 cookies

1 C. figs, de-stemmed, soaked 10 minutes	
1/2 C. dates, pitted	*1/4 C. shredded coconut*
1 C. pecans, soaked 2 minutes	*1 T. raw tahini*
1/2 C. walnuts, soaked 2 minutes	*1/2 C. raisins, soaked 2 minutes*

1. In a food processor, blend the figs first. Add remaining ingredients and blend again.
2. Form into small cookies and place in the refrigerator to solidify.

> **"...The principle of nonviolence necessitates complete abstention from exploitation in any form."**
>
> MAHATMA GANDHI (1869-1948) ~ Hindu pacifist, spiritual leader

> "The highest realms of thought
> are impossible to reach without first attaining
> an understanding of compassion."

SOCRATES (469-399 B.C.)
Greek philosopher

Just Desserts

For baking tips, see Baking Guide, pages 10–11

Just Desserts

*"The average age (longevity) of a meat-eater is 63.
I am on the verge of 85 and still at work as hard as ever.
I have lived quite long enough and am trying to die, but
I simply cannot do it. A single beef-steak would finish me,
but I cannot bring myself to swallow it.
I am oppressed with a dread of living forever.
That is the only disadvantage of vegetarianism."*

GEORGE BERNARD SHAW (1856–1950)
Anglo-Irish author and playwright
1925 Nobel Prize recipient

Apple Pie
yields 1 pie

Crust

1 3/4 C. whole wheat pastry flour	1/2 C. oil
1/4 C. soy powder or pastry flour	1 t. vanilla
1/4 C. orange juice	1 T. sweetener

1. Sift flour and soy powder into a bowl. Remove any bran.
2. In a separate bowl, whisk wet ingredients together, including sweetener.
3. Mix dry ingredients into the wet. Dough should be wet enough to hold together and dry enough not to stick to your fingers. It is best to use this dough immediately for easy rolling. (Or chill sealed until ready to use.)
4. Split dough in half, leaving one half slightly larger. Roll each half between two pieces of wax paper, (dampen a flat surface and place wax paper on it, flattening to remove bubbles) or use flour to keep dough from sticking. Roll from the center outward, until even, about 1/8" thick. Place the larger rolled dough in a pie plate and gently press it into the plate, covering the sides and bottom.

Filling

5-6 medium apples	1 1/2 t. cinnamon
(preferably rome beauty)	1/4 C. dry sweetener
1 t. vanilla	a dash of nutmeg & allspice

5. Peel and core apples. Cut into bite-sized pieces. Mix with remaining ingredients.
6. Place apples into pie crust. Cover with the second piece of rolled dough, seal edges with fingers or a fork, and make a few air holes on the top with a fork. Bake in a pre-heated oven at 350° for 25–30 minutes, until crust is golden-brown.

Apple Crisp
yields one 9" x 12" baking casserole

8 C. apples, peeled and sliced	1 C. sweetener (maple syrup)
1/2 C. cashew milk or soy milk	1/4 t. nutmeg
2 C. rolled oats	1/4 t. allspice
1 3/4 C. pastry flour	1 t. cinnamon
	1/2 C. oil or vegan margarine (melted)

1. Cover the bottom of a baking dish with the sliced apples.
2. Pour 1/2 C. cashew milk over apples or use soy or rice milk. (2/3 C. cashews blended with one quart water will make a blender of cashew milk or use one rounded teaspoon of cashew butter blended with 1/2 C. water)
3. Mix together all dry ingredients, including sweetener.
4. Add oil or melted vegan margarine to dry mixture and mix well. Crumble over the top of the apples, covering them thoroughly.
5. Bake in a pre-heated oven at 350° for about 40 minutes, until browned on top and apples are soft (test with a fork).

Apple Turnovers
yields 10-12 small turnovers

<u>Filling</u>
5 C. apples, peeled,
   cut into small pieces
1 1/2 t. cinnamon
1/4 t. nutmeg
1/4 t. allspice
1/4 C. dry sweetener

<u>Dough</u>
1 3/4 C. whole wheat pastry flour
1/4 C. soy powder (or pastry flour)
1/4 t. cinnamon
1/4 C. orange juice (cold)
1/2 C. oil
1 t. vanilla
1 T. sweetener

1. Filling: Mix together apples, spices and sweetener. Set aside.
2. Dough: Mix dry ingredients together in a bowl.
3. In a separate bowl, whisk orange juice, oil, vanilla and sweetener. Mix well.
4. Slowly pour dry mixture into wet batter. Mix thoroughly, using your hands at the end to knead in flour. Dough should not be too dry so that it falls apart, but dry enough not to stick to your fingers. It is best to use this dough immediately for easiest rolling or chill (well sealed) until use.
5. On wax paper, roll dough into a long rectangle and cut into squares (about six).
6. Place the apple filling in the squares one at a time and fold the dough corner to corner, making a triangle. Seal the edges. (It can be folded any way as long as it seals the apples in). Using a fork, make holes in the top.
7. Place the turnovers on a lightly oiled tray, or on baking paper. Bake in a pre-heated oven for 30 minutes at 350° until golden-brown on top and bottom.

Chocolate Mousse
serves 3-4

1 lb. (2 C.) soft tofu
2-3 T. oil (mild-flavored oil)
1 T. almond butter or tahini
6 T. sweetener
1 C. non-dairy chocolate chips (optional - see page 278)

5 T. cocoa powder
2 T. carob powder
1/3 C. maple syrup
1 t. vanilla

1. Melt chocolate chips - see page 11. Rinse and drain tofu.
2. In a food processor, using the "S" shaped blade, blend all ingredients until smooth and creamy, scraping sides with a spatula periodically. Chill in parfait glasses. Serve.

"The question is not, 'Can they reason?' nor, 'Can they talk?' but, 'Can they suffer?'"

JEREMY BENTHAM (1748-1832) ~ English philosopher
An Introduction to <u>The Principles of Morals and Legislation</u>, 1789

Rich Chocolate Mousse
serves 3

1 C. vegan chocolate chips (p. 278)	4 T. maple syrup
1/3 C. water	2 T. oil
2 T. carob powder	5 T. dry sweetener
2 T. cocoa powder	1/2 C. soft tofu, mashed

1. Melt chocolate chips - see page 11. Rinse and drain tofu then mash.
2. In a food processor, using the "S" shaped blade, first blend carob and cocoa powder with water and the melted chips. Add remaining ingredients and blend thoroughly.
3. Scrape the sides of the food processor with a rubber spatula then whiz again.
4. Pour into three parfait glasses and refrigerate for a few hours. Serve chilled.

Chocolate Pie
yields one 11" pie

Crust

1/4 C. oil	1 1/2 C. whole wheat pastry flour
1/8 C. + 1 T. orange juice	1/2 t. baking soda
1/4 C. dry sweetener	

1. In a bowl, whisk together oil, orange juice and sweetener.
2. In a separate bowl, sift flour and baking soda. Add dry ingredients to wet and mix.
3. Chill batter for a few minutes to make rolling easier. With a rolling pin, roll out dough into a circle larger than the pie dish (see page 11).
4. Pat evenly into an oiled pie plate. Bake in a pre-heated oven at 350° for 5-8 minutes.

Filling

1 C. chocolate chips (page 278)	3/4 C. cocoa powder (or half carob powder)
2-2 1/2 C. (1 lb.) tofu	1/2-3/4 C. dry sweetener
1/3-1/2 C. oil	1/2 t. vanilla
1/2 C. maple syrup	1 T. arrowroot powder
	1/2 t. sea salt (optional)

1. Melt chocolate chips before blending - see page 11. Rinse and drain tofu.
2. In a food processor, using the "S" shaped blade, blend all ingredients together. (If using cocoa, more sweetener is needed than with carob.)
3. Pour into pre-baked pie shell. Bake at 350° for 30-35 minutes until cream filling cracks. Chill 3-4 hours allowing filling to solidify before serving.

"The more we come in contact with animals and observe their behavior, the more we love them..."

IMMANUEL KANT (1724-1804) ~ German philosopher

Banana Dream Pie
yields one 9" pie

Crust
2 C. whole wheat pastry flour
1/2 C. dry sweetener
1/4 t. sea salt
1/2 t. cinnamon
1/3 C. oil or vegan margarine
1 1/2 T. maple syrup
1/2 t. vanilla
1 t. molasses

Filling
4 bananas (ripe; brown spotted is best)
1 t. vanilla
1/4 C. fresh lemon juice
1/2 C. oil
1 1/4 C. dry sweetener
1/4 C. maple syrup (optional)
1/2 t. sea salt
2 C. silken tofu (or soft), rinsed & drained
1 T. arrowroot powder

1. Sift the dry crust ingredients together. Mix in the oil or margarine, maple syrup, vanilla and molasses. Work together into a uniform consistency.
2. Oil a 9" pie plate. Press dough evenly into the bottom and up the sides.
3. In a food processor, using the "S" shaped blade, blend the filling ingredients until smooth and creamy.
4. Pour batter into the crust. Bake in a pre-heated oven at 350° for 20–25 minutes, until crust is golden-brown. Cool and refrigerate for 3–4 hours before serving.

Pumpkin Pie
yields 2 pies

Crust: *(use Pie Crust recipe page 228)*
Split dough in half, roll out and place in two pie plates, evenly covering the sides and bottom. Pre-bake at 350° for six minutes.

Filling
1 (29 oz.) can pumpkin
1 3/4 C. tofu, rinsed and drained
1/2 C. oil
3 t. egg replacer (dry)
2 t. cinnamon

1 t. ground ginger
1 1/4 C. dry sweetener
1 t. sea salt
1–1 1/2 t. vanilla
1/2 t. ground cloves/all spice (optional)

1. In a food processor, blend all Filling ingredients together, using the "S" shaped blade.
2. Pour into pre-baked pie shells and smooth down. Bake at 350° for 25–35 minutes.
3. Let cool and chill for at least four hours before serving.

"I do not regard flesh-food as necessary for us at any stage and under any clime in which it is possible for human beings ordinarily to live. I hold flesh-food to be unsuited to our species."

MAHATMA GANDHI (1869-1948) ~ Hindu pacifist, spiritual leader

Liberty's Chocolate Cream Pie
yields one 8" pie

> 2 C. vegan chocolate chips (p. 276)   1/4 C. dry sweetener
> 1 silken tofu, rinsed and drained   1 T. vanilla

1. Melt chocolate chips (see page 11). In a food processor, using the "S" shaped blade, blend all ingredients until smooth.
2. Make Apple Pie Crust - page 228. This will yield two 8" crusts. Double the filling to make two pies. Or, to use excess dough, roll it out, cut into strips and top with cinnamon and sweetener. Bake with the pie shell, below.
3. Split dough in half. Roll one half into a round and place in a pie dish, evenly covering the sides and bottom, making a lip at the top. Pre-bake crust at 350° for 6-10 minutes until golden-brown. Let cool.
4. Pour filling into baked crust. Refrigerate 45 min. Top with Whipped Dream (pg. 242)

"Cheesecake" Custard Pie
yields one 9" pie

Crust
1/4 C. orange juice   2 C. whole wheat pastry flour
1/3 C. oil   1 1/2 t. baking soda
1/2 C. dry sweetener

1. In a bowl, whisk orange juice, oil and sweetener. Sift pastry flour and baking soda.
2. Pour dry ingredients into wet and stir to make a dough.
3. Chill for 5-10 minutes. Roll between two pieces of wax paper from the center out. Place into an oiled pie plate, evenly pressing it around sides and bottom.
4. Bake in a pre-heated oven for five minutes at 350° then remove from oven.

Filling
2 1/2 C. mashed tofu   7 T. dry sweetener
1/3 C. oil   1/2 t. vanilla
6 T. nutritional yeast   1/2 t. sea salt
6 T. fresh lemon juice   2 T. arrowroot powder
2 T. maple syrup   1 t. egg replacer

1. Rinse and drain tofu. Blend all ingredients in a food processor, using the "S" shaped blade.
2. Pour into pie shell and bake at 350° for 35 minutes or until crust is golden-brown.
3. Cool and refrigerate, allowing to solidify before serving.

"All great truths begin as blasphemies."

GEORGE BERNARD SHAW (1856-1950) ~ Anglo-Irish author and playwright
1925 Nobel Prize recipient

Sweet Brown Rice Pudding
serves 8

3 1/2 C. water	1/4 C. maple syrup
1 C. short grain brown rice (dry)	1 1/2 C. non-dairy milk (soy/rice/nut)
1/2 t. sea salt	1 t. vanilla extract
1/2 C. raisins	1/2 t. cinnamon
1/2 C. dry sweetener	

1. In a medium-sized pot, bring water to a boil. Stir in rice and salt. Reduce heat to low. Cover and simmer for 45–50 minutes or until rice is very soft. Uncover and boil gently for five minutes or until most of the water evaporates. Stir in raisins, sweeteners, milk and vanilla. Mix well.
2. Cook 12–15 minutes, on medium-low heat, until rice absorbs most of the milk and mixture is thick (pudding will thicken as it cools).
3. Pour into a shallow, heat-safe bowl. Allow to cool. Add cinnamon and stir. Chill, stirring occasionally. Serve.

Carob Pudding
yields 5 cups

1 1/4 C. tofu, rinsed & drained	1/2 C. carob powder
1 1/4 C. cashew butter	3/4-1 C. dry sweetener
water, to blend	5 T. arrowroot powder
2 t. vanilla	

1. In a blender, blend tofu and cashew butter with water, to a creamy, thick milk consistency. (Start with one cup of water and add as needed.) Add remaining ingredients and blend thoroughly.
2. Pour into a saucepan and heat on low, stirring continuously until it bubbles through the center. When it bubbles, it will be thickened. Do not boil. Pour immediately into small cups, let cool, refrigerate and serve chilled.

"First it was necessary to civilize man in relation to man. Now it is necessary to civilize man in relation to nature and the animals."

VICTOR HUGO (1802-1885) ~ French poet, novelist and playwright

Jewish Noodle Pudding
yields 1 medium-sized baking dish

1 lb. flat wide noodles (not egg)
1 lb. (2 C.) firm tofu
1/2 C. sweetener
1/4 C. soy milk or cashew milk
1/3 C. oil
1/4 C. tahini

1 T. vanilla
1 t. cinnamon
nutmeg, a pinch
2/3 C. raisins, (soaked in water
    15 minutes and drained)

1. In a large saucepan, cook noodles in plenty of boiling water for 10–12 minutes.
2. Rinse and drain tofu then place in a medium-sized bowl and mash well. Add sweetener, soy milk, oil, tahini, vanilla, cinnamon and nutmeg. Fold in and mix very well. Mix in soaked raisins.
3. Place cooked noodles in a casserole dish and add tofu mixture, tossing lightly. Bake in a pre-heated oven at 325° for 25 minutes. Sprinkle cinnamon on top.

• Variation ~ Add half a cup of chopped apricots or apples.

Vanilla Maple Pudding
serves 2-3

1/2–3/4 lb. (1–1 1/2 C.) tofu
4 T. maple syrup
1 T. oil

2 T. tahini
3–4 T. fructose (or other dry sweetener)
1 1/2 t. vanilla

1. Rinse and drain tofu. In a food processor, using the "S" shaped blade, process all ingredients, periodically scraping the sides with a rubber spatula.
2. Blend until creamy smooth. Pour into cups. Chill and allow to solidify before serving.

• Variation ~ Layer in a parfait glass with chocolate mousse (see pages 229 & 230).

"This is what you shall do: Love the Earth, and Sun, and animals. Hate tyrants, argue not concerning God, have patience and indulgence towards the people; re-examine all you have been told at school or church, or in any books, and dismiss whatever insults your own soul."

WALT WHITMAN (1819-1892) ~ American poet and essayist

Heavenly Carob Cake
yields two 9" cake pans

2 C. thick tofu milk (see page 10)	3 C. whole wheat pastry flour
2/3 C. oil	3/4 C. carob (or cocoa powder), sifted
2 t. vanilla	(if using cocoa, add a bit more sweetener)
1/2 C. maple syrup	1 1/2 t. baking soda
1 1/2 C. dry sweetener	1/2 t. sea salt

1. In a blender, blend one cup of rinsed soft tofu and 1–1 1/2 cups of water to make tofu milk. Start with a small amount of water, adding more until you reach two cups.
2. Add oil, maple syrup, vanilla and sweetener to the blender and blend well.
3. In a bowl, sift all dry ingredients and mix.
4. Pour the blender mixture into the bowl and mix well. Batter will be loose.
5. Pour batter into two small oiled cake pans, filling half-way, leaving room for rising.
6. Bake in a pre-heated oven at 350° for approximately 35 minutes, or until a toothpick comes out dry. Cool before slicing. Use this recipe to make a double layer cake:
   • Frost one cake, place the second one on top, then frost the top and sides.
   • Use this recipe for making cupcakes, as well. Pour batter into an oiled muffin tin.

'Peacetime' Cake
yields one 9" cake

The 'wartime' cake emerged when eggs and milk were rationed during the World Wars. Here's the updated version.

[handwritten: 2 sweet potato / 1 C. Applesauce / 1 cup water / 1 8 yogurt / no raisins]

Wet	Dry
1 C. dry sweetener	2 C. whole wheat flour
1 1/4 C. + 2 t. water	1 t. baking soda
1/3 C. oil	1 t. baking powder
2 C. raisins	1/2 t. salt
	1/2 t. nutmeg
	2 t. cinnamon
	1/2 t. ground cloves

1. Oil and flour a cake pan.
2. In a saucepan, mix all wet ingredients. Boil for three minutes. Cool.
3. Sift flour, baking soda and powder. Combine with salt & spices in a mixing bowl. Stir.
4. Add wet to the dry and mix.
5. Pour batter into cake pan and bake in a pre-heated oven at 325° for 50 minutes.

> **"It is almost a definition of a gentleman to say he is one who never inflicts pain."**
>
> CARDINAL NEWMAN (1801-1890) ~ English Cardinal

Ambrosia Cake
yields two 9" cakes

2 1/2 C. dry sweetener	3 C. pastry flour
1/2-3/4 C. oil	2 t. baking soda
2 1/2 C. tofu milk (see page 10)	1 T. baking powder
2 t. vanilla	1/2 t. sea salt
1 t. almond extract	1 C. shredded coconut
1 t. lime (or lemon) extract	

1. Mix together wet ingredients including sweetener.
2. In a separate bowl, sift remaining dry ingredients. Add shredded coconut. Mix.
3. Mix the dry into the wet. Divide batter into two lightly oiled and floured cake pans.
4. Bake in a pre-heated oven at 350° for 45 minutes or until a toothpick comes out dry.

- Serve with a white frosting and/or strawberry glaze (page 238) over the frosting.
- Omit almond extract and shredded coconut to make a pound cake.

Carrot Cake
yields two 9" cakes

1 C. thick tofu milk (see below)	1/2 t. allspice
3/4 C. oil	2 t. cinnamon
1 3/4 C. dry sweetener	1/8 t. ground cloves
4 C. whole wheat pastry flour	1 C. raisins
1 1/2 t. baking soda, sifted	1 3/4 C. carrots, grated

1. In a blender, blend 4 oz. rinsed tofu and half a cup water to make one cup of thick tofu milk. Add oil and sweetener and blend.
2. In a large bowl, mix the dry ingredients. Mix in the raisins and carrots.
3. Pour wet mix into the dry ingredients and stir well.
4. Pour into two small cake pans or a large baking dish. (Use a spatula to get all the batter.) Bake in a pre-heated oven at 350° for 40-50 minutes or until a toothpick comes out dry. Spread the following frosting over the cake once cooled:

2 C. tofu, rinsed & drained	
1 C. cashew butter	3/4 t. cinnamon
1 1/2 C. dry sweetener	1-2 T. maple syrup

In a food processor, blend all ingredients. Chill before spreading on cake.

> *"It should not be believed that all beings exist for the sake of the existence of man..."*
>
> MAIMONIDES (Rabbi Moses ben Maimon) (1135-1204) ~ Spanish-born rabbi, physician, philosopher, scholar

Chocolate Zucchini Cake
yields two 9" cakes

Dry
4 T. cocoa powder
2 1/2 C. pastry flour
1/4 t. sea salt
1/2 t. baking powder
1 1/4 t. baking soda, sifted

3/4 C. oil
2 C. dry sweetener
2 T. soy powder & 4 T. water
3/4 C. tofu milk (see page 10)
1 t. vanilla
2 C. grated zucchini

1. In a bowl, sift and combine all <u>Dry</u> ingredients. Stir.
2. In a separate bowl, whisk oil, sweetener, soy mixture, tofu milk and vanilla.
3. Mix the dry with the wet together well. Add grated zucchini to batter. Mix.
4. Pour into two oiled 9" cake pans. Bake in a pre-heated oven at 350° for 30–40 minutes or until a toothpick comes out dry.

• Optional ~ Top with half a cup of dairy-free carob/chocolate chips and bake.

Vanilla Cake
yields two 9" cakes

2 1/2 C. tofu milk (see below)
1 T. vanilla
1 t. almond extract
3/4 C. oil
2 C. dry sweetener

3 3/4 C. whole wheat pastry flour, sifted
2 t. baking soda, sifted
2 t. baking powder, sifted
1/2 t. sea salt

1. In a blender, make tofu milk by blending 1/2 cup rinsed tofu with 1 1/2 cups of water.
2. In a bowl, whisk together all ingredients in the first column.
3. Combine dry ingredients. Add the dry to the wet batter. Mix well.
4. Pour batter into two lightly oiled cake pans, filling each half-way.
5. Bake at 350° in a pre-heated oven for 40–45 minutes, or until a toothpick comes out dry.

• Mix tahini/cashew butter with maple syrup, to taste, for a quick and easy frosting.

> *"The fact is that there is enough food in the world for everyone. But tragically, much of the world's food and land resources are tied up in producing beef and other livestock-food for the well-off, while millions of children and adults suffer from malnutrition and starvation."*
>
> DR. WALDEN BELLO
> Executive Director, Food First, Institute for Food and Development Policy

Marble Cake
yields two 9" cakes

2 1/2 C. thick tofu milk (see below)	3 3/4 C. pastry flour
1 T. vanilla	2 t. baking soda
1 t. almond extract	2 t. baking powder
3/4 C. oil	1/2 t. sea salt
2 C. dry sweetener	

1. In a blender, blend 1/2 cup rinsed soft tofu with 1 1/2 cups of water. Add water and/or tofu until you reach the 2 1/2 cup line on the blender.
2. In a bowl, whisk together all ingredients in the first column including sweetener.
3. Sift together dry ingredients. Add the dry to the wet batter. Mix well.
4. Split batter in half. Pour one half into two oiled cake pans, filling one side only.
5. Add the following ingredients to the remaining batter in the bowl. (If too thin, add more flour, if too thick, add more milk):

> 1/3 C. carob or cocoa powder
> 1/4 C. sweetener (add more sweetener if using cocoa powder)
> 1/4 C. tofu milk

6. Add the carob batter to the other side of each cake pan and gently swirl or "marblize".
7. Bake at 350° in a pre-heated oven for 40-45 minutes or until a toothpick comes out dry.

Holiday Fruitcake
yields two 9" round cakes or a 9" x 13" rectangle

2/3 C. oil	
2 C. dry sweetener	8 oz. (1/2 C.) tofu, rinsed and drained
2 t. vanilla	1 1/2 C. water
1/2 t. almond extract	1/2 C. raisins
1 1/2 T. orange juice	1/2 C. walnuts, chopped
3 3/4 C. whole wheat pastry flour	1/2 C. dates or figs, chopped
1 1/2 t. baking soda	1/2 C. apple, diced (or banana)

1. In a bowl, whisk together the oil, sweetener, vanilla, almond extract and juice.
2. In a separate bowl, sift together the flour and baking soda.
3. In a blender, blend the tofu and water.
4. Add dry ingredients and the tofu mixture alternately to the wet ingredients. Stir well. Fold in the raisins, chopped nuts and fruit. Pour batter into oiled and floured pans.
5. Bake in a pre-heated oven at 350°. For small round cake pans, bake for 25-30 minutes. For a rectangle, bake for 35-40 minutes or until a toothpick comes out dry. Ice with White Frosting (page 240) or Cashew Icing (page 242).

• Optional ~ Add grated orange peel to the frosting/icing.

Crumb Cake
yields two 9" cake pans

4 C. whole wheat pastry flour	1 C. walnuts, chopped
2 C. dry sweetener	1 3/4 C. tofu milk (see below),
1 t. cinnamon	mixed with 4 t. vinegar
1 t. ginger powder	1 1/2 t. baking soda, sifted
1/2 t. nutmeg	2 t. baking powder, sifted
2/3 C. oil	2 T. egg replacer,
1 C. raisins	mixed with 4 T. water

1. Sift flour and combine with sweetener and spices in a bowl.
2. Mix in oil and set aside two cups of this crumbly mixture.
3. Stir raisins and walnuts into the remaining crumbly mixture.
4. For tofu milk, blend 1/2 C. rinsed tofu with 1 1/4 cups of water + vinegar in a blender.
5. Add tofu milk, baking soda, baking powder and egg replacer mixture to batter. Mix.
6. Oil two small cake pans and pour thick batter into them. Sprinkle the two cups of crumbly mixture on top.
7. Bake in a pre-heated oven at 375° for 40 minutes or until a toothpick comes out dry.

"Cheesecake"
yields 8 slices

Crust	Filling
2 C. whole wheat pastry flour	1 lb. (2 C.) tofu (silken or soft)
1 t. baking powder	1/4 C. fresh lemon juice
1/4 t. sea salt	1/4 t. sea salt
1/4 C. dry sweetener	1 t. arrowroot powder
1/8 C. maple syrup	1/2-3/4 C. dry sweetener (fructose)
1/3 C. oil (safflower)	1/2 t. vanilla
2 T. water/orange juice	2 T. nutritional yeast

1. Sift the flour, baking powder and salt into a bowl. Mix the remaining crust ingredients in a separate bowl. Add the dry to the wet and mix. Rinse and drain tofu.
2. Press dough into a 9" pie pan. Bake in a pre-heated oven for 5-7 minutes at 350°.
3. In a food processor, blend the filling ingredients until smooth. Pour into the crust.
4. Return to the oven for 15-20 minutes, or until the tofu turns pale yellow. Remove. Let cool and chill before serving.

> *"The great aim of culture is the aim of setting ourselves to ascertain what perfection is, and to make it prevail."*
>
> MATTHEW ARNOLD (1822-1866) ~ English poet and essayist

Strawberry Tall Cake
yields two short or one tall cake

Cake

2 1/2 C. tofu milk (see below)	3 3/4 C. pastry flour (whole wheat)
3/4 C. oil	2 t. baking soda
1/2 t. almond extract	2 t. baking powder
1 T. vanilla	1/2 t. sea salt
1 T. orange juice	1 t. orange rind, grated
2 C. dry sweetener	1 t. lemon juice (optional)

1. In a blender, blend half a cup rinsed soft tofu with 1-1 1/2 cups of water. Add tofu or water until you reach the 2 1/2 C. line on the blender.
2. Whisk together all ingredients in the first column.
3. Sift together flour, baking soda and powder. Combine with remaining ingredients.
4. Add the dry to the wet batter and mix.
5. Pour batter into two oiled cake pans, filling each half-way.
6. Bake at 350° in a pre-heated oven for 40–45 minutes or until a toothpick comes out dry.

Frosting

Frosting	Strawberry Glaze
2 C. soft tofu, rinsed & drained	1 pint fresh strawberries, sliced
1/2 C. sweetener	2 T. arrowroot powder
1/2 C. cashew butter	2 T. strawberry jam
1 t. vanilla	1 C. fresh strawberries, sliced

1. In a food processor, using the "S" shaped blade, blend the frosting ingredients until creamy.
2. In a saucepan, on medium-low, heat 1 pint sliced strawberries with arrowroot and jam until the arrowroot thickens (approx. 20 minutes), stirring often. Do not boil.
3. To make one tall cake, use both cakes. For two short cakes, cut each cake in half horizontally (when cooled) using a sharp, serrated knife.
4. Spread cashew frosting on bottom layer. Pour enough of the strawberry glaze to cover the frosting. Put the second layer of cake on top of this and fully frost the top and the sides with the cashew frosting. Lay out fresh sliced strawberries on frosting then pour the glaze on top letting it drip down the sides.
5. Serve immediately or refrigerate until serving.

White Cake Frosting
frosts 2 cakes

1 1/3 C. soft tofu, firmly packed	4–5 T. dry sweetener
1 T. cashew butter	(fructose makes a whiter frosting)
2 T. maple syrup	

Rinse and drain tofu. In a food processor, using the "S" shaped blade, blend all ingredients together. Chill to solidify before using.

Chocolate/Carob Frosting
frosts 2 cakes

1 1/3 C. tofu (pressed into cup)	4 t. cashew butter
4 T. maple syrup	5 T. dry sweetener
2 T. carob powder	1 T. cocoa powder

Rinse and drain tofu. In a food processor, using the "S" shaped blade, blend all ingredients together until smooth and creamy. Chill before using.

Macadamia Nut Frosting
frosts 2 cakes

1 C. soft tofu	3/4 C. dry sweetener + 1/3 C. maple syrup
1 C. macadamia nut butter	1 t. vanilla

Rinse and drain tofu. In a food processor, using the "S" shaped blade, blend all ingredients until smooth and creamy. Chill before using.

Melted Chocolate Chip Frosting
frosts 1-2 cakes

1/4 C. water (or non-dairy milk)	1/4 C. carob powder
1-2 C. non-dairy chocolate chips	1/2 C. dry sweetener

Melt chocolate chips (see page 278) with remaining ingredients in a small pot but do not boil. Stir. Pour over cake. Allow to cool and solidify. Refrigerate until serving.

Peanut Butter Frosting
frosts 2-3 cakes

2 C. soft tofu, rinsed & drained	2 t. vanilla
1/2 C. peanut butter	1/4 C. maple syrup
1 1/2 C. dry sweetener	1/4 C. tahini

In a food processor, using the "S" shaped blade, blend ingredients thoroughly. Chill.

> ***"Slowly but surely, humanity realizes the dreams of the wise."***
>
> ANATOLE FRANCE (1844-1924) ~ French novelist, poet and critic
> 1921 Nobel Prize recipient

Whipped Dream (non-dairy whipped cream)

1/4 C. soy milk (thick) *2 T. vanilla*
1/4 C. dry sweetener *3/4 C. oil*

1. Pour soy milk (Vitasoy™ Creamy Original) into a blender, keeping it just under the tips of the blade. Add sweetener and vanilla.
2. Start by blending this mixture then turn blender onto high speed, slowly adding oil. Soy milk will thicken up to a "whipped cream" consistency. Use on your favorite desserts. Great as a topping for Liberty's Chocolate Cream Pie, page 232.

Cashew Icing

1 C. cashew butter *1 C. dry sweetener*
8 oz. (1/2 C.) soft tofu, rinsed & drained *2 t. vanilla*

Blend all ingredients in a food processor, using the "S" shaped blade.

Carob Sundae Sauce

1/2 C. water (or non-dairy milk) *3–4 T. peanut butter*
4 T. carob powder *1 T. rice syrup*
2 T. dry sweetener (or maple syrup)

In a blender, blend all ingredients until smooth and creamy. Pour over homemade Banana-Peanut Butter 'Nice Cream' (see page 215).

Chocolate Sauce

2 squares unsweetened non-dairy baking chocolate
1/3 C. water *3 T. vegan margarine (page 274)*
1/2 C. dry sweetener *1/2 t. vanilla*

1. Melt chocolate squares in water over low heat. Stir constantly.
2. Add sweetener. Bring to a boil for two minutes or until slightly thickened.
3. Add margarine and vanilla. Simmer and stir. Cool.

**"All that is needed for the triumph of evil,
is that good men do nothing."**

EDMUND BURKE (1729-1797) ~ Irish-born English statesman, orator and writer

Frozen Carob Fudge

1/2 C. water
6 T. carob powder
4 T. dry sweetener

4-5 T. peanut butter
2 T. rice syrup or sorghum

1. In a food processor, using the "S" shaped blade, blend all ingredients.
2. Pour into a small, shallow, plastic container. Cover and freeze.

Nutty Chocolate Chip (or Raisin) Cookies
yields 35

2 1/2 C. whole wheat pastry flour
1 t. baking soda, sifted
2 t. baking powder, sifted
2 C. rolled oats (quick cooking)
1 T. egg replacer
1 1/2-1 3/4 C. dry sweetener

3/4 C. vegetable oil
2/3 C. thick tofu milk (1/2 C. tofu,
    blended with 1/4 C. water)
2 t. vanilla
10 oz. non-dairy chocolate chips or raisins
1 C. walnuts, chopped

1. Sift flour, baking soda & baking powder into a bowl. Combine with oats and egg replacer. Rinse and drain tofu. In a blender, blend with water to make thick tofu milk. Add sweetener, oil and vanilla and blend until smooth.
2. Add wet mixture to dry and stir. Add chocolate chips (or raisins) and walnuts. Mix.
3. Form into cookies and place onto an oiled cookie sheet (or use baking paper). Bake in a pre-heated oven at 350° for 12-13 minutes.

Almond Cookies
yields 34

2 1/2 C. almonds, ground
2 C. whole wheat pastry flour, sifted
1 t. baking soda, sifted
1/2 t. baking powder, sifted

1/2 C. soy/rice milk (see page 10)
1 t. almond oil or extract
3/4 C. oil
1 t. vanilla
1 1/2-2 C. dry sweetener

1. Combine dry ingredients (except sweetener) in a bowl.
2. Blend sweetener with remaining wet ingredients in a blender or with a whisk.
3. Add dry ingredients to the wet. Mix. Form into cookies. Place on lightly oiled baking sheets. Bake in a pre-heated oven at 350° for about 10 minutes or until golden-brown.

"What wisdom can you find that is greater than kindness?"

JEAN-JACQUES ROUSSEAU (1712-1778) ~ Swiss-born French philosopher and author

Peanut Butter Carob Chip Cookies
yields 20

3 T. soy milk
1 t. vanilla
1/2 T. molasses
1 1/2 t. egg replacer
   (mixed with 2 T. water)
1/4 C. margarine (page 274)
   at room temperature

1/2 C. peanut butter
1 1/4 C. dry sweetener
1 3/4 C. flour
1/2 t. baking powder
1/2 t. baking soda
1/2 t. sea salt
3/4 C. non-dairy carob chips (page 278)

1. Combine liquid ingredients, vegan margarine, peanut butter and sweetener in a bowl and whisk.
2. In a separate bowl, sift together flour, baking powder, baking soda and salt.
3. Add dry to the wet and mix well. Fold in carob chips.
4. Roll into balls, place on a cookie sheet and flatten with a fork. Bake at 350° in a pre-heated oven for 7-8 minutes or until golden-brown.

Fluffy Carob Cookies
yields 20

2 1/4 C. whole wheat pastry flour
7 T. carob powder
1 t. baking soda
1/2 C. maple syrup

1/2 C. dry sweetener
1/2 C. oil
2 t. vanilla
1/4 C. tofu, rinsed and drained

1. Pre-heat oven to 350°. In a bowl, sift flour, carob and baking soda.
2. Rinse and drain tofu. In a blender, blend tofu with sweeteners, oil and vanilla.
3. Add wet mixture to the dry and mix well.
4. Drop a tablespoon of batter per cookie onto an oiled cookie sheet or baking paper.
5. Bake for 8-10 minutes or until cracks appear on top and the bottom begins to harden.

   • Variation ~ Before baking, fold 3/4 C. carob chips into batter.

"Women who eliminate dairy products from their diet often experience great improvement in their menstrual cycle. One study found that women with PMS consumed five times more dairy products than women without PMS."

JOHN ROBBINS ~ American author, Pulitzer Prize Nominee for <u>Diet for a New America</u>, author, <u>The Food Revolution</u>, Conari Press 2000

Carob Coconut Cashew Cookies
yields 24

2 1/2 C. pastry flour	**Blender Ingredients**
6 T. carob	1/4 C. oil
1/2 t. baking soda	1/2 C. cashew butter
1/2 C. shredded coconut	1/2 C. water
1/2 t. egg replacer	1/2 T. vanilla
	1 C. dry sweetener

1. Into a bowl, sift flour, carob and baking soda. Add shredded coconut and egg replacer and stir.
2. In a blender, blend remaining ingredients. Pour wet ingredients into the dry. Mix.
3. Oil a cookie sheet (or use baking papers). Form batter into 24 small cookies (roll the batter into balls then press down on sheet).
4. Bake in a pre-heated oven at 350° for 10-15 minutes.
5. Rotate trays while baking. Cookies are done when small cracks appear on the top and the bottom has hardened a bit. Allow to cool before serving.

Coconut Cookies
yields 24

1/2 C. maple syrup	1 1/2 t. almond extract
1/2 C. dry sweetener	3 C. pastry flour
3/4 C. oil	1 1/4 t. baking soda
2 t. vanilla	1 1/2 t. baking powder
2 T. soy powder	3/4 C. shredded coconut
& 4 T. water (mixed well)	

1. Combine sweeteners, oil, vanilla, soy powder mixture and almond extract; whisk well.
2. Sift dry ingredients into a separate bowl, except coconut. Add coconut and stir.
3. Add dry ingredients to the wet and mix. Roll into cookies and place on a lightly oiled baking sheet (or on baking paper).
4. Bake at 350° in a pre-heated oven for 12-15 minutes or until bottom and top are golden-brown. Allow to cool and harden before eating.

> *"You cannot make yourself feel something you don't feel.*
> *But you can make yourself do right, in spite of your feelings."*
>
> PEARL S. BUCK (1892-1973) ~ American author

Thumbprint Cookies
yields 1 dozen

1 1/4 C. whole wheat pastry flour	1/3 C. oil
1/2 t. baking soda	1/3 C. sweetener
1 C. walnuts, finely chopped	1/2 t. vanilla
1 T. egg replacer,	1/2 t. almond extract
mixed with 2 T. water	5 oz. fruit-sweetened jam (page 278)

1. Sift together flour and baking soda in a mixing bowl. Add chopped walnuts.
2. Mix the water and egg replacer with the oil, sweetener, vanilla and almond extract.
3. Add the liquid to the dry. Mix well and chill in the freezer for 5–10 minutes.
4. Roll dough into small balls and flatten somewhat on an oiled cookie sheet or baking paper. Press thumb gently into center. Fill with jam.
5. Bake in a pre-heated oven at 350° for 10–13 minutes.

Light and Fluffy Spice Cookies
yields 30

4 C. whole wheat pastry flour	1/2 C. maple syrup
1 t. egg replacer	1 T. vanilla
1 1/2 t. baking soda	1/2 C. oil
1 T. cinnamon	1/4 C. tofu, rinsed and drained
1/2 t. nutmeg	1/2–3/4 C. dry sweetener
1 t. allspice	1 C. raisins (soaked 10 min and drained)

1. In a bowl, sift flour, egg replacer, baking soda and spices.
2. In a blender, blend remaining ingredients, except the raisins soaked in water.
3. Pour wet mixture into dry and add raisins. Mix well. If batter is sticky, add a bit more flour.
4. Roll into balls and flatten onto an oiled cookie sheet (or use baking papers).
5. Bake at 350° in a pre-heated oven for approximately 10 minutes or until cookies are golden-brown and cracks appear on top.

> *"I will not kill or hurt any living creature needlessly,*
> *nor destroy any beautiful thing,*
> *but will strive to save and comfort all gentle life,*
> *and guard and protect all natural beauty upon the earth."*
>
> JOHN RUSKIN (1819-1900) ~ English author

Holiday Spice Cookies
yields 3 dozen

2/3 C. oil	1 t. baking soda
1 1/4 C. dry sweetener	4 t. cinnamon
1/4 C. tahini & 1/2 C. water	1/4 t. allspice
1 T. vanilla	1/8 t. nutmeg
4 C. whole wheat pastry flour	1 C. raisins (rinsed and drained)

1. In a large bowl, combine oil, sweetener, tahini and water mixture and vanilla. Mix well.
2. In a separate bowl, sift the flour, baking soda and spices. Stir in raisins.
3. Mix the dry mixture into the liquid mixture and stir to a smooth consistency.
4. The batter should be fairly dry. Roll batter into small balls and form into cookies. Place on an oiled cookie sheet. Bake in a pre-heated oven at 350° for 8–10 minutes, until bottoms are slightly browned.

Carob Chip Cookies
yields 32

4 C. whole wheat pastry flour	3/4 C. tofu, rinsed & drained
1 t. baking soda	1/2 C. maple syrup
2/3 C. oil	1/2 t. vanilla
1/8 C. water	1 C. non-dairy carob chips (page 278)
1/3+ C. dry sweetener	

1. In a bowl, sift together pastry flour and baking soda.
2. In a blender, blend remaining ingredients, except for carob chips.
3. Pour wet mixture into the dry and mix thoroughly. If batter is sticky, add a bit more flour. Add the carob chips and mix. Shape into cookies and place them on a lightly oiled cookie sheet (or use baking paper).
4. Bake in a pre-heated oven at 350° until the cookies crack a bit on top (approximately 10 minutes). Rotate trays half-way through, so they bake evenly on the top and bottom.

> *"....Why is compassion not part of our established curriculum, an inherent part of our education? Compassion, awe, wonder, curiosity, exaltation, humility—these are the very foundation of any real civilization..."*
>
> YEHUDI MENUHIN (1916-1999) ~ world-renowned violinist

Chips A' High Cookies
yields 30–35

4 C. whole wheat pastry flour	3/4+ C. oil (mild-flavored oil)
1/2 t. baking soda	2 t. vanilla (or maple syrup)
1/4 t. sea salt	1 1/4 C. dry sweetener
1 T. baking powder	1/8–1/4 C. maple syrup
2 T. egg replacer mixed with	1/4 C. soy milk
1/3 C. water or soy/rice milk	1 1/4 C. vegan chocolate chips (see pg. 278)

1. In a bowl, sift together flour, baking soda, salt and baking powder.
2. In a separate bowl, mix egg replacer mixture, oil, vanilla, sweeteners and soy milk.
3. Add dry mixture to the wet batter. Mix. Fold in chocolate chips.
4. Form into cookies and place onto a lightly oiled cookie sheet (or use baking papers).
5. Bake in a pre-heated oven at 350° for 10–15 minutes or until cracks appear on top. Bottoms should be lightly browned.

Oatmeal Chewies
yields 18–24 large cookies

2/3 C. oil	1 t. baking soda
3/4 C. dry sweetener	1/3 t. sea salt
3/4 C. maple syrup	3/4 t. cinnamon
1/2 C. water	4 t. soy powder
2 t. vanilla	6 C. oats
2 C. whole wheat pastry flour	1 1/2 C. raisins

1. With a whisk, blend together oil, sweeteners, water and vanilla until fluffy.
2. Sift together flour, baking soda, sea salt, cinnamon and soy powder. Add dry to the wet and stir. Add oats and raisins and mix thoroughly. Shape into cookies and place on an oiled cookie sheet (or use baking papers).
3. Bake in a pre-heated oven at 350° for 12–17 minutes or until golden-brown on the bottom.
   • Optional ~ Add 1–2 teaspoons of maple or almond flavoring.

*above: **Pumpkin Pie** (page 231) ~ below right: **Heavenly Carob Cake** (page 235)*
*below left: **Rich Chocolate Mousse** (page 230) layered with **Whipped Dream** (page 242)*

> *"...There slowly grew up in me an unshakable conviction that we have no right to inflict suffering and death on another living creature, unless there is some unavoidable necessity for it."*
>
> ALBERT SCHWEITZER, M.D. (1875-1965) ~ Alsatian philosopher and medical missionary, 1952 Nobel Prize recipient

Tootie Fruitie Thumbprint Cookies
yields 25

4 C. whole wheat pastry flour
1 t. baking soda
1/8 C. water
1/4 C. maple syrup
1 C. oil

2 T. lemon/lime peels, grated
1/4 C. tofu, rinsed & drained
3/4 C. dry sweetener
1 t. vanilla
10 oz. fruit-sweetened jam (page 278)

1. In a bowl, sift flour and baking soda.
2. Mash tofu and blend well in a blender with remaining ingredients, except for the jam.
3. Pour wet mixture into the dry and mix. If batter is too sticky, add a little more flour.
4. Roll into little balls and flatten somewhat on an oiled cookie sheet, (or use baking papers.) Put a thumb print in the middle of each and fill with half a teaspoon of jam.
5. Bake in a pre-heated oven at 350° for 10-15 minutes or until golden-brown.

Christmas Gingerbread Cookies
yields 30

1/4 C. oil
1/2 C. dry sweetener
3/4 C. molasses
1/3 C. water
3 1/2 C. whole wheat pastry flour

1 t. baking soda
1/2 t. allspice
1 t. cinnamon
3/4 t. ginger powder
1/2 t. ground cloves
1/4 t. sea salt (optional)

1. Whisk the wet ingredients, including sweetener, together in a bowl.
2. In a separate bowl, sift the dry ingredients (starting with pastry flour).
3. Pour wet ingredients into the dry and mix thoroughly.
4. Cover the batter and refrigerate for several hours.
5. Roll out dough and use cookie cutters to form shapes.
6. Place the cookies on a lightly oiled cookie sheet (or use baking papers). Bake in a pre-heated oven at 350° for 10-15 minutes or until golden-brown.

> *"It ill becomes us to invoke in our daily prayers the blessings of God, the Compassionate, if we in turn will not practice elementary compassion towards our fellow creatures."*
>
> MAHATMA GANDHI (1869-1948) ~ Hindu pacifist, spiritual leader

Outrageous Cookies
yields 2 dozen

3 C. whole wheat pastry flour	3/4 C. oil
1 T. baking powder	1 C. dry sweetener
1/2 t. sea salt	2 T. maple syrup
1/2 t. baking soda	2 t. vanilla
2 T. egg replacer,	1/2 C. raisins or non-dairy carob chips
mixed with 3 T. water	1/2 C. walnuts, chopped

1. Sift flour, baking powder, salt and baking soda into a bowl. Mix wet ingredients, including sweeteners. Add the dry to the wet, then add raisins and walnuts. Mix.
2. Roll into balls and flatten onto an oiled cookie sheet (or use baking papers).
3. Bake in a pre-heated oven at 350° for 14–15 minutes. Allow to cool before serving.

 • Use a non-dairy margarine (see page 274) in place of oil for a butter-type cookie.

Chocolate Walnut Cookies
yields 20

2 T. maple syrup	2 1/2 C. flour (spelt or whole wheat pastry)
3/4 C. oil or margarine	1/2 T. baking powder
1 t. vanilla	1/2 t. baking soda
1 1/2 C. dry sweetener	3/4 C. cocoa powder
1/2 t. sea salt	1 C. walnuts, chopped

1. In a blender, blend all liquid ingredients with sweetener and salt.
2. In a bowl, sift flour, baking powder, baking soda and cocoa.
3. Add wet to dry and mix thoroughly. Fold in walnuts. Roll into balls and flatten onto an oiled cookie sheet (or use baking papers).
4. Bake in a pre-heated oven at 350° for 8–12 minutes.

above: **Liberty's Chocolate Cream Pie** *(page 232)* ~ *below left:* **Carrot Cake** *(page 236)*
below right: **Brownies** *(page 252),* **Outrageous** *and* **Chocolate Walnut Cookies** *(page 249)*

"People are the only animals that drink the milk
of the mother of another species.
All other animals stop drinking milk altogether after weaning.
It is unnatural for a dog to nurse from a mother giraffe;
it is just as unnatural for a human being
to drink the milk of a cow."

MICHAEL A. KLAPER, M.D. ~ American author and international lecturer

Oatmeal Cookies
yields 28

6 C. oats	2/3 C. oil
2 C. whole wheat pastry flour	2/3 C. water
1 1/2 t. baking soda	1/4 C. soft tofu, rinsed & drained
1/2 t. sea salt	2 t. vanilla
2 t. cinnamon	1 C. raisins
2 C. dry sweetener	

1. Place oats in a large bowl. Sift in flour, baking soda, salt and cinnamon, stir.
2. Blend the sweetener, oil, water, tofu and vanilla in a blender. Pour the wet into the dry and mix well. Fold in the raisins and mix again.
3. Form the dough into cookies and place on oiled baking sheets (or use baking papers). Bake in a pre-heated oven at 350° for 15 minutes.

Wheat–Free Chocolate Chip Cookies
yields 1 dozen

<u>Wet</u>	<u>Dry</u>
1 T. vanilla	2 C. spelt flour
1/3 C. oil	1/2 t. baking soda
1/2 C. tofu, rinsed & drained	1/2 t. baking powder
1/4 C. rice or soy milk	<u>Add</u>
1 C. dry sweetener	1 C. carob/chocolate chips (dairy-free)

1. In a blender, blend the first four ingredients. Pour into a large bowl. (Using a rubber spatula, scrape sides of the blender to get all the mixture.) Add sweetener and mix.
2. In a separate bowl, sift dry ingredients and mix. Mix the dry into the wet ingredients.
3. Add chips to the dough and gently stir.
4. Roll or spoon out into 1/2" balls and flatten onto an oiled and floured cookie sheet.
5. Bake in a pre-heated oven at 350° for 10–15 minutes or until golden-brown.

• Variation ~ Use 1/2 cup raisins and 1/2 cup chopped nuts instead of chips.
• Variation ~ Use 1 T. ground flaxseed mixed with 3 T. boiled water instead of oil for an oil-free cookie.

> *"It is madness to think that one can solve a problem with the same thinking that created it."*
>
> ALBERT EINSTEIN (1879-1955) ~ German-born American physicist
> 1921 Nobel Prize recipient

Lemon Walnut Cookies
yields 2 dozen

3 1/4 C. whole wheat pastry flour
2 t. baking powder
2 T. egg replacer (dry)
1/2 t. sea salt
1/2 t. baking soda
4 T. maple syrup

3 T. lemon rind
3-4 T. fresh lemon juice
3/4 C. oil
2 t. vanilla
1 C. dry sweetener
1 1/2 C. walnuts, chopped

1. Sift dry ingredients (except sweetener) into a bowl. Blend the remaining ingredients (except walnuts) in a blender.
2. Add wet mixture to the dry and mix, folding in walnuts at the end.
3. Shape into small balls and flatten onto an oiled cookie sheet (or use baking papers).
4. Bake in a pre-heated oven at 350° for 12-15 minutes, until bottoms are golden-brown.

Vanilla Cakies
yields 2 dozen

1/2 C. oil
1/2 C. maple syrup
2 T. egg replacer
    mixed with 2 T. water

1 1/2 T. vanilla
2 1/8 C. whole wheat pastry flour
1/2 t. baking soda

1. In a blender, blend oil, maple syrup, egg replacer mixture and vanilla.
2. In a bowl, sift together the flour and baking soda. Pour the wet into the dry and mix.
3. Drop batter by the spoonful onto an oiled cookie sheet. Bake in a pre-heated oven at 375° for approximately 10 minutes or until bottom is crispy brown. Allow to cool.

Brownies
yields 8-9

1/2 C. non-dairy margarine (pg. 274)
2/3 C. cocoa
2 T. egg replacer
1 C. soy milk
2 C. dry sweetener

1/2 t. sea salt
1 t. vanilla
2 C. whole wheat pastry flour
1 C. walnuts, chopped

1. Melt margarine in a small saucepan on the stove. Mix in cocoa until creamy.
2. In a mixing bowl, whisk egg replacer and soy milk. Add sweetener, salt, and vanilla. Mix well, adding the melted margarine and cocoa.
3. Add flour to the wet mixture and mix well. Fold in walnuts.
4. Spread into a 9" x 12" oiled and floured baking pan.
5. Bake in a pre-heated oven at 350° for 25 minutes or until a toothpick comes out dry.

Carob Chip Pecan Squares
yields one 7" square baking pan

3/4 C. whole wheat pastry flour	1/3 C. dry sweetener
1/2 t. baking soda	1 t. vanilla
1 T. soy powder & 3 t. water, mixed	1/2 C. pecan halves (sliced)
1/3 C. oil	1/2 C. non-dairy carob chips (page 278)

1. Sift flour and baking soda together in a bowl.
2. Blend wet ingredients together, including the sweetener.
3. Combine the wet and dry mixtures, stirring in pecans and carob chips.
4. Pour into a lightly oiled 7" square shallow baking pan. Spread out to cover bottom. Bake in a pre-heated oven at 350° for 15–20 minutes or until lightly browned. Let cool in pan then cut into squares.

Zappy Orange and Ginger Squares
Contributed by Wild Ginger Restaurant - Vegan Village, United Kingdom

	Topping
1/2 C. non-dairy margarine (or oil)	
2 T. rice syrup and/or maple syrup	1/3 C. non-dairy margarine (page 274)
1/2 C. dry sweetener	1 t. ground ginger
2 t. ground ginger	1 T. maple or rice syrup
1 orange, juiced (save rind)	orange rind (saved from juicing)
1 1/8 C. (or 9 oz.) rolled oats	1/2 C. rice syrup or liquid sweetener

1. Melt margarine and mix with syrup, dry sweetener, ginger and orange juice. (Grate orange rind and keep for topping.) When dissolved, add oats and mix well.
2. Spread on an oiled baking tray and level out. Bake in a pre-heated oven at 375° for 20 minutes or until golden-brown. Leave to cool.
3. To make the topping, blend melted margarine, ginger and syrup together. Add orange rind and rice syrup. Mix well. Make sure there are no lumps.
4. Spread over cooled oat base. Refrigerate. Cut into squares and serve.

"The time will come when men such as I will look upon the murder of animals as they now look upon the murder of men."

LEONARDO DA VINCI (1425-1519) ~ Italian sculptor, artist and inventor

Sweet Tarts
yields 17

4 C. whole wheat pastry flour
1 t. baking soda
3/4 C. oil
2 lime or lemon peels, grated
1/2 C. tofu (not firm)

2 t. vanilla
1/4 C. water
1 C. maple syrup and/or dry sweetener
fruit-sweetened jam (to fill tarts with)
   (see page 278)

1. In a bowl, sift together flour and baking soda. Rinse and drain tofu.
2. In a blender, blend oil, grated citrus rinds, tofu, vanilla, water and sweetener.
3. Pour wet mixture into the dry. Mix together thoroughly until batter no longer sticks to fingers. Oil one or two muffin tins (enough for 17 tarts).
4. Fill each muffin cup by pressing in the dough, leaving room in the middle for jam.
5. Bake in a pre-heated oven at 350° for 10 minutes. Remove and drop 1 t. of jam in each tart's center. Place back in the oven for 7-9 minutes and bake. Allow to cool.
6. Run a small knife around the edge of each tart to pop it out.

Maple Pecan Biscotti
yields 2 loaves, sliced

1/2 C. pecans, finely chopped
   (use almonds or a mix of both)
1/2 C. soft tofu, rinsed & drained
1/4 C. maple syrup
1/4 C. safflower oil
2 t. vanilla

1/4 C. dry sweetener
3 C. whole wheat pastry flour
1 t. baking powder
1 t. baking soda
1/4 t. salt

1. In a food processor, using the "S" shaped blade, chop nuts finely. Set aside.
2. In food processor, blend tofu, the remaining wet ingredients and dry sweetener.
3. Add pecans/almonds and one cup of whole wheat pastry flour to processor; whiz.
4. Take dough out of food processor, place in a bowl. Sift in remaining flour, baking soda and powder and salt. Mix. The dough should be firm but not dry. Add more flour if needed.
5. Place dough on an oiled baking tray and mold into two long loaves about three inches wide.
6. Bake in pre-heated oven at 375° for 20-25 minutes, until golden-brown.
7. Remove from oven. Let cool and cut, while warm, into 3/4 inch thick pieces and place back on to the baking tray. In oven, toast each side for 4-5 minutes.

> *"To see what is right and not to do it, is want of courage."*
>
> CONFUCIUS (551-479 B.C.) ~ Chinese political and ethical philosopher

Easy Biscotti
yields 2 loaves

3 1/2 C. whole wheat pastry flour	1 t. vanilla
1 t. each: baking powder/soda	1 t. almond extract
1 C. dry sweetener	4 T. tahini & 5 T. water, mixed
1/2 C. oil	1/4 C. orange juice

1. In a medium-sized bowl, sift flour, baking powder and baking soda.
2. In a separate bowl, mix together sweetener and all liquid ingredients. Slowly add the liquid ingredients to the dry, and mix until you get a dough-like texture. Use enough flour so it is not sticking to your fingers. If too dry, add a bit more liquid.
3. Divide dough into two sections and form into separate long loaves. Pre-heat oven to 350°. Place on a lightly oiled baking sheet and bake for 25–35 minutes or until golden-brown.
4. Take out, let cool and slice loaves, while warm, into pieces about an inch thick.
   - Optional ~ For a drier slice, toast in the oven for four minutes on each side.
   - Optional ~ Add 1/2 cup chopped walnuts and raisins to dough.

Carob Coconut Bars
yields one 8" x 8" pan

<u>Crust</u>

1 1/2 C. oats	1 T. egg replacer + 1 1/2 T. water, mixed
1/2 C. dry sweetener	1 t. vanilla
1/2 C. whole wheat pastry flour	<u>Topping</u>
1 1/2 t. baking powder	1 C. non-dairy carob chips (page 278)
1/4 t. baking soda	1/2 C. walnuts
2 T. maple syrup	1 C. shredded coconut
1/3 C. oil or vegan margarine	1/4 C. maple syrup
1/4 t. sea salt	1 t. vanilla

1. In a bowl, sift the flour, baking soda and baking powder. Add the remaining <u>Crust</u> ingredients, mixing thoroughly. Press firmly into a lightly oiled pan or pie plate.
2. Stir together topping ingredients. Spread evenly over bottom layer, pressing lightly together.
3. Bake in a pre-heated oven at 350° for 25 minutes, until golden-brown. Remove from oven and cool before serving.

> *"The animals of the world exist for their own reasons.*
> *They were not made for humans any more than blacks*
> *were made for whites, or women for men."*
>
> ALICE WALKER ~ American author, <u>The Color Purple</u>

Danish Pastry
yields 2 loaves

2 T. active dry yeast	1 t. lemon rind
1 T. dry sweetener	1/2 C. hot water
1/2 C. lukewarm water	4 3/4 C. whole wheat pastry flour, sifted
1/3 C. (additional) dry sweetener	4+ T. oil
1/2 C. maple syrup	1/3 C. dry sweetener (additional)
3/4 C. thick soy milk (see page 10)	2 T. cinnamon
or other non-dairy milk	1 t. nutmeg
1 t. sea salt	1/2 C. raisins, chopped
1/2 C. oil	1 C. nuts, chopped

1. In a small bowl, combine the yeast, one tablespoon dry sweetener and the warm water. Let rise until doubled in size, about 15 minutes (see page 11).
2. In a large bowl, combine 1/3 cup of sweetener, maple syrup, soy milk, sea salt, oil, lemon rind and the hot water. Mix well. Add the yeast mixture. Gradually add the sifted flour in 4 parts, mixing well each time. Cover and allow to rise for 20 minutes.
3. Turn dough onto a well-floured board and knead for approximately 10 minutes until satiny smooth, adding flour as needed.
4. Place in an oiled bowl and oil the top of the dough. Cover and allow to rise for approximately one hour, until doubled in volume. Punch the dough down.
5. Divide the dough in half; roll out one half on a floured board into a 9" x 12" rectangle. Cover with 1-2 tablespoons of oil. Sprinkle with half of the dry sweetener, cinnamon, nutmeg, chopped raisins and nuts.
6. Roll up, like a jelly roll, starting along the longest side; pinch ends. Place on an oiled cookie sheet. Repeat with the other half of the dough. Allow to rise for approximately one hour, until doubled in size.
7. Bake in a pre-heated oven at 325° for 20–30 minutes, watching carefully to prevent burning.

Glaze

3 T. sorghum or liquid sweetener	1 T. date sugar or dry sweetener
3 T. oil	1/4 C. chopped nuts

8. Combine liquid sweetener, oil and date sugar in a saucepan. Bring to a boil over medium heat. When finished, spread the hot glaze over the warm danish.
9. Sprinkle with chopped nuts. Partially cool and serve.

"There is no escaping the harsh reality that many of the methods employed in the commercial production of honey are cruel and repugnant and provide an overwhelming case for ethical vegans to reject the use of this product and its derivatives."

ARTHUR LING ~ President/Managing Director of Plamil Foods

Fruit Pastry
yields 3 loaves

1 C. maple syrup
1-2 t. vanilla
1 C. oil
1/4 C. tofu
1-2 lemon/orange rinds, grated

4 C. whole wheat pastry flour
1 t. baking soda
3/4 C. fruit-sweetened jam (page 278)
   or apple sauce, for filling

1. Rinse and drain tofu. In a blender, blend the first five ingredients.
2. Sift flour and baking soda together into a bowl and stir.
3. Add wet ingredients to the dry and mix thoroughly. The batter should not stick. If it is sticky, add a small amount of flour and mix. Chill before rolling out.
4. Split batter into three equal balls. Place one ball at a time between two pieces of wax paper. Roll out into a rectangle, using a rolling pin, from the center outward.
5. Place four tablespoons of jam or apple sauce on half the dough and roll up lengthwise into a loaf, tucking ends in.
6. Place each loaf on an oiled baking sheet (three on a tray) and spread apart evenly.
7. Place on the bottom shelf of a pre-heated oven at 350° and bake for 15-20 minutes. Switch to the upper shelf and bake to a golden-brown crisp (about 15 more minutes).
8. Cut into slices before the loaves are totally cooled. (When they harden they become more difficult to slice.)

Pumpkin Bread-Cake
yields 1 bread pan

1/3 C. oil
1/8 C. soy milk (see page 10)
1 C. canned pumpkin
4 1/2 t. egg replacer & 6 T. water
2 1/4 C. whole wheat pastry flour

1 1/4 C. dry sweetener
1 t. baking soda, sifted
2 t. cinnamon
1/2 t. sea salt
1/2 C. raisins

1. In a blender, blend oil, soy milk, pumpkin and egg replacer/water mixture.
2. Sift flour and combine with remaining dry ingredients (not raisins) into a bowl.
3. Add wet to the dry, mixing lightly, and fold in raisins.
4. Bake in a pre-heated oven at 350°, in a small baking dish or loaf pan for 45-55 minutes, or when a toothpick comes out dry.

---

*"We cannot have peace among men
whose hearts delight in killing any living creature.
By every act that glorifies or even tolerates such delight
in killing, we set back the progress of humanity."*

RACHEL CARSON (1907-1964) ~ American author, Silent Spring

Banana Bread
yields 1 loaf

1 C. dry sweetener	1 t. baking soda
3 bananas, mashed	1/2 t. cinnamon
1/2 C. oil	1/2 C. walnuts, chopped
2 1/2 C. whole wheat pastry flour	1/2 C. raisins

1. In a bowl, mix sweetener, bananas and oil. In a separate bowl, sift dry ingredients.
2. Mix dry and wet batter together. Add walnuts and raisins. Mix again.
3. Pour into an oiled and floured loaf pan. Bake in a pre-heated oven at 350° for 45-60 minutes, or until a paring knife/toothpick comes out dry.

Rogolos
yields 15-20

Dough	Filling
2 C. whole wheat pastry flour	1/2 C. pecans
2 T. egg replacer	1/2 C. walnuts
1/4 C. orange juice	1/4 C. maple syrup
1/4 C. apple sauce	1/2 C. raisins
1/4 C. oil	1 T. cinnamon
1/2 t. sweetener	1/2 t. allspice

<u>Dough</u> *You can also substitute Apple Pie crust, page 228.*
1. Sift flour and egg replacer together in a bowl and mix.
2. Mix the wet dough ingredients in a separate bowl. (For an even healthier treat, substitute more apple sauce for the oil.)
3. Mix the dry into the wet. (You may need to use your hands at the end to mix all the flour in.) Dough should be dry enough so that it does not stick to your fingers.
4. Roll dough out (on wax paper or a floured board) into two flattened and very thin rectangles.

<u>Filling</u>
5. Chop the nuts into fine pieces. Mix nuts with the rest of the filling ingredients and spread on the rolled out dough. Roll lengthwise, pinch ends together and place on a baking sheet.
6. Bake in a pre-heated oven at 350° for 30-40 minutes until lightly browned on top and bottom. Let cool and cut into 1-2 inch rounds while still warm.

> *"You put a baby in a crib with an apple and a rabbit. If it eats the rabbit and plays with the apple, I'll buy you a new car."*
>
> HARVEY DIAMOND ~ American author, co-author, <u>Fit for Life</u>

Tart Baked Apples – Low Fat
yields 4

4 tart apples (Granny Smith)
1 T. fresh lemon juice
1/2 t. cinnamon

1/4 C. brown rice syrup
1 t. vanilla
1/3 C. orange juice
1/3 C. golden raisins

1. Use hard, firm apples. Remove the stems and cores. Place in a baking dish.
2. Squeeze lemon juice over apples then sprinkle with cinnamon, sweetener and vanilla.
3. Top with orange juice and raisins. Bake (uncovered) in a pre-heated oven at 350° for 30 minutes.

Hot 'Mochalate'
makes 4 cups

2 C. soy milk
2 C. water
4 T. cocoa

3 1/2 T. coffee substitute (page 280)
4 T. sweetener
1/8 t. vanilla

In a small saucepan, heat all ingredients on low. Serve hot.
• Variation ~ Chill and serve on ice or with a scoop of non-dairy ice cream (page 275).

Hot Carob Espresso Amaretto Beverage
yields 1/2 blender

a dash of almond flavor
2 T. carob
1/2 T. vanilla powder
  (or 1/4 T. liquid vanilla)

1 1/4 T. coffee substitute (page 280)
2 T. tahini
2 T. maple syrup
2 C. boiling hot water

In a blender, blend all ingredients. Serve with dessert or after a meal.

"Animals are God's creatures, not human property, nor utilities, nor resources, nor commodities, but precious beings in God's sight."

REV. DR. ANDREW LINZEY ~ Anglican (Episcopalian) priest, professor of theology
chaplain Oxford University, author of 13 books

Carob Mint Beverage
yields 2 1/2 cups

2 C. boiling hot water
2 T. carob powder
3 T. tahini
2 T. molasses

1 T. maple syrup
1/8 t. mint extract
1 t. vanilla

In a blender, blend the above ingredients until smooth, then serve.

Pineapple Heaven Drink
yields 2 1/2 cups

1 C. frozen banana (peeled), sliced
   (see page 217)
2 C. fresh pineapple, chopped
3/4 C. fresh orange juice

1/8 t. almond extract
a dash of vanilla
3 T. maple syrup

In a blender, blend the above ingredients until creamy. Add a handful of ice cubes and blend again. Serve.

Carob Peanut Butter Protein Drink
yields 2 cups

1 C. soy/rice milk
1 1/2 T. carob powder
2-3 T. peanut butter
1 banana

1-2 T. sweetener
1 T. vegan protein powder
   (see page 281)

In a blender, blend the above ingredients until creamy. Add a handful of ice cubes and blend again. Serve.

"A study of 45,619 male health workers by Harvard School of Public Health found that men with the highest intake of potassium, contained in fruits and vegetables, reduced their risk of kidney stones by 50 percent, while those who ate the most animal protein increased their risk by 33 percent."

NEW ENGLAND JOURNAL OF MEDICINE ~ March 25, 1993

Banini or Vanilla (Malted) Shake
yields 1 blender

ice cold water
4 bananas, peeled & frozen, sliced
   (see page 217)

1/4 C. tahini
1 T. maple syrup
1 t. vanilla

In a blender, start with one cup of ice cold water. Add the remaining ingredients and blend. If too thick, add more water. Sweeten to taste.

• Suggested variations ~ strawberry, carob, carob-mint

Creamy Chocolate Milk
yields 4 cups

1/2-2/3 C. cashew pieces (raw)
1 C. water
5 t. carob or cocoa powder
1 T. sweetener

1/8 t. vanilla
1/2-1 T. maple syrup
2 C. ice cold water
1/2 t. tahini

In a blender, blend the cashew pieces with one cup of water and homogenize to a creamy consistency. Use a rubber spatula to push the small cashew pieces from blender sides into the mixture. Add remaining ingredients. Blend and serve.

Almond Cashew Drink
yields 2 glasses

1/3 C. raw cashew pieces
1 T. almond butter
2/3 C. ice water

1-2 T. sweetener
1 t. almond extract
1 C. ice water (additional)

In a blender, purée the first three ingredients.
Add the remaining ingredients. Blend until smooth and serve.

• Use raw or roasted cashew pieces and almond butter, according to taste.

> *"In order to get meat, we have to kill. And we are certainly not entitled to any other milk except the mother's milk in our infancy."*
>
> MAHATMA GANDHI (1869-1948) ~ Hindu pacifist, spiritual leader

A New Paradigm

A
New
Paradigm

> "*Very little of the great cruelty shown by men can really be attributed to cruel instinct. Most of it comes from thoughtlessness or inherited habit. The roots of cruelty, therefore, are not so much strong as widespread. But the time must come when inhumanity protected by custom and thoughtlessness will succumb before humanity championed by thought. Let us work that this time may come.*"
>
> **ALBERT SCHWEITZER, M.D. (1875–1965)**
> **Alsatian philosopher and medical missionary**
> **1952 Nobel Prize recipient**

Time For A New World

Time for a new world
We're waking up to a brighter dream
Time for a new world
The morning sounds have a new world theme
And they sing of a life
That is gentle and high
Of a day that shall rise
With the sun in the sky

Time for a new world
Where love lifts us 'til we can see the light
Time for a new world
A world in which everything is right
If enough people cared
We all would be free
From a dream that is shared
Comes reality
Time for a new world

"There is no force powerful enough to stem the tide of an idea whose time has come. We can no longer, in good conscience or in good health, continue to use animals for food.

The vegan concept is not a fad that will pass with time. It is a necessary shift in thinking, that will lead to a heightened empathy and concern for others. It is the expansion of compassion, which is the single most important step in the next evolution of humankind.

When we consider the wolf and the elephant, the shark and the ox, the weasel and the deer, we find that it is not the size or strength of animals, but how they obtain their food, that determines whether their nature is violent or gentle.

We humans are also animals. Therefore, it is how our food is obtained that determines our own nature: violent or gentle. A gentle human nature is essential if we are to evolve; and we must evolve, if we are to survive."

Light
Co-founder & President
Gentle World

What We Know
Excerpts from <u>THE FOOD REVOLUTION</u> ~ *John Robbins* ~ *Conari Press*

Cholesterol
- Blood cholesterol levels of vegetarians compared to non-vegetarians: 14% lower
- Blood cholesterol levels of vegans compared to non-vegetarians: 35% lower
- Risk of death from heart disease for vegetarians compared to non-vegetarians: Half
- Chicken has about as much cholesterol as beef. There is simply no escaping the correlation between meat consumption and cholesterol levels.

High Blood Pressure
- People with high blood pressure are 7 times more likely to suffer a stroke, 4 times more likely to have a heart attack and 5 times more likely to die of congested heart failure than people with normal blood pressure.
- High blood pressure in meat eaters compared with vegetarians: 13 times higher
- Patients with high blood pressure who achieve substantial improvement by switching to a vegetarian diet: 30–75%
- Incidence of high blood pressure among senior citizens in the U.S.: More than 50%
- Incidence of high blood pressure among senior citizens in countries eating traditional low-fat plant-based diets: Virtually none

Cancer
- Number of lives lost to colon cancer each year in the U.S.: 55,000
- Risk of colon cancer for women who eat red meat daily compared to those who eat it less than once a month: 250% greater
- Risk of colon cancer for people who eat red meat once a week compared to those who abstain: 38% greater
- Risk of colon cancer for people who eat poultry once a week compared to those who abstain: 55% greater
- Risk of colon cancer for people who eat poultry four times a week compared to those who abstain: 200–300% greater
- Risk of colon cancer for people who eat beans, peas or lentils at least twice a week compared to people who avoid these foods: 50% lower

Dairy Products
- Countries with the highest consumption of dairy products: Finland, Sweden, United States and England
- Countries with the highest rate of Osteoporosis: Finland, Sweden, United States and England
- Children with chronic constipation so untreatable that it can't be treated successfully by laxatives, who are cured by switching from cow's milk to soy milk: 44%

"A loving heart is the truest wisdom."

CHARLES DICKENS (1812-1870) ~ English novelist

Environment

· Amount of greenhouse-warming carbon gas released in one day by driving a typical American car: 3 kilograms
· Amount released by clearing and burning enough Costa Rican rainforest to produce beef for one hamburger: 75 kilograms
· Next to carbon dioxide, the most destabilizing gas to the planet's climate is methane. Concentrations of atmospheric methane are now nearly triple what they were when they began rising a century ago. The primary reason is beef production.
"Livestock account for 15–20% of global methane emissions." - Worldwatch Institute

Water

· Water required to produce 1 lb. of California foods, according to Soil & Water specialists, University of California Agricultural Extension, working with livestock advisors:

1 pound of lettuce	23 gallons	1 pound of apples	49 gallons
1 pound of tomatoes	23 gallons	1 pound of chicken	815 gallons
1 pound of potatoes	24 gallons	1 pound of pork	1,630 gallons
1 pound of wheat	25 gallons	1 pound of beef	5,214 gallons
1 pound of carrots	33 gallons		

World Hunger

· U.S. corn eaten by people: 2%   · U.S. corn eaten by livestock: 77%
· U.S. farmland producing vegetables: 4 million acres
· U.S. farmland producing hay for livestock: 56 million acres
· U.S. grain and cereals fed to livestock: 70%
· Humans who could be fed by the grain and soy eaten by U.S. livestock: 1,400,000,000
· World's population living in the U.S.: 4%
· World's beef eaten in the U.S.: 23%

Mad Cow Disease

According to the FDA, only two-thirds of licensed feed mills are ever inspected, and more than 20% of these mills do not follow FDA rules designed to keep Mad Cow disease at bay. "Worse," noted a prominent meat industry journal, "there are about 8,000 feed mills that aren't even licensed at all, and less than one-half of those have ever had an FDA inspection."

Compassion

"I do not believe that anyone's true health can be sustained by eating products produced through systems that depend on the relentless and systematic suffering of billions of our fellow creatures...We are not just physical beings with a need for so many grams of iron a day. I believe we are also spiritual beings, with a need for respect and compassion, with a need to make our caring visible, with a need to love and to honor life."

"The vegan paradigm will inspire a heightened spiritual awareness, purify the body, and make possible personal and planetary healing unprecedented in human history."

SUN ~ Co-founder Gentle World, A Newer Age

Healthful Hints

For those who want to reduce oil consumption:
  Sauté with a little water, rather than oil (or mix with water to stretch).
  When baking, replace some of the oil with an equal amount of apple sauce.
  When baking cookies, replace oil with apple juice.

When possible, bake rather than fry.

Steam vegetables lightly; avoid overcooking.

For easier digestion, soak beans overnight, then drain and rinse them before cooking.

Avoid using aluminum-coated cookware; traces of aluminum may taint the food.

Eat foods in their natural, raw state as much as possible.

Avoid genetically modified, chemically sprayed and irradiated foods.

Eat a variety of colors from the vegetable kingdom to ensure a variety of vitamins and minerals.

Eat fruit alone; don't mix with vegetables. The body produces different enzymes to digest fruits and vegetables. These enzymes work better alone.

When possible, use cayenne pepper instead of black pepper. Cayenne aids in blood circulation.

Slippery Elm Bark is an herb from the inner bark of an elm tree that coats the stomach. It is great for an upset stomach. The Soothie Smoothie recipe: 1 C. boiled water, 1 T. slippery elm, 1 t. sweetener, 1 t. tahini, 1/4 banana and 1/2 t. vanilla whizzed in a blender.

Golden Seal and Myrrh is an herbal combination, excellent as a mouthwash and for the gums.

Wheatgrass juice is an excellent source of fresh, live vitamins, minerals, and chlorophyll. It is a potent mouthwash that draws out toxins from the gums and teeth, and is helpful in relief of toothache pain. 1 oz. of wheatgrass juice is an ample portion with which to begin.

"Vitamin D is normally produced within the body after sunlight exposure to the skin. If one does not get regular sun exposure, or lives in a northern area, fortified vegan foods, such as cereal and milk alternatives are available."

NEAL BARNARD, M.D. ~ President, Physicians Committee for Responsible Medicine
author, Turn Off The Fat Genes

Raw garlic is a natural antibiotic that may be included in the diet on a regular basis.

Peppermint tea aids digestion and relieves flatulence.

To relieve hiccups, eat a quarter of an orange.

Hot water with lemon or orange juice, along with a dash of cayenne pepper, is great for alleviating cold symptoms.

Aloe plant leaves are filled with a jelly-like substance that soothes and heals the skin, especially when applied to burns and bites.

Ear candles, found in health food stores, help relieve wax buildup in the inner ear. See page 281 for ear candle companies.

Wild Yam extracts, in the form of skin creams, found in health food stores, are a source of natural progesterone for menopausal women with no negative side effects. They have a molecular structure that is the same as the progesterone found in the female body. Some creams are not vegan. See page 281 for companies that market vegan wild yam extracts.

Echinacea is an herbal antibiotic that strengthens the immune system.

Short, periodic fasting is helpful to the body. It gives our ever-working digestive system a break, and allows time for cleansing, detoxifying and healing. High colonics, fasting and fruit cleansing diets are highly beneficial when evolving from an animal-based to a plant-based diet.

Take a brisk walk in the fresh air and sunshine for your exercise. Spending time with nature, breathing clean air and drinking pure water are essential for vibrant health.

"If you are serious about a vegan diet, start reading labels at the grocery store and look for hidden ingredients. At first you might feel overwhelmed. It seems as though there are animal ingredients - lard, whey, dried milk, egg whites - in everything from bread to margarine and even some veggie burgers. But don't be discouraged - you'll quickly become familiar with ingredients that are truly vegan. Eventually you'll have a shopping list of the products you want to eat."

VIRGINIA MESSINA, MPH, R.D. and MARK MESSINA, Ph.D
<u>Total health for You and Your Family; The Vegetarian Way</u>
Crown Trade Paperbacks, New York

Vitamin B-12

The Vegan Society

To be truly healthful, a diet must be best not just for individuals in isolation but must allow all six billion people to thrive and achieve a sustainable co-existence with the many other species that form the "living earth." From this standpoint, the natural adaptation for most (possibly all) humans in the modern world is a plant-based diet. In choosing to use fortified foods or supplements, vegans are taking their B12 from the same source as every other animal on the planet – micro-organisms – without causing suffering to any sentient being or causing environmental damage.

The only reliable plant-based sources of B12 are foods fortified with B12 (including some plant milks, some soy products and some breakfast cereals) and B12 supplements. Vitamin B12, whether in supplements, fortified foods, or animal products, comes from micro-organisms.

Very low B12 intakes can cause anemia and nervous system damage. Most vegans consume enough B12 to avoid anemia and nervous system damage, but many do not get enough to minimize the potential risk of heart disease or pregnancy complications. To get the full benefit of a plant-based diet, do one of the following:

1) Eat fortified foods 2 or 3 times a day to get at least 3 micrograms of B12 a day
2) Take one B12 supplement daily providing at least 10 micrograms
3) Take a weekly B12 supplement providing at least 2000 micrograms.

If relying on fortified foods, check the labels carefully to make sure you are getting enough B12. For example, if a fortified plant milk contains 1 microgram of B12 per serving then consuming three servings a day will provide adequate vitamin B12. Others may find the use of B12 supplements more convenient and economical.

The less frequently you obtain B12 the more you need to take, as B12 is best absorbed in small amounts. The recommendations above take full account of this. There is no harm in exceeding the recommended amounts or combining more than one option.

In over 60 years of experimentation only B12 fortified foods and B12 supplements have proven themselves as reliable plant-based sources of B12, capable of supporting optimal health. It is very important that all vegans ensure they have an adequate intake of B12, from fortified foods or supplements.

Claimed sources of B12 that have been shown through direct studies of vegans to be in-adequate include human gut bacteria, spirulina, dried nori, barley grass and most other seaweeds.

Certified vegan B12 with Folic Acid Supplements: VegLife™ - Nutraceutical Corp.
(800) VEG-0250

Feeding Your Pets

We have experimented for many years with feeding animals and have found it easy for dogs to enjoy and thrive on a plant-based diet. Cats require extra supplementation, see below.

To ensure that your dogs get enough protein and calcium, feed them a varied diet of tofu, legumes, grains, potatoes, seitan, tempeh, some T.V.P. (see Glossary) and vegetables. Approximately 40% of their diet should be a source of protein, such as well-cooked legumes (garbanzo beans, lentils, split peas, soy beans, etc.), tofu, seitan or potatoes.

A large portion of their dinner can be well-cooked grains; millet, rice, quinoa, barley, oats, pasta, blended corn, etc. (a source of carbohydrates and protein). A tablespoon of bran in their dinner aids bowel elimination. Some veterinarians recommend adding pumpkin seed milk and liquid Kyolic® Garlic (available in a plain liquid formula without whey) or 1/2 to 1 clove of diced raw garlic in their dinner bowl to prevent and decrease worms and other intestinal parasites. Grated raw vegetables, such as carrot, beet, cabbage & sprouted lentils should be included in their meal for fiber. Add some sprouts for vitality.

Oil requirements are met mostly with avocado, which they love. Other sources include 1–2 tablespoons of tahini or vegetable oil and/or raw wheat germ for a shiny coat. Supplement the meal with Red Star™ Vegetarian Support Formula nutritional yeast, Bragg™ Liquid Aminos, a small amount of (food grade) flax seed oil or soaked flax seeds and sometimes a sprinkle of spirulina. Calcium requirements are met with tahini or finely chopped raw greens and from the vitamins and minerals found in canned vegetarian dog foods. Dogs enjoy nori (and other sea vegetables) in bite-sized pieces. Food should be served warm or at least at room temperature. Always serve their meals with a fresh bowl of water. Please note that onions (in large amounts) and chocolate (in small amounts) can be toxic to dogs.

There are also several completely plant-based dog foods. We mix a little canned food into their meals, as they find it irresistible! There are several brands of canned and dry foods that are 100% nutritionally complete (see page 284). Best of all is homemade, fresh food, similar to what you yourself will be eating. You can feel confident that on a plant-based diet, your dog will have a sleek, clean body, clean teeth and a healthy coat.

Cats are more difficult. However, it is possible to feed them a plant-based diet. By nature they are true carnivores, unlike dogs. To avoid serious consequences, a cat's diet <u>must be</u> supplemented with a product containing taurine and certain essential fatty acids. Vege-Cat™, made by Harbingers of a New Age, has had great success. Evolution Diet for cats or Veganpet are other options. A favorite meal of cats includes mashed tofu with nutritional yeast and kelp with 'Vege-Cat'. Other additions include well-cooked chick peas, seaweeds of all kinds, avocado, bread, ground seitan, oatmeal and quinoa.

Look forward to your pet becoming gentler, healthier, cleaner and even more lovable.

<u>RECOMMENDED READING/ADVICE</u>
<u>Vegetarian Dogs and Cats</u> by James Peden <u>www.vegepet.com</u>
<u>Vegetarian Dogs: Towards a World Without Exploitation</u> by Verona Re-Bow & Jonathan Dune
<u>www.vegetariandogs.com</u>
Contact Sandy Anderson for advice on feeding cats vegan <u>www.veganpet.com.au</u>

Animal-Based Products and Ingredients

Meat, fowl, fish and lard involve the killing of animals.

Dairy - "Sweet gentle Bessie is hardly contented at all. She has been denied the natural life of a cow and the pleasures of foraging, ruminating and caring for her young (who are often taken from her at birth to be made into veal). She has been bred, medicated, implanted with hormones, artificially inseminated and kept perpetually pregnant to provide one thing only - continual milk production...When at last she is unable to keep up the demanded level of milk production, drained and exhausted, Bessie will be packed into a crowded truck for transport to her final destination - the meat processing plant."

JOANNE STEPANIAK
The Uncheese Cookbook

Eggs - "Ninety-eight percent of egg-laying hens are housed in battery cages (World Poultry Science Journal, 3/93). Typically, four or five egg-laying hens live in a cage with a wire floor area about the size of a folded newspaper... All free-range, factory farmed and egg-laying animals who don't die from disease are trucked to the slaughterhouse."

VEGAN OUTREACH
"Why Vegan"

Honey - Honey is a concentrated sugar, obtained by robbing bees of the fruits of their labor. When bee keepers take their honey, bees are left with little to eat, or are given an inferior substitute, usually sugar water with antibiotics, as a replacement. From time to time, their hives are smoked out, killing many bees in the process. Honey also carries the risk of botulism, and raw honey is particularly known for breeding bacteria, parasites and viruses. Honey is regurgitated insect food, not intended for human consumption.

Gelatin(e) is a protein dissolved from bones, skin and hide trimmings. It is an ingredient in many food products as well as capsules for medicines and vitamins. (Vegetable-based capsules are sold at health food stores - see page 279.) Gelatin is sometimes used in clearing wines.

White refined sugar is often filtered through bone charcoal (carbonized bone char), derived from cattle. Bone char is a by-product of the gelatin production industry.

Rennet or Rennin is the lining of a calf's stomach, used to coagulate cheese.

Casein or caseinate, sodium caseinate, potassium caseinate. The main protein of cow's milk. Most soy cheeses contain casein.

> *"Within 24 hours of birth, more than 90% of calves are taken away from their mothers forever."*
>
> ERIK MARCUS ~ Vegan: The New Ethics of Eating McBooks Press

Animal-based ingredients found on labels in food items

- **Whey** (derived from milk) - used in margarine, baked goods, cleaning products, etc.
- **Nonfat dry milk, Lactic acid** (when from milk) - by-products of the dairy industry.
- **Beeswax, bee propolis, honey, royal jelly** - all made by bees for the use of bees.
- **Calcium Stearate** is often derived from hogs or cows as an anti-caking agent.
- **Non-dairy creamers** often contain dairy or casein.
- **Lecithin** can be from eggs. Soya lecithin is used more widely.
- **Cod liver oil and anchovy paste** (found in Worcestershire Sauce).
- **Beef bouillon and chicken stock**
- **Diglycerides and Monoglycerides** may be lard (animal fat) unless otherwise noted by "vegetable derived" or something to that effect. Glyceride is a chemical name for fat.
- **Pepsin** from hogs' stomachs is a clotting agent, found in some cheeses and vitamins; with the same uses as rennet. (Plant rennets are available as an alternative.)
- **Albumin** - protein derived, most often from egg whites, used as a food binder.
- **Carminic acid, Carmine** is a red pigment extracted from crushed cochineal insects. To produce 1 lb. of this dye, 70,000 insects are crushed.
- **Vitamins** may have animal sources. Totally vegetarian formulas are available. Vitamin D3 is made from fish oil, or sometimes lanolin (wool fat).
- **Lipase** - an enzyme from the stomachs, etc., of young farm animals. May be in some vitamins. Vegetable enzymes are alternatives.

Other Animal-Based Items

Leather and suede, furs, wool, silk, down, lanolin, tallow, stearic acid, collagen, keratin, elastin, hydrolyzed animal protein, placenta, urea, pearls, ivory, sable brushes, boar bristles, catgut, sperm oil, musk oil, mink oil, shark cartilage, squalene, calcium carbonate, angora and cashmere.

Many soaps, candles, glues & adhesives, cleaning products, pharmaceuticals, fertilizers cosmetics and toiletries may contain animal products or be tested on animals.

For a more comprehensive listing of animal-based products and ingredients, see our website: www.gentleworld.org

"As long as humans have lived upon this planet, they have lived in fear of the violence of other humans. In a new paradigm of reverence for life, that fear will be replaced by trust; and trust will lead to love; the only true religion; the source of all healing."

SUN ~ co-founder Gentle World, <u>A Newer Age</u>

Plant-Based Alternatives

Non–Dairy Milks

Blue Diamond Almond Breeze® ~ Original, vanilla, & chocolate. A gluten-free, cholesterol-free and lactose-free beverage. *Blue Diamond Growers* (800) 987-2329 www.bluediamond.com

Rice Dream™, Soy Dream™ ~ *Imagine Foods* (800) 333-6339 www.imaginefoods.com

Vitasoy™ ~ (800) 848-2769 or (800) VITASOY www.vitasoy-usa.com

Edensoy®, EdenBlend® ~ *Eden Foods* (800) 248-0320 www.edenfoods.com

Westsoy™ ~ *Westbrae* (800) 769-6455 www.westsoy.com

Silk™ Soymilk, Silk Nog & Silk Creamer ~ *White Wave, Inc.* (800) 488-9283 www.whitewave.com

Pacific Almond, Oat, Soy, Rice and Multi-Grain Milks ~ *Pacific Foods of Oregon* (503) 692-9666 www.pacificfoods.com

Soy Moo ~ *Health Valley* (800) 423-4846 www.hain-celestial.com

Cheese Alternatives

Red Star Nutritional Yeast™ ~ 'Vegetarian Support Formula' is fortified with B-12. Use it to make 'cheezy' toppings and gravies. *Red Star Co.* (800) 558-7279 www.redstaryeast.net

VeganRella™ ~ *Rella Good Cheese Co.* (800) 238-3947 www.rella.com

Soymage™ Grated Parmesan Cheese Alternative, Soy Singles, Mozzarella/Cheddar Slices, Cream Cheese, Sour Cream ~ *Soyco Foods* (800) 808-2325 www.galaxyfoods.com

'Chreese' & Nacho Cheese Dips ~ *Road's End Organics* (802) 888-4130 www.chreese.com

Vegan Gourmet™ ~ It melts! *Follow Your Heart* (818) 348-3240 www.imearthkind.com

Butter Replacements

Spectrum Natural Spreads™, Spectrum Organic Shortening™ ~ (800) 995-2705 www.spectrumnaturals.com

Earth Balance Buttery Spread ~ *GFA Brands* (201) 568-9300 www.earthbalance.net

The Natural Food Store Soy Bean Margarine ~ *Kettle Foods* (503) 364-0399

Shedd's Willow Run Soy Margarine ~ (800) 735-3554

Non-Dairy Yogurt

WholeSoy® Creamy Cultured Soy ~ Certified vegan (415) 495-2870 www.wholesoy.com

Silk Cultured Soy™ ~ *White Wave, Inc.* 800) 488-9283 www.whitewave.com

Nancy's Cultured Soy Yogurt ~ 7 vegan varieties - the plain soy has honey. *Nancy's* makes dairy yogurt; check labels. *Springfield Creamery* (541) 689-2911 www.nancysyogurt.com

---

"All the arguments to prove human superiority cannot shatter this hard fact: in suffering, the animals are our equals."

PETER SINGER ~ Australian author, <u>Animal Liberation</u>

Non–Dairy Ice Cream

Organic Soy Delicious™ (Purely Decadent line contains beet sugar (not filtered through bone char), *It's Soy Delicious!™, Sweet Nothings™* ~ *Turtle Mountain* (541) 338-9400 www.turtlemountain.com

Rice Dream/Soy Dream™ ~ The pint containers, pies and bars are vegan. (Trace amounts of dairy can be found in the varieties that contain chocolate or carob due to processing equipment.) *Imagine Foods* (800) 333-6339 www.imaginefoods.com

Tofutti™ Super Soy Supreme ~ *Tofutti Brands* (908) 272-2400 www.tofutti.com Please note: All other Tofutti frozen dessert products contain non-vegan sugar.

WholeSoy® Glacé ~ Certified vegan. (415) 495-2870 www.wholesoy.com

Soy Cream ~ *Double Rainbow Ice Cream Co.* (800) 489-3580 www.doublerainbow.com

FreeZees Nutcreem ~ (928) 636-9419 info@freezees.com www.freezees.com

Meat Substitutes

Vegi-Deli® Pepperoni (3 flavors), *Slice of Life®, Vegi-Jerky* ~ *Green Options, Inc.* (888) 473-3667 info@vegideli.com www.vegideli.com

Tofurky Jurky, Tofurky ~ *Turtle Island Foods* (800) 508-8100 www.tofurky.com

Yves Veggie Cuisine® ~ All meat analogs (bologna, salami, pepperoni, turkey, and ham slices) are vegan & B-12 fortified. ('The Good Slices' cheese contains casein; a milk protein.) *Yves Fine Foods* Canada. (800) 667-9837 www.yvesveggie.com

Tofu Pups®, Lean Links™, Smart Deli Slices®, Savory Seitan™, Foney Baloney, Meatless Gimme Lean!, Sausages, Hot Dogs, many more ~ Some products have egg whites. *Lightlife Foods* (800) SOYEASY (769-3279) www.lightlife.com

UnTurkey™, UnSteak-out, Breast of UnChicken, BBQ Unribs, The UnKabobs ~ *Now & Zen* (800) 335-1959 www.nowandzen.com

Sandwich Slices, Lemon Broil Tempeh, Stir Fry Seitan/Meat of Wheat Chicken Style & Baked Tofu ~ *White Wave Inc.* (800) 488-9283 www.whitewave.com

Heartline Meatless Meats, Stonewall's Jerquee ~ *Lumen Foods* (800) 256-2253 www.soybean.com

Wild Dogs ~ Hot dog alternative (800) 499-8638 www.wildwoodharvestfoods.com

Natural Touch® Tuno ~ Tuna alternative. *Kellogg Co.* (800) 557 6525 www.kelloggs.com

Bac'uns ~ Alternative to bacon bits. *Frontier Co-op* (800) 669-3275 www.frontiercoop.com

Chicken-free Patties/Nuggets/Buffalo Wings ~ www.healthiswealthfoods.com

Meatless Riblets/Savory Herb Chick'n Grill/Meatless Breakfast Sausage ~ Other products not vegan. *Garden Burger Inc.* (800) 636-0109 www.gardenburger.com

Veggie Ribs, Chicken Chunks & Soy Burger Mix, Soy Ball & Loaf, Soy Taco Mix, Soy Chili Mix & Soy BBQ Mix ~ *Harvest Direct* (800) 838-2727 hdirect@usit.net

Mayonnaise

Vegenaise™ ~ *Follow Your Heart* (818) 348-3240 www.followyourheart.com

Nayonaise™ ~ *Nasoya* (800) 229-TOFU www.nasoya.com

Egg Replacement

Ener-G® Foods Egg Replacer ~ *Ener-G Foods* (800) 331-5222 www.ener-g.com (See Baking Guide on page 17 for other egg replacement ideas.)

Burgers

HempNut™ Smoked Burger ~ (707) 571-1330 www.TheHempNut.com
SuperBurgers™ ~ All vegan products! *Turtle Island* (800) 508-8100 www.tofurky.com
Yves Veggie Burgers ~ Two varieties. www.yvesveggie.com
Grilled Hamburger Style® ~ *Garden Burger, Inc.* (800) 636-0109
www.gardenburger.com
Natural Touch Vegan Burger™ ~ *Kellogg Co.* (800) 557-6525 www.kelloggs.com
Boca Burger's Vegan™ ~ Only one kind is vegan. *Boca Foods Co.* www.bocaburger.com
Lightburgers™ ~ *Lightlife Foods* (800) SOYEASY (769-3279) www.lightlife.com
Original Tofu-Vegie Burger ~ (800) 499-8638 www.wildwoodharvestfoods.com
NewMenu Vegi-Burger ~ *Nasoya* (800) 229-TOFU www.nasoya.com
Soyburg USA ~ *Pleasant Farms* (800) 499-9616 www.soyburgusa.com

Breakfast Cereals and Waffles

*Nature's Path Multigrain, Millet-Rice, Mesa Sunrise, Fruit Juice Corn Flakes, Hemp/
Soy Plus, Optimum Power & Slim, 8 Grain Sesame, Buckwheat Wild Berry, & 4
EnviroKids Cereals* ~ Others contain honey. (604) 940-0505 www.naturespath.com
*Health Valley Brown Rice Flakes, Amaranth Flakes, Fiber 7 Flakes, Oat Bran Flakes
& Breakfast Bars* ~*Health Valley* (800) 423-4846 www.hain-celestial.com
LifeStream Toaster Waffles ~ *Nature's Path* (604) 940-0505 www.naturespath.com
Teddy Puffs ~ *Healthy Times* (877) 548-2229 htbaby80@aol.com
*Shredded Spoonfuls, Puffins, Bite-Size Shredded Oats, Shredded Wheat, Corn Flakes,
Breakfast O's, Brown Rice Crisps, Soy Essence, Crispy Wheat* ~ Others contain honey.
Barbara's Bakery (707) 765-2273 www.barbarasbakery.com
Flax Plus Multi-Bran Cereal ~ *LifeStream Natural Foods* www.naturespath.com
Puffed Kashi, Kashi Breakfast Pilaf® & Kashi Go® ~ *The Kashi Co* (858) 274-8870
Kamut Whole Grain Cereal ~ *Arrowhead Mills* www.hain-celestial.com
*Erewhon - Aztec, Corn Flakes, Kamut Flakes, Fruit 'n Wheat, Crispy Brown Rice,
Wheat Flakes, Raisin Bran, Banana O's, Apple Stroodles, Barley Plus, & assorted
Instant Oatmeals* ~ 20 vegan choices! *U.S. Mills* (781) 444-0440 www.usmillsinc.com
Puffed Kashi, Kashi Breakfast Pilaf® & Kashi Go® ~ *The Kashi Co* (858) 274-8870
All Natural Waffles ~*Van's International Foods* (310) 320-8611 www.vansintl.com
Peace Cereals ~ Maple-Raisin has honey. *Golden Temple* (800) 225-3623 goldentemple.com
Soy-N-Energy Organic Cereals ~ B-12 fortified. www.theorganicgardenfood.com

Tempeh and Tofu (Soy Products)

SuperBurgers, Tempeh and Tofurky ~ *Turtle Island* (800) 508-8100 www.tofurky.com
Lightlife Foods ~ (800) SOYEASY (769-3279) www.lightlife.com
Nasoya Tofu ~ Organic or enriched with B-12, etc. (800) 229-TOFU www.nasoya.com
White Wave ~ *White Wave, Inc.* (800) 488-9283 www.whitewave.com
Wildwood Harvest Foods ~ Not all vegan. (800) 499-8638 www.wildwoodharvestfoods.com
Smoke and Fire™ ~ organic tofu in 5 varieties. (413) 528-1877 www.smokeandfire.com
SoyBoy™ ~ *Northern Soy, Inc.* (585) 235-8970 www.SoyBoy.com

Flour

Giusto's ~ A full line of all-natural bakery ingredients. (888) 873-6566 www.giustos.com
Arrowhead Mills ~ High quality flours. www.hain-celestial.com

Breads

French Meadow Bakery ~ All vegan. (877) NO-YEAST www.frenchmeadowbakery.com
Ezekiel 4:9 Bread, Rice Pecan Bread, Rice Almond & Millet Bread ~ Other varieties may contain honey. *Food for Life® Baking Co.* (800) 797-5090 www.food-for-life.com
Manna Bread™ ~ *Nature's Path* (604) 940-0505 www.naturespath.com
Natural Ovens® of Manitowoc Wisconsin ~ The 100% whole wheat contains honey. *Natural Ovens* (800) 558-3535 www.naturalovens.com
Pacific Bakery ~ All vegan. (760) 757-6020 www.pacificbakery.com
Heavenly Soy & Flax ~ Many other varieties contain honey. *Rainier Natural Bakery* (253) 833-4369 www.rainiernaturalbakery.com
Alvarado Bakery ~ Vegan & sprouted bread. (707) 585-3293 www.alvaradostreetbakery.com

Cookies, Baked Goods, Desserts

Organica™ ~ *Organica Foods* (toll-free) 877-OH SO YUM www.organicafoods.com
Sun Flour Baking Co. ~ (916) 488-4150 www.sunflourbaking.com
The Alternative Baking Co. ~ (916) 488-9725 www.alternativebaking.com
Carob Iced Spelt Donuts & Cookies ~ *Nutrilicious Natural Bakery* (800) 835-8097 www.nutrilicious.com
Cinnamon Rolls, Chocolate Chip Cookies, Hip Whip, Chocolate Mousse Hip Whip & a line of Fancy Cakes ~ *Now & Zen* (800) 335-1959 www.nowandzen.com
Alaine's Bakery ~ All products are vegan. *Alaine's Bakery* (800) 718-1115
La Dolce Vegan ~ (845) 628-4060 www.ladolcevegan.com
Friendly Foods ~ Dry baked goods mixes. Canada. (403) 217-6059 www.friendlyfoods.com
Clif Bars ~ Other products are not vegan. (800) 884-5254 www.clifbar.com
Frankly Natural Bakers ~ (800) 727-7229 www.franklynatural.com
Amazake Pudding ~ *Grainaissance* (800) 472-4697 www.grainaissance.com
Barbara's Bakery Whole Wheat Fig Bars & Snackimales ~ *Barbara's Bakery* (707) 765-2273 www.barbarasbakery.com
Gummi Bears, Sprinkles, Brown Rice Snacks ~ *Edward & Sons Trading Co.* (805) 684-8500 www.edwardandsons.com
Nana's Originals ~ (800) 836-7534 www.healthycrowd.com
Mrs. Denson's Chocolate Chip Macaroon/Quinoa Macaroon/Date Walnut/Oatmeal Raisin ~ Other varieties are not vegan. (800) 219-3199 www.mrsdensonscookies.com
Power Pouches ~ *Snacks for Corporate Giving* (707) 677-9163 www.allinharmony.com
Simple Treats ~ (toll-free) (866) 33-VEGAN www.simpletreats.com
Boulder Bar ~ (800) EAT-1-NOW www.boulderbar.com
Bumble Bars ~ (888) 453-3369 www.bumblebar.com
Taro Dream ~ (808) 987-8823 or (808) 885-1766 tarodream@msn.com
Desserts by Rebecca ~ Request no white refined sugar. www.vegan-desserts.com
Allison's Cookies™ ~ *Allison's Gourmet* (818) 991-2149 www.allisonsgourmet.com
Only Fruit™ Mince ~ The vegan alternative to the holiday favorite. *Wax Orchards* (800) 634-6132 www.waxorchards.com

Salad Dressings

Nasoya Creamy Dill, Creamy Italian, Sesame Garlic, Garden Herb ~ *Nasoya* (800) 229-TOFU www.nasoya.com
Annie's Naturals - Goddess, Organic Green Garlic, Shiitake & Sesame, Gardenstyle Check labels; 9 vegan choices. ~ *Annie's Naturals* (800) 434-1234 www.anniesnaturals.com

Chocolate and Carob Products Without Dairy or White Sugar

Tropical Source 100% Dairy-Free Chocolate (bars and chips), *Ah!Laska Chocolate Syrup* ~ *Nspired Foods* (510) 686-0116 www.nspiredfoods.com
Sunspire Dairy-Free Organic Chocolate Chips ~ *Sunspire* (510) 569-9731
Trace amounts of dairy may be found in the product due to processing.
www.nspiredfoods.com
Rapunzel Pure Organics Dairy-Free Chocolate Bars, Rio Bar ~ *Rapunzel Pure Organics*
Semi-sweet & Bittersweet bars only. (800) 207-2814 www.rapunzel.com
Chatfield's Carob/Chocolate Morsels ~ Due to processing, may contain trace amounts of dairy. Grain sweetened, dairy-free recipe. *American Natural Snacks*
www.ans-natural.com
Green & Black's Organic ~ Maya Gold, Hazelnut & Currant, Dark Chocolate Bars
Fairtrade. *Belgravia Imports* (800) 848-1127 www.greenandblacks.com
Fudge Topping ~ Six flavors. *Wax Orchards* (800) 634-6132 www.waxorchards.com

Fruit Spreads and Jams *(No white refined sugar)*

Sorrel Ridge ~ *Allied Old English* (800) 225-0122 www.alliedoldenglish.com
Wax Orchards ~ Fruit spreads, fruit butters & fruit syrups. No pectin or preservatives.
All fruit sweetened and thickened. (800) 634-6132 www.waxorchards.com
Natural Value Spreadable Fruit NaturalVal@aol.com www.naturalvalue.com

Sweeteners/White Refined Sugar Alternatives

The Ultimate Sweetener® ~ (800) THE-MEAL or (805) 962-2221 www.ultimatelife.com
Rapadura® ~ *Rapunzel Pure Organics* (800) 207-2814 www.rapunzel.com
Organic Sucanat® ~ *Wholesome Foods* (800) 680-1896 www.wholesomesweeteners.com
Shady Maple Farms ~ *Shady Maple Farms* (905) 206-1455 info@shadymaple.ca
Maple Grove Farms of Vermont, Inc. ~ (802) 748-5141 www.maplegrove.com
Spring Tree (maple syrup) ~ *Specialty Brands of America* (802) 254-8784
www.springtree.com
Maple Valley® Syrup & Granules ~ Organic. (800) 760-1449 www.maplevalleysyrup.com
Fruitsource® ~ *Advanced Ingredients, Inc.* (888) 238-4647 info@advancedingredients.com
Plantation Molasses ~ *Allied Old English* (800) 225-0122 www.alliedoldenglish.com
Sweet Dreams® Rice Syrup ~ *Lundberg Family Farms* (530) 882-4551 www.lundberg.com
Malt Barley Syrup ~ *Eden Foods* (888) 441-EDEN www.edenfoods.com
Sorghum ~ *Arrowhead Mills* www.hain-celestial.com
Agave Nectar Light ~ *Western Commerce* (626) 333-5225 www.wcommerce.com
Stevia Extract ~ *Innovative Natural Products* (800) 893-7467 www.inovatprod.com
White Stevia Powder ~ *NuNaturals, Inc.* (888) 753-4372 www.nunaturals.com
Sweet Cloud Organic Brown Rice Malt Syrup & Organic Barley Malt Syrup ~
Great Eastern Sun (828) 665-7790 www.great-eastern-sun.com
Date Sugar ~ *Jaffe Brothers* (760) 749-1133 www.organicfruitsandnuts.com
Chatfield's Date Sugar ~ *American Natural Snacks* (904) 825-2039 www.ans-natural.com
Florida Crystals® ~ *Florida Crystals Corporation* (800) 558-8836 www.floridacrystals.com
SlimSweet!™ ~ *TriMedica, Inc.* (800) 800-8849 www.trimedica.com
Fruit Sweet™ pear, pineapple and peach juice *Pear Sweet™* concentrated pear juice ~
Wax Orchards (800) 634-6132 www.waxorchards.com

Nut Butters, Nuts, Tahini

Maranatha ~ (510) 686-0116 www.maranathanutbutters.com
Health Trip Organic Nut Butter ~ *NSpired* (800) 299-0048 www.nspiredfoods.com
Once Again Nut Butters ~ (888) 800-8075 www.onceagainnutbutter.com
Living Tree Community Foods ~ (800) 260-5534 www.livingtreecommunity.com
HempNut™ Peanut Butter ~ toll-free: (877) HEMP NUT www.TheHempNut.com
Natural Value Organic Peanut Butter naturalval@aol.com www.naturalvalue.com

Salt Flavorings or Substitutes

San-J Tamari ~ *San-J International* (800) 446-5500 www.san-j.com
Bragg™ Liquid Aminos ~ (800) 446-1990 www.bragg.com
Real Salt® ~ *Redmond Minerals, Inc.* (800) 367-7258 www.realsalt.com

Recommended Oils

Barlean's Organic Flax Oil ~ (800) 445-FLAX (3529) www.barleans.com
Spectrum Oils ~ (800) 995-2705 or (707) 778-8900 www.spectrumnaturals.com
Oils of Aloha Macadamia Oil ~ (800) 367-6010 www.oilsofaloha.com
Lucini Italia Cold-Pressed Olive Oil ~ (888) 558-2464 www.lucini.com
Aptera Extra Virgin Cold-Pressed Olive Oil ~ (801) 273-8078 www.apteraimports.com
Sadeg Organic Olive Oils ~ *Nick Sciabica & Sons, Inc.* (800) 551-9612 www.sciabica.com
Rapunzel Pure Organics ~ 100% certified organic. (800) 207-2814 www.rapunzel.com

Unpasteurized Miso Products

Cold Mountain Miso ~ *Miyako Oriental Foods* toll-free (877) 788-MISO
www.coldmountainmiso.com
Miso Master Organic Miso ~ *The American Miso Co.* for *Great Eastern Sun*
(828) 665-7790 www.great-eastern-sun.com
Westbrae Miso ~ *Westbrae* (800) 769-645 www.westbrae.com
Miso Cups ~ *Edward & Sons Trading Co.* (805) 684-8500 www.edwardandsons.com

Bouillon Cubes (Instant Broth)

Vegan Bouillon & Broth ~ *Rapunzel Pure Organics* (800) 207-2814 www.rapunzel.com
Organic Country ~ *Edward & Sons Trading Co.* (805) 684-8500 www.edwardandsons.com
Balanced Mineral Bouillon ~ *Dr. Bronner's* (760) 743-2211 www.drbronner.com
Edward & Sons ~ *Edward & Sons Trading Co.* (805) 684-8500 www.edwardandsons.com

Pasta Products

Ancient Harvest Quinoa Pasta ~ *The Quinoa Corporation* (310) 217-8125
www.quinoa.net
Vita Spelt ~ Wheat-free. *Purity Foods* (800) 997-7358 www.purityfoods.com
DeBoles ~ Jerusalem artichoke pasta. (800) 749-0730 www.hain-celestial.com
Natural Value Organic Pasta ~ naturalval@aol.com www.naturalvalue.com
Eden Foods ~ Spaghetti sauce with honey is not vegan. Many pastas including
wheat-free varieties & many other vegan products. *Eden Foods* (800) 248-0320
www.edenfoods.com

Sea Vegetables

Maine Coast Sea Vegetables ~ (207) 565-2907 www.seaveg.com
Emerald Cove Sea Salads ~ *Great Eastern Sun* (828) 665-7790 www.great-eastern-sun.com

Teas and Coffee Substitutes

San Francisco Herbs and Natural Food ~ (800) 227-2830 www.herbspicetea.com
San Francisco Herbs (teas) ~ (800) 227-4530 www.sfherb.com
Traditional Medicinals Tea ~ (800) 543-4372 www.traditionalmedicinals.com
Yogi Teas ~ *Golden Temple* (800) 225-3623 www.goldentemple.com
Kaffree Roma ~ *Worthington Foods/Kellogg Co.* (800) 557-6525 www.kelloggs.com
Pero/Cafix ~ *International Foods* (201) 909-0808 www.internaturalfoods.com
Raja's Cup™ ~ *Maharishi Ayur-Ved Products* (800) 255-8332
Teeccino Vanilla Nut ~ (800) 498-3434 www.teeccino.com
Organic Haiku Tea Line ~ *Great Eastern Sun* (828) 665-7790 www.great-eastern-sun.com
Long Life Teas ~ *Country Life* (800) 887-4096 www.long-life.com
All Goode Organics (teas) ~ (888) 980-8884 www.allgoodeorganics.com

Sauces

The Wizard's™ Vegetarian Worcestershire Sauce (no anchovy), **Rainforest Organic** ~
Edward & Son's Trading Co. (805) 684-8500 www.edwardandsons.com
Bar-B-Q Sauces (2 varieties) ~ *Annie's Naturals* (800) 434-1234 www.anniesnaturals.com
Drew's Salsa, Caribbean Sauce & Asian Sauce ~ (800) 228-2980 www.chefdrew.com
Café Yumm!™ Sauces ~ *Rising Sun Farms* (800) 888-0795 www.risingsunfarms.com
Muir Glen Organic Tomato Products ~ Some products have honey. (800) 832-6345
Seeds of Change Ketchup ~ (888) 762-7333 www.seedsofchange.com
Edward & Sons ~ *Edward & Sons Trading Co.* (805) 684-8500 www.edwardandsons.com
Wax Orchards ~ Chutneys, barbeque sauce & plum sauce. Good for stir-frys.
(800) 634-6132 www.waxorchards.com

Quick and Easy Meals in a Cup or Carton

Dr. McDougall's Right Foods ~ (707) 254-3700 www.rightfoods.com
Casbah ~ *Sahara Natural Foods* (510) 352-5111 www.hain-celestial.com

Non-Irradiated Spices and Herbs

San Francisco Herbs and Natural Food ~ (800) 227-2830 www.herbspicetea.com
San Francisco Herbs Teas ~ (800) 227-4530 www.sfherb.com
Frontier Herbs ~ (319) 227-7996 www.frontierherb.com
Spice Garden, Spike™ Seasoning and Vegit™ ~ *Modern Products of Milwaukee WI.*
Herbamare™/Trocomare™ ~ Sea salt with herbs. *Bioforce America* www.bioforce.ca
The Spice Hunter ~ (800) 444-3061 www.spicehunter.com

opposite: **'Let There Be Light'** *by Sky Weil*
quote by: **JOHN STUART MILL** *(1806-1873) ~ English author and philosopher*

"It often happens that the universal belief of one age, a belief from which no one was free or could be free without an extraordinary effort of genius or courage, becomes to a subsequent age, so palpable an absurdity, that the only difficulty is to imagine how such an idea could ever have appeared credible."

"*The vegetarian ideal as a concept which embodied a moral imperative – 'thou shalt not kill for food' – made its first impact on history in India and Greece in 500 B.C., within the lifetimes of both The Buddha and Pythagoras.*"

"It often happens that the universal belief of one age, a belief from which no one was free or could be free without an extraordinary effort of genius or courage, becomes to a subsequent age, so palpable an absurdity, that the only difficulty is to imagine how such an idea could ever have appeared credible."

"The vegetarian ideal as a concept which embodied a moral imperative – 'thou shalt not kill for food' – made its first impact on history in India and Greece in 500 B.C., within the lifetimes of both The Buddha and Pythagoras."

Non-Alcoholic Vanilla

Pure Vanilla Powder ~ *Nielsen-Massey Vanillas* (800) 525-PURE www.nielsenmassey.com
Spicery Shoppe ~ (800) 4-FLAVOR www.flavorchem.com

Varied Special Products

Organic Quinoa ~ *The Quinoa Corporation* (310) 217-8125 www.quinoa.net
Bob's Red Mill ~ Full line of quality grains. (800) 553-2258 www.bobsredmill.com
SuperFruit™ ~ Jello alternative. *Hain-Celestial Food Group* www.thehainfoodgroup.com
Mochi ~ Bake & serve rice popovers. *Grainaissance* (800) 472-4697 www.grainaissance.com
Baby's Herbal Garden ~ Organic baby food (Apple Yogurt Parfait is not vegan).
Healthy Times (877) 548-2229 htbaby80@aol.com
Wally's Natural Products ~ Paraffin ear candles. (800) 215-1566 www.wallysnatural.com
The Date People ~ A wide variety of veganically grown dates. (760) 359-3211 Niland, California.
American Health & Nutrition ~ Many vegan/organic products. www.organictrading.com
Dixie Diners Chicken Not! & many products ~ (800) BEEF NOT www.dixiediner.com
Amy's No Cheese Vegan Pizza ~ (707) 578-7188 www.amys.com
Vegicaps Non-Gelatin Capsules ~ GS Technologies, Inc. (800) 645-2246 or (516) 599-2442

Healthy Food Supplements

The Ultimate Meal® ~ (800) THE-MEAL (843-6325) or (805) 962-2221 www.ultimatelife.com
Spirulina Pacifica ~ *Nutrex Inc.* (800) 453-1187 www.nutrex-hawaii.com
Earthrise™ Spirulina ~ *Earthrise* (800) 949-RISE www.earthrise.com
The Supreme Meal™ and Peaceful Planet High Protein Energy Shake ~ Certified vegan.
VegLife™ Nutraceutical Corporation (800) VEG-0250
NutriBiotic® Prozone and Rice Protein Drink ~ (800) 225-4345 www.nutribiotic.com
e3Live ~ Blue-green algae. Truffles are not vegan. (888) 800-7070 www.e3live.com

Herbal Supplements and Vitamins

VegLife® ~ All certified vegan. *Nutraceutical Corporation* (800) 669-8877
www.nutraceutical.com
Born Again™ ~ Vegan products for menopause. *At Last Inc.* (800) 527-8123 www.alast.com
Twinlab 'Vegetarian Formula' Sublingual B-12 Dots ~ *Twin Laboratories, Inc.*
Read label; non-vegetarian formula dots contain gelatin. (800) 645 5626 www.twinlab.com
Liquid Vitamin B12 ~ *Innovative Natural Products* (800) 893-7467 www.inovatprod.com
Wild Yam Creme ~ (no beeswax) *Wise Essentials, Inc.* (800) 705-9473 www.wiseessentials.com
Pioneer Nutritional ~ 50% is certified vegan. (800) 458-8483 www.pioneernutritional.com
Indian Meadow Herbals ~ (888) 464-3729 www.imherbal.com
Maca Magic™ Superfood ~ Maca root from Peru (541) 846-6222 www.herbs-america.com
Life Flow Progesta-Care (for menopause) & **Maca** ~ (888) 999-7440 www.life-flo.com
Lifestyle Daily Foods Vitamin/Mineral/Herb Formula ~ (800) 848-2542 www.megafood.com

opposite: 'Wishing Star' by Sky Weil
quote by: **COLIN SPENCER** ~ *British writer and publisher*
<u>*The Heretic's Feast: A History of Vegetarianism*</u>, Fourth Estate, London 1994

Vegetable Based Soaps

Dr. Bronner's Magic Soaps ~ *Dr. Bronner's* (760) 743-2211 www.drbronner.com
Auromére Ayurvedic Soaps ~ *Auromére, Inc.* (800) 735-4691 www.auromere.com
Avalon Organic Glycerin Soaps ~ All products vegan. *Avalon Natural Products*
(707) 769-5120 www.avalonnaturalproducts.com
Rainbow Aloe-Oatmeal Bar, Rainbow Antibacterial Soap ~ *Rainbow Research*
(800) 722-9595 www.rainbowresearch.com
Nature's Gate Organics Shower/Bath Gel ~ *Levlad, Inc* (800) 327-2012 www.levlad.com
Aura Cacia Bath Soaps ~ *Aura Cacia* (800) 437-3301 www.auracacia.com
Coconut Coast Natural Products ~ (800) 210-1668 www.ccnphawaii.com
Aptera Olive Oil Soap ~ *Aptera Imports* (801) 273-8078 www.apteraimports.com
Tea Tree Vegetable Bar Soap ~ *Tea Tree Therapy, Inc.* (800) 990-4221 teatree@pacbell.net
Clearly Natural ~ (800) 274-7627 www.clearlynaturalsoaps.com
San Francisco Soap Company ~ Milk & Honey bar is not vegan. (800) 254-8656
Kiss My Face™ Olive Oil Bar, Organic Bar Soaps & Liquid Moisturizing Soaps ~
Kiss My Face Corporation (800) 262-5477 www.kissmyface.com
Vermont Soapworks ~ 1 contains honey. toll-free: (866) 762-7482 www.vermontsoap.com
Kirk's Castile Soap ~ *Kirk's Natural Products* (800) 82-KIRKS www.kirksnatural.com
Wild Body Butter Soap ~ *Ecco Bella Botanicals* (877) 696-2220 www.eccobella.com
Sappo Hill ~ (800) 863-7627 www.sappohill.com
Harvest Soaps ~ Not all vegan; 10 vegan soaps. (877) 373-SOAP www.harvestsoaps.com

Lip Balms *(no beeswax)*

Hemp Nut, Inc. ~ toll-free: (877) HEMP-NUT www.TheHempNut.com
Azida Lip Balm ~ *Azida, Inc.* (800) 603-6601 www.azida.com
Vegan Hemp Balm ~ *Merry Hempsters* (888) SEED-OIL www.merryhempsters.com

Hair Care Products

Tea Tree Oil, Tall Grass & Forest Essence Shampoos ~ All products are vegan.
Jason Natural Products (800) JASON-05 www.jason-natural.com
Aubrey Organics ~ A few are not vegan. (800) 282-7394 www.aubrey-organics.com
Herbal Shampoo & Conditioner, Forest Pure Conditioner ~ *Nature's Gate/Levlad Inc.*
(800) 327-2012 www.levlad.com
ShiKai® Original Formula & Dry Hair Shampoo ~ (800) 448-0298 www.shikai.com
Beauty Without Cruelty, Avalon Organic Botanicals Therapeutic Shampoos & Conditioners ~
Avalon Natural Products (800) 227-5120 www.avalonnaturalproducts.com
**Kiss & Go Shampoo, Everyday Care Shampoo & Conditioner, Olive & Aloe Shampoo
& Conditioner** ~ *Kiss My Face Corp.* (800) 262-5477 www.kissmyface.com
Emerald Forest Shampoo & Botanical Conditioner - *Natural Nectar* (949) 495-6693
Head Shampoo & Conditioner ~ *Pure & Basic* (800) 432-3787 www.pureandbasic.com
Avalon Organic Botanicals Therapeutic Shampoos and Conditioners ~
Avalon Natural Products (800) 227-5720 www.avalonnaturalproducts.com
Henna Highlighting Shampoo ~ *Rainbow Research* (800) 722-9595 www.rainbowresearch.com
Sleepy Hollow® Oil-Free Shampoo & Conditioner ~ *Mill Creek* (310) 366-2772
Labels read 'no animal by-products', but some contain beeswax. www.millcreekbotanicals.com
Peppermint Tea Tree Shampoo & Conditioner/Natural Shampoo/Herbal Conditioner ~
Essential Wholesale (503) 252-9639 www.essentialwholesale.com
Herbal Essences Conditioner ~ *Clairol, Inc.* (800) 252-4765 www.clairol.com

Oral Care Products

Eco-DenT ~ (Pain Relief Formula contains bee propolis.) *Eco-DenT International* (888) ECO-DENT www.eco-dent.com

Nature's Gate Toothpastes ~ *Nature's Gate/Levlad* (800) 327-2012 www.levlad.com

AuroMére ~ *Auroméré Ayurvedic Imports* (800) 735-4691 www.auromere.com

Plant-Gel & Salt Toothpaste w/ Baking Soda ~ *Weleda* (800) 241-1030 www.weleda.com

Tom's of Maine Baking Soda Toothpaste with Fluoride & Vegetable Wax Floss ~ Some toothpastes contain bee products. (207) 985-2944 www.toms-of-maine.com

Vicco Toothpaste ~ *Lotus Brands* (800) 824-6396 www.lotuspress.com

The Natural Dentist Whitening/Gentle Herbal Toothpaste ~ Other varieties not vegan. *Woodstock Natural Products* (800) 615-6895 www.thenaturaldentist.com

Rembrandt Naturals™ ~ *Den Mat Corp.* (800) 548-3663 www.rembrandt.com

Tea Tree Therapy™ Whitening Toothpaste, Toothpaste w/ Baking Soda, Tea Tree Pure Oil, Mouthwash ~ *Tea Tree Therapy, Inc.* (800) 990-4221 teatree@pacbell.net

Squigle Enamel Saver ~ *Squigle, Inc.* (610) 645-5556 www.homesteadmarket.com

Jason Pure Natural & Organic® Toothpaste & Power Smile™ ~ *Jason Natural Cosmetics* (800) JASON-05 www.jason-natural.com

Triple Action Toothpaste ~ *Kiss My Face Corp.* (800) 262-KISS www.kissmyface.com

Moisturizers and Body Care Products

ShiKai All Natural Hand & Body Lotions (800) 448-0298 www.shikai.com

Beauty Without Cruelty *Avalon Natural Products* (800) 227-5120 www.avalonnaturalproducts.com

Aura Cacia Aromatherapy Massage Oils ~ (800) 437-3301 www.auracacia.com

CamoCare ~ *Abkit, Inc.* (800) CAMOCARE www.camocare.com

Nature's Gate Herbal Moisturizing Lotion, Skin Therapy Lotions ~ *Tea Tree, Hemp, Colloidal Oatmeal* Many, but not all, vegan. *Levlad, Inc.* (800) 327-2012 www.levlad.com

Kiss My Face ~ Some products contain honey. (800) 262-5477 www.kissmyface.com

Aubrey Organics ~ Most products are vegan. (800) 282-7394 www.aubrey-organics.com

Stonybrook Botanicals™ Oil-Free Body Lotion ~ *Rainbow Research Inc.* (800) 722-9595

Abra Therapeutics Moisturizing Lotions ~ (800) 745-0761 www.abratherapeutics.com

Island Essence Hawaiian Body Lotions ~ (888) 878-3800 www.islandessence.com

Woman Wise™ Wild Yam Hand & Body Therapy ~ *Jason Natural Cosmetics* No animal derivatives or testing in any products. (800) JASON-05 www.jason-natural.com

Rich Moisturizer ~ *Morganics* (800) 820-9235 www.morganics.com

Tea Tree Therapy™ Hand & Body Lotion ~ *Tea Tree Therapy, Inc.* (800) 990-4221

Emerald Forest® Botanical ~ *Natural Nectar* (949) 495-6693

Niora Naturals ~ (800) 882-9887 www.niora.com

Hemp Lotion/Herbal Lotion/Massage Oil ~ (503) 252-9639 www.essentialwholesale.com

Swiss Herbal Beauty ~ Certified vegan. (206) 624-6464 www.swissherbalbeauty.com

Earth–Friendly Cleaning Products

The following products contain no animal ingredients and are not tested on animals:

Planet ~ *Planet, Inc.* (800) 858-8449 www.planetinc.com

Bi-O-Kleen ~ (800) 240-5536 www.bio-kleen.com

Sal Suds ~ *Dr. Bronner's Magic Soaps* (760) 743-2211 www.drbronner.com

Earth Friendly Products ~ (800) 335-3267 www.ecos.com

Life Tree Products ~ *Life Tree Products, The Terrapin Co.* (707) 588-0755

*Seventh Generation Cleaning Product*s ~ www.seventhgen.com

Morganics ~ (800) 820-9235 www.morganics.com

Citra-Solv™, Citra-Suds™, Citra-Dish™, Citra-Clear™ ~ *Shadow Lake, Inc.* (800) 343-6588 www.shadowlake.com

New Age ~ *New Age Products* (888) 7NEWAGE (763-9243) or (707) 459-5969

Ecover ~ (800) 449-4925 www.ecover.com

Citri-Glow™ Cleaners ~ *Mia Rose* (800) 292-6339 www.miarose.com

Allens Naturally ~ (800) 352-8971 www.allensnaturally.com

Country Save ~ *Country Save* (360) 435-0896 www.countrysave.com

Simple Green ~ Hand cleaner gel is not vegan. (800) 228-0709 www.simplegreen.com

Pet Care Products

Harbingers of a New Age ~ Vegan pet food supplement. (406) 295-4944 www.vegepet.com

Evolution Diet Pet Food ~ *Evolution Diet* (800) 659-0104 www.petfoodshop.com

'Vegetarian Dog Formula' (canned & dry) ~ *Natural Life* (800) 367-2391 www.nlpp.com

Mr. Barkey's & Mr. Pugsly's Dog Biscuits and Vegetarian Feast Formula (canned) ~ *Pet Guard* (800) 874-3221 www.petguard.com

Wow Bow Baking Manufacturers (dog biscuits) ~ (800) 326-0230 www.wow-bow.com

F & O Alternative Pet Products ~ (877) 376-9056 www.vegancats.com

Nature's Recipe 'Vegetarian Canine' ~ *Heinz Co.* (800) 843-4008 www.naturesrecipe.com

Hokamix 30 Herb blend for dogs/cats. ~ *Naturmix, USA* (800) 825-1669 www.naturmix.com

Sun Blocks and Sun Care Products

The Hemp Nut ~ (707) 571-1330 www.TheHempNut.com

Titania ~ *Aubrey Organics* (800) 282-7394 www.aubrey-organics.com

Bronzo Sensualé ~ (800) 991-2226 www.bronzosensuale.com

Cosmetics

Beauty Without Cruelty ~ One product has keratin; another silk protein. The rest of the line is vegan. *Avalon Natural Products* (800) 227-5120 www.avalonnaturalproducts.com

---

*"Now does not nature produce enough
simple vegetarian food for thee to satisfy thyself?
And if thou art not content with such, canst thou not
by mixture of them make infinite compounds?"*

LEONARDO DA VINCI (1425-1519) ~ Italian artist, sculptor, scientist, inventor

Non-Leather Shoes

Payless Shoe Stores ~ Many man-made material shoes and hiking boots (Rugged Outback) (800) 426-1141 www.payless.com (See www.gentleworld.org for mail order companies)

Gardening Supplies

Vegan Mix ~ 100% natural fertilizer. *Down to Earth* (888) 251-2334
Seeds of Change ~ 100% organic seeds. (800) 957-3337 www.seedsofchange.com

Have-a-Heart Traps

Cruelty-free Rodent Traps ~ *Lehman's Catalog* (888) 438-5346
Humane Smart MouseTrap ~ *People for The Ethical Treatment of Animals* (800) 483-4366

Synthetic Artist Brushes

Daler-Rowney, *distributor of* **Robert Simmons** ~ (609) 655-5252 www.daler-rowney.com
The company makes synthetic sable bristle artist brushes.
Winsor & Newton ~ The synthetic brushes have yellow handles with white bristles.
Winsor & Newton (732) 562-0770 www.winsornewton.com
Loew-Cornell ~ White nylon and golden taklon. (201) 836-7070 www.loew-cornell.com

---

"We divert our attention from disease and death as much as we can; the slaughterhouses are huddled out of sight and never mentioned, so that the world we recognize officially in literature and in society is a poetic fiction far handsomer, cleaner and better than the world that really is."

WILLIAM JAMES, M.D., LLD. (1842-1910)
American psychologist, philosopher and teacher

Cruelty-Free Companies

The Ultimate Life®
Based in Santa Barbara CA; was founded, is owned and managed by Sam Gerard, a dedicated vegan & environmentalist. It manufactures the following products:
The Ultimate Meal® ~ a potent and complete source of nourishment in powder form.
The Ultimate Meal Bar® ~ a potent and complete source of nourishment.
The Ultimate Acidophilus® ~ helps create friendly bacteria for a healthy digestive system.
The Ultimate FloraZyme® ~ helps digest cooked, processed or gas-producing foods.
The Ultimate Defense® ~ antioxidants to help the body and mind deal with stress.
The Ultimate Blue-Green® ~ combination of organic Hawaiian spirulina and blue-green.
The Ultimate Sweetener® ~ 100% birch sugar which tastes like sugar. Safe even for diabetics. Call (800) THE-MEAL (843-6325) or (805) 962-2221 or visit www.ultimatelife.com
Turtle Mountain ~ Certified vegan frozen desserts: Organic Soy Delicious™ sandwiches & quarts, It's Soy Delicious!™, Sweet Nothings™ (541) 338-9400 www.turtlemountain.com
Vegi-Deli™ ~ 3 flavors of pepperoni meat analogs and Vegi-Deli slices, Vegi-Jerky, Slice of Life® *Green Options, Inc.* is based in San Francisco at (888) 473-3667 www.vegideli.com
Turtle Island Foods ~ SuperBurger™, Tofurky™ Feast, Deli Slices & Jurky, tempeh. Non-GMO. *Turtle Island Foods* (800) 508-8100 www.tofurky.com info@tofurky.com
Organica™ *Foods* ~ 4 varieties of the ultimate cookie experience! No hydrogenated oils or refined sugars, GMO-free. toll-free: (877) OH SO YUM www.organicafoods.com
Sun Flour Baking Co. ~ 22 cookie varieties; 9 gluten/wheat-free, gingerbread men. mail@sunflourbaking.com Sacramento, CA. (916) 488-4150 www.sunflourbaking.com
Now and Zen™ ~ A wholefood manufacturer of cookies & fancy cakes (served on United Airlines when ordering a vegan meal), 'Savory Select' meat substitutes (one has wine) and the 'Unturkey'. San Francisco, CA. (800) 335-1959 www.nowandzen.com
The Alternative Baking Co. ~ Large cookies. (916) 488-9725 www.alternativebaking.com
Dr. Bronner's Balanced Mineral Bouillon & All-Purpose Soaps & Sal-Suds ~ Biodegradable & pure castile. Escondido, CA. (760) 743-2211 www.drbronner.com
Maine Coast Sea Vegetables ~ A variety of certified organic sea vegetables & sea vegetable products. Franklin, Maine (207) 565-2907 www.seaveg.com
Lumen Foods ~ Makers of Heartline Meatless Meats. (800) 256-2253 www.soybean.com
Harbingers of a New Age ~ Food supplements for feeding cats a vegan diet, as well as dogs. Troy, Montana. (406) 295-4944 www.vegepet.com
Evolution Diet Pet Food ~ Quality ingredients, pet food company. Based in St.Paul, MN. (800) 659-0104 info@petfoodshop.com www.petfoodshop.com
Road's End Organics ~ 'Chreese' non-dairy cheese alternative in packets (add boiling water) and Nacho Cheese Dips in a jar. Morrisville, CT. (802) 888-4130 www.chreese.com
The Date People ~ A wide variety of veganically grown dates. (760) 359-3211 California.
Vegan Essentials ~ Toiletries, cosmetics, household & pantry products. Wauwatosa, WI. (877) 881-6477 or (414) 607-1953 www.VeganEssentials.com
(Mention Gentle World when ordering; 7% of the profit will be donated to Gentle World.)
Morganics ~ Cleaners, shampoos, etc. Scottsdale, AZ. (800) 820-9235 www.morganics.com

Allens Naturally ~ Cleaning/laundry products. (800) 352-8971 www.allensnaturally.com

Friendly Foods ~ Dry baked goods mixes. Canada (403) 217-6059 www.friendlyfoods.com

WholeSoy® ~ Certified vegan frozen glacé and non-dairy yogurts. www.wholesoycom.com

VegTime, Inc. ~ Makers of heat & eat Handi-Pies. (415) 921-8925 www.vegtime.com

La Dolce Vegan ~ Cookies. (845) 628-4060 www.ladolcevegan.com
ladolcevegan@rcn.com

Nutrilicious Natural Bakery ~ Organic spelt (wheat-free) donuts and assorted cookies made with healthy ingredients that taste incredible! (800) 835-8097 www.nutrilicious.com

Born Again™ ~ Products for natural menopause & PMS relief. MSM cream & soap. *At Last Inc.* is based in Ardsley, N.Y. (800) 527-8123 info@atlastnaturals.com
www.alast.com

Jason Natural Cosmetics ~ Offers an extensive range of personal and beauty care products, truly botanical in origin. (800) JASON-05 www.jason-natural.com

Dr. McDougall's ~ A leading authority on nutrition offers a large variety of 'meals in a cup'. *Dr. McDougall's Right Foods,* San Francisco, CA. (707) 254-3700 www.rightfoods.com

Simple Treats ~ Cookies, brownies & muffins. Eastham, MA. toll-free: (866) 33-VEGAN www.simpletreats.com simpletreats@earthlink.net

Allison's Cookies/Brownies™ ~ Gourmet, organic, with unrefined sweeteners delivered to your door! Wheat-free options. *Allison's Gourmet* (818) 991-2149 www.allisonsgourmet.com

Nana's ~ Healthy cookies & snacks, gluten-free options & tropical treats. No refined sugars; sweetened with Fruittrim®. Organic. San Diego, CA. (800) 836-7534 www.healthycrowd.com

Alaine's Bakery ~ Baked goods sold at Wild Oats & Whole Foods Markets. (800) 718-1115

Ginny's Vegan Foods ~ Roasted Pepper Chili, Savory Soy Chili, Ratatouille, Mexican Stew. (603) 788-3975 www.ginnysveganfoods.com ginny@ginnysveganfoods.com

Azida, Inc. ~ Hemp oil body/hair care products. *Azida, Inc.* (800) 603-6601 www.azida.com

Niora Naturals ~ Adult acne treatment & moisturizer, anti-aging skin care, hand & body lotions. *Niora Naturals* is based in Sweet Home, OR. (800) 882-9887 www.niora.com

Bronzo Sensualé ~ A full range of sun & skin care products using a carrot formula. Miami, FL. (800) 991-2226 www.bronzosensuale.com suntan@bronzosensuale.com

Swiss Herbal Beauty ~ Certified vegan & organic facial creams, bath/body/baby products, toners/skin cleansers. Seattle, WA. (206) 624-6464 www.swissherbalbeauty.com

The Organic Garden™ ~ Soy products/cereals. www.theorganicgardenfood.com
Trademark of *American Health & Nutrition.* www.organictrading.com

All in Harmony ~ Organic, fair-trade gift collections for corporate or personal giving. (707) 677-9163 allinharmony@cox.net www.allinharmony.com

---

"Average weight of vegan adults compard to non-vegetarian adults: 10-20 pounds lighter"

JOHN ROBBINS ~ American author, Pulitzer Prize Nominee for Diet for a New America, author, The Food Revolution, Conari Press 2000

Quinoa Corporation ~ Organic quinoa, pasta products and ready-made food. Produces organic corn polenta; several flavors. *Quinoa Corporation* (310) 217-8125 www.quinoa.net

Pleasant Farms ~ Makers of Soyburg USA. 3 flavors of soy burgers, soy loaf, and 2 entrée frozen dinners. Pasadena, CA. (800) 499-9616 www.soyburgusa.com

Vegan Mercantile ~ One stop on-line shopping. www.VeganMercantile.com

DifferentDaisy.com ~ Vegan webstore. (740) 820-3146 www.differentdaisy.com

Vegan Street ~ Shop with compassion at www.veganstreet.com or call (773) 252-0026

Sappo Hill ~ Soaps. Ashland, OR. (800) 863-7627 www.sappohill.com

Kirk's Castile Soap ~ Kirk's Natural Products (800) 82-KIRKS www.kirksnatural.com

Clearly Natural Soap ~ Petaluma, CA. (800) 274-7627 www.clearlynaturalsoaps.com

Coconut Coast Natural Products ~ Handmade soap. (800) 210-1668 www.ccnphawaii.com

Smoke and Fire™ ~ Organic tofu in 5 varieties. (413) 528-1877 www.smokeandfire.com

Pacific Bakery ~ Yeast-free/organic/vegan breads - (760) 757-6020 www.pacificbakery.com

SoyBoy™ ~ Northern Soy, Inc. (585) 235-8970 www.SoyBoy.com

"....We treat them as sticks or stones, as trees and other non-sentient things that are not possessed of organs or sense and feeling. We are wrong in this; they are not things, but beings. We forget the wonderful likeness that exists between us and these 'lower' creatures. We neglect the fact that their brains are much like our brains, their muscles like our muscles, their bones like our bones, that they digest as we digest, that they have hearts that beat as ours beat, nerves that thrill as ours thrill, that they possess to a wonderful degree the same faculties, the same appetites and are subject to the same impulses as we. An ox, a sheep, can hear, see, feel, smell, taste and even think, if not as well as man, at least to some degree after the same fashion....A horse or a cow can learn, remember, love, hate, mourn, rejoice and suffer, as human beings do...."

JOHN HARVEY KELLOGG, M.D., LLD, FACS (1852-1943)
American director of Battle Creek Sanitarium, educator of the medical profession, author of 50 books

Recommended Reading

Gentle World Publications:
The Cookbook For People Who Love Animals
Vegan Nutrition: Pure and Simple

The Food Revolution: How Your Diet Can Help Save Your Life and The World ~ John Robbins
Diet for A New America ~ John Robbins
Reclaiming Our Health ~ John Robbins, HJ Kramer Publisher
Beyond Beef: The Rise and Fall of the Cattle Culture ~ Jeremy Rifkin
Out of the Jungle ~ H. Jay Dinshah, American Vegan Society
Mad Cowboy ~ Howard Lyman
The Most Noble Diet ~ George Eisman
Tofu Cookery ~ Louise Hagler
The Vegan Source Book ~ Joanne Stepaniak
The Uncheese Cookbook ~ Joanne Stepaniak
The Saucy Vegetarian ~ Joanne Stepaniak
The Vegan Kitchen ~ Freya Dinshah, The American Vegan Society
The Compassionate Cook ~ Ingrid Newkirk; National Director: P.E.T.A.
The Power of Your Plate ~ Neal Barnard, M.D.
Eat Right, Live Longer ~ Neal Barnard, M.D.
Turn Off The Fat Genes ~ Neal Barnard, M.D.
Food for Life ~ Neal Barnard, M.D.
Love Yourself Thin ~ Victoria Moran
Prisoned Chickens; Poisoned Eggs ~ Karen Davis
The Sunfood Diet Success System ~ David Wolfe
Eating For Beauty ~ David Wolfe
Vegan Nutrition; A Survey of Research ~ Gill Langley, Ph.D., U.K.
The Sexual Politics of Meat ~ Carol J. Adams
Vegan: The New Ethics of Eating ~ Erik Marcus

Videos

A Diet for All Reasons ~ with Michael Klaper, M.D.
    (dist: Paulette Eisen Nutritional Services) (310) 289-4173
Diet for A New America ~ hosted by John Robbins, based on his book
Truth or Dairy ~ The Vegan Society, U.K.
The Witness ~ Tribe of Heart www.tribeofheart.org mail@tribeofheart.org

Recommended Kitchenware

Blenders

Hamilton Beach/Procter-Silex ~ 16 speed, maximum power blender. Quick clean setting. *Procter-Silex* is based in Washington, NC., at (800) 851-8900.

Osterizer® ~ 10 speed, five-cup, scratch-resistant, dishwasher safe, glass jar with plastic lid. Ice crushing power. *Sunbeam-Oster Corporation* (800) 882-5842.

Food Processors

KitchenAid® ~ 11 cup Ultra Power and Professional Food Processor. *KitchenAid®*, based in Greenville, OH., can be reached at (800) 541-6390.

Cuisinart® Deluxe 11 ~ Introduced in 1973, this is one of the most practical and well-designed kitchen appliances--the ideal tool for the home chef. It has an 11 cup capacity bowl. *Cuisinart®*, based in Stamford, CT., can be reached at (800) 726-0190 or (203) 975-4600.

Krups Master Pro Deluxe® ~ Fine quality machine. Krups North America, Inc. is based in Closter, N.J. (800) 526-5377. Look for their products in finer stores nationwide.

Power Pro® Food Processor ~ 400 watts of power. Large 6 cup bowl. Economical. To reach Black and Decker call (800) 231-9786 or look for their products nationwide.

Vita-Mix

A powerful total nutrition center that performs amazing food feats at the flip of a switch. Vita-Mix is a powerful blender and a versatile machine that enables you to make whole food juice, smoothies, soups or non-dairy ice cream in about a minute. It cooks sauces without lumping, curdling or scorching. It easily chops salad bar items. It will purée half a cup of baby food as well as it will two quarts. It also makes nut butters. For more information call the Vita-Mix Corporation, based in Cleveland, OH., at (800) 848-2649 or www.vitamix.com

Cookware

Cuisinart® Stainless Steel Cookware ~ 25 years of culinary excellence, markets 'Everyday Stainless Steel Cookware®'. 100% aluminum-free with wide hand-grips for easy lifting. Hand-polished & mirror-finished in top quality 18/10 stainless steel, with copper bottoms for fast, even heating. The tight-fitting covers seal in flavor & nutrients. Dishwasher and oven-safe, it comes with a lifetime warranty. *Cuisinart™*, your kitchen resource, is based in Stamford, CT. and can be reached at (800) 726-0190 or (203) 975-4600.

Farberware® Classic Series Stainless Steel Cookware ~ a standard in American kitchens for generations. The cookware has a "full-cap" stainless steel over aluminum base. Farberware Cookware Division is based in Vallejo, CA. For more information call (800) 809-7166. www.farberwarecookware.com

All-Clad Stainless Steel Cookware ~ The stainless collection features a magnetic stainless exterior. The cooking surface is hand-polished 18/10 stainless steel that will not react with food. The inner core is pure aluminum, not just at the bottom, but all the way up the sides. All three layers are bonded together for optimum heat conductivity. All styles feature long, stay-cool handles. They are dishwasher-safe, easy to care for, and come with a lifetime guarantee. Based in New York, N.Y., Patrice Tanaka & Co. can be reached at (212) 229-0523. www.allclad.com

LeCreuset® ~ Makers of colorful enamel-coated cast-iron for use in oven/microwave to table, and freezer to oven. A product of France, this elegant designed stoneware resists chipping and staining. Le Creuset of America, Early Branch, S.C. (877) 273-8738 www.lecreuset.com

CorningWear™ ~ *CorningWear* products are ideal pieces for preparing, cooking and serving in one beautiful dish. They're also safe for repeated microwave and oven use, are non-staining, non-warping, odor-resistant and dishwasher compatible. For more information, call CorningWear's consumer division at (800) 999-3436. www.worldkitchen.com

VapoSeal Cookware ~ 7-ply stainless steel cookware/bakeware designed for nutrient retention. Vapo-Seal Cookware is <u>not</u> found in retail stores. Based in Harrisonburg, VA. (800) 434-4628

WearEver® ~ Durable porcelain coated (non-stick). Economical, lightweight, easy-clean & great for low-fat cooking. *The Mirro Company,* Manitowoc, WI. (800) 518-6245

Lodge Cast Iron ~ Cookware, skillets, bakeware. Great for corn bread. New cast-iron cookware needs to be seasoned; an easy process. Lodge Manufacturing, South Pittsburgh, TN. (423) 837-7181

Presto Pride® Pressure Cooker ~ Heavy gauge stainless steel for quick pressure cooking that preserves flavors, colors and nutrients. For information on Presto small appliances call Customer Service at (715) 839-2209.

Bread-Making Machines

Home Bakery Traditional™ ~ Superior kneading & baking technologies. Custom baking cycles. *Zojirushi America Corporation* Based in Commerce, CA. at (323) 722-1700 www.zojirushi.com

Juicers

Krups Optifruit Juice Extractor ~ Easy to assemble, operate, and clean. Krups products are found in stores nationwide or call *Krups North America, Inc.*, based in Closter, N.J. at (800) 526-5377.

Toaster Ovens

Toast-R-Oven ~ Bakes, broils, toasts, browns, defrosts, re-heats. Economical. *Black & Decker* can be reached at (800) 231-9786.

Steamers

Krups Optisteam® ~ Multi-purpose steamer. *Krups North America, Inc.* Closter, N.J. (800) 526-5377 .

Good Earth Steam Pot ~ A *Joyce Chen* product. Order from *Oriental Pantry* at (800) 828-0368 oriental@orientalpantry.com

Equipment

Saladacco ~ Makes spiral cuttings, fine strips, and thin vegetable slices, as well as mincing onion. Based in Camarillo, CA., *SCI Cuisine International* can be reached at (805) 482-0791.

Presto Professional Salad Shooter® ~ For information call Customer Service at (715) 839-2209.

Joyce Chen Oriental Cookware Products ~ "Eastern Cookware for the Western kitchen" Woks, Peking pans, stove-top ceramic casseroles and tea kettles, Japanese stoneware mortar and pestle, cutting boards, chopsticks, Japanese cutlery, etc. *Oriental Pantry* is a retail mail order source for Joyce Chen Products. Based in Acton, MA., they can be reached at (800) 828-0368.

OXO – Good Grip Kitchen Tools ~ A variety of high quality stainless steel kitchen tools, serving utensils, gadgets, and cutlery. A division of *General Housewares*, based in New York, N.Y., OXO. (800) 545-4411 or (212) 242-3333. oxo@ghc.com

Wheatgrass Juicers

The Green Power juice extractor, with its powerful Twin Gear Technology, easily makes chlorophyll-high juice from wheatgrass, barley grass, alfalfa and other grasses as well as juice from therapeutic herbs, fibrous plants, pulpy fruits and leafy vegetables. It also has practical accessories that allow you to make mochi, baby food, frozen fruit sorbet, etc. It is made for life with its precision 1/4 horsepower motor. Order from *Green Power International*, 12020 Woodruff Ave., Suite C, Downey, CA. 90241 or call: (888) 254-7336 or (562) 940-4241. service@greenpower.com

Wheateena Wheatgrass Juicers ~ Manufactured in the U.S., these juicers are sturdy, efficient, and reliable. They come in many models; commercial and compact electric, as well as manual. The machines are especially designed to juice wheatgrass, sprouts, herbs and make nut butters. UL & NSF approved. Serving the health food market since 1966, the Sundance Industries, Inc., P.O. Box 1446, Newburgh, N.Y., can be reached at (914) 565-6065.

Miracle Wheatgrass Juicers ~ These machines are plastic and lightweight. Miracles Exclusives, Inc. market a commercial as well as a smaller electric model and a stainless steel hand juicer. The company has a catalog and a wide selection of juice extractors, stainless steel cookware, grain mills, grinders, pasta makers, dehydrators, sprouters and more. Based in Port Washington, New York, order by phone at (800) 645-6360.

A special thank you to Sony Corporation of America
for donating a digital camera to Gentle World, Inc.,
making it possible for us to have
an alternative to gelatin-based photography.
Visit their website at www.sony.com

"New opinions are always suspected and usually opposed, without any other reason, but because they are not already common."

JOHN LOCKE (1632-1704) ~ English philosopher

About the Authors

Gentle World is a non-profit educational organization, incorporated in Florida in 1979, based in Hawai'i since 1989. Its purpose is to enhance the quality of life, by educating the public as to the health, environmental and spiritual benefits of a plant-based diet and lifestyle.

Toward that end, Gentle World has served as a source of information since its inception. Member-volunteers have offered free seminars, cooking classes, and meals to thousands of interested people. They authored <u>The Cookbook for People Who Love Animals</u> and published two books by Michael A. Klaper M.D.: <u>Vegan Nutrition, Pure and Simple</u> and <u>Pregnancy, Children and the Vegan Diet</u>. They created and catered two Celebrity Vegetarian Banquets in Hollywood, California, inspiring those who are an inspiration to others. In Maui, they established "The Vegan Restaurant".

Presently, Gentle World is in the process of developing two New Paradigm centers: one on the Big Island of Hawai'i, and another on the North Island of New Zealand.

<u>www.gentleworld.org</u>
gentle@aloha.net
PO Box 238, Kapa'au HI. 96755

Index of Quotes

Prayer for Gentleness to All Creatures

"To all the humble beasts, there be,
to all the birds on land and sea,
Great Spirit, sweet protection give
that 'free & happy' they may live.
And to our hearts the rapture bring
of Love for every living thing.
Make us all one kin, and bless
our ways with God's own gentleness."

JOHN GALSWORTHY (1867-1933) ~ British playwright and novelist
1932 Nobel Prize for Literature

~ Notes ~